FEMINIST JUDGMENTS: REWRITTEN CRIMINAL LAW OPINIONS

"Is it possible to be both a judge and a feminist?" *Feminist Judgments: Rewritten Criminal Law Opinions* answers that question in the affirmative by rewriting seminal opinions that implicate critical dimensions of criminal law jurisprudence, from sexual assault law to provocation to cultural defenses to the death penalty. Right now, one in three Americans has a criminal record, mass incarceration and overcriminalization are the norms, and our jails cycle through about 10 million people each year. At the same time, sexual assaults are rarely prosecuted at all, domestic violence remains pervasive, and the distribution of punishment, and by extension justice, seems not only raced and classed but also gendered. We have had #MeToo campaigns and #SayHerName campaigns, and yet not enough has changed. How might all of justice look different through a feminist lens. This book answers that question.

Bennett Capers is the John D. Feerick Research Professor of Law at Fordham Law School, where he is also the Director of the Center on Race, Law, and Justice. He has published widely in law journals on the intersection of race, gender, and criminal justice and is the author of *The Prosecutor's Turn* (Metropolitan Books). His commentary and op-eds have appeared in *The New York Times*, *The Washington Post*, and other journals.

Sarah Deer is a citizen of the Muscogee (Creek) Nation of Oklahoma. Deer was named a MacArthur Fellow in 2014 and a Carnegie Fellow in 2020. She teaches at the University of Kansas, where she holds a joint appointment in Women, Gender, and Sexuality Studies and the School of Public Affairs and Administration. Her efforts to address crime on Indian reservations have received national awards from the American Bar Association and the Department of Justice.

Corey Rayburn Yung is William R. Scott Research Professor at the University of Kansas School of Law and a former Lisa Goldberg Fellow at the Harvard Radcliffe Institute. His scholarship about criminal law, sexual violence, and policing has influenced state criminal justice reform measures and has been cited by courts across the country, including the Supreme Court of the United States.

Feminist Judgments Series

Editors

Bridget J. Crawford
Elisabeth Haub School of Law at Pace University

Kathryn M. Stanchi
University of Nevada, Las Vegas William S. Boyd School of Law

Linda L. Berger
University of Nevada, Las Vegas William S. Boyd School of Law

Advisory Panel for Feminist Judgments Series

Kathryn Abrams, *Herma Hill Kay Distinguished Professor of Law, University of California, Berkeley, School of Law*

Katharine T. Bartlett, *A. Kenneth Pye Professor of Law, Duke University School of Law*

Mary Anne Case, *Arnold I. Shure Professor of Law, The University of Chicago Law School*

April L. Cherry, *Professor of Law, Cleveland-Marshall College of Law*

Margaret E. Johnson, *Professor of Law, University of Baltimore School of Law*

Sonia Katyal, *Chancellor's Professor of Law, University of California, Berkeley, School of Law*

Nancy Leong, *Associate Professor of Law, University of Denver Sturm College of Law*

Rachel Moran, *Michael J. Connell Distinguished Professor of Law and Dean Emerita, University of California, Los Angeles School of Law*

Angela Onwuachi-Willig, *Chancellor's Professor of Law, University of California, Berkeley, School of Law*

Nancy D. Polikoff, *Professor of Law, American University Washington College of Law*

Daniel B. Rodriguez, *Dean and Harold Washington Professor, Northwestern University Pritzker School of Law*

Susan Deller Ross, *Professor of Law, Georgetown University Law Center*

Dean Spade, *Associate Professor of Law, Seattle University School of Law*

Robin L. West, *Frederick J. Haas Professor of Law and Philosophy, Georgetown University Law Center*

Verna L. Williams, *Judge Joseph P. Kinneary Professor of Law, University of Cincinnati College of Law*

Feminist Judgments: Rewritten Criminal Law Opinions

Edited by

BENNETT CAPERS

Fordham University, New York

SARAH DEER

University of Kansas

COREY RAYBURN YUNG

University of Kansas

CAMBRIDGE
UNIVERSITY PRESS

University Printing House, Cambridge CB2 8BS, United Kingdom

One Liberty Plaza, 20th Floor, New York, NY 10006, USA

477 Williamstown Road, Port Melbourne, VIC 3207, Australia

314–321, 3rd Floor, Plot 3, Splendor Forum, Jasola District Centre, New Delhi – 110025, India

103 Penang Road, #05–06/07, Visioncrest Commercial, Singapore 238467

Cambridge University Press is part of the University of Cambridge.

It furthers the University's mission by disseminating knowledge in the pursuit of education, learning, and research at the highest international levels of excellence.

www.cambridge.org
Information on this title: www.cambridge.org/9781316515112
DOI: 10.1017/9781009091978

© Cambridge University Press 2023

This publication is in copyright. Subject to statutory exception and to the provisions of relevant collective licensing agreements, no reproduction of any part may take place without the written permission of Cambridge University Press.

First published 2023

A catalogue record for this publication is available from the British Library.

A Cataloging-in-Publication data record for this book is available from the Library of Congress

ISBN 978-1-316-51511-2 Hardback
ISBN 978-1-009-09597-6 Paperback

Cambridge University Press has no responsibility for the persistence or accuracy of URLs for external or third-party internet websites referred to in this publication and does not guarantee that any content on such websites is, or will remain, accurate or appropriate.

Contents

Advisory Panel for Feminist Judgments: Rewritten
Criminal Law Opinions   *page* ix

Notes on Contributors   xi

Introduction and Overview   1

PART I   GENDERED JUSTICE   5

1   **McQuirter v. State**   7
    Commentary: *Grayce Zelphin*
    Judgment: *Cortney Lollar*

2   **People v. Berry**   26
    Commentary: *Carolyn B. Ramsey*
    Judgment: *Susan D. Rozelle*

3   **Coker v. Georgia**   50
    Commentary: *Catherine M. Grosso and Barbara O'Brien*
    Judgment: *Madalyn K. Wasilczuk*

4   **Oliphant v. Suquamish Indian Tribe**   69
    Commentary: *Adam Crepelle*
    Judgment: *Melissa L. Tatum*

5   **State v. Rusk**   89
    Commentary: *JoAnne Sweeny*
    Judgment: *Michelle J. Anderson*

6   **People v. Wu**   110
    Commentary: *John Felipe Acevedo*
    Judgment: *Leti Volpp*

7	**Winnebago Tribe of Nebraska v. Bigfire** Commentary: *Ann E. Tweedy* Judgment: *Sarah Deer*	131
8	**Commonwealth v. Blache** Commentary: *Marie-Amélie George* Judgment: *Ben A. McJunkin*	168

PART II   GENDER ON TRIAL   189

9	**State v. Williams** Commentary: *Kim Hai Pearson* Judgment: *Addie C. Rolnick*	191
10	**State v. Walden** Commentary: *Lisa R. Avalos* Judgment: *Sarah L. Swan*	214
11	**State v. Norman** Commentary: *Joan H. Krause* Judgment: *Martha R. Mahoney*	230
12	**Whitner v. State** Commentary: *Ruqaiijah Yearby* Judgment: *Aziza Ahmed*	253
13	**United States v. Nwoye** Commentary: *Sherri Lee Keene* Judgment: *Mary D. Fan*	263
14	**Erotic Services Provider Legal Education and Research Project v. Gascon** Commentary: *Aya Gruber and Kate Mogulescu* Judgment: *I. India Thusi*	282

Advisory Panel for *Feminist Judgments: Rewritten Criminal Law Opinions*

Libby Adler, Professor of Law and Women's, Gender and Sexuality Studies, Northeastern University

Donna Coker, Professor of Law & Dean's Distinguished Scholar, Miami School of Law

Frank Rudy Cooper, William S. Boyd Professor of Law, University of Nevada, Las Vegas

Anne Coughlin, Lewis F. Powell, Jr., Professor of Law, University of Virginia

Brandon Davis, Assistant Professor of Law and Society, University of Kansas

Joshua Dressler, Professor Emeritus of Law, The Ohio State University

Mary Fan, Professor of Law, University of Washington

Aya Gruber, Professor of Law, University of Colorado Boulder

Angela Harris, Distinguished Professor of Law, UC Davis

Aviva Orenstein, Professor of Law, Indiana University Bloomington

Angela Riley, Professor of Law, UCLA

Deborah Tuerkheimer, Professor of Law, Northwestern University

Deborah Weissman, Reef C. Ivey II Distinguished Professor of Law, University of North Carolina

Stephanie Wildman, Professor Emerita Santa Clara University

Notes on Contributors

John Felipe Acevedo is Assistant Professor in Residence at University of Alabama School of Law. He earned his Ph.D. in history from The University of Chicago, where he wrote his dissertation on the criminal law and procedure of the Seventeenth-Century Massachusetts Bay colony. He earned his J.D. from the University of Southern California Gould School of Law where he was a fellow in the Center for Law, History, and Culture. He received his undergraduate degree in history with honors from California State University at San Bernardino. Professor Acevedo was previously an Assistant Professor at the University of La Verne College of Law and a Visiting Assistant Professor at Barry University School of Law. In addition he has taught law at the University of Southern California Gould School of Law and Chicago-Kent College of Law. He has also taught undergraduate courses on American history and historical theory at the University of Chicago. Professor Acevedo's research interests focus on remedies to police misconduct, the concept of dignity takings, and the history of criminal law and procedure in the British Empire. His work examines the interplay between law and society from both a contemporary and historical focus

Aziza Ahmed is Professor of Law at Boston University School of Law. Her scholarship examines the intersection of law, politics, and science in the fields of constitutional law, criminal law, health law, and family law. This work advances multiple scholarly conversations including those related to law and social movements, race and the law, and feminist legal theory. Professor Ahmed joins BU Law from University of California Irvine School of Law and UCI and Northeastern University School of Law. Professor Ahmed has been Visiting Professor at the University of Chicago Law School, Bennett Boskey Visiting Professor at Harvard Law School, visiting scholar at the Harvard Law School Petrie-Flom Center for Health Law Policy Biotechnology, and Bioethics, and Law and Public Affairs Fellow at Princeton University. She is the author of the forthcoming book *Feminism's Medicine: Law, Science, and Social Movements in the AIDS Response*, published by Cambridge University Press, and coeditor of the forthcoming handbook *Race, Racism, and the Law*, published by

Edward Elgar Publishing. Professor Ahmed earned a B.A. from Emory University, a J.D. from the University of California, Berkeley School of Law, and an M.S. in Population and International Health from the Harvard School of Public Health.

Michelle J. Anderson is the tenth president of Brooklyn College. Previously, she was Dean at City University of New York School of Law, a professor at Villanova Law, and a visiting professor at Georgetown Law Center and Yale Law School. Anderson holds a B.A. from the University of California, Santa Cruz, and a J.D. from Yale Law School, where she was notes editor on the *Yale Law Journal*. Following law school, she clerked on the US Court of Appeals for the Ninth Circuit for Judge William Norris. Anderson is a leading scholar on rape law. She is an adviser to the American Law Institute's project to reform the Model Penal Code on sexual offenses and a consultant to its campus sexual misconduct project. She is the recipient of numerous honors, including the Champion of Justice Award from Brooklyn Legal Services and the Diversity and Inclusion Champion Award from the New York City Bar.

Lisa R. Avalos is an Associate Professor of Law and holds the Hermann Moyse, Sr. Professorship at Louisiana State University Paul M. Hebert Law Center, where she has taught since 2018, primarily in the areas of criminal law and procedure, sex crimes, and professional ethics. Her scholarship has appeared or is forthcoming in the *University of Illinois Law Review, Case Western Reserve Law Review, Brooklyn Law Review, Nevada Law Journal, Michigan Journal of Gender & Law, Vanderbilt Journal of Transnational Law, Fordham International Law Journal*, and others. She has written opinion pieces for *The Guardian*, appeared on BBC Radio and Louisiana Public Radio, and has been quoted in numerous publications including *The Guardian, Huffington Post, Time Magazine, BuzzFeed, Cosmopolitan*, and *Vice News*. She earned her J.D. at New York University School of Law and holds a Ph.D. from Northwestern University. She thanks the editors for their thoughtful comments.

Adam Crepelle is an assistant professor of law at the Antonin Scalia Law School, George Mason University and Director of the Tribal Law & Economies Project and the Law & Economics Center. He is also an associate professor of law at Southern University Law Center (SULC), as well as the Campbell Fellow at the Hoover Institution at Stanford University. Adam is an enrolled citizen of the United Houma Nation, and serves as a judge on the Court of Appeals for the Pascua Yaqui Tribe.

Mary D. Fan is the Jack R. MacDonald Endowed Chair Professor of Law at Washington University School of Law. Professor Mary D. Fan's expertise includes criminal law and procedure, evidence, privacy, and immigration. Her research and teaching are informed by her experiences as a federal prosecutor in the Southern District of California and as an associate legal officer at a United Nations criminal tribunal. She is the author of numerous articles, including most recently, *The Right to Benefit from Big Data as a Public Resource* in the *NYU Law Review* (2021) and two books: *Camera Power: Proof, Policing, Privacy, and Audiovisual Big Data*

(Cambridge University Press, 2019) and *Perilous Science: Lessons from Firearms Violence Research on Knowledge in Political Minefields* (Stanford University Press, forthcoming 2022). Her scholarship has been cited by judges, including US Supreme Court Justice Sonia Sotomayor, and in media venues such as *The New York Times*.

Marie-Amélie George is Associate Professor at Wake Forest University School of Law and an expert on LGBTQ rights. Her scholarship has appeared in numerous law reviews and peer-reviewed journals, and she is a three-time recipient of the Dukeminier Award, which recognizes the most influential sexual orientation and gender identity scholarship in the United States. She received her Ph.D. in history from Yale University, her J.D. from Columbia Law School, and her M.St. in Women's Studies from the University of Oxford. Prior to joining the Wake faculty, she was the Berger-Howe Fellow in Legal History at Harvard Law School and an Associate in Law at Columbia Law School. Before entering academia, Professor George worked as a domestic violence prosecutor at the Miami State Attorney's Office and as a litigation associate at Paul, Weiss, Rifkind, Wharton & Garrison in New York.

Catherine M. Grosso teaches the Michigan State University College of Law. Her interdisciplinary scholarship examines the role of race and other extralegal factors in criminal investigations, trials, and the administration of capital punishment. Much of her research documents the persistent role of race in jury selection and in charging and sentencing decisions relating to capital punishment. Another line of work empirically evaluates the success of death penalty statutes in fulfilling the Eighth Amendment narrowing requirements. Professor Grosso is also an associate editor of the National Registry of Exonerations. The Registry "collects, analyzes and disseminates information about all known exonerations of innocent criminal defendants in the United States, from 1989 to the present." The Registry provides a virtual home for exoneration stories and also an accessible, searchable statistical database about the cases. Grosso was copresident of the Society of American Law Teachers (SALT) from 2020–22.

Aya Gruber is a professor of law at University of Colorado, where she teaches and writes in the areas of criminal law and procedure, critical theory, feminism, and comparative/international law. Her scholarship focuses primarily on feminist efforts to strengthen criminal law responses to crimes against women. Her widely taught and frequently cited articles combine insights from practicing as a public defender with extensive research to articulate a feminist critique of punitive and authoritarian laws on violence against women. Her articles appear in leading journals, including *California Law Review*, *Northwestern Law Review*, and *Iowa Law Review*. She is the author of the book *The Feminist War On Crime: The Unexpected Role of Women's Liberation in Mass Incarceration* (University of California Press, 2020), which tells the story how feminists, in their quest to secure women's protection from domestic violence and rape, became soldiers in the war on crime and contributors to mass incarceration It sketches a path forward for young women, activists, and lawmakers to oppose violence against women without reinforcing the American prison state.

Sherri Lee Keene is Associate Professor of Law, Legal Practice at Georgetown University Law Center and previously the Director of the Legal Writing Program at University of Maryland Carey School of Law. Professor Keene received her law degree from New York University School of Law, which she attended as a Root-Tilden-Snow public interest scholar, and graduated from Spelman College with a degree in Sociology. Prior to teaching, Professor Keene handled criminal appeals at the Federal Public Defender's Office for the District of Maryland. Her experiences as a public defender influence her teaching and scholarship. Professor Keene's writing focuses on the intersection of criminal law, advocacy, and psychology, and she considers how negative stereotypes and stock stories about African Americans can unconsciously influence the perceptions of police and other actors in the criminal justice system. Her recent work explores how seemingly neutral laws can mask biased thinking, rather than afford opportunities for such thinking to be meaningfully challenged.

Joan H. Krause is Dan K. Moore Distinguished Professor of Law, University of North Carolina School of Law; Professor (Secondary Appointment), Department of Social Medicine, University of North Carolina School of Medicine; and Adjunct Professor, Health Policy and Management, Gillings School of Global Public Health. She received her B.A. with Honors in Political Science from Yale University and her J.D. with Distinction from Stanford Law School, and previously taught at Loyola University Chicago School of Law and the University of Houston Law Center. She joined the University of North Carolina in 2009, was named Dan K. Moore Distinguished Professor of Law in 2011, and served as Associate Dean for Faculty Development from 2012 to 2016. She has published widely on issues of health law, criminal law, and women and the law.

Cortney Lollar is the Norman and Carole Harned Law and Public Policy Professor the University of Kentucky Rosenberg College of Law, where she teaches in the areas of criminal law, criminal procedure, and evidence. She is a graduate of Brown University and New York University School of Law. She previously represented adult and juvenile defendants at the Federal Defender Program in Atlanta, Georgia, and the Public Defender Service for the District of Columbia. She served as a research assistant to the United Nations Special Rapporteur on Violence Against Women and provided invited testimony before the Department of Defense Judicial Proceedings Panel on sexual assault in the military. Her work has appeared in journals such as the *Virginia Law Review*, *Minnesota Law Review*, and *Iowa Law Review*, and has been cited by the US Supreme Court as well as other federal and state courts.

Martha R. Mahoney is Professor of Law and Dean's Distinguished Scholar at the University of Miami School of Law. A former community organizer, she was a founding member of the San Francisco Women's Health Collective. Professor Mahoney's work on violence against women includes *Misunderstanding Judy Norman: Theory as Cause and Consequence*, 51 CONN. L. REV. 671 (2019); *Oppression or Victimization? Women's Lives, Violence, and Agency, in* The Public Nature of Private Violence 59, 79 (Martha Albertson Fineman & Roxanne Mykitiuk eds., 1994); *EXIT: Power and the Idea of Leaving in Love, Work, and the Confirmation Hearings*, 65 S. CAL. L. REV. 1283 (1992); and *Legal Images of Battered Women: Redefining the Issue of Separation*, 90 MICH. L. REV. 1 (1991). Her work also includes *Whiteness and Women, in Practice and Theory: A Reply to Catharine MacKinnon*, 5 YALE J.L. & Feminism 217 (1993); Martha R. Mahoney, John O. Calmore, and Stephanie M. Wildman, *Social Justice: Professionals, Communities, and Law* (West Academic, 2nd ed. 2013); and articles on class and race.

Ben A. McJunkin is an associate professor of law at the Sandra Day O'Connor College of Law at Arizona State University. He is also the Associate Deputy Director of ASU Law's Academy for Justice. Professor McJunkin teaches and writes on the criminalization of sexual violence and the policing of marginalized communities. His research routinely seeks to connect legal doctrines with broader themes in moral philosophy and gender theory. His work in substantive criminal law, in particular, questions how the legal regulation of sex and sexuality shapes, and is shaped by, societal narratives about gender identity and sexual injury.

Kate Mogulescu is an associate professor of clinical law at Brooklyn Law School. She directs the Criminal Defense & Advocacy Clinic, which she launched in 2017. Her work and scholarship focus largely on gender, sentencing, and reentry issues in the criminal legal system, with a focus on gender-based violence, intimate partner abuse, sex work, and human trafficking. Before starting the Clinic, Professor Mogulescu worked as a public defender at The Legal Aid Society for 14 years. Professor Mogulescu has founded several projects, including the Exploitation Intervention Project (2011), the Survivor Reentry Project (2016), and the Survivors Justice Project (2020). She offers critical analysis of carceral approaches to violence and harm and advocates extensively against the criminalization of vulnerable and exploited people.

Barbara O'Brien is a professor at the Michigan State University College of Law, where she teaches classes in criminal law and procedure. She is currently the Editor of the National Registry of Exonerations, which "collects, analyzes and disseminates information about all known exonerations of innocent criminal defendants in the United States, from 1989 to the present." The Registry provides a virtual home for exoneration stories and also an accessible, searchable statistical database about the cases. Professor O'Brien's scholarship applies empirical methodology to legal issues, such as identifying predictors of false convictions and understanding prosecutorial decision-making. Her most recent work examines the persistent role of race in jury selection and in charging and sentencing decisions relating to capital punishment. An ongoing National Science Foundation project with Professor Catherine Grosso applies conversation analysis to assess ways in which race influences voir dire in capital cases.

Kim Hai Pearson is Professor of Law and serves as the Associate Dean of Academic Affairs and Program Innovation at Gonzaga University School of Law. From 2016 to 2018, Professor Pearson was the Associate Dean of Faculty Research and Development at Gonzaga Law. Prior to joining Gonzaga Law in 2010, she held a Law Teaching Fellowship at the Williams Institute housed at the University of California Los Angeles (UCLA)Law School where she taught Law and Sexuality, Legal Scholarship, and Family Law. Recently, she completed an M.St. degree in International Human Rights Law at Oxford University. Her current research and writing projects focus on identity, legal classifications, and children in domestic and international movement. In her earlier work, Professor Pearson wrote about the impact of identity classification for domestic family law purposes, particularly unfair treatment and outcomes for racial, religious, and sexual minority children and parents.

Carolyn B. Ramsey is a professor of law at University of Colorado School of Law, where she teaches and writes about criminal law, criminal procedure, domestic violence, gender issues, and legal history. She earned her J.D. with distinction from Stanford Law School and clerked for Chief Judge Marilyn Hall Patel of the US District Court for the Northern District of California and Judge Paul J. Kelly, Jr., of the US Court of Appeals for the Tenth Circuit. In addition to her law degree, Professor Ramsey received an M.A. in history and further graduate training as a social historian at Stanford University. This background stimulates her interest in the relationship between law and social norms. She publishes widely in well-regarded law journals and has a book forthcoming with Cambridge University Press about the history of criminal justice responses to intimate-partner violence.

Addie C. Rolnick is the San Manuel Band of Mission Indians Professor of Law at the University of Nevada, Las Vegas, William S. Boyd School of Law. She is the Faculty Director of the Indian Nations Gaming & Governance Program and the Associate Director of the Program on Race, Gender & Policing. She is also a member of the National Academy of Sciences Ad Hoc Committee on Reducing Racial Disparities in the Criminal Justice System. Her areas of expertise include Native children in juvenile justice and child welfare; Native people's encounters with tribal, federal, and state criminal systems; and equal protection-based attacks on Indigenous rights. Prior to joining UNLV in 2011, she was the inaugural Critical Race Studies Law Fellow at UCLA School of Law. Before that, she represented tribal governments as a lawyer and lobbyist in Washington, DC. She earned her J.D. (2004) and M.A. (2007) in American Indian Studies from UCLA and her B.A. (1999) from Oberlin College.

Susan D. Rozelle is Professor of Law at Stetson University College of Law, teaching Criminal Law, Evidence, Criminal Procedure, and Criminal Responsibility Seminar. Her work on provocation has been cited by the Law Commission for England and Wales in its Report to Parliament recommending reform to the law of murder and manslaughter, and her work on death qualification was cited by US Supreme Court Justice Stephen Breyer. Professor Rozelle has presented at scholarly conferences across the country, from Georgetown University Law Center to the University of California, Berkeley and is a featured legal commentator in the popular press. She serves on the Editorial Board of the ABA Criminal Justice Magazine, the Executive Board of the AALS Section on Women in Legal Education and is the founder and chair of the Teaching Materials Network. She is past chair of the AALS Criminal Justice Section, and AALS Section for the Associate Deans.

Sarah L. Swan is an associate professor at Rutgers Law School (Newark). She teaches and writes in the areas of torts, criminal law, family law, and local government law. Her scholarship focuses on issues of third-party responsibility, and her publications include articles in the *Harvard Law Review*, *Michigan Law Review*, *Duke Law Journal*, *UCLA Law Review*, and *Vanderbilt Law Review*, among others.

JoAnne Sweeny is a professor of law at University of Louisville School of Law, where she teaches lawyering skills and writing for practice. Prior to coming to Louisville, she was a Westerfield Fellow at Loyola University New Orleans College of Law, where she taught legal research and writing as well as a seminar in comparative constitutional law. After graduating Order of the Coif from the University of Southern California Law School, she clerked for the Honorable Ferdinand F. Fernandez at the Ninth Circuit Court of Appeals. Professor Sweeny then practiced as an employment litigator at Manatt, Phelps & Phillips, LLP before returning to academia. In 2009, she completed her Ph.D. in law at Queen Mary, University of London. Professor Sweeny's current scholarly interests include freedom of expression, feminist jurisprudence, and comparative constitutional law. Some of Professor Sweeny's most recent research has focused on the legal considerations behind the #MeToo movement, how rape myths infiltrate the criminal justice system, and the intersection between freedom of expression and technology.

Melissa L. Tatum is a research professor of law at the University of Arizona College of Law, where she also serves as Graduate Advisor for students in the Indigenous Peoples Law and Policy Program and teaches in the American Indian Studies Graduate Interdisciplinary Program. Professor Tatum is the author or coauthor of seventeen law review articles and four books, including two textbooks which have been adopted by a variety of law, Indian Studies, and tribal governance programs. She has contributed chapters to the leading treatise on Federal Indian Law, as well as to three books exploring various aspects of comparative Indigenous peoples law. She has served on the Southwest Intertribal Court of Appeals, edited multiple volumes of tribal court opinions including for the Navajo Nation and the Muscogee (Creek) Nation, and has trained law enforcement and court personnel across the US in issues relating to the Violence Against Women Acts.

I. India Thusi is a professor of law at the Indiana University Maurer School of Law with a joint appointment at the Kinsey Institute. Her research examines racial and sexual hierarchies as they relate to policing, race, and gender. Her articles and essays have been published or are forthcoming in the *Harvard Law Review*, *NYU Law Review*, *Northwestern Law Review* (twice), *Georgetown Law Journal*, *Cornell Law Review Online*, among others. Among other acknowledgments throughout her career, Thusi was selected as a Fulbright US Global Scholar for 2020–23. Her paper "Reality Porn" was selected for the 2020 Stanford/Harvard/Yale Junior Faculty Forum, and she was recognized as a Top 40 Rising Young Lawyer by the American Bar Association in 2019. Her most recent paper was selected for the 2021 Equality Law Scholars Workshop.

Ann E. Tweedy is a professor of law at University of South Dakota Knudson School of Law. She is a noted scholar on tribal civil rights and tribal jurisdiction, as well as on bisexuality and the law. Before coming to University of South Dakota, she served as an in-house attorney for Muckleshoot Tribe and as an adjunct professor for University of Tulsa College of Law. Professor Tweedy has also taught at Michigan State University College of Law, California Western School of Law, and Hamline University School of Law (now Mitchell Hamline), where she served as an Associate Professor. She also previously served as a Tribal Attorney for Swinomish Indian Tribal Community and as an Associate Attorney and as Of Counsel at Kanji & Katzen, PLLC. After law school, she clerked for Ninth Circuit Judge Hon. Ronald M. Gould and for Oregon Court of Appeals Judge Hon. Rex Armstrong (retired). Her work in practice focused primarily on natural resources law and environmental law in the context of protection of Tribal treaty resources. She is also an award-winning poet, having published one full-text length book (The Body's Alphabet) and three chapbooks. Professor Tweedy holds a J.D. from the University of California Berkeley School of Law (Order of the Coif) and an MFA in Creative Writing from Hamline University.

Leti Volpp is the Robert D. and Leslie Kay Raven Professor of Law in Access to Justice at Berkeley Law School and is a renowned scholar of immigration law and citizenship theory. She researches immigration and citizenship law with a particular focus on how law is shaped by ideas about culture and identity. Her publications have appeared in *Columbia Law Review*, *Constitutional Commentary*, *Berkeley La Raza Law Journal*, the *Oxford Handbook of Citizenship*, *UC Irvine Law Review*, *UCLA Law Review*, *Fordham Law Review*, and *differences: A Journal of Feminist Cultural Studies*, among others. She is the editor of *Looking for Law in All the Wrong Places: Justice Beyond and Between* (with Marianne Constable and Bryan Wagner)

(Fordham University Press, 2019) and *Legal Borderlands: Law and the Construction of American Borders* (with Mary Dudziak) (Johns Hopkins University Press, 2006). Volpp's honors include two Rockefeller Foundation Humanities Fellowships, a MacArthur Foundation Individual Research and Writing Grant, the Association of American Law Schools Minority Section Derrick A. Bell, Jr., Award, and the Professor Keith Aoki Asian Pacific American Jurisprudence Award.

Madalyn K. Wasilczuk is an assistant professor of law at the University of South Carolina School of Law. She teaches the Juvenile Justice Clinic and courses focused on the criminal legal system, race, policing, and prisons. Previously, Professor Wasilczuk taught at Louisiana State University Paul M. Hebert Law Center. She has also worked at the Cornell Center on the Death Penalty Worldwide and the Defender Association of Philadelphia. In addition to her domestic defense work, Professor Wasilczuk has served as a fellow with International Legal Foundation in Myanmar and Tunisia, engaged in human rights advocacy at the United Nations, and defended and investigated death penalty cases in Malawi and Tanzania. She earned her J.D. from New York University School of Law and her B.A. with honors in International Studies from American University.

Ruqaiijah Yearby is the Kara J. Trott Professor in Health Law at Moritz College of Law at The Ohio State University. She remains an affiliate faculty member of Saint Louis University's Institute for Healing Justice and Equity. Recently, Professor Yearby authored a report entitled, "Protecting Workers that Provide Essential Services" and coauthored, "Racism is a Public Health Crisis. Here's How to Respond." Using empirical data, her research explores the ways in which discrimination prevents vulnerable populations from attaining equal access to quality health care, resulting in health inequities. Her work has been cited in *The Oxford Handbook of Public Health Ethics* (Oxford University Press, 2019), Dolgin and Shephard, *Bioethics and the Law* (Aspen, 4th ed 2019), and Mark Hall, et al., *Health Care Law and Ethics* (Aspen, 9th ed 2018). She earned her B.S. in Honors Biology from the University of Michigan, M.P.H. from Johns Hopkins School of Public Health, and her J.D. from Georgetown University Law Center.

Grayce Zelphin is a senior staff attorney at the ACLU of Northern California, where she leads impact litigation and policy initiatives focused on racial and economic justice. Prior to joining the ACLU, she served as the inaugural Director of Judicial Clerkships at University of California Berkeley School of Law and spent several years in private practice at two international law firms. Grayce is a former law clerk to the Honorable Consuelo B. Marshall (US District Court for the Central District of California) and the Honorable Ann Claire Williams (US Court of Appeal for the Seventh Circuit). She earned her J.D. from UC Berkeley School of Law, and her B.A. in Critical Race Theory: Public Policy & Law from UCLA.

Introduction and Overview

BENNETT CAPERS, SARAH DEER, AND
COREY RAYBURN YUNG

How would feminist judges change the way in which we conceive of criminal law? Would the application of feminist jurisprudence change the answer to difficult criminal law problems? These are questions at the core of this text on rewritten opinions in criminal law.

This book is a part of a series that seeks to apply feminist critique to commonly taught cases. The first text in the series, *Feminist Judgments: Rewritten Opinions of the United States Supreme Court*, published in 2016, focused on watershed cases involving gender and sexuality. This inspired the development of several discipline-specific feminist opinions. A book of reimagined feminist court opinions related to criminal law seemed the obvious next step.

Law students rarely have the opportunity to truly think critically about lasting alternatives to the status quo of the criminal justice system; they spend most of their time learning what the law *is* rather than what the law *could be*. The publication of rewritten opinions can help students, practitioners, and scholars think outside the patriarchal box of standard criminal law cases and influence the intellectual growth of future jurists. As Robin West reminds us, "feminist legal theory is a normative field of scholarship as well as being descriptive and critical."[1] This volume illustrates how normative feminist legal theory can be, and the difference it can make.

One might think that the primary feminist intervention in American criminal law would be through reform of rape and domestic violence laws. Certainly well-known legal feminist theorists, such as Catharine MacKinnon, have advanced feminist arguments designed to address the subordination of women that is embedded in the foundation of American law. But feminist theories don't start or stop at the question of violence. Put differently, one of the ambitions of this book is to show readers the difference feminist analysis can make beyond the expected categories of sexual violence, domestic violence, and reproductive rights. The contributors show

---

[1] ROBIN WEST, *Introduction to the Research Handbook on Feminist Jurisprudence*, in RESEARCH HANDBOOK OF FEMINIST JURISPRUDENCE 1, 1 (Robin West, Frederick Haas, & Dorothea S. Clark, eds., 2019).

that feminist jurisprudence also offers significant insights into areas of criminal law without a self-evident relationship to gender such as self-defense, provocation for manslaughter, cultural defenses, and the role of punishment itself. Quite simply, this book demonstrates how feminist reasoning could have changed the development of criminal law writ large. To that end, the cases in this volume go beyond examining sexual violence and domestic violence, behavior during pregnancy, child abuse and neglect, self-defense and provocation, capital punishment and sex work. The cases and accompanying commentary also address such foundational criminal law principles as the act requirement and *mens rea*, the state's police power, the rules of legality, and punishment. In doing so, this book highlights the importance and influence of perspective, background, and preconceptions on the reading and interpretation of the governing criminal law. Feminism challenges theories that approach criminal law as a neutral system for addressing deviant behavior. Feminism answers that criminal law is far from neutral in its application. Beyond this, feminist jurisprudence brings into sharp focus imbalances of power between the state, victims, and defendants, imbalances which are exacerbated not only by gender, but also by race, class, disability, and other forms of identities.

While the rewritten cases in the volume are bound by the precedent and sources that existed at the time of each opinion, the opinions and commentaries are also written against the backdrop of feminist thinking now. For example, the #MeToo movement for starters, which has demanded a revision of how we view sexual harassment and assault. Equally important is the attention given to female victims of police violence, and the #SayHerName movement. The confirmation of Amy Coney Barrett to the US Supreme Court raises issues about abortion rights and with it the criminalization of terminations. Beyond this, the abolition movement and movement to defund the police have called attention to what has been termed "carceral feminism." Indeed, some of our contributors are actively engaged in significant critique of the entire criminal justice system – in particular, police misconduct and overincarceration. There have even been calls to decriminalize domestic violence, seeking extrajudicial solutions that allow for addressing violence against women without resorting to the overly punitive approaches of mandatory arrest and hefty carceral sentences.

One thing that makes this volume stand out is that it reflects multiple approaches to feminist thinking. That said, there is a unifying principle: that feminist ways of thinking matter, and can make a difference. The book is proof that incorporating feminist theories and methods into criminal law cases *is* consistent with judicial duties and accepted methods of interpretation. It's also proof that feminist thinking can enrich and deepen the process by which judicial decisions are made.

There are two more things to say about this book. First, it is divided into two sections: Gendered Justice and Gender on Trial. The first section focuses on cases where a feminist perspective may inform the court's reasoning even though there is not an obvious gendered dynamic to the criminal complainant (if there is one) and the defendant. In contrast, the second section, Gender on Trial, highlights cases where the gender identity of the complainant and/or victim is central to the facts of the cases.

Second, we want to emphasize that this is the first book in the *Feminist Judgments* series that includes a focus on Federal Indian law and tribal law. We've included a case issued by the Winnebago Tribal Supreme Court in 1998 with facts markedly similar to the United States Supreme Court case *Michael M. v. Supreme Court*. In addition, we have included the infamous US Supreme Court Indian law case, *Oliphant v. Suquamish*, decided in 1978, which prohibits tribal nations from prosecuting non-Indians. This case has been widely critiqued by Indigenous feminists who are seeking to restore criminal authority over anyone who is violent or abusive, regardless of Indian status. Finally, we've included a state court case in which Indian parents were convicted of manslaughter for failing to take a child to the doctor. The parents' hesitancy came in part because they justifiably feared that state social services would remove the child from the home. While this volume might, at first glance, come across as tribal-heavy, that is only because the treatment of Indigenous people has for too long been ignored by the legal canon and by feminist legal theory. This book seeks to begin us on a path of righting that wrong.

PART I

Gendered Justice

1

Commentary on *McQuirter v. State*

GRAYCE ZELPHIN

In 1953, the Alabama Court of Appeals decided *McQuirter v. State* and held that evidence based on racial and gender stereotypes was sufficient to support a conviction for an attempt to commit an assault with the intent to rape.[1] The opinion is disturbing to a modern legal reader because its analysis relies so comfortably on the blackness of the defendant and the whiteness of the purported female victim to cast otherwise innocuous movements as both criminal and sexual. This decision is frequently cited in law school classrooms to expose the ugly recent history of race, and particularly anti-Black racism, in American criminal law. *McQuirter* also raises concerns about the reliability and validity of criminalizing an *attempt* in the absence of criminal action, in effect making criminal liability dependent on presumed or expressed bad intentions without any *actus reus* (culpable action) or *corpus delicti* (concrete evidence of a crime). While this opinion often makes its way into criminal law textbooks, *McQuirter* is rarely viewed from a feminist perspective or evaluated for its anti-feminist implications. Rewriting *McQuirter* from a feminist perspective illuminates how analysis of gender cannot be abstracted from race, and the importance of considering race and intersectionality when pursuing feminist objectives.

The historical context of the *McQuirter* opinion is not easily severable from the conclusions that it drew based on gendered racial identities. This case was handed down when *Plessy v. Ferguson* was the law of the land,[2] one year before *Brown v. Board of Education* famously rejected segregation in public schools,[3] and two years before the gruesome murder of Emmett Till, a 14-year-old African-American boy who was viciously mutilated and murdered for allegedly whistling at a white woman (which the woman later admitted never happened).[4] In other words, at the

---

[1] *McQuirter v. State*, 63 So.2d 388 (Ala. Ct. App. 1953).
[2] *Plessy v. Ferguson*, 163 U.S. 537 (1896), overturned by *Brown v. Board*, 357 U.S. 483 (1954).
[3] *Brown*, 347 U.S. 483.
[4] Library of Congress, NAACP Records (1955), www.loc.gov/exhibits/naacp/the-civil-rights-era.html#obj9. After the murder, the accuser recanted her story, affirming that the young boy was killed based on racial animus alone.

time the Alabama Court of Appeals decided *McQuirter*, Jim Crow segregation was in full effect and public policy was unashamedly built around an entrenched assumption that Black men were a persistent and severe threat to white women.

Pre-Civil Rights era Alabama, rife with anti-Black hostility and vehement animus toward the idea of Black men interacting with white women, laid the framework under which *McQuirter* was decided. While a contemporary reader may easily recognize that overt reliance on race- and gender-based stereotypes would not survive legal scrutiny in the modern era,[5] the opinion's signature deference to racism and sexism was considered commonsense in 1953 in Alabama, and throughout the United States. In fact, *McQuirter* was a product of the same Alabama court system that convicted and sentenced the "Scottsboro Boys" to death preceding the US Supreme Court's opinion in *Powell v. Alabama*.[6] Twenty years later in 1953, little had changed in the Alabama judiciary. The Alabama judiciary was still entirely white and nearly 100 percent male (there was one white female appellate judge).[7] Black people were (as they still are) systematically removed from serving as jurors.[8] Interracial sex and marriage were criminal acts expressly prohibited by the Alabama Constitution.[9] And, as factored into the original *McQuirter* opinion, Black men accused by white women were presumptive rapists or sexual predators.

While public policy and the broad acceptability of overt racism have changed since 1953, the racial and gender dynamics at the root *McQuirter v. State* plague our criminal legal system today.

THE ORIGINAL OPINION

In *McQuirter*, the Alabama Court of Appeals reviewed and affirmed a lower opinion that convicted McQuirter (no first name given, nor is he ever accorded the title

---

[5] *See, e.g., Buck v. Davis*, 580 U.S. __ (2017); *People v. Robinson*, No. 14CA1795, 2017 WL 4684157, at *4 (Colo. App. October 19, 2017) (noting that the rule applied in *McQuirter* is "now defunct"), cert. granted, No. 17SC823, 2018 WL 2772788 (Colo. June 11, 2018).

[6] *Powell v. Alabama*, 287 U.S. 45 (1932). The "Scottsboro Boys" were nine Black teenaged boys, mostly unacquainted and unrelated, who happened to be on the same freight train in Scottsboro, Alabama in 1931. The moniker "Scottsboro Boys" was created by media coverage as these boys' lives were thrown into complete disarray and put in grave danger because they were accused of raping two white women on that train. The National Museum of African American History & Culture, "The Scottsboro Boys," https://nmaahc.si.edu/blog/scottsboro-boys. The boys were charged, tried (after narrowly escaping being lynched), and sentenced to death without counsel or due process. Despite glaring errors in the investigation, procedures, and logic underlying the case, and the recantation of one of the women who initially made the accusation, the boys' charges and sentences were largely upheld at all levels of the Alabama court system before being reversed by the US Supreme Court due to procedural errors. Powell, 287 U.S. at 45.

[7] A History of the Alabama Judicial System. https://judicial.alabama.gov/docs/judicial_history.pdf (The first Black appellate judge in Alabama, Oscar Adams, was not appointed until 1980).

[8] Equal Justice Initiative, "Illegal Racial Discrimination in Jury Selection: A Continuing Legacy" (2010), https://eji.org/wp-content/uploads/2019/10/illegal-racial-discrimination-in-jury-selection.pdf.

[9] ALA. CONST. of 1865, art. IV, § 31 (1901). In fact, Alabama did not remove its constitutional restriction on miscegenation until 2000.

"Mr." even though the prosecutrix is repeated addressed as "Mrs.") of an attempt to commit an assault with the intent to rape in a brief two-page opinion.[10]

The very first line of the opinion was used by the court to put McQuirter's race and gender front and center: "Appellant, a Negro man, was found guilty."[11] The court explained that McQuirter had been indicted with an *assault* with the intent to rape but was found guilty of an *attempt* to commit an assault with intent to rape. The court then recited the underlying facts that were presented and accepted as evidence in the trial court. First among these, was that "Mrs. Ted Allen" was "a white woman" who was with "her two children and a neighbor's little girl" drinking Coca-Cola at a diner.[12] To accord both the accuser and accused equal dignity, I will refer to him as McQuirter and her as Allen.

The court then recounted Allen's testimony. Allen and the children were walking home when she noticed McQuirter sitting in the cab of a parked truck. As Allen passed the truck, she heard McQuirter say something unintelligible and he opened the truck door and placed his foot on the running board. Allen testified that after she passed the truck, McQuirter followed her down the street. Allen became uncomfortable, and when she reached the nearby home of a neighbor, she stopped and turned in toward their house. Allen believed that McQuirter was two or three feet from her when she turned into this neighbor's house. Allen then waited for McQuirter to pass. Approximately ten minutes later, Allen proceeded walking toward her house, and McQuirter came in her direction from behind a telephone pole. She told the children to run to a house owned by another neighbor, Lewis Simmons (presumably a white cisgender man), to tell him to come and meet her. Allen testified that once McQuirter saw Simmons, he turned and went back down the street to the intersection and leaned on a stop sign across the street from Allen's home. Allen watched McQuirter from Simmons's porch for about thirty minutes, then McQuirter left, and Allen walked home.

The court found that Allen's testimony was corroborated by her young daughter and by Simmons. The daughter testified that McQuirter was within six feet of Allen as she and the children approached the first neighbor's house. The daughter also testified that there was a while when she didn't see McQuirter at the intersection. Simmons testified that the little girls ran up on his porch and said a Negro was after them. He also testified that he walked down the sidewalk to meet Allen and saw McQuirter walk down the street before stopping at the intersection (in front of Allen's home) for approximately thirty minutes.

The court considered, and accepted, the testimony of three (presumably white cisgender male) police officers, who said McQuirter confessed his intent to rape Allen after being arrested and held in jail.

---

[10] *McQuirter*, at 388.
[11] *Id.*
[12] *Id.* at 389.

McQuirter's testimony told a completely different story with respect to his intent, but largely the same story with respect to his movements. McQuirter testified that he did not intend to interact with Allen, and in fact, moved to avoid her. McQuirter testified that he and Bill Page, a friend, carried a load of junk-iron from Monroeville to Pensacola, and on their way back to Monroeville, they stopped in Atmore. They parked the truck near the "Tiny Diner" and rode to the Front in a cab. McQuirter returned to the truck around 8:00 p.m. and waited for approximately thirty minutes before deciding to look for Page. As he walked down the street, he saw Allen and the children. He turned around and waited until he thought they had left, then he walked up the street toward the Front. When he reached the intersection, he decided he did not want to go back to the Front and he sat around there for a few minutes. He eventually decided to return to the Front, where he stayed until he returned to the truck and was arrested. McQuirter denied following Allen, making any gesture toward her or the children, or making the statements testified to by the officers.

After reciting this evidence, the court provided minimal analysis. The court held that the evidence "was sufficient to warrant the submission of the question of defendant's guilt to the jury, and was ample to sustain the judgment of conviction."[13] Citing a much earlier case, *Burton v. State*, 8 Ala. App. 295 (1913), the court explained that under Alabama law, a conviction for an attempt to commit an assault with intent to rape was justified if the jury was satisfied "beyond a reasonable doubt that [McQuirter] intended to have sexual intercourse with [Allen] against her will, by force or by putting her in fear." The court held that intent was a question to be determined by a jury, and established law at the time held that "[i]n determining the question of intention the jury may consider social conditions and customs founded upon racial differences, such as that the prosecutrix was a white woman and defendant was a Negro man."[14] The court then tersely held that the introduction of the officers' statements was proper because there were facts from which a jury could reasonably infer that the crime had been committed.[15] The "facts" being simply that McQuirter was a Black man who walked in some proximity to a white woman.

THE FEMINIST JUDGMENT

Rewriting *McQuirter* from a feminist perspective provides an opportunity to confront *racialized* gender stereotypes and to engage in race-conscious intersectional analysis. While reading the original *McQuirter* opinion makes plain that McQuirter's race is the key factor upholding his conviction, the outcome of the

---

[13] Id.
[14] Id.
[15] Id.

original opinion is also tied to the white femaleness of the purported victim and the white patriarchal gaze built into rape laws. The monumental failing of the original opinion from a feminist perspective is that it completely failed to provide any critical analysis of race or gender – much less the intersection between these identities. While the court easily accepted that it could consider McQuirter's race and gender, it provided no context or guidance on *how* these identities should be considered or their relevance to a correct and legally sound outcome. Instead, the opinion relied on what the original authoring judge took as plain common sense: Because McQuirter was a Black man, this was evidence he intended to rape Allen, because she was a white woman. The feminist opinion of Professor Cortney Lollar, writing as Judge Lollar, digs deeper into the analysis of race and gender and exposes that flawed assumptions based on McQuirter's identities should not impact the outcome of McQuirter's case. By separating race and gender stereotypes from the evidence of what *happened* (a brief walk down the street), Lollar satisfyingly rejects McQuirter's conviction for assault with the intent to rape as unsupported by evidence.

Lollar's rewritten opinion first sets up the facts much differently than in the original *McQuirter* opinion and acknowledges that McQuirter and Allen's testimony is consistent. Where the original *McQuirter* opinion suggested that McQuirter's actions were suspicious, stating McQuirter followed Allen down the street and then waited by Allen's home, Lollar avoids interjecting controversy where it is unsupported by the facts. The rewritten opinion states that both McQuirter and Allen acknowledged that they walked down the same street, did not exchange words or come in contact, and there was no reason to believe that McQuirter knew the intersection upon which he stood was across from Allen's home. Lollar correctly identifies that the singular dispute between Allen and McQuirter was the interpretation of McQuirter's intentions. By laying out the facts in this manner, the rewritten opinion is able to separate out the facts of what happened from the facts derived from McQuirter and Allen's identities.

With the factual record simply and plainly established, Lollar's opinion then fleshes out the notably anti-feminist legal standard under which McQuirter was convicted. Lollar highlights the specific intent and force required for a conviction of assault with intent to rape under Alabama law. By doing so, she exposes the nearly insurmountable evidentiary bar that courts normally required for a man to be convicted of an assault with an intent to rape. Citing 1875 precedent, Lollar explains that to convict, the evidence must show that the defendant intended not only to "gratify his passion" on a woman, but also that he intended to do so with "force" and "notwithstanding any resistance on her part."[16] This troubling standard does not take into account the perspective of the female victim, but is instead rooted in a male-centric conception of the thin line between rape and sex, "adjudicating the level

---

[16] Quoting *McNair v. State*, 53 Ala. 453, 455, 456 (1875).

of acceptable force starting just above the level set by what is seen as normal male sexual behavior....".[17] The question then rests on what *amount* of sexual violence should be permissible (not whether sexual violence should be permissible at all) and how strongly a woman rejected this violence. While traditional feminists are likely to recognize that this standard harms women, it may be less obvious to some that it also feeds anti-Blackness. The root of "normal male sexual behavior" masking deference to whiteness – allowing for Black male behavior to be considered inherently abnormal, and "normal male sexual behavior" to be particularly aggressive when aimed at Black women.

Lollar then summarizes and compares two factually similar cases, *State v. Massey*, 86 N.C. 658 (1882) and *Dorsey v. State*, 24 S.E. 135 (Ga. 1899). While these cases are from different states, the relevant criminal codes are nearly identical, and the actions of the male defendants were notably more aggressive and verbal toward their alleged victims. Still, both resulted in a court refusing to uphold a conviction for a man charged with assault with the intent to rape. Lollar first uses *Massey* to highlight how a white woman's testimony of a white man running after and threatening to kill her and her children was *not* evidence of an intent to rape, but only "raised a suspicion" and was therefore insufficient to be heard by a jury.[18]

Lollar then discusses *Dorsey*, a case in which a Black male defendant allegedly threatened a white woman while holding a gun and chasing her for several yards.[19] Lollar compares McQuirter's actions to the much more aggressive actions of Dorsey; the rewritten opinion also adds that Allen was with three children and in a residential area where neighbors were readily at hand – suggesting that this should further negate the likelihood of McQuirter's intention to rape. While it seems that the rewritten opinion aims to highlight the gap between the facts in *Dorsey* and *McQuirter* (to make clear that McQuirter's conviction should *not* be upheld), this analysis disappointingly steps briefly into the white male gaze of rape laws. It does this by shifting the analysis of McQuirter's intent and actions to the feasibility he might successfully victimize Allen. Under a feminist analysis, the "rapeability" and context of a woman should not factor into whether she is, in fact, a victim. A feminist lens would instruct that if Allen were alone and in a dark alley, this would not make McQuirter more, or less, guilty.

However, Lollar's examination of *Dorsey* provides valuable context and legal analysis that is sorely lacking from the original opinion. Where the original opinion cites *Pumphrey v. State*, 156 Ala. 103, 107–108 (1908) and concludes that "social customs" founded on "race differences … can be properly taken into consideration," Lollar's

---

[17] Catharine A. MacKinnon, *Feminism, Marxism, Method, and the State: Toward Feminist Jurisprudence*, 8 SIGNS 635, 649 (1983).
[18] Quoting *Massey v. State*, 86 N.C. at 661.
[19] Despite its factual similarity and implication on the cases cited in the original *McQuirter* opinion, *Dorsey* was not cited in the original *McQuirter* opinion.

rewritten opinion takes one step further and uses *Dorsey* to identify *how* such evidence can be taken into consideration. This leads to the revelation that *Dorsey* clarified that race may be considered only *to rebut a presumption that the accused man sought to obtain the consent of the female*.[20] This rule is problematic with respect to race *and* gender. It is anti-feminist as it protects white men from claims of assault by providing a presumption of consent. And it is racist as this presumption evaporates merely based on Blackness. Still, Lollar effectively uses *Dorsey's* narrowing of the *Pumphrey* rule to make clear that evidence of race alone – even following persuasive legal precedent in 1953 Alabama – was insufficient to convict one of an offense.

The cursory acceptance of racial stereotypes – specifically the stereotype that Black men are sexual predators of white women – is a defining characteristic of the original *McQuirter* opinion. Lollar's feminist rewriting explicitly rejects this. While acknowledging and giving heed to the unavoidable precedent under which this case arose, Lollar addresses the long history of targeting, prosecuting, and killing Black men wrongly charged with rape or attempted rape of white women. Citing the prevalence of lynching (extrajudicial and legally sanctioned) and giving a brief history lesson on the Black Codes (laws explicitly based on race, permitting castration or death for Black men convicted of a rape or assault against a white woman), Lollar urges against the use of anti-Black racism, now thinly veiled as considerations of "social custom," in rape and assault with intent to rape cases. Pushing back on the trope of Black men being sexual predators of white women also raises a feminist challenge to the law's obsession with some types of rapes, and dismissal of others.[21] Lollar simply and clearly rejects that analysis of intent be colored by race stating: "either the facts are sufficient to support a finding of intent or they are not."

Lollar's rewritten opinion also directly addresses and advances the feminist objective that women's claims of sexual violence should be taken seriously. Acknowledging the deeply racialized context of the *McQuirter* case, however, Lollar attempts to employ an intersectional lens,[22] and remarks that while women should be heard, the legal system has not welcomed claims of sexual violence equally. Lollar affirms Allen's reporting and calls on women to come forward with claims regardless of whether a perpetrator is Black or White, noting that if White men were prosecuted equally for behavior deemed unacceptable by Black men, the legal standards would evolve to be more equitable. She also points out that the legal system frequently fails to honor or believe allegations made by Black women – discrediting their voices and undermining the validity of rape laws.

---

[20] *Dorsey*, 34 S.E. at 137.
[21] *See* Dorothy E. Roberts, *Rape, Violence, and Women's Autonomy*, 69 CHI.-KENT L. REV. 359 (1993), at 364–365.
[22] *See* Kimberlé Crenshaw, *Demarginalizing the Intersection of Race and Sex: A Black Feminist Critique of Antidiscrimination Doctrine, Feminist Theory and Antiracist Policies*, 139 U. CHI. LEGAL F. 157–160 (1989) (explaining intersectional analysis).

Lollar's bold feminist and anti-racist voice is a marked difference from the original *McQuirter* opinion, and she refuses to embrace Allen's discomfort (or the court's discomfort) with Black men as a reason to punish McQuirter. However, it would also be interesting to look more closely at the centrality of Allen's whiteness in this case, and how white feminism, broadly, has used the criminal justice system to perpetuate anti-Blackness. Allen, a self-purported victim of attempted sexual violence uses her race to wield the power of a legal system which traditionally disempowers women. Claims of rape or attempted rape have long been misused to weaponize race using the veneer of protecting women,[23] particularly in the context of white women accusing Black men of (or, in the case of McQuirter, merely intending to) rape.[24] Critical race theorist Kimberlé Crenshaw has noted that this can be attributed to the fact that rape laws "generally do not reflect male control over female sexuality, but *white* male regulation of *white* female sexuality."[25] This means that women who benefit from white supremacy have not been innocent bystanders in developing criminal rape laws that disproportionately target Black men.[26] Quite the opposite. The weaponizing of race and pitting of the law's regulation of white women against anti-racism remains salient in discourse around race and gender and the criminalization of Black men. This is exemplified by the modern day "Karen" – a pejorative term describing white women using their privileged racial identity to threaten, harm, or wield entitlement when interacting with nonwhite persons.[27] The testimony of Allen against McQuirter feeds into this vein. Her testimony pushes a version of feminism (white woman protectionism) as a justification for another's punishment – and it is successful not just because McQuirter is Black, but because she is white.[28] Allen's role in bringing criminal charges against McQuirter are not blameless. Critiquing Allen's use of the criminal justice system gives an opportunity to challenge and expose this pattern. On an even broader scale, Allen's problematic role in seeking to punish McQuirter (and assert her privilege) could be used to highlight that criminal punishment may never be the answer to promoting equal rights for women. Instead, we should be raising the profile of the anti-essentialist feminist script that rejects incarceration, embraces abolition, and seeks to improve

---

[23] *See* DIANE MILLER SOMMERVILLE, RAPE AND RACE IN THE NINETEENTH-CENTURY SOUTH (2004).
[24] Crenshaw, *supra* note 22.
[25] *Id.*, at 157.
[26] Bennett Capers, *The Unintentional Rapist*, 87 WASH. U. L. REV. 1345, 1387 (2010).
[27] Hellen Lewis, *The Mythology of Karen*, THE ATLANTIC, Aug. 24, 2020. www.theatlantic.com/international/archive/2020/08/karen-meme-coronavirus/615355/. Widely distributed social media videos have frequently cast "Karens" into the spotlight for illegitimately crying rape or fear, typically of Black men. *See, e.g.*, *Video Shows White Woman Calling Police on Black Man in Central Park*, NEW YORK TIMES, May 27, 2020. www.nytimes.com/video/us/100000007159234/amy-cooper-dog-central-park-police-video.html.
[28] Not only is Allen white, but she benefits from additional class privileges which sharpen her abilities to guide the law's impact on her situation and surroundings. *See* Khiara M. Bridges, *White Privilege and White Disadvantage*, 105 VA. L. REV. 449 (2019).

the lives of all women,[29] while rejecting any form of feminism that benefits from the criminalization of the Black body.

Still, Lollar's feminist opinion easily cures the original *McQuirter* opinion's cursory and logically unsound conclusion. Lollar makes plain that McQuirter's act of "[w]alking down the street and occasionally stopping is not evidence of criminality." Lollar further dismisses the officers' conflicting statements regarding McQuirter's alleged after-the-fact confession of intent, finding that their admission was based on *corpus delecti* that was simply not there. By calling out the facts (or lack thereof), and conducting a robust female-centered analysis, Lollar's opinion expunges the racist and anti-feminist outcome of the original *McQuirter* opinion – despite, and even working within, the hostile laws in operation in 1953 Alabama. Creating this precedent would have been a monumental win, and an important early shift toward race-consciousness, for feminist jurisprudence.

While criminal jurisprudence has shifted away from explicitly using race as a proxy for guilt, the ugly partnership between race and rape laws persists. This partnership has been deeply entrenched into the American psyche through media as well as law. The prevailing myth of Black men as rapists and white women as victims persists, and feeds into the presumptive guilt of Black men for simply being.[30] Even more troublingly, this continuing myth silences the stories of those who are, in fact, most likely to be victims of sexual violence – Black women.[31] Black women continue to be dually victimized – both grossly under protected by the law and over policed,[32] while remaining on the margins of public discourse and legal analysis. The criminal legal system perpetuates this. Unfortunately, while the "social custom" evidence rejected by Lollar in the *McQuirter* rewrite may have disappeared from the pens of appellate jurists, it persists in the offices of prosecutors who evaluate whether to bring rape and sexual assault cases. In those offices, where charging decisions are often the ultimate arbiter of culpability, the cases deemed "winnable" are still governed by who is a presumptive rapist (nonwhite men) and who is a valid victim (white women). There is much more work to be done toward the goal of rape laws and jurisprudence that are neither anti-Black nor anti-Woman. Perhaps one part of the answer is more Black feminist judges.

---

[29] See I. India Thusi, *Feminist Scripts for Punishment*, 134 HARV. L. REV. 2449 (2021) (Book Review of AYA GRUBER, THE FEMINIST WAR ON CRIME: THE UNEXPECTED ROLE OF WOMEN'S LIBERATION IN MASS INCARCERATION (2021)).

[30] This presumptive guilt extends well beyond of the context of rape law. Black men have been killed by law enforcement for actions as innocuous as McQuirter's walk down an Alabama street even without a white woman present – Trayvon Martin for walking in his own Florida neighborhood with skittles, Philando Castile for sitting in his own car with his girlfriend and her young child.

[31] Linda Meyer Williams, *Race and Rape: The Black Woman as Legitimate Victim*, ERIC CLEARINGHOUSE (1986), available at https://eric.ed.gov/?id=ED294970.

[32] KIMBERLÉ CRENSHAW, PRISCILLA OCEN, AND JYOTI NANDA, BLACK GIRLS MATTER: OVERPOLICED AND UNDERPROTECTED (2015).

MCQUIRTER V. STATE, 63 SO.2D 388 (ALA. APP. 1953)

JUDGE CORTNEY LOLLAR DELIVERED THE OPINION OF THE COURT

The question before the court is whether the actions of the appellant, McQuirter, were sufficient to support his conviction for attempt to commit an assault with the intent to rape. Finding the evidence before the court insufficient, we reverse.

I

The facts in this case are largely uncontested. Around 8 o'clock in the evening on a summer night in June, 1951, Mrs. Ted Allen – whose first name is not noted in the record – and her two children, along with the daughter of a neighbor, were enjoying a Coca-Cola at the Tiny Diner in Atmore, Alabama. Upon leaving the diner to walk home, Allen observed Mr. McQuirter – whose first name is similarly not noted in the record – sitting in the cab of a parked truck. As will be discussed further below, precedent compels us to note that Allen is a White woman and McQuirter a Black man. Allen and the children walked past where McQuirter was sitting in his truck. Around the time Allen passed McQuirter, he opened the door to the truck, placing his foot on the running board. According to Allen's testimony, she thought McQuirter said something "unintelligible" to her as she passed. At some point after that, McQuirter got out of his truck and began to walk in the same direction as Allen and the children.

Allen reached a friend's house and "turned in," as she felt uncomfortable having McQuirter behind her. She then waited ten minutes for McQuirter to pass. Once she proceeded on her way, Allen saw McQuirter again. She testified that at this point, she told her children to run to another neighbor's house and tell him to come meet her. The neighbor, Lewis Simmons, came and met her, and according to Allen, McQuirter then went back down the street to an intersection and leaned on a stop sign. The stop sign, it turned out, was across the street from Allen's home, though there is no suggestion that McQuirter knew or had any reason to know this fact. Allen stayed on her neighbor's porch for about thirty minutes, at which point McQuirter left and she went home.

Appellant McQuirter testified to largely the same facts, differing only in his description of his intentions. McQuirter testified that he and Bill Page had been delivering junk-iron in Pensacola. On their way back to Monroeville, they decided to stop in Atmore. They parked the truck near the Tiny Diner and took a cab to the Black section of town, called the "Front." Around 8:00 p.m., McQuirter came back to the truck and sat in the cab for about thirty minutes. He then decided to go back to the Front to try and find Bill Page. He saw Allen and the children go by as he turned to get out of the truck. As a consequence, he waited until he thought they were gone. Then he walked up the street toward the Front. When he reached the aforementioned intersection, he decided he didn't want to go, so he stayed there a few minutes before ultimately deciding he would go on to the Front, where he stayed for twenty-five to thirty minutes before returning to his truck.

McQuirter denied deliberately following Allen, making any gesture toward her or her children, and making any statements to officers after his arrest. In fact, no witness testified to any exchange of words between McQuirter and Allen, any gestures made by McQuirter toward Allen, or any efforts by McQuirter to pursue or chase Allen. The evidence on these points is undisputed. The only dispute between Allen and McQuirter is as to McQuirter's intentions.

The jury also heard from several other witnesses. One of Allen's daughters testified, adding little to contradict either Allen's or McQuirter's testimony. According to Allen's daughter, at one point, McQuirter was within six feet of her mother as they initially approached the first friend's porch. The daughter also testified that there was a period of time during which she didn't see McQuirter at the intersection.

The jury heard from Simmons, who similarly observed McQuirter on the street after the children came to him and told him "a Negro was after them." Simmons said he observed McQuirter on the street in front of Mrs. Allen's home for approximately thirty minutes. Again, this point was uncontested.

The only conflicting testimony, and the critical testimony, was that of three police officers, who testified to statements purportedly made by McQuirter after his arrest. Officer Clarence Bryars testified that McQuirter said he drove to Atmore "with the intention of getting him a white woman that night." Chief W. E. Strickland, corroborated by Chief Deputy Norvelle Seals, testified that McQuirter made several statements in the jail, including that he didn't know what was the matter with him; he was drinking a little; that (contrary to Officer Bryars' testimony) he sat in the truck and made up his mind that he was "going to get the first woman that came by"; and that Allen was that woman. Strickland and Seals also alleged that McQuirter further stated he was "going to carry her in the cotton patch and if she hollered he was going to kill her."

Two character witnesses testified on McQuirter's behalf, telling the jury that McQuirter had a reputation for truth and veracity, as well as for peace and quiet.

The jury convicted and assessed a fine of $500. McQuirter now appeals arguing the trial court erred in denying his motion for a new trial on the ground that the verdict was contrary to the evidence, and in refusing the general affirmative charge. We address these issues in turn.

II

Alabama law establishes that to have sufficient evidence to justify an attempt to commit an assault with the intent to rape, the prosecution must prove beyond a reasonable doubt that the defendant intended to have sexual intercourse with the complaining witness against their will, by force or putting them in fear. *Morris v. State*, 25 So.2d 54, 32 Ala. App. 278 (Ala. App. 1946); *Burton v. State*, 62 So. 394, 8 Ala. App. 295 (Ala. App. 1913). Intent is judged by the facts and circumstances presented at trial.

Case law clearly establishes that an assault with an intent to rape requires proof beyond a reasonable doubt both that McQuirter "desired to gratify his passion upon [Allen's] person," and that he intended to do so in a "forcible" manner, "notwithstanding any resistance on her part." *See McNair v. State*, 53 Ala. 453, 455, 456 (1875). The accused must "us[e] or purpose to use force ... in accomplishing the gratifications of his passions," *id.* at 456, leaving "no reasonable doubt of his intention to gratify his lustful desire against the consent of the female and notwithstanding resistance on her part. This principle is well supported by our own decisions, and we accept it as the law." *Pumphrey v. State*, 156 Ala. 103, 106 (1908). Intent may be inferred from the circumstances. *Id.*

The Alabama Supreme Court previously has accepted that "upon the question of intention ... social customs, founded on race differences ... might properly be taken into consideration." *Id.* at 107–108. In so ruling, however, the Alabama Supreme Court relied on an 1893 Georgia case, *Jackson v. State*, 91 Ga. 322 (1893), a case whose premise was drawn into question by the Georgia Supreme Court a mere six years later. *See Dorsey v. State*, 108 Ga. 477 (1899) (discussed further below). This alone should lead us to question the notion that "social customs, founded on race differences" should play any role in our consideration of an intent to rape.

The facts of this case resemble the facts found by the court in a North Carolina case, *State v. Massey*, 86 N.C. 658 (1882), although even under Allen's version, McQuirter's conduct was not nearly as insistent as the defendant's purported conduct in *Massey*. In that case, according to the North Carolina court, a young woman left her house around 8:00 a.m., intending to visit her mother-in-law, who lived about a mile north. She was also accompanied by her two children, one in a baby carriage and the other five to six years old. They passed Massey's home, and were about halfway to her mother-in-law's when she heard someone say, "halt I intend to ride in that carriage." The complainant turned and saw Massey, and said, "sir?" He replied, "if you don't halt a minute, I'll kill you when I get hold of you." She began to run, and testified that he ran after her, telling her to stop and threatening to kill her if she didn't. When she reached her mother-in-law's gate, he was gone. When she first saw Massey, he was about 75 yards away from her.

North Carolina law, like Alabama law, requires proof beyond a reasonable doubt that the defendant "intended to gratify his passion on the person of the woman, and that he intended to do so, at all events, notwithstanding any resistance on her part." The *Massey* court queried, "Even conceding that the defendant pursued the prosecuting witness with the intent of gratifying his lustful desires upon her, does it follow that he intended to do so 'forcibly and against her will'?" 86 N.C. at 661.

As our colleagues in North Carolina point out, "that is an essential element of the crime, and must be proved. It must be established by evidence that does more than raise a mere suspicion, a conjecture or possibility, for 'evidence which merely shows it *possible* for the fact in issue to be as alleged, or which raises a mere *conjecture* that it is so, is an insufficient foundation for a verdict, and should not be left to the jury." *Id.* On the facts of that case, which for purposes of this opinion we accept as presented by the North Carolina court, and which, as presented, were undoubtedly more indicative of guilt than in McQuirter's case, the *Massey* court found, "there is no evidence ... from which a jury might reasonably come to the conclusion that the defendant intended to have carnal knowledge of the person of the prosecutrix, at all hazards and against her will. At most, the circumstances only raised a suspicion of his purpose, and therefore should not have been left to the consideration of the jury." *Id.*

The race of the parties is not discussed in *Massey*, leading to the presumption that both the complainant and defendant were White. However, in another similar case, the Georgia Supreme Court, as per the usual custom, noted that the complainant was White and defendant Black, as in the instant case. *Dorsey v. State*, 34 S.E. 135, 136 (Ga. 1899). And yet the *Dorsey* court reached a similar conclusion to the *Massey* court – in the process, significantly limiting the Georgia court's ruling in *Jackson*. In *Dorsey*, a woman was walking alone along a public road in the country, on her way to her father-in-law's house. According to the complainant, at a point in the road with no dwellings nearby, a man appeared from behind some bushes at the side of the road with a gun in his hand and said, "I have got you where I have wanted you for a long time." *Id.* He was approximately 20 to 25 yards away at this point. According to her testimony, she turned and fled, and he pursued her for 70 to 75 yards, only ceasing his pursuit when they came in sight of her husband, who was working in a field near the side of the road. *Id.* The accused then ran off. *Id.* He was never closer to the complainant than 10 to 15 yards away, and he did not make any attempt to shoot or injure her. *Id.*

The language of Georgia's assault with intent to rape statute again mirrors Alabama's and North Carolina's. And according to the Georgia high court, "the evidence does not show an intention on the part of the accused to have carnal knowledge of Mrs. Vines forcibly and against her will." *Id.* As an initial matter, the Georgia court pointed out that there was insufficient evidence to establish the defendant intended to have carnal knowledge of the prosecutrix forcibly and against her will. Rather, the defendant may have had some other objective, criminal or not. As the court put it,

> An intention to do any one of three things might be inferred from [the] evidence,— rob, frighten, or rape,—or there might have been some other motive for his conduct difficult to conjecture. It is not sufficient that the intent to do one may as likely be presumed as an intention to commit the others; but the question is, is the intention to commit the crime charged "more likely to be true than any other"?....

Now, can it be said that this evidence points with a greater degree of certainty to an intention to commit rape than to any other act? ... If he did not desire to commit this offense, what was his desire? We do not know. Possibly to rob, possibly to frighten, possibly something else; but we are not willing to say that his conduct showed, beyond a reasonable doubt, that there was more of an intention to commit one than the other. And, if it points to one with as great a degree of certainty as another, that which is the least heinous will be presumed to have been intended. This follows logically from the presumption of innocence which the law raises in favor of a person charged with crime. (*Id.* at 136)

The case before us raises similar questions. Setting aside McQuirter's purported statements to the police, which we'll return to momentarily, the evidence that McQuirter intended "to gratify his lustful desire against the consent of the female and notwithstanding resistance on her part," *Pumphrey v. State*, 156 Ala. 103, 106 (1908), is nonexistent, especially given that the prosecutrix was with her two children and the daughter of a neighbor, and that, even under her version of the facts, McQuirter followed her in a residential area where neighbors were readily at hand.

Of course, there remains the issue of racial differences, which precedent binds us to acknowledge. *Pumphrey v. State*, 156 Ala. at 107–108. We again find Georgia's discussion in *Dorsey* persuasive. The Court began by acknowledging the racial differences between the prosecutrix and the defendant and noting the Georgia common law's recognition that race "may ... be properly considered ... to rebut any presumption that might otherwise arise in favor of the accused that his intention was to obtain the consent of the female." *Dorsey*, 34 S.E. at 137. Yet the court nevertheless emphasized, "No decision of this court has ever been made in which it was held that evidence of [race]... was sufficient to convict one of the offense for which the accused was charged." *Id.* at 137. Indeed, the court surveyed its past cases and found that its decisions "tend to establish the opposite conclusion," that is, that race alone is insufficient to establish intent to rape. *Id.*

Still, it is worth acknowledging here that the role of race weighs heavily in the case before us. As previously noted, our courts have held that, "upon the question of intention ... social customs, founded on race differences ... might properly be taken into consideration." *Pumphrey*, 156 Ala. at 107–108. We therefore take this opportunity to urge trial courts to refrain from relying on racially based "social custom" evidence in the context of rape or attempted rape allegations, particularly as such evidence tends to inject an unfounded presumption of Black male guilt into the factfinding calculus. Dating back to the days of slavery, Black men have been wrongly portrayed in White society as insatiable sexual predators: *See, e.g.*, Arthur Raper, The Tragedy of Lynching 50 (1933) ("[A]ccording to the popular estimate, all Negroes are essentially alike and are inclined to commit certain crimes, chief of which is the rape of white women."). As a consequence of this pervasive and condemnable viewpoint, which is largely accepted in White society, close to one thousand Black men have been lynched:[33] see Ida B. Wells-Barnett, Lynch Law in All Its Phases 12–13 (1892) (calculating that over a seven-year period leading up to 1892, 728 Black Americans were lynched, and that in the first half of 1892, no fewer than 150 had met the same fate), many due to precisely the type of accusation in this case – accusations of sexual overtures toward White women. The allegations and trial court conviction in McQuirter's case cannot be removed from that context.

Certainly since *Powell v. Alabama*, 287 U.S. 45 (1932), where the lack of process for nine Black youth accused of raping two White women was on full display, the procedural protections provided for Black men accused of serious crimes have become more present, in theory at least. But the extrajudicial killings and terror Black men continue to face upon the allegation of rape by a White woman, or even an allegation of a perceived sexual advance far short of rape, cannot be overestimated. As a court, we must reject and condemn presumptions solely based on skin color or race. Especially when a legal sentence of death is the possible, and indeed often the probable, result if the allegation is against a Black man by a White woman. For this reason, we consider Allen and McQuirter's racial identities with caution and consciously reject presumptions based on racial stereotypes.

To be clear, we are not suggesting that we remove race from explicit consideration only to permit jurors and trial judges implicitly to take it into account. Our previous conversion of explicitly race-based criminal prohibitions to race-neutral ones has not done much to transform the judicial landscape. The Black Codes in existence through 1866 permitted the death penalty or castration for rape when the person convicted was Black and the accuser White. *See, e.g.*, Alabama Code of 1852 (death penalty for rape of a White woman by a slave or free Black); Mississippi 1857 Statute (death penalty for attempted carnal connection with or rape of a White female under fourteen by a slave); Tennessee 1858 Law (death by hanging for rape of a free White woman by a slave or free Black); Missouri 1825 Statute (castration for rape or attempted rape by a Black or mulatto); Arkansas Code of 1838 (death penalty for assault with intent to commit rape by a Black or mulatto). Federal law ultimately invalidated these Codes because they explicitly permitted differential treatment of Black and White individuals under the law. *See* U.S. Const., amend. XIV; Civil Rights Act, ch. 31, 14 Stat. 27 (1866); Freedmen's Bureau Act, ch. 200, 14 Stat. 176 (1866).

---

[33] In fact, the number proved to be much higher. According to the Equal Justice Initiative's 2017 Lynching in America report, 4,425 individuals in at least twenty states were victims of racial terror lynchings between 1877 and 1950. EQUAL JUSTICE INITIATIVE, LYNCHING IN AMERICA: CONFRONTING THE LEGACY OF RACIAL TERROR (3rd ed. 2017), https://lynchinginamerica.eji.org/report/. Although more than 80 percent of lynchings between 1889 and 1918 occurred in the South, lynchings were not unique to southern states; they occurred in at least eight other states. *Id.* Approximately 25 percent of Black lynching victims were accused of sexual assaults. *Id.*

And yet, as we see here, the presence of facially race-neutral rape and assault with intent to rape statutes has not cured the almost singular focus on race in the context of rape allegations lodged against Black men by White women, both in the legal and extralegal landscape. See, e.g., Raper, at 21; James H. Chadbourn, *Plan for Survey of Lynching and the Judicial Process*, 9 N.C. L. Rev. 330, 332–333 (1931). In fact, Alabama courts continue to have to take special precautions to protect Black men accused of rape from extrajudicial threats that stem from these unfounded yet deeply rooted racial stereotypes. *Thompson v. State*, 117 Ala. 67 (1898) (change of venue granted for Black defendant accused of rape because threats of mob violence threatened defendant's imminent death or would pressure jury into convicting). Extrajudicial lynchings are but one in a line of egregious and deadly practices against Black men accused of raping White women that began during slavery and continued during the Black Codes. See, e.g., William Reynolds, *The Remedy for Lynch Law*, 7 Yale L. J. 20, 20 (1897).

In acknowledging this racial legacy, we emphasize the need for trial courts to be extraordinarily cautious in how they consider race when evaluating allegations of attempted rape lodged by a White woman against a Black man. Permitting consideration of social customs based on race in an evaluation of whether intent to rape is present allows deep-rooted racial stereotypes to flourish and shape the contours of our criminal jurisprudence, as well as the future lives of those who may be falsely accused. Certainly, jurors' views are influenced by the social mores of their surrounding communities, and inevitably, those views will shape the verdicts they reach not only in rape and assault with intent to rape cases, but in all cases. However, the fact that some in our communities endorse extrajudicial lynching and presumptive viewpoints about an individual's actions or sexual desires based on race does not mean we can or should sanction those ungrounded beliefs in our legal analysis.

If the evidence is insufficient to find intent to rape when considered in the context of a White man accused of assault with intent to rape a White woman, it likewise is insufficient to find intent when a Black man is accused of the identical crime. Neither the accused's race nor any "social custom" should change the intent analysis. Either the facts are sufficient to support a finding of intent or they are not.

This is not to discount Allen's allegations in this case. Too often women have been and continue to be silenced or disregarded when alleging rape, attempted rape, or assault with intent to rape, particularly when the allegations are aimed at White men. The disregard and disrespect for women's claims of rape, attempted rape, and assault with intent to rape are even more profound for Black and other non-White women, who can make extraordinarily credible allegations, only to have prosecutors and courts deem their claims incredible and unworthy of belief. We see this downplaying of women's claims of nonconsent in the legal requirements that a defendant must act with force and a victim must resist in order for the encounter to be viewed as a criminal rape. If neither force nor resistance is present, in many jurisdictions, no rape has occurred. If the allegations come from a Black woman, even when there is clear proof of force, resistance, and nonconsent, and abundant evidence of intent, her claims are dismissed out of hand. Marital rape continues to be permissible in most jurisdictions, as it is in our own. *Cf.* Anonymous, 206 Ala. 295, 297 (1921) (recognizing that marriage confirms an implied consent to sexual intercourse with one's spouse). Likewise, our jurisprudence presumes that a woman's lack of chastity negates an argument of nonconsent. *Story v. State*, 178 Ala. 98, 102–103 (1912). In short, most of the parameters built into our rape, attempted rape, and assault with intent to rape statutes pay little heed to a woman's perspective, a problem that is compounded exponentially for women who are not White due to the very "social customs" to which we decline to give deference today.

The one context in which our legal system consistently encourages a woman's voice crying rape is when the accusation is lodged by a White woman against a Black man. Numerous other assaults with intent to rape, attempted rapes, and actual rapes are never reported to police or to anyone because women know that these allegations will rarely be pursued or punished. By endorsing primarily allegations by White women against Black men, our legal system implicitly condones assaults of a sexual nature conducted by White men against women. Moreover, in failing to honor or believe even the most compelling allegations of assaults and rapes made by Black women against White men, the criminal legal system sends the unmistakable message that Black women are not valued. The legal system's discrediting of certain voices and convenient use of others undermines the very validity of our system of laws.

We hope this opinion begins a dialogue that encourages courts and lawyers to be more cognizant of these issues and to act with deliberate attention to race and gender dynamics when considering a rape, attempted rape, or assault with intent to rape allegation. Although many powerful factors, systemic and personal, may prevent someone from reporting a rape or attempted rape, including a very real threat of danger from the person accused, the barriers to an effective prosecution should not include unfounded racial prejudices and sex-based stereotypes. The only way our system can become the fair and just system for which we strive is if we continue to challenge the dangerous race- and sex-based presumptions that persistently work to undermine an equitable system of justice.

All of that said, on the facts of this case, we find the evidence insufficient to support McQuirter's conviction. On these facts, no reasonable jury could find beyond a reasonable doubt that the State met its burden of proving McQuirter had the intent to rape Allen. As the *Massey* court noted, "Every man is presumed to be innocent until the contrary is proved, and it is a well-established rule in criminal cases, that if there is any reasonable hypothesis upon which the circumstances are consistent with the innocence of the party accused, the court should instruct the jury to acquit, for the reason the proof fails to sustain the charge." *Massey*, 86 N.C.

at 660–661. Indeed, the testimony here is consistent and provides ample hypotheses upon which the circumstances are wholly consistent with innocence. According to Allen's and Simmons's testimony, McQuirter followed behind Allen, never approaching her, never speaking to her, and never threatening her with a weapon or words. McQuirter is accused of nothing more than walking in some proximity to Allen. "Undoubtedly the right of locomotion, the right to remove from one place to another according to inclination, is an attribute of personal liberty, and the right, ordinarily, of free transit from or through the territory of any state is a right secured by the 14th Amendment and by other provisions of the Constitution." *Williams v. Fears*, 179 U.S 270, 274 (1900). Walking down the street and occasionally stopping is not evidence of criminality. Thus, there is nothing in the record, other than inadmissible second-hand statements, to support a conclusion that McQuirter intended to have sexual intercourse with Allen *at all*, much less "against her will, by force or by putting her in fear," or that he "intended to gratify his lustful desires" against Allen's resistance. The prosecution's primary evidence of intent was McQuirter's race, and that simply is no basis on which to conclude intent was present.

III

The Alabama Supreme Court has long held, "The foundation of every criminal accusation, the primary fact, is the *corpus delicti* – the fact that the particular offense, whether it be treason, murder, or other felony, or a misdemeanor, has been committed. Without this fact, there cannot be a guilty agent." *Matthews v. State*, 55 Ala. 187, 191 (1876). When the only evidence of the crime is the extra-judicial confession of the defendant, uncorroborated by other evidence of the *corpus delicti*, the statement itself should not be admitted at trial. *Id.* at 192, 194.

McQuirter contests the admission of the statements he purportedly made to law enforcement in this case. Defense counsel asserts that the officers' testimony was inadmissible because there was "no attempt or overt act toward carrying that intent into effect." In light of our findings in Part II related to McQuirter's lack of intent, we construe this objection to be an objection to the admission of a confession when the *corpus delicti* has not been sufficiently proven to authorize admitting it at trial.

A careful consideration of the evidence adduced at the trial in this case leads us to the conclusion that, independent of the purported admissions and confessions of defendant, there is no legitimate inference that McQuirter attempted to commit an assault with the intent to rape Allen. Therefore, "there was no evidence of the corpus delicti sufficient to authorize the admission in evidence of defendant's confessions, or to authorize his conviction of the crime charged." *Id.*

Consequently, the trial court's admission of the officers' unsubstantiated statements, despite no evidence of McQuirter's intent to commit a rape, was in error. These statements were improperly admitted and thus, McQuirter's conviction, which could only be based on his purported statements, cannot stand.

We also note that McQuirter denies making the incriminating statements testified to by the officers. Although we do not seek to impugn the officers, we do note that the circumstances of McQuirter's "confessions" raise more questions than they answer. However, since McQuirter did not raise that issue on appeal, we defer to another day any discussion of how confessions are obtained, and whether confessions under circumstances such as McQuirter's are truly voluntary under the Due Process Clause.

IV

For the reasons articulated herein, we reverse McQuirter's conviction as unsupported by the evidence.

2

Commentary on *People v. Berry*

CAROLYN B. RAMSEY

Many feminists critique the heat-of-passion defense as a gender-biased means of mitigating murder to voluntary manslaughter for provoked killings.[1] In its traditional form, which some states still use, the doctrine recognizes only a few types of adequate provocation by the victim that historically were understood as affronts to male honor.[2] The judge plays a strict gatekeeping role, precluding the jury from considering the partial defense in cases that fall outside approved categories or involve lapses of time sufficient for the formation of deliberate, premeditated intent to kill.[3] Of the "nineteenth-century four,"[4] the adultery category raises the greatest concern that the defense entrenches sexist victim-blaming in the facially neutral law of homicide.[5]

People v. Berry – a California case decided in 1976[6] – became emblematic of a shift to a broader version of the defense. This version does not require any specific type

---

[1] See, e.g., Caroline Forell, *Gender Equality, Social Values and Provocation Law in the United States, Canada, and Australia*, 14 AM. U. J. GENDER SOC. POL'Y & L. 27, 43–44 (2006); Emily L. Miller, *(Wo)manslaughter: Voluntary Manslaughter, Gender, and the Model Penal Code*, 50 EMORY L. J. 665, 665–669, 693 (2001).

[2] See, e.g., *Riggs v. State*, 138 So. 3d 1014, 1024 (Ala. 2013); *People v. Hernandez*, 562 N.E.2d 219, 226 (Ill. App. Ct. 1990). For the defense's roots in male conceptions of honor, see JEREMY HORDER, PROVOCATION AND RESPONSIBILITY 26–29 (1992).

[3] Carol S. Steiker, *Justice vs. Mercy in the Law of Homicide, The Contest between Rule-of-Law Values and Discretionary Leniency from Common Law to Codification to Constitution*, 47 TEX. TECH. L. REV. 1, 4 (2014).

[4] These four categories were: "(1) a violent assault; (2) an unlawful arrest; (3) mutual combat; (4) the sight of the accused's wife in the act of adultery." Donna K. Coker, *Heat of Passion and Wife Killing Men Who Batter/Men Who Kill*, 2 S. CAL. REV. L. & WOMEN'S STUD. 71, 80 (1992). Some states recognized a fifth category of serious injury to a close relative. See, e.g., *Girouard v. State*, 583 A.2d 718, 721 (Md. 1991).

[5] JENNY MORGAN, WHO KILLS WHOM AND WHY: LOOKING BEYOND THE LEGAL CATEGORIES 39 (Vic. L. Reform Comm. Occasional Paper, 2002); Laurie J. Taylor, Comment, *Provoked Reason in Men and Women: Heat of Passion Manslaughter and Imperfect Self-Defense*, 33 UCLA L. REV. 1679, 1692–1697 (1986). See Susan D. Rozelle, *Controlling Passion: Adultery and the Provocation Defense*, 37 RUTGERS L. J. 197, 228–229 (2005) (arguing that there is no "act justification" for killing an unfaithful spouse).

[6] *People v. Berry*, 556 P.2d 777 (Cal. 1976).

of provocation, and it relaxes or removes the cooling-time limit.[7] A similar statutory defense known as "extreme mental or emotional disturbance" (EMED), which a substantial minority of states borrowed from the Model Penal Code (MPC),[8] shares both these attributes with *Berry*.[9] Collectively, these changes decrease judicial gatekeeping and give juries vast discretion to find a defendant guilty of manslaughter, instead of murder. Yet, if the traditional provocation defense expresses sexist values and produces substantively unequal results along gender lines, the trend that *Berry* and the MPC exemplify is arguably worse.[10]

Berry involved a defendant who killed his wife after she allegedly provoked him over a two-week period by confessing her infidelity, taunting him sexually, threatening to leave him, and finally, screaming when she discovered him in the apartment they formerly shared. Reversing Albert Berry's first-degree murder conviction,[11] the California Supreme Court held that the trial judge should have instructed the jury on voluntary manslaughter, which California law defined as "the unlawful killing of a human being, without malice ... upon a sudden quarrel or heat of passion."[12]

The events leading to the homicide demonstrated Berry's past violence against his wife, Rachel, including two prior choking incidents; the evidence also showed that Berry waited for twenty hours in her apartment with a precut ligature before he strangled her to death.[13] Yet, focusing on Rachel's supposedly provocative conduct and suicidal ideation, the California Supreme Court held that the jury should have been invited to consider whether Berry's emotional state made the killing less blameworthy.[14] Rachel's cumulative provocation of her husband "could arouse a passion of jealousy, pain and sexual rage in an ordinary man of average disposition such as to cause him to act rashly from this passion."[15] Therefore, failure to give a voluntary manslaughter instruction constituted reversible error.

The California Supreme Court's approach to the provocation defense in *Berry* was not unprecedented. Several states, including California, had already eliminated the requirement that provoking behavior must fit precisely into an

---

[7] *Id.* at 780–781.
[8] MPC § 210.3(1) (b) (1962). About twenty states now use some version of the EMED test. Steiker, *supra* note 3, at 6.
[9] The MPC actually eliminates the provoking-act requirement altogether and expands the defendant's qualifying mental state to include mental disorders and other emotional distress besides hot-blooded passion. *See* Carolyn B. Ramsey, *Provoking Change: Comparative Insights on Feminist Homicide Law Reform*, 100 J. CRIM. L. & CRIMINOLOGY 33, 55–56 (2010) [hereinafter Ramsey, *Provoking Change*]; Steiker, *supra* note 3, at 5–6.
[10] Victoria Nourse, *Passion's Progress: Modern Law Reform and the Provocation Defense*, 106 YALE L. J. 1331, 1335–1339, 1384–1390 (1997). *See* Ramsey, *Provoking Change*, *supra* note 9, at 84–88.
[11] *Berry*, 556 P.2d at 783.
[12] CAL. PEN. CODE § 192 (1972).
[13] *See Berry*, 556 P.2d at 780–781.
[14] *Id.*
[15] *Id.*

established category, such as witnessing the spouse in the act of adultery.[16] That said, in California, two conflicting lines of cases had developed as to whether "mere words" could constitute adequate provocation. One held that insults, words of reproach, and offensive gestures do not rise to the level of "serious and highly provoking injury."[17] However, a second line of cases – exemplified by the 1946 opinion, *People v. Valentine* – interpreted California's penal code to have abandoned such common-law limitations.[18]

Berry adopted the second approach. Citing *Valentine*, the appellate opinion stated that words might suffice to inflame the passion of an "ordinary man." The *Berry* court also reframed the defendant's narrative, which had focused on a physical struggle, holding "ample evidence ... support[ed] the conclusion that [Berry's] ... passion was the result of the *long course* of provocatory [sic] conduct by Rachel."[19] California courts continue to cite *Berry* for these aspects of its analysis;[20] however, few other states recognize cumulative provocation.[21] *Berry* appears in myriad criminal law textbooks, although the expansive approach to manslaughter mitigation it illustrates remains a minority doctrine in the United States.[22] Its prominence stems largely from the feminist outrage it has elicited.

Suggesting that silencing a woman by strangling her is an understandable response to her assertion of agency or autonomy in a relationship, the *Berry* opinion crystallized several of criminal law's patriarchal tendencies. It retained the common-law emphasis on how sexual betrayal might lead a man to kill in partially justifiable rage. But it also bore the influence of the emerging, excuse-based strand that unmoored manslaughter mitigation from traditional limits, including what qualifies as provocation and how long uncontrollable emotions can stay hot.[23] The focus of this latter strand is the excusable overthrow of reason by distress; the reformed law ostensibly avoids value judgments about victim misconduct. Yet judges now give voluntary manslaughter instructions in cases of victims who simply chose to file for divorce, get a restraining order, or decline a date.[24]

---

[16] *People v. Valentine*, 169 P.2d 1, 14–15 (Cal. 1946); *People v. Logan*, 164 P. 1121, 1122–1123 (Cal. 1917). See also *Mack v. State*, 63 Ga. 693, 696–697 (1879); *Maher v. People*, 10 Mich. 212, 222 (1862).

[17] *People v. Mendenhall*, 67 P. 325, 326 (Cal. 1902); *People v. Bruggy*, 93 Cal. 476, 481 (1892); *People v. Turley*, 50 Cal. 469, 471 (1875).

[18] *Valentine*, 169 P.2d at 11–14.

[19] *Berry*, 556 P.2d at 781 (emphasis added).

[20] See, e.g., *People v. Vasquez*, 2019 WL 667721 (2019), at *3.

[21] Michal Buchandler-Raphael, *Fear-based Provocation*, 67 AM. U. L. REV. 1719, 1744 & n.115, 779 & n.348 (2018) (noting two states that recognize cumulative provocation).

[22] Most American states now steer a middle course, centered on the concept of "reasonableness," which gives the jury more discretion than the nineteenth-century doctrine did, but still allows the judge a gatekeeping role with regard to cooling-time and adequate provocation. See Steiker, *supra* note 3, at 4–5.

[23] See *People v. Borchers*, 325 P.2d 97, 102 (Cal. 1958) (recognizing the concept of cumulative provocation).

[24] Nourse, *supra* note 10, at 1333–1335, 1343, 1347–1350 & tbls. A & B.

States that have followed this trend permit, or even encourage, jurors to empathize with defendants whose rage stemmed from their inability to control an intimate partner – or some other morally dubious reason – in a much wider array of situations than the traditional doctrine contemplated. Despite the provocation defense's compassion for cuckolded husbands, nineteenth- and early twentieth-century courts rarely allowed juries to extend mitigation to a man's act of revenge against a wife or lover based on mere separation, jealousy, or suspicion of unfaithfulness,[25] and by the nineteenth century, the adultery category also applied to a husband's infidelity.[26] Indeed, Victorian norms held male defendants to stricter standards of self-control than female defendants.[27] *Berry*, by contrast, undermined even the paternalistic protection criminal law had offered women who sought to end a relationship before second-wave feminist reforms addressed domestic violence.

Today, neither the heat-of-passion defense nor EMED are expressly gendered. Modern jurisdictions use the term "reasonable person" as a yardstick.[28] Hence, EMED and the provocation doctrine in *Berry* offend principles of substantive rather than formal equality. The disparate *impact* on the basis of gender (not distinctions on the face of the law) and the law's implied embrace of chauvinistic values animate calls to abolish or reform these defenses.[29] American men are four times more likely to kill an intimate partner of any gender than women are.[30] Additionally, empirical research indicates that men typically kill their partners to exercise control over them, while women most often use lethal violence when they fear being killed or injured.[31] Some women retaliate violently against partners who have left them, but such cases are comparatively rare.[32] A defense that extends mercy when jealous rage

---

[25] Carolyn B. Ramsey, *Domestic Violence and State Intervention in the American West and Australia, 1860–1930*, 86 IND. L. J. 185, 225–228 (2011) [hereinafter Ramsey, *Domestic Violence*].

[26] The law of early modern England and its colonies defined adultery as intercourse with a married or espoused woman; a married man could not commit adultery by sleeping with a single female. *See* R. v. *Mawgridge* (1706) 84 Eng. Rep. 1107, 1115 (QB), Kel. 119, 137–138; MARY BETH NORTON, FOUNDING MOTHERS AND FATHERS: GENDERED POWER AND THE FORMING OF AMERICAN SOCIETY 342 (1996).

[27] While men were punished for murder if the alleged provocation fell outside any recognized category or enough time had passed for a reasonable *man* to cool off, nineteenth-century courts and juries tended to favor mitigation or acquittal in women's cases with less regard for doctrinal boundaries. Ramsey, *Provoking Change*, *supra* note 9, at 49–51; Ramsey, *Domestic Violence*, *supra* note 25, at 250–254.

[28] Nourse, *supra* 10, at 1384–1385.

[29] HORDER, *supra* note 2, at 186–187, 194, 197; Forell, *supra* note 1, at 29–30; Morgan, *supra* note 5, at 7; Nourse, *supra* note 10, at 1338; Ramsey, *Provoking Change*, *supra* note 9, at 106.

[30] James Alan Fox & Emma E. Fridel, *Gender Differences in Patterns and Trends in U.S. Homicide, 1976–2017*, 6 VIOLENCE & GENDER 27, 29 tbl.1 (2019).

[31] *Id.* at 28; Morgan, *supra* note 5, at 23–29.

[32] *See, e.g.*, Michael Granberry, *Broderick Found Guilty of Murder in Second Degree*, L.A. TIMES (Dec. 11, 1991, 12:00 a.m.), available at https://www.latimes.com/la-me-broderick11dec1191-story.html and https://perma.cc/2W95-ZT4C (describing Betty Broderick's conviction for the fatal shooting of her unfaithful ex-husband and his new wife).

or another emotion leads to homicide, without any rules about the timing or reason for the killing, thus perpetuates hyper-masculine values.

THE FEMINIST JUDGMENT

What if *Berry* had been decided differently? In her thoughtful judgment, Professor Susan D. Rozelle (writing as Justice Rozelle) imagines how the opinion would have unfolded had the court affirmed Berry's murder conviction. Such a holding would have drawn a line between a heat-of-passion killing and a deliberate murder, between a killer overwhelmed by sudden emotion and a strangler who snuffed out his spouse's life as the culmination of prior choking incidents. Along the way, Rozelle disposes of further claims, including Berry's argument that evidence of his prior bad acts and Rachel's fear that he would kill her was inadmissible. The judgment also describes the facts in a way that corrects the sexist slant of the real California Supreme Court.

Rozelle's handling of the provocation claim constitutes the feminist core of the judgment. After rejecting Berry's threshold arguments that domestic homicides are "inherently crimes of passion" and that a man cannot lie in wait in his own home to kill his victim, Rozelle provides a three-pronged analysis to support her ruling that no provocation instruction was required. First, she holds that the twenty hours Berry spent waiting for Rachel amounted to sufficient cooling time to preclude his heat-of-passion claim as a matter of law. She remarks that Berry had moved out, underscoring that this was a "separation" murder.[33] Rachel sought to get her husband arrested for choking her and might have soon divorced him. Berry thus had both the time and the motive for deliberate, premeditated murder.

Next, Rozelle offers cautious guidance on the "verbal provocation" issue. Declining to reinstate the traditional "mere words" limit, she explains that a reactive scream differs from words spoken during a heated dispute. This reasoning dovetails with the revised holding on state-of-mind evidence of Rachel's fear, which was probative of whether Berry lay in wait and emerged, unseen, to choke Rachel from behind. By allowing evidence that Rachel feared Berry, the feminist judgment bolsters the prosecution theory that her scream (which the appellate court emphasized *sua sponte*) constituted a reaction to the defendant's attack, rather than the last taunt in a course of provocative behavior.

Third, Rozelle concludes that expert testimony about Berry's rage was insufficient to establish several elements of the provocation defense, including the requirement that an ordinary, reasonable person would have become similarly emotional. Staying close to the briefs, the rewritten opinion steers clear of several questions

---

[33] Martha R. Mahoney, *Legal Images of Battered Women: Redefining the Issue of Separation*, 90 Mich. L. Rev. 1, 65 (1991). ("Separation assault is the attack on the woman's body and volition in which her partner seeks to prevent her from leaving, retaliate for the separation, or force her to return.")

that often trouble readers of the real case. For example, Rozelle does not disturb the expert witness's characterization of the victim (whom he had never examined) as suicidal and mentally unbalanced. Displaying typical judicial deference to an expert witness, the rewritten judgment avoids criticizing the leeway Dr. Blinder was given to psychoanalyze and blame Rachel and other women in Berry's life.

Rozelle nevertheless denies that testimony by Berry and Blinder warranted an instruction on "sudden quarrel or heat of passion" and emphasizes that Berry's idiosyncrasies had no bearing on the requisite provocation or the cooling-time limit. She also holds that there was not enough evidence of Berry's diminished capacity to necessitate an instruction on this alternate basis for mitigation.[34] The lasting significance of her opinion might be its refusal to categorize domestic homicides as inherently hot-blooded crimes and its reassertion of objective constraints on cooling time. Rozelle also establishes the admissibility of important evidence about the context of intimate-partner homicide, validating the view of the prosecutor and the jury that Berry was a calculating killer.

Rozelle's evidentiary rulings harmonize with the insight of battered women's advocates that jurors need information about the abusive relationship beyond the narrow facts of the charged incident. This context helps jurors and others in the criminal legal system determine the identity of the primary or predominant abuser in the relationship. The real *Berry* opinion underlined the victim's alleged pattern of provocation, not the defendant's repeated efforts to choke her. The rewritten judgment deems evidence of Berry's prior strangulation of Rachel and his assault on his previous spouse admissible to demonstrate his motive, intent, and patterned behavior. The jury's verdict that Berry was a fully culpable murderer makes sense considering his use of escalating physical violence to regain power and control in his marriage. The prior-acts evidence bolstered another aspect of the prosecution's theory: Berry was on probation for stabbing his second wife; he killed Rachel, at least in part, because criminal charges for the nonfatal choking incidents might have revoked his probation. Several states now have special statutes on the admissibility of prior-acts evidence in domestic violence cases.[35] Had courts more readily admitted such evidence for nonpropensity purposes in the 1970s and 1980s, specific provisions might not have been necessary to ensure that juries understand the context of intimate assaults.

Rozelle's judgment affirms the narrative of Berry as a deliberate murderer – the story that the jury chose to believe at trial. However, her opinion avoids boldly restructuring the provocation defense according to feminist values or explaining how expansive versions of it excuse lethal violence in morally problematic, sexist

---

[34] California voters abolished the diminished capacity defense in 1981 after its successful use by Dan White – the assassin of San Francisco Mayor George Moscone and LGBTQ leader Harvey Milk, who was the city's first openly gay Supervisor. Dr. Martin Blinder, the expert who testified for Berry, also appeared for the defense in White's case. Ramsey, *Provoking Change*, supra note 9, at 79 n.226.

[35] *See, e.g.*, COLO. REV. STAT. ANN. §18-6-801.5 (West 2020); CAL. EVID. CODE ANN. § 1109 (West 2006).

ways. Rozelle does not elucidate the need, from a feminist perspective, for judicial gatekeeping on the cooling-time limit and the bounds of adequate provocation. Nor does she reject the concept of cumulative provocation outright, choosing instead to distinguish an earlier case, *People v. Borchers*,[36] on the facts. The theoretical insights behind Rozelle's holdings remain largely unspoken, though she has taken a stronger stance against a broad provocation defense elsewhere.[37] Her meticulous rewrite of *Berry* thus stops short of being overtly feminist.

THE CHANGING FEMINIST CONVERSATION

From the perspective of radical feminism, the expanded heat-of-passion defense – with its acceptance of male rage as "ordinary" and its tacit suggestion that myriad types of female revolt partially excuse homicide – tightened the grip of patriarchal power. Yet dominance theory is not the only lens to scrutinize provocation. The ability of homophobic, xenophobic, and racist killers to shelter under *Berry* or EMED gives anti-subordination theorists cause for concern,[38] while others note that a narrower doctrine satisfies a mix of retributive, utilitarian, and expressive goals.[39] Furthermore, even if the liberalization of the defense was well-intentioned and informed by contemporary psychology, reframing wanton aggression as explicable and excusable offends values of nonviolence central to the feminist movement.

The feminist conversation about criminal law is changing, and in recent decades, some feminists have parted company with provocation's critics. These new perspectives fall into several overlapping categories. First, commentators have resurrected an old worry that cooling-time limits preclude heat-of-passion mitigation for long-term abuse survivors and other sympathetic defendants.[40] Second, mass incarceration injects new urgency into debates about substantive criminal law and the punishment of violence.[41] It is argued that "progressive scholars must liberate themselves from the dogma that the heat-of-passion defense is inherently a woman-hating doctrine" and focus their critiques instead on the violence the state inflicts on marginalized people, especially Black men.[42] These thorny issues have no easy answers, but they demand thoughtful discussion.

Proposals for reforming heat-of-passion mitigation are often "ratchet-up" solutions that would "make it harder for *any* murder defendant to invoke the provocation

---

[36] 325 P.2d 97 (Cal. 1958).
[37] See Rozelle, *Controlling Passion*, supra note 5, at 200–201, 226, 233.
[38] See, e.g., CYNTHIA LEE, MURDER AND THE REASONABLE MAN: PASSION AND FEAR IN THE CRIMINAL COURTROOM 17–45, 61–63, 67–95, 137–174, 253, 277 (2003).
[39] Nourse, *supra* note 10, at 1401 n.402.
[40] See, e.g., Buchandler-Raphael, *supra* note 21, at 1733, 1766. See also Taylor, *supra* note 5, at 1714, 1734.
[41] DAVID ALAN SKLANSKY, A PATTERN OF VIOLENCE: HOW THE LAW CLASSIFIES CRIMES AND WHAT IT MEANS FOR JUSTICE 1–3, 230–232 (2021).
[42] Aya Gruber, *A Provocative Defense*, 103 CALIF. L. REV. 273, 302 (2015).

defense."[43] As to the objection that a curtailed doctrine would disadvantage battered women, abused children, and others who use self-protective violence out of fear, one rejoinder is that the availability of provocation claims is only a stop-gap. Reforming "perfect" and "imperfect" self-defense law to address defects in the required elements and ensure that the jury hears probative evidence about the victim's past violence would enable abuse survivors charged with murder to make cognizable claims for acquittal or mitigation.[44] Such doctrines might fit their cases better, in terms of facts and feminist values, than trying to shoehorn them into a *Berry* or EMED framework. At the same time, refusal to confront instances when women use force in unjustifiable and inexcusable ways does not strengthen feminism. The goal should be to ensure the law avoids formal and substantive inequality, not to prevent women's convictions for serious crimes in all cases.

The second concern – the "train wreck of mass incarceration"[45] – might prompt questions about whether redressing racial inequity should trump redressing gender inequity when it comes to punishing violence. But these harms often intersect, complicating the analysis. Should gender-violence victims – including women of color, whom intimate-partner homicide disproportionately affects[46] – have to wait for justice until the structural sources of criminality are eliminated? A key aspect of the solution involves determining which types of violence warrant imprisonment and which could be handled in other ways.[47] For example, the imprisonment of many domestic abusers convicted of nonfatal offenses might lead to unemployment and other stressors predictive of femicide[48] in the short run without keeping their victims safe in the long run. By contrast, murder stands alone as the ultimate, irreparable crime against the body; there are reasons to believe it always warrants serious punishment relative to lesser homicides and myriad other crimes. Consequently, murder and its defenses must be defined with great care.

Whether or not EMED and broad heat-of-passion instructions widely result in lesser convictions and lighter sentences for chauvinistic killers, *Berry* perpetuated harmful gender stereotypes. It also created the potential for inconsistent, biased application in future cases and sent a morally deficient message about which homicides deserve mercy. For that reason, Justice Rozelle's painstaking effort to rewrite the opinion takes a step in the right direction.

---

[43] Aya Gruber, *Murder, Minority Victims, and Mercy*, 85 U. COLO. L. REV. 129, 149–150 (2014) (emphasis added).

[44] Ramsey, *Provoking Change*, supra note 9, at 88, 100–104.

[45] SKLANSKY, *supra* note 41, at 2.

[46] Emily Pertrosky et al., CDC, *Racial and Ethnic Differences in Homicides of Adult Women and the Role of Intimate Partner Violence – United States, 2003–2014*, 66 MORBIDITY & MORTALITY WKLY. REP. 741, 742–743, 745 (2017), available at https://www.cdc.gov/mmwr/volumes/66/er/pdfs/mm6628a1.pdf.

[47] Carolyn B. Ramsey, *The Stereotyped Offender: Domestic Violence and the Failure of Intervention*, 120 PENN. ST. L. REV. 337, 361 (2015).

[48] See Jacquelyn C. Campbell et al., *Risk Factors for Femicide in Abusive Relationships: Results from a Multisite Case Control Study*, 93 AM. J. PUB. HEALTH 1089, 1092 (2003).

PEOPLE V. BERRY, 556 P.2D 777 (CAL. 1976)
JUSTICE SUSAN D. ROZELLE DELIVERED THE OPINION OF THE COURT

Defendant Albert Berry acknowledges having strangled his wife to death; it is the first-degree murder conviction he appeals. His arguments on that point are without merit, and we affirm.

I. FACTS AND BACKGROUND

Before she ever met the defendant, the victim, Rachel Pessah, had married an American in her native Israel. At 17, she moved with him to the United States, and three years later, he died in a tragic accident. In January 1974, Rachel was an immigrant, newly widowed, and 20 years old when she met the 46-year-old defendant, Albert Berry.

Berry had been married before, as well. He testified that his first wife left him when he was incarcerated at Attica State Prison; his second wife left after he was sent to the Sonoma County Jail. "I stabbed her four times," he offered. After release on probation from that incarceration, he lived with other women, each arrangement lasting only briefly. With respect to one, Berry's expert witness, psychiatrist Dr. Martin Blinder, testified on direct that Berry "put his foot through [her] stereo ... [and went] to jail for this." With respect to another, on direct Berry testified, "She locked me out one day. I broke her door down."

A few months later, Berry met Rachel, and they married on May 27, 1974. Three days after the wedding, Rachel traveled to Israel alone, where she stayed for six weeks. While there, Dr. Blinder testified, she sent Berry two letters. The first stated she loved and missed him, the second that "he forced her to marry him and she expected him to be out of the house when she got back." When she returned on July 13, 1974, she "immediately beg[an] screaming at him that he had forced her to marry him and had ruined her life," and "taunted him about sex she purportedly had with a man in Israel." Dr. Blinder's testimony then turned briefly lyrical before resuming a more prosaic tone:

> On into the night taunts and tirades continue. Finally, exhausted, the Defendant asked his wife to please shut up so he could get some sleep, he had to go to work the next morning. She continues. Finally, he grabs her around the neck and chokes her until she almost faints.
>
> The next ten days are characterized by bitter fights over his purported possessiveness and abuse of her. Yet it is coupled with active sexuality. All the while they are fighting, they are having intercourse, which is not unusual in these kinds of love-hate relationships.

During this time, Dr. Blinder continued, Rachel "would threaten to tell [Berry's] Probation Officer about his assault upon her on the 13th." Berry's testimony aligned with this version of the facts, and added that Rachel also "kept in about ... wanting a divorce."

On the evening of July 22, Berry and Rachel saw a movie and returned around midnight on July 23. Berry testified they had "done some heavy petting," before Rachel again taunted him with her feelings for the other man. "I think I might be pregnant by him and if I have sexual intercourse with you, I don't know whether it will be your baby or his." "I don't want to hear it," he says he replied, and announced he was leaving. "I hate you," Berry testified Rachel told him. "You don't even care for your own children. You never do anything for your own children, try to get in touch with them. How do you expect me to think that you care for me?" In response, Berry testified on direct, "I blanked out. I grabbed her and choked her" until "[s]he became unconscious."

He revived her, he said, and they talked for two hours. Rachel "said she was going to report the incident to the police," and Berry moved his belongings into a locker at the Greyhound Bus station before going to Reno. He called and spoke to Rachel on July 24. She told him she had reported the strangulation from the day before to the police, "they had taken photographs [of her injuries] and there was a warrant for [his] arrest." Berry "tried to talk her out of it," calling again on July 25, in an effort to convince her to drop the charges. He testified that she told him "she never wanted to see me again." She said, he testified on direct, "that I would kill her."

Berry's testimony continued, narrating the events that led up to the killing. He went back to the apartment on July 25 to speak to Rachel, he said. He saw her enter, change clothes, and then leave again. After she was gone, he entered the apartment. For the next 20 hours, Berry waited. He cut a black electrical cord and set it out. He left only once, getting more cigarettes and returning promptly to the apartment.

When Rachel arrived around 11:00 or 11:30 in the morning on July 26, Berry testified, "She saw me and she said, 'Hello.' I said, 'Hello.' She said, 'I suppose you have come here to kill me.' And I said 'Yes.' And then again I said, 'No.' And then I said, 'Yes,' again." Then, "I said, 'I really have come to talk to you.'" Then Rachel screamed, and Berry said he tried to stop her from screaming. "She wouldn't stop," he explained. "We struggled and the next thing I knew I had a telephone cord around her neck."

Berry was arrested on August 1 in San Francisco. He confessed that the murder was intentional, that he planned it, and stated they had an "open and shut case" for first degree murder. At trial, however, he testified that the part of his confession that said he planned to kill Rachel was false, and he "was bent on self-destruction" when he gave it.

At trial, Berry presented a theory of the case centered on his assertion that he killed Rachel in a fit of "uncontrollable rage." Berry himself and his expert, Dr. Blinder, were Berry's only witnesses. Dr. Blinder's testimony focused heavily on Berry's history of dependence on women Dr. Blinder called "provocative," including Rachel and her taunts. Dr. Blinder also testified, however, that Berry did indeed intend to kill Rachel on July 26, and that the killing was due to a "growing, malignant, persistent, enduring kind of impulse. I don't see it as a sudden impulse, and thus I see the homicidal thoughts as recurring. I would suspect that they may have been in evidence even weeks before this." The bulk of Dr. Blinder's testimony concerned his opinion that Berry was motivated by rage rather than reason. Berry testified similarly, in that although he often stated he had killed Rachel on "impulse" in a "sudden rage," when asked on cross why he had cut the black cord while waiting for her in the apartment, he admitted "I had thought about it." He also admitted telling police the reason he switched from the precut, black cord to the telephone cord when strangling Rachel to death. The black cord, he said, "kept slipping out of my hands."

The jury found Berry guilty of both the July 23 assault and of murder in the first degree for the killing committed three days later. Berry appealed, the Court of Appeal affirmed with modification, and Berry now appeals to this Court. His claims are numerous, and we address each in turn. Ultimately, however, we reject all but the modification made by the Court of Appeal: Berry correctly objects to the erroneous inclusion of his prior felony conviction in the judgment. The State concurs on this point, and we affirm the modified judgment, which strikes reference to the prior felony conviction.

II. ASSAULT

Berry was convicted of assault by means of force likely to produce great bodily injury, Cal. Pen. Code § 245(a), for strangling Rachel into unconsciousness on July 23, three days before he strangled her to death. He claims error in the trial court's failure to instruct *sua sponte* on simple assault as a lesser and included offense. Simple assault is "an unlawful attempt, coupled with a present ability, to commit a violent injury on the person of another," Cal. Pen. Code § 240 (1976).

There was no error. "[T]he trial court may properly refuse to instruct upon simple assault where the evidence is such as to make it clear that if the defendant is guilty at all, he is guilty of the higher offense [of felonious assault]." *People v. McCoy* (1944) 25 Cal. 2d 177, 187–188. Berry himself testified that on July 23, he "choked her [until] she became unconscious." Berry did not merely "attempt" to injure Rachel on that date, as would befit an instruction on simple assault. According to his own uncontradicted testimony, he strangled her until he rendered her unconscious. This is unquestionably "force likely to produce great bodily injury," as befits the felonious assault instruction given, Cal. Pen. Code § 245(a), and therefore the court properly refused the lesser included instruction on simple assault. *People v. McCoy*, 25 Cal. 2d at 187–188. There being no other contentions concerning the assault conviction, the judgment as to that count is affirmed as modified by the exclusion of reference to the prior felony.

II. FIRST-DEGREE MURDER

A. *Admission of Rachel's Statement Regarding her Fear of Berry*

Berry next contends the trial court erred by allowing into evidence the rebuttal testimony of Paul Cummins, the assistant district attorney for San Francisco, that Rachel told him she feared Berry would kill her when she asked Cummins that Berry be arrested. Admitted under the state of mind exception to the hearsay rule, Evidence Code § 1250(a), Berry claims error because Rachel's state of mind was "irrelevant ... not at issue in this case."

Rachel's state of mind was at issue because her "expressions of fear were relevant to an issue of fact raised by the defense." People v. Lew (1968) 68 Cal. 2d 774, 780. The prosecution here presented evidence of Berry's lying in wait to support the first-degree murder charge, Cal. Pen. Code § 189. This included proof that Berry had waited in Rachel's apartment for 20 hours for her to arrive, and that when she did so, he strangled her from behind with a black electrical cord he had cut to serve as a ligature while he was waiting. There was no sign of a struggle. Berry had no injuries. There were no scratches or bruising that a struggling victim might inflict on an assailant who approached openly. Nor did anything appear out of place in the apartment. No furnishings had been knocked over, no belongings scattered as they might have been if the victim had seen her assailant reach for her throat and tried to escape or fight back. None, that is, but a key to the front door, found on the floor near the entryway. This, too, the prosecutor argued, supported the claim of lying in wait for a surprise attack from behind.

Berry, in contrast, claimed he had not planned to kill Rachel, but that when she unlocked her door, she saw him in the kitchen area. "[S]he said, 'Hello.' I said, 'Hello.' She said, 'I suppose you have come here to kill me.' And I said, 'Yes.' And then again I said, 'No.' And then I said, 'Yes,' again." And then, Berry testified, "I said, 'I really have come to talk to you.'" Rachel "let out a scream. I grabbed her by the shoulder and tried to stop her from screaming. She wouldn't stop. We struggled, and the next thing I knew I had a telephone cord around her neck." On cross-examination, he admitted strangling her first with his hands, second with the black cord he had cut in advance, and then thirdly with the telephone cord.

Evidence that Rachel was afraid of Berry and fearful he would kill her is relevant to a fact Berry placed at issue with his testimony. Had Rachel seen a person she believed was going to kill her waiting for her inside her apartment, it is less likely that she would have simply said "hello," as Berry claims she did, and more likely that she would have struggled or tried to flee. The fact that no evidence of either struggle or attempted flight appeared made it more likely that Berry instead had been lying in wait for Rachel. Because lying in wait is an element of the first-degree murder charge the prosecution sought to prove under Cal. Pen. Code § 189, and because Berry's testimony raised the issue of whether Berry instead greeted Rachel openly in support of his claim that the killing was unplanned, evidence of Rachel's fear was properly admitted on rebuttal.

Berry relies on *Lew* to support the assertion that Cummins's testimony was wrongly admitted, but this reliance is misplaced. In *Lew*, the defendant claimed the victim was shot accidentally. According to Lew's version of events, he had picked her up from her parents' place and the two had run some errands when the victim asked about a pair of "earmuffs" in the vehicle. Lew explained those were ear protection, which "naturally led into a conversation about guns." *Id.* at 776. The victim then said she wanted to shoot Lew's gun, and he compliantly drove them to his apartment so they could get it. Lew testified that the two snuggled on his couch together, and that he then handed the weapon to her, removing the clip as he did so. The clip fell, and Lew said he was bending down to retrieve it when he heard the gun go off. The implication of this testimony was that the victim must have accidentally shot herself. *Id.* at 776. The prosecution, in contrast, offered hearsay statements regarding the victim's fear of Lew, and on appeal, we held those statements to be relevant and at issue. If she were afraid of Lew, then it would be unlikely for her to suggest the two of them go get his gun. *Id.* at 780. As in the case at bar, *Lew* exemplifies a situation where the defendant's evidence makes the victim's state of mind relevant.

The hearsay was nevertheless inadmissible in *Lew* because, although state of mind was at issue in the case, the contested evidence there was heavily comprised of statements regarding the defendant's past acts. This raised concern that the statements were used impermissibly, to prove the defendant had in fact done those prior acts, rather than permissibly, to prove the victim's state of mind. *Id.* at 781. By way of explanation, *Lew* quoted the legislative comment to Evidence Code § 1250, as follows:

> Statements of a decedent's then existing fear — i.e., his state of mind — may be offered under Section 1250, as under existing law, either to prove that fear when it is itself in issue or to prove or explain the decedent's subsequent conduct. Statements of a decedent narrating threats or brutal conduct by some other person may also be used as circumstantial evidence of the decedent's fear — his state of mind — when that fear is itself in issue or when it is relevant to prove or explain the decedent's subsequent conduct; and, for that purpose, the evidence is not subject to a hearsay objection because it is not offered to prove the truth of the matter stated..... *But when such evidence is used as a basis for inferring that the alleged threatener must have made threats, the evidence falls within the language of Section 1250(b) and is inadmissible hearsay evidence.* (emphasis added).

Id. at 781 n.3.

This aspect of *Lew*, however, does not apply to the facts before us today. The facts in *Lew* involved statements that referred to Lew's past actions – specifically, his past threats. In *Lew*, the victim's fear of Lew was elucidated through the testimony of witnesses who said that the victim told them Lew had threatened to kill her, had threatened her parents, had bought the victim a cemetery plot, and had displayed a gun. *Id.* at 777–778. In the case at bar, in contrast, the contested hearsay refers entirely to Rachel's beliefs about Berry: that he is a violent man, that she fears him, that she fears he will kill her. No prior actions by Berry were relayed through Cummins's testimony. Moreover, in the case at bar, the past actions that likely provided the basis for Rachel's fear had already been admitted by Berry himself in his testimony, in which he described his prior strangulations of Rachel on July 13 and 23. Berry also testified that Rachel had threatened to report him to his probation officer for strangling her on July 13. He testified that she told him she had reported the strangulation on July 23. And he testified that Rachel told him she was afraid he would kill her. Because (1) there is no evidence of past acts communicated by the hearsay, and because (2) even if the jury were to infer any past acts to supply a reasonable basis for Rachel's fear, the past acts inferred would be the prior strangulations that Berry admits, together with (3) Berry's own testimony on direct that Rachel had told him she was afraid he would kill her, there was no error in admitting proof of Rachel's fear. This testimony falls squarely within the state of mind exception. It does not require the jury to accept as true any past acts, and if it did, the past acts in question would be those that Berry himself offered.[49] Berry's first claim of error with respect to the first-degree murder charge lacks merit.

B. *Admission of Other Acts Evidence*

Berry next claims the trial court erred in admitting evidence of Berry's prior conviction for having stabbed his second wife, Carol. Citing *People v. Haston* (1968) 69 Cal. 2d 233, 244, he notes that "evidence of other crimes is inadmissible when it is

---

[49] We pause to note – and this is only dicta, as it is not at issue in the case before us – that in a different and significant way, the reasoning of *Lew* is mistaken, as is the legislative commentary it cites. To the extent that testimony consists of threats communicated by the defendant, those statements are not hearsay at all. This is so for two reasons. First, they are statements made by, and offered against, a party. EVIDENCE CODE § 1220. As a party, Berry was free to explain or deny having said any words attributed to him by another. Second, the words were offered, not for their truth, but because they were said. *See People v. Henry* (1948) 86 Cal. App. 2d 785, 789; EVIDENCE CODE § 1200 (defining hearsay as "evidence of a statement that was made other than by a witness while testifying at the hearing and that is offered to prove the truth of the matter stated"). Threats are not simply words, relevant only insofar as they are either true or false. Instead, threats are actions taken that have particular legal significance. *See* CAL. PEN. CODE § 422 (criminalizing threats). Therefore, they are not hearsay, but "operative facts." *People v. Patton* (1976) 63 Cal. App. 3d 211, 219 (holding statements defendant made "constituted the substantive offense with which he was charged, and therefore were 'operative facts'"). Threatening someone is a thing done in the world that can be observed and reported the same way witnesses can report any other observations of acts in the world they witnessed. Thus, even if in repeating Rachel's words as to her mental state (which is all that happened here), Cummins also had repeated Rachel repeating Berry's threats (which did not happen here), still there would have been no error. Each layer of this hypothetical hearsay-within-hearsay is justified. Rachel's recitation of what Berry said would have been permissible both because Berry himself said it, and because what Berry said was admissible as an operative fact. And Paul Cummins's testimony repeating what Rachel had told him would be permissible as proof of her state of mind. She was afraid of Berry, which explains why she was reporting him to the authorities and asking for him to be arrested in the first place. And, as previously explained, her fear was at issue in the case because Berry's version of the facts, in which he greeted her openly and they exchanged "hellos" before he strangled her, raised it.

offered solely to prove criminal disposition or propensity on the part of the accused to commit the crime charged, because the probative value of such evidence is outweighed by its prejudicial effect." While this is the general rule, Evidence Code § 1101(b) nevertheless permits other acts when offered instead to prove motive, intent, plan, and the like. The trial judge expressly – and correctly – ruled that Berry's prior act of stabbing his second wife could be admitted for those reasons. *See People v. Beamon* (1973) 8 Cal. 3d 625, 632.

With respect to motive, the prosecution argued that Berry killed Rachel not only because she was leaving him,[50] but also out of anger over her threats to report his strangling of her on July 13 to his probation officer, and retaliation for her report of the strangling on July 23. The bare fact that Berry was on probation for a prior offense is both relevant and necessary to proving that portion of his motive relating to his anger over her threats to report – and her actual report of – Berry's strangling her. Existence of this motive also speaks to the likelihood that Berry acted from the sort of premeditation and deliberation that supports a first-degree murder charge, rather than from impulse, as would befit a second-degree murder or voluntary manslaughter charge. He and Rachel were not arguing when, in the heat of the moment, he killed her. He wanted her dead before he saw her that day, which is why he was waiting in her apartment for her with a cut electrical cord.

In addition to admissibility regarding motive, Berry's prior act also was admissible as to intent. Berry's stabbing of his second wife, Carol, after she taunted him with her desire for another man, tended to show a pattern – arguably the very same pattern Berry sought to prove – of his violent and emotional relationships with women. Both in his earlier marriage and in this one, Berry "had been rejected, made threats and retaliated. The jury was entitled to conclude that his retaliatory state of mind, occurring under similar circumstances, was the same in both instances; to find that his actions toward [both victims] were conscious, intentional, revengeful and malicious." *People v. Bufarale* (1961) 193 Cal. App. 2d 551, 558–559.

The defense goal throughout trial was not to contest the killing, but to demonstrate that Berry repeatedly became involved with women who rejected him the way his mother had. Berry and Dr. Blinder both offered vivid testimony regarding Berry's stabbing of his second wife, as well as of his violence towards other women. Again, the defense goal was to paint Berry's life as a recurring cycle of passionate and violently reactive relationships, in contrast with the prosecution's theories that Berry killed Rachel after cold-blooded premeditation and deliberation and lying in wait. Most compellingly, then, we note that Berry himself offered testimony that he had stabbed his second wife, Carol, repeatedly in the stomach. As such, he is in a poor position to complain about its admission. The observation in *Henry* is equally apropos here: "Not only does this case come within the exception thus provided, but

---

[50] The prosecution received support on this point from Dr. Blinder, who agreed on recross it was "reasonable to say that he killed because she was going to leave him."

the material matter is also amply covered in the statements and admissions made by the appellant personally. Neither error nor prejudice appears in this regard." *Henry*, 86 Cal. App. 2d at 789. This claim, too, fails.

An excessive number of cross-examination questions are complained of, in addition. Almost all were permissible as evidence of motive or intent, or as straightforwardly falling under the scope of matters raised on direct; these do not merit individual discussion.[51] With respect to those that were, in fact, objectionable, the trial judge sustained objections and took corrective measures. A question regarding the statement by one Owen Snodgrass, for example, was stricken from the record, and the jurors were instructed that questions are not evidence. "It must be presumed that the jurors acted in accordance with the instructions and disregarded the question." *People v. Rocha* (1971) 3 Cal. 3d 893, 901.

Of the myriad cross-examination questions Berry calls out on appeal, only one caused us a moment's pause. The first question the prosecutor asked Berry was "How much money did you take from Rachel's purse after you murdered her?" Continued reading, however, reveals that although this was clearly objectionable, the prosecutor's word choice was thoughtless rather than malicious. "This is cross-examination. It is a leading question. It is allowed," he said.

"That is true," acknowledged the judge, "but it is compound. 'After you killed her,' perhaps."

"That is why I asked," the prosecutor replied. "After you killed, after you murdered her, is what I said."

At this, Berry's counsel interjected, "Legal conclusion."

"He admits killing her but he does not admit murder," the judge elaborated.

"I can rephrase it," said the prosecutor. "How much money did you take from Rachel's purse after you killed her?"

"Thirty-three dollars," Berry answered.

This recitation reveals that all present treated the prosecutor's word choice the way the trial judge treated it: as a mistake rather than as a deliberate violation. The jury heard the exchange in its entirety, including the judge's clear elucidation of the concern and the prosecution's corrected query. Berry raises nothing now to contradict this understanding, and we see nothing; therefore, we defer to the trial judge's first-hand observations of the prosecutor's demeanor. Berry did not ask for anything more from the judge at the time, *see* Evidence Code § 353 (requiring timely objection to preserve error for appeal), and the full exchange encompassed one-half of one page out of a several-hundred-page transcript. In the grand scheme of the entire

---

[51] One example suffices: Berry asserts error in the prosecution's cross-examination regarding his dishonorable discharge from military service. This was manifestly *not* error. Indeed, Berry objected to this at trial, but when the trial judge reminded him that Dr. Blinder had testified earlier that Berry said he had been honorably discharged, he withdrew the objection. Berry raises no additional concerns with respect to this incident in his appeal, and we see none. Therefore, we reject this claim and those like it, as well.

trial, we easily conclude that this admitted error was harmless beyond a reasonable doubt. *See People v. Morse*, 70 Cal. 2d 711, 730–731 (1969).

C. *Voluntary Manslaughter Instruction*

The last significant claim Berry raises on appeal is that his request for a voluntary manslaughter instruction was wrongly denied. This claim, too, lacks merit, but because Berry attacks the judge's denial at every possible step of the analysis, and because of the disturbingly frequent and widespread misapplication of the voluntary manslaughter doctrine, we respond in exacting detail.

Voluntary manslaughter is defined as "the unlawful killing of a human being, without malice ... upon a sudden quarrel or heat of passion." Cal. Pen. Code § 192 (1972). As an initial matter, then, voluntary manslaughter contrasts with both first- and second-degree murder in that voluntary manslaughter does not include malice aforethought. *See People v. Bender*, 27 Cal. 2d 164, 180 (1949). Consequently, a jury's finding that malice aforethought was *not* present precludes a murder conviction, *see People v. Castillo*, 70 Cal. 2d 264, 270 (1969), and defendants are entitled to voluntary manslaughter instructions when there is sufficient evidence to support that lesser charge, *see People v. Carmen*, 36 Cal. 2d 768, 773 (1951). Indeed, "it is reversible error to refuse a manslaughter instruction in a case where murder is charged, and the evidence would warrant a conviction of manslaughter." *Id.* Berry claims sufficient evidence existed on the record to show he was entitled to a voluntary manslaughter instruction due to the absence of malice aforethought for two reasons: (1) he was suffering from a diminished capacity at the time of Rachel's death, and (2) the killing was done in a sudden heat of passion. Both rationales fail.

1. Diminished Capacity

"Malice aforethought" is the legal concept separating murder from manslaughter. *People v. Conley*, 64 Cal. 2d 310, 321 (1966). The diminished capacity doctrine explains that "mental defect, disease, or intoxication" may negate malice aforethought and thereby preclude a murder conviction when "because of mental defect, disease, or intoxication ... the defendant is unable to comprehend his duty to govern his actions in accord with the duty imposed by law." *Id.* at 322. Berry's assertion that he was entitled to a jury instruction on voluntary manslaughter on this ground fails because there was no evidence Berry suffered from diminished capacity. Indeed, Dr. Blinder testified that Berry was sane, of "bright normal" intelligence, did not suffer from a mental illness, and was capable of understanding his actions and their seriousness. He testified that Berry was capable of harboring malice, premeditating, and deliberating, and that Berry intended to kill Rachel when he strangled her to death. No contrary evidence on these points appeared.

This case resembles *People v. Morse*, 70 Cal. 2d 711 (1969), in which the defendant failed to offer sufficient evidence to establish diminished capacity, thus eliminating the need for voluntary manslaughter instruction. *See id.*, at 735–736. Fundamentally, there was no evidence that Berry suffered from a "mental defect, disease, or intoxication." The conclusion is even clearer here than it was in *Morse*. There, the defendant at least offered evidence of a personality disorder. *Id.* Dr. Blinder's testimony recited Berry's manifest lack of any such thing, instead affirming Berry's capacity to understand, bear malice, premeditate, and deliberate. Dr. Blinder went so far as to offer his opinion that Berry not only intended to kill Rachel when he strangled her to death, but that Berry's "homicidal thoughts … may have been in evidence even weeks before" the killing.

Although Dr. Blinder also testified that Berry's relationships with women, including Rachel, fit a "clinical pattern" "dating back to the way his mother dealt with him," this does not provide support for the kind of mental defect, disease, or intoxication necessary to find diminished capacity and corresponding lack of malice aforethought. As we explained in *Morse*, the evidence here, too,

> provides no basis whatsoever for a finding that defendant's act was accomplished in the absence of malice aforethought. Nowhere is it intimated that defendant lacked an awareness that his act was contrary to the laws of society. Rather, the testimony of [defendant's psychiatrist expert witness] posits such awareness and proceeds upon the theory that defendant's personality disorder and the effects of his environment rendered him disinclined to or incapable of conforming his conduct accordingly. Such a state of mind cannot amount to an absence of malice aforethought as we have defined that term in Conley. Though defendant's conduct may in fact have been in some sense "psychologically predictable," under the present law of the State of California this fact does not of itself affect his criminal liability.

Id. at 736. We necessarily conclude that Berry's request for instruction on voluntary manslaughter in the context of diminished capacity was properly denied.

2. Provocation

Berry's next challenge to the denial of his request for voluntary manslaughter instruction rests on his claim that there was sufficient evidence of provocation to send this question to the jury. His reply brief states, "It is a known fact among criminal lawyers and jurists that a first-degree murder conviction in a domestic homicide is a rarity. They are inherently crimes of passion, and an acquittal or manslaughter conviction is quite common. Respondent's contention then that the evidence of guilt was overwhelming (as applied to first degree murder) is inherently untenable." In other words, Berry asserts, strangling one's wife is statistically unlikely to be characterized as committing first-degree murder, because domestic homicides are "inherently crimes of passion."

While it is sadly true that perpetrators of violence against those whom they purport to love are neither prosecuted nor convicted at the same rate as perpetrators of violence against other victims, the law does not differentiate. There is no exception to first-degree murder based on the relationship between the perpetrator and the victim, nor does the provocation doctrine automatically apply on that basis.

First-degree murder as charged by the prosecution here consists of (1) the unlawful killing of a human being with malice aforethought, Cal. Pen. Code, § 187; (2) which malice consists of a deliberate intent unlawfully to kill, Cal. Pen. Code, § 188; (3) perpetrated by lying in wait or by any other kind of willful, deliberate, and premeditated killing, Cal. Pen. Code § 189. Nothing in our criminal code changes any of those elements based on the identities of the defendant and the victim, nor on any relationship between them. Murder victims run the gamut from stranger to loved one, and the fact that Rachel was Berry's wife when he killed her, like the fact that they had separated, is not legally relevant to the prosecution's burden of proving the elements of first-degree murder.

Berry claims that the fact that he was in his own home is relevant to the element of lying in wait, however, and that the instruction on lying in wait therefore should not have been given. "[I]n order to constitute lying in wait the elements of waiting, watching and concealment must be present," *People v. Merkouris*, 46 Cal.2d 540, 559 (1956). And Berry declares in his opening brief, "Certainly a man in his own house can't be in concealment."

First, we note that it certainly is possible to conceal oneself in one's own home. Children play hide and seek in their houses, and fugitives hide from law enforcement. There is no reason first-degree murderers cannot conceal themselves likewise, and unfortunately sometimes they do. In *People v. Morse*, 60 Cal.2d at 656, we upheld the giving of an instruction on murder by lying in wait in precisely this situation. The defendant, Morse, stated he had

> picked up the rock in his front yard early Sunday morning with the intent to kill someone. After his mother let him into the house and they had each retired to their respective sleeping quarters, defendant called to her, perhaps saying "Hey, come here for a second." He waited in the dark of the bedroom corridor until she arose and opened her bedroom door; then he struck her.
>
> The instruction concerning murder by lying in wait appropriately stemmed from these events; the record affords evidence of defendant's intention to kill and of his perpetration of his mother's murder by means of lying in wait for the opportune moment to strike.

Id. Berry is simply wrong in claiming it is not possible to lie in wait in one's own home.

Second, we note that according to Berry's own testimony, he had moved out by the time of the killing. On June 23, Berry took his things and stored them in a Greyhound bus station locker. When he returned to the apartment, he waited until

Rachel left before letting himself in, and there were dissolution of marriage papers on the kitchen table. Concealed or not, while he waited for Rachel's return with the cord he admitted on cross he "had thought about" using to strangle her, he was far less clearly in his own house than the defendant had been when we upheld the giving of an instruction on lying in wait in *Morse*.

Finally, we note that even if Berry were still living in the apartment, there was ample evidence to support a finding of the concealment inherent in lying in wait. Although Berry testified that he and Rachel greeted each other and discussed his intent to kill her before she screamed and he strangled her, this was not the only evidence presented on the issue. Berry also testified that he saw Rachel go into the apartment, but instead of trying to catch up to her or calling out, he waited for her to leave before he entered unseen by her. The marks on Rachel's throat were consistent with having been strangled from behind. There were no marks on Berry, as one would expect if there had been the struggle he first said there was,[52] and as he testified he had received when he strangled her before. Nothing was out of place in the apartment aside from the key found on the floor by the front door, itself consistent with Rachel's having dropped it after being attacked from behind the moment she entered. This collection of evidence more than suffices to support the jury's verdict, and for all these reasons, Berry's allegation of error in giving the instruction on lying in wait fails, as well.

Berry next contends he was entitled to jury instructions on voluntary manslaughter because the killing was committed in a heat of passion, pointing to Dr. Blinder's testimony "that the victim was very provocative and in his opinion precipitated the homicide by being who she was." Again, while it is true that courts must instruct on all relevant legal principles, including lesser included offenses fairly raised by the facts presented at trial, *People v. Sedeno*, 10 Cal. 3d 703, 715 (1974), where no evidence appears to support any lesser included offenses, trial courts are under no obligation to provide such instruction. *Id.* That the victim allegedly "had it coming" or "asked for it" does not satisfy the provocation doctrine's requirements for mitigating murder to manslaughter. Neither does "being who she was" establish a legally cognizable provocation.

Instead, the sort of provocation that can serve to mitigate murder to manslaughter "must be such as would naturally be aroused in the mind of an ordinary, reasonable person, under the given facts and circumstances, or in the mind of a person of ordinary self-control." *People v. Taylor*, 197 Cal.App.2d 372, 379 (1961) (*citing People v. Bridgehouse*, 47 Cal.2d 406, 413 (1956)). The doctrine has been described as requiring a provocation that "would render an ordinary man of average disposition likely

---

[52] Oddly, Berry maintained there was no struggle on cross-examination: "No struggle?" "That is correct." "No screaming?" "That is correct." "She just watched as you proceeded to strangle her to death, is that correct?" "That is correct." Dr. Blinder's testimony is in accord with the no-struggle version: "'I suppose you have come to kill me.' 'Yes,' he says. He wraps a cord around her neck and strangles her. There is virtually no struggle."

to act rashly or without due deliberation and reflection, and from this passion rather than from judgment." *Id.* at 380 (*citing People v. Brubaker*, 53 Cal.2d 37, 44 (1959); *People v. Borchers*, 50 Cal.2d 321, 329 (1958)). It bears emphasis here "that [any] evidence of defendant's extraordinary character and environmental deficiencies [is] manifestly irrelevant to the inquiry." *Morse*, 70 Cal. 2d at 735. The peculiarities of the defendant, whether created by nature or nurture, have no bearing on whether an ordinary, reasonable person of average disposition and ordinary self-control would be provoked to act from passion rather than judgment. Lastly, provocation mitigation precludes the presence of a "cooling period." *Taylor*, 197 Cal.App.2d at 380. Once hot blood has had time to cool, the law requires that it does so. A killing committed after reason has had opportunity "to resume its empire" is murder, not manslaughter. *People v. Wells*, 10 Cal.2d 610, 618 (1938).

The relevant test, then, is whether "the 'heat of passion' was reasonably and justifiedly engendered, [and] 'hot blood had not had time to cool' before the fatal act was committed." *Taylor*, 197 Cal.App.2d at 380 (*quoting Wells*, 10 Cal. 2d at 618–619). Note that here, too, nothing delineates any differences in applicability based on the identities of perpetrator and victim, nor on any relationship between them.

There is no doubt that Berry's defense focused on his emotions. He himself testified that "sudden rage and impulse came over" him, and Dr. Blinder testified that Berry acted in a "rage" that was dominated by "the feeling rather than the thought." With passion as his theme, Berry claims error in the judge's denial of his request for an instruction on voluntary manslaughter as a lesser included offense.

This claim fails, too. Provocation requires more than passion. As we have stated, it requires the passion flow from the sort of event that would provoke an ordinary, reasonable person of average disposition and ordinary self-control to act on that passion rather than on judgment, and it requires the lack of a cooling period. *Taylor*, 197 Cal.App.2d at 380. The evidence offered at trial fails to justify the giving of this instruction at every step of the analysis: The type of provocation was itself insufficient; Berry's evidence spoke to his own peculiarities, placing him well outside what can be expected of an ordinary, reasonable person of average disposition; and there was indisputably a cooling period. We address each of these in turn.

First, in his brief, Berry contends that he was subject to many instances of provocative conduct by Rachel, culminating in a struggle in the kitchen:

> He is the only person alive who was present when the victim was killed, so obviously his testimony should be allowed as much weight as a jury is willing to give it on whether there was a struggle and, if so, whether it was the type of sudden quarrel which gives rise to adequate provocation to reduce guilt to voluntary manslaughter.

We have reviewed the record thoroughly, and there is nothing to support the contention that this struggle – if there was one, given Berry's contradictory testimony on the question – could have been "the type of sudden quarrel which gives rise to adequate provocation to reduce guilt to voluntary manslaughter."

In Berry's Reply Brief, he cites to page 307, line 7 of the transcript to support his claim that the jury should have been given an opportunity to find provocation. That line reflects Berry's testimony on cross that "[s]udden rage and impulse came over me." Additional context is useful. A few lines down, the prosecution asked, "You weren't arguing with her that day that you called her, were you?"

A: "No."
Q: "What caused the sudden rage?"
A: "Just looking at her. I don't know. It just came."
Q: "Was it the same type of sudden rage that came over you when you stabbed your second wife, Carol?"
A: "I suppose you could say so."

"Just looking at her" is not adequate provocation.

Berry's testimony on direct is equally unavailing. He testified that he strangled Rachel when she screamed; that she did so after he told her he was, in fact, there to kill her; and that he had strangled her to unconsciousness twice before. Even taking all of the defense evidence as true, Rachel's screams and any struggle that followed were a rational response to a credible threat, not legally cognizable provocations. It would make a mockery of the provocation doctrine to hold that the screams and struggles of a victim on being attacked could serve as the sort of event that "would render an ordinary man of average disposition likely to act rashly or without due deliberation and reflection, and from this passion rather than from judgment," *Taylor*, 197 Cal.App.2d at 380. As such, we decline to so hold.

Next, Berry's evidence fails to support his request for a voluntary manslaughter instruction in that the proof offered at trial focused on his particular upbringing, history, and temperament. The defense went to some pains to elaborate on Berry's childhood, his relationship with his mother, and the unhealthy nature of his relationships with women ever since – including Dr. Blinder's professional opinion that Berry's relationship with Rachel was "kind of a suicidal-homicidal bag." As we have stated, "evidence of defendant's extraordinary character and environmental deficiencies [is] manifestly irrelevant to the inquiry." *Morse*, 70 Cal. 2d at 735.

The proper question "is whether or not the defendant's reason was, at the time of his act, so disturbed or obscured by some passion – not necessarily fear and never, of course, the passion for revenge – to such an extent as would render ordinary men of average disposition liable to act rashly or without due deliberation and reflection, and from this passion rather than from judgment." *People v. Logan*, 175 Cal. 45, 49 (1917). Although we held in *People v. Borchers*, 50 Cal.2d 321, 328 (1958), that "a series of events over a long period of time" can support a finding of provocation, the events in *Borchers* differ markedly from those at bar. The defendant, Borchers, testified that after giving his fiancé, Dotty, a symbolic wedding ring and access to his bank accounts, he took out a large insurance policy for the benefit of Dotty and Tony, the little boy she was raising and whom they planned to adopt. *Id.* at 323–324.

He later became suspicious of two men who were "hanging around" Dotty. *Id.* at 324. He hired an investigator, who told Borchers the men were "big-time hoodlums," conspiring with Dotty to kill Borchers for the insurance money, and that Dotty was taking money from Borchers and giving it to one of the men, with whom she was having sex. *Id.* at 324–325. Borchers testified that Dotty admitted to sleeping with the man, but that he believed the man frightened her into it. *Id.* at 325. Dotty was suicidal, Borchers said, at one point declaring "she wished she were dead … and 'These men will stop at nothing,' and she attempted to jump from the car as they were driving." *Id.* Four days later, as they were again driving down the road, Borchers testified, Dotty said "she would commit suicide and wanted me to shoot Tony. I told Dotty without Tony and without her, as far as I was concerned, there was nothing." *Id.* Dotty then removed Borchers's gun from the glove compartment, loaded it, pointed it at him, "and told him he better stop the car, she was going to shoot him. Then she pointed it at herself." She begged Borchers "to shoot her, Tony, and himself" over and over again while Borchers tried to calm her down, all while still driving the car. *Id.* at 329. He testified that he managed to take the gun from her "very carefully" and

> put my arm with the gun in it on the back … of the seat. I had thought of throwing it in the back, but I didn't want to throw it back there, and I didn't want to make too much of a point so that she would feel I actually tried to take the gun away from her. I was trying to do it as carefully as I could. But I didn't throw it in the back seat and if I only had.

Id. at 325–326. Borchers testified that Dotty continued to demand he kill her, saying "Go ahead and shoot, what is the matter, are you chicken." And he shot her. *Id.* at 326.

We need not belabor the differences between the nature of the alleged provocations in *Borchers* and those in the case at bar. Suffice it to say that Borchers offered evidence that, if believed by the fact-finder, would demonstrate he was overwhelmed by credible threats to his own life and to the lives of his loved ones. In contrast, Berry's evidence, if believed by the fact-finder, demonstrated that he was enraged because (1) Rachel refused to have sex with him, loved another man, and wanted to divorce Berry; and (2) she not only threatened to report his strangling her on July 13 to his probation officer, but also did report his strangling her on July 23 to police. In other words, Berry choked Rachel, first into unconsciousness on July 23, and later to her death on July 26, not because she had done anything criminal, or even anything that the law would call "wrong," but instead because she rejected him and because she reported his previous violence against her to law enforcement. *Logan*, 175 Cal. at 49 (stating that "passion for revenge" is a disqualifying form of passion). There are many reactions that a reasonable man with an ordinary disposition may have to this, but choking her to death is not among them.

Lastly, and again in contrast to the defendant in *Borchers*, Berry was not entitled to a provocation instruction because there was a cooling period. In the moments immediately before Borchers shot Dotty, she had pointed a gun at him and repeatedly insisted he kill her, Tony, and himself. In the case at bar, even if Rachel's conduct in the weeks prior to the killing could serve as adequate provocation (which we do not hold), Berry's claim still would fail for ample cooling time. Berry spent twenty hours alone in the apartment. He left only to fetch cigarettes. He cut an electrical cord, which he admitted on cross he had thought about using to strangle Rachel, and he waited. When Rachel entered, she asked if he was there to kill her. He said "yes," she screamed, and he killed her. Whether Berry's blood had in fact cooled or no – and there was ample evidence it had – the relevant inquiry is whether a reasonable person's blood would have cooled. *Taylor*, 197 Cal. App. 2d at 380. The law does not characterize a killing that any defendant commits after so much time alone with his thoughts as a heat-of-passion manslaughter. For this reason, too, the denial of instruction on voluntary manslaughter was not error.

Berry's numerous additional contentions likewise lack merit, and the judgment of conviction as modified by the Court of Appeal is affirmed.

3

Commentary on *Coker v. Georgia*

CATHERINE M. GROSSO AND BARBARA O'BRIEN

The United States Supreme Court issued its opinion in *Coker v. Georgia* onto a still unsettled Eighth Amendment landscape.[1] Five years prior to *Coker*, the court in *Furman v. Georgia* famously found the death penalty as practiced in Georgia and across the United States arbitrary and unconstitutional.[2] State governments almost immediately adopted new death penalty statutes based on the American Law Institute's model intended to guide the discretion of prosecutors and jurors as they identify cases where the death penalty would be appropriate.[3] Georgia prosecuted Coker under one of the newly minted statutes.[4] The *Coker* opinion emerges from and hews closely to the narrow path defined during that tumultuous period for death penalty jurisprudence.

FACTUAL AND LEGAL ISSUES

Ehrlich Anthony Coker was a white man born in Atlanta, Georgia, in 1949. He experienced a turbulent homelife[5] and faced minor criminal charges and probation beginning at age fifteen. He finished tenth grade before enlisting in the army. He served three years in Korea and was honorably discharged. He married and had a son upon return. Shortly thereafter, however, Coker pled guilty to rape, kidnapping, and aggravated assault, receiving two life sentences plus 28 years. He also pled guilty

---

[1] 433 U.S. 584 (1977) (plurality opinion).
[2] *Furman v. Georgia*, 408 U.S. 238 (1972).
[3] AMERICAN LAW INSTITUTE, MODEL PENAL CODE § 210.6 (section withdrawn in 2009). *See* CAROL S. STEIKER & JORDAN M. STEIKER, COURTING DEATH 43–44, 61–63, 283 (2016) (documenting the history of the Model Penal Code death penalty statute).
[4] The Supreme Court decided *Gregg v. Georgia*, and its companion cases, upholding the new death penalty statutes on July 2, 1976. 418 U.S. 153 (1976). *See also Proffitt v. Florida*, 428 U.S. 242 (1976); *Jurek v. Texas*, 428 U.S. 262 (1976); *Woodson v. North Carolina*, 428 U.S. 280 (1976); and *Roberts v. Louisiana*, 428 U.S. 325 (1976).
[5] SHERI LYNN JOHNSON, *Coker v. Georgia: of Rape, Race, and Burying the Past*, *in* DEATH PENALTY STORIES 172 (John H. Blume and Jordan M. Steiker, eds., 2009). The brief history presented here draws heavily on Professor Johnson's wonderful chapter.

to an additional prior rape and murder. The court again sentenced him to a life sentence plus twenty more years of incarceration.[6]

While serving those sentences, Coker escaped from prison and committed the crimes at issue in the case before the Supreme Court. During his escape, Coker fled and unlawfully entered the home of Allen and Elnita Carver, a young white couple with a three-week-old baby. He threatened the couple with a "board" and a kitchen knife, tied up Mr. Carver in the bathroom, and raped Mrs. Carver. He forced Mrs. Carver to leave with him in the family car.[7]

After he was recaptured, Georgia filed capital charges against Coker. The newly minted Georgia rape statute authorized the death penalty for aggravated rape so long as jurors found in a separate sentencing hearing one of three aggravating circumstances present. These aggravating circumstances looked to the defendant's prior record, the presence of a second capital felony in the same offense, or evidence of torture, depravity of mind, or aggravated battery.[8]

Coker's attorney unsuccessfully challenged the constitutionality of a death sentence for rape under *Furman v. Georgia*, before a jury found him guilty, rejected his insanity plea, and ultimately sentenced Coker to death. Coker appealed all the way to the United States Supreme Court, arguing that a death sentence was a disproportionate and unconstitutional punishment for the rape of an adult woman.

THE US SUPREME COURT OPINION

The plurality opinion in *Coker v. Georgia* held that death was a "grossly disproportionate and excessive punishment for the crime of rape and ... therefore forbidden by the Eighth Amendment as cruel and unusual punishment."[9] Justice White, joined by Justices Stewart, Blackmun, and Stevens, drew heavily on the understanding of the Eighth Amendment articulated in *Weems v. United States*, a 1910 decision. *Weems* recognized that the court's understanding of cruelty reflected an evolving understanding of the meaning of the Eighth Amendment prohibitions.[10]

In *Coker*, the court articulated a framework for assessing that evolving understanding. The court first assessed the frequency with which states imposed a death sentence for rape, noting "at no time in the last 50 years have a majority of the states authorized death as a punishment for rape."[11] The court then reviewed state statutes from the preceding five years. Sixteen states authorized a death sentence for rape at the time of *Furman*. After *Furman* invalidated those statutes, three states reauthorized a death sentence for rape post-*Furman*: North Carolina, Louisiana,

---

[6] *Id.* at 173.
[7] *Coker, supra* note 1, at 587.
[8] GA. CODE ANN. § 26–3102 (Supp. 1976).
[9] *Coker, supra* note 1, at 592.
[10] *Weems v. United States*, 217 U.S. 349 (1910).
[11] *Coker, supra* note 1, at 593.

and Georgia. The Supreme Court found North Carolina's and Louisiana's initial post-*Furman* statutes unconstitutional.[12] While both states amended their murder statutes to authorize a death sentence under the court's new guidance, neither reauthorized death as a penalty for rape. At the time the court decided *Coker*, Georgia was the only jurisdiction that authorized death for rape of an adult woman. Two other states, Florida and Mississippi, authorized a death sentence for the rape of a child.[13]

The court also examined the record of juror decision making as an objective measure of popular opinions on the authorization of the death penalty for rape. It considered that Georgia juries had imposed only six death sentences in sixty-three eligible cases under the new law.

The court then turned to its "own judgment." In later cases, the court would use similar reasoning to assess whether a death penalty in a particular context served the purposes of punishment.[14] The *Coker* plurality relegated that analysis to a footnote, however. It concluded that given how infrequently rape was punished by death "in almost all of the States and in most of the countries around the world," the punishment could not be considered "indispensable."[15]

The court concluded from this analysis that "death is indeed a disproportionate punishment for the crime of raping an adult woman" because the victim survives.[16] The court, in a section remarkably clinical in tone, explained that rape is the "ultimate violation of self" and "highly reprehensible." It recognized that rape violates the "personal integrity and autonomy of the female victim" and is a violent crime "often accompanied by physical injury" and "mental and psychological damage."[17] The court concluded, however, that rape does not compare with murder because "for the rape victim, life may not be nearly so happy as it was, but it is not over and normally is not beyond repair."[18]

The plurality opinion avoided any mention of the long history of racism in the prosecution and punishment of rape, just as the court had in the overwhelming majority of the other death penalty cases of the era.[19] As Sheri Lynn Johnson noted, "Prior to *Coker*, it was impossible to think about rape and capital punishment without thinking about race; it was impossible to think about race and capital punishment without thinking about rape."[20] Nothing in the opinion gives even a clue of this history.

---

[12] *Woodson v. North Carolina*, 428 U.S. 280 (1976); *Roberts v. Louisiana*, 428 U.S. 325 (1976).

[13] Tennessee initially authorized a death sentence for rape of a child in its post-*Furman* death penalty statutes, but the initial Tennessee statute was found unconstitutional and the revised statute omitted the rape of a child provision.

[14] *See, e.g., Atkins v. Virginia*, 536 U.S. 304, 318–322 (evaluating whether deterrence or retribution can be advanced by authorizing a death penalty for people with developmental disabilities); *Kennedy v. Louisiana*, 554 U.S. 407, 420–421 (2008) (same with respect to cases involving rape of a child).

[15] *Coker, supra* note 1, at 591 n.4 ("We observe that in the light of the legislative decisions in almost all of the States and in most of the countries around the world, it would be difficult to support a claim that the death penalty for rape is an indispensable part of the States' criminal justice system.").

[16] *Id.* at 597 (citing *Weems*).

[17] *Id.* at 597–598.

[18] *Id.* at 597–598.

[19] STEIKER & STEIKER, *supra* note 3, at 101–104.

[20] Johnson, *supra* note 5, at 195.

The court knew this history from decades of litigation. The NAACP Legal Defense Fund represented Coker and included an appendix documenting the racist history of punishment for rape in Georgia.[21] An amicus brief drafted by Ruth Bader Ginsburg presented this long history in detail.[22] Professor Johnson concluded that the court intentionally picked this case – one with a white defendant and white victim – over two similarly aggravated Georgia rape cases on the docket at the same time with Black defendants and white victims, so as to avoid discussing race.[23]

Justices Brennan and Marshall separately and briefly concurred in the judgment on the basis that the death penalty is unconstitutional in all instances. Their votes combined with the plurality to form a majority holding the Georgia rape statute unconstitutional.

Chief Justice Burger, joined by Justice Rehnquist, dissented. Chief Justice Burger first objected that "the Court ... overstepped the bounds of proper constitutional adjudication by substituting its policy judgment for that of the state legislature."[24] He returned to this theme throughout the opinion, lamenting the loss of state laboratories to experiment with the death penalty to evaluate its deterrent and retributive weight with respect to rape.[25]

He then recounted the crime and Coker's criminal history in detail, and concluded that the majority "takes too little account of the profound suffering the crime imposes upon the victims and their loved ones."[26] Burger questioned whether the five tumultuous years immediately following *Furman* reflected a changing sentiment with respect to the authorization of a death sentence for rape or compromise under pressure. History, he argued, showed that rape had frequently been punished by death.[27]

Burger criticized the majority's proportionality analysis for lacking depth and for its inappropriate return to the retributive "eye for an eye" justification for punishment. He argued that state legislatures could rationally identify rape as a heinous and dangerous crime that merits a death sentence regardless of the damage suffered by the victim.

---

[21] Brief for the Petitioner, *Coker v. Georgia*, No. 75-5444 (filed Dec. 9, 1976) (available on Westlaw at 1976 WL 181481), at 1a (Appendix A).

[22] Brief Amici Curiae of the American Civil Liberties Union, the Center for Constitutional Rights, the National Organization for Women Legal Defense and Education Fund, the Women's Law Project, the Center for Women Policy Studies, the Women's Legal Defense Fund, and Equal Rights Advocates, Inc., *Coker v. Georgia*, No. 75-5444 (filed Dec. 3, 1976) (available on Westlaw at 1976 WL 181482), 18–19.

[23] See Johnson, *supra* note 5, at 195. ("Two other Georgia capital rape defendants, John Eberheart and John Hooks, were before the Supreme Court on petition for a writ of certiorari at the same time as was Ehrlich Coker. In fact, the petitioners in those cases were filed before Coker's.")

[24] *Coker*, 433 U.S. at 604 (Burger, dissenting).

[25] Id. at 618–619.

[26] Id. at 612.

[27] Id. at 614.

Forty-five years after publication, *Coker* is cited most often to affirm the prohibition on authorizing a death sentence for a crime that does not result in death or to support a proportionality argument. *Kennedy v. Louisiana* (2008) is an example of the former; the court declared unconstitutional a statute authorizing a death sentence for rape of a child. The proportionality argument citations appear often in cases assessing proportionality of punishment both as to the crime and the offender[28] and even in cases not involving the death penalty.[29]

THE FEMINIST JUDGMENT

Professor Madalyn Wasilczuk, writing as Justice Wasilczuk, begins with a careful restating of the facts from the perspective of Elnita Carter. She organizes the narrative from Mrs. Carter's perspective: We learn of her age, her recent birthing of a child, and her health. Every other statement of the facts starts with the life or criminal history of Ehrlich Carter. The plurality, the dissent, Brief for Petitioner, and Brief for the Respondent all start by recounting Coker's criminal history and the details of his several crimes. The Brief for the Petitioner provides a more complete account of the events in the Carter's house.

In Wasilczuk's account, Mrs. Carter "did what Ehrlich Coker demanded," rather than having it done to her. Mrs. Carter "emerged from the harrowing incident with her life," rather than having her life spared. This framing does not undermine the horror of the crime, but it gives Mrs. Carter more agency, more voice than any previous presentation. Using this frame, Wasilczuk situates the case properly at the intersection of racism and sexism. None of the original opinions acknowledged either the Petitioner's argument that the "roots of [acceptance of the death penalty for rape] have lain in racial, not penal considerations" or calls from amici to reject the death penalty for rape "as a vestige of an ancient, patriarchal system in which women were viewed both as the property of men and as entitled to a crippling 'chivalric protection.'"[30] Wasilczuk uses these arguments and the evidence provided as the foundation for her argument.

Wasilczuk's opinion highlights the selective lens with which the majority reviews the historical use of the death penalty to punish rapists. The court, she argues, "peers at the penalty's decay without considering the origin of the rot." Wasilczuk proceeds to document courts' tendency when enforcing rape laws to rely on antiquated notions of a woman's value as rooted in her chastity and in the property interests of white men. She then contrasts those pronouncements about the law's commitment

---

[28] See Johnson, *supra* note 4, at 183–190 (reviewing cases).
[29] See, e.g., *Graham v. Florida*, 560 U.S. 48, 60–61 (2010) (citing *Coker* in a case holding that the Eighth Amendment prohibits imposition of life without parole sentence on juvenile offender who did not commit homicide).
[30] Brief Amici Curiae for the ACLU et al., *supra* note 22, at 11.

to protecting sanctity of women's virtue with statistics demonstrating the inadequacies of rape laws, noting the relatively low conviction rate in rape prosecutions and the host of evidentiary requirements reflecting suspiciousness of victims' stories. In so doing, Wasilczuk presents rape laws, and the enforcement of them, in the political context in which they have always operated.

Wasilczuk then ties the law's view of women as "objects who could be soiled, broken, or valueless as a result of rape" to its history of treating enslaved people as chattel who carry "a presumption of criminality." Moreover, she notes that rape law's ostensible reverence for "women" was reserved exclusively for white women, as "[e]nslaved Black women lived outside the bounds of protection of rape laws entirely." She then argues that the modern use of the death penalty for rape – while based on facially race-neutral laws – exhibits the same discriminatory patterns it did in the past.

Wasilczuk points out the plurality opinion's failure to note that the court's first attempts to regulate the death penalty arose in cases where Black men and boys were falsely charged with raping white women. Wasilczuk references the important cases of the Scottsboro boys, who were falsely convicted of raping two white women after they all hitched a ride on a train along the Tennessee/Alabama border. The nine defendants faced rape charges and lynch mobs. They all had been sentenced to death in just three days.[31]

The Supreme Court's review of these proceedings led to important rulings on the requirements for due process and adequate legal representation. All nine of the Scottsboro defendants were exonerated after extraordinary efforts.[32] Had Wasilczuk's opinion been written today, the statistics on discrimination in the prosecution of rape cases would be much the same, though based on more complete data. According to a 2017 report by the National Registry of Exonerations, a Black prisoner serving a sentence for sexual assault is three-and-a-half times more likely to be innocent than a white sexual assault convict.[33]

Ehrlich Coker remains in prison in Georgia at the time of this writing, having passed his seventieth year and survived the global coronavirus pandemic that began in 2020. Perhaps unsurprisingly, a Google search for Elnita Carver repeatedly reports on this case – Coker's story. We do not learn how Mrs. Carver recovered or survived. We know nothing of her subsequent choices. Cases always capture the actors at a single moment. Yet, it seems at least possible that Wasilczuk's deliberate framing of Mrs. Carver as a protagonist and a survivor rather than a passive victim

---

[31] *Powell v. Alabama*, 287 U.S. 45, 49–50 (1932).
[32] *See* Meghan Barrett Cousino, *Clarence Norris*, THE NATIONAL REGISTRY OF EXONERATIONS: EXONERATIONS BEFORE 1989, www.law.umich.edu/special/exoneration/Pages/casedetailpre1989.aspx?caseid=238.
[33] Samuel R. Gross, Maurice Possley, & Klara Stephens, *Race and Wrongful Convictions in the United States*, The National Registry of Exonerations (Mar. 7, 2017), www.law.umich.edu/special/exoneration/Documents/Race_and_Wrongful_Convictions.pdf.

might have empowered a different narrative, perhaps more like those articulated by the survivors of Harvey Weinstein or Larry Nassar.

COKER V. GEORGIA, 433 U.S. 584 (1977)
JUSTICE MADALYN K. WASILCZUK, DELIVERS THE JUDGMENT OF THE COURT.

Elnita Carver was 16 years old when Ehrlich Coker raped her. She had given birth less than three weeks earlier and was still weak and bleeding from the delivery. Ehrlich Coker knew that – Mrs. Carver's newborn son was in the bassinet in the bedroom she shared with her husband – but he declared it was "time again" for her to have sex and forced himself upon her, threatening her with the four-inch steak knife he had placed on her nightstand. She cried, and Ehrlich Coker demanded Mrs. Carver tell her husband, tied up in the adjoining bathroom, that she wasn't being hurt. Mrs. Carver did what Ehrlich Coker demanded time and time again and emerged from the harrowing incident with her life.

Mrs. Carver testified at trial that she followed Mr. Coker's commands out of fear for her safety and that of her infant son and 16-year-old husband. At Coker's direction, Mrs. Carver went to the bedroom, grabbed a white halter top blouse for Coker to tie up her husband, tied her husband's hands, tied up her husband's hands again with pantyhose after the halter top ripped, locked the back door and turned out the lights, fetched a kitchen knife from the sink, felt around the ash trays for a cigarette butt for Coker to smoke, poured Coker a glass of tea, handed Coker her husband's billfold, got the car keys, told her husband Coker wasn't hurting her, took her clothes off, laid on the bed, got on top of Coker, gave Coker directions to Atlanta, got in the car, showed Coker how to crank the car, unlocked the door, and pointed out a dirt road. During neither the trial nor the sentencing did anyone ask Mrs. Carver how the incident affected her physically, emotionally, or psychologically. The only passing reference to someone inquiring about Mrs. Carver's well-being is that a police officer asked whether she was okay as they apprehended Mr. Coker, and Mrs. Carver nodded in response. She was later taken to the hospital.

Our judgment in this case does not reflect our opinion of whether Erlich Coker deserves to die for his crimes against Elnita Carver. Instead, in this case we review whether U.S. states, consistent with the Eighth Amendment, can be entrusted with the punishment of death for rape.

Just last term, we upheld the states' power to kill as punishment for murder on the grounds that adequate procedures could guide the hand of justice. Our decisions in *Gregg v. Georgia*, 428 U.S. 153 (1976); *Proffitt v. Florida*, 428 U.S. 242 (1976); *Jurek v. Texas*, 428 U.S. 262, 263 (1976); *Woodson v. North Carolina*, 428 U.S. 280 (1976); and *Roberts v. Louisiana*, 428 U.S. 325 (1976), upheld the death penalty as punishment for murder only when it aligns with the "evolving standards of decency that mark the progress of a maturing society" and "accord[s] with the dignity of man." In so doing, we held that the current Georgia death penalty statute cured the infirmities of the one struck down in *Furman* because it contained adequate safeguards to channel jurors' and judges' discretion and constrain the freakish and wanton imposition of the penalty that had previously plagued our country. *Id.* at 188–189, 196–198 (citing *Furman*, 408 U.S. at 309–310 (White, J., concurring), 313 (Stewart, J., concurring) (1972)). Those safeguards, we found, would restrain the death penalty, making it consistent and reasonable in application rather than cruel and unusual.

Yet judges and juries continue to impose the death penalty for rape with the cruelty and unusualness of a lightning strike. *Furman v. Georgia*, 408 U.S 238, 309 (Stewart, J., concurring). The excessive punishment is neither decent nor dignified. Therefore, we hold that the death penalty for rape is unconstitutional. I further believe that our reasoning applies to the death penalty more broadly. Therefore, I concur in the opinions of Mr. Justice Brennan and Mr. Justice Marshall.

I.

The State of Georgia prosecuted Erlich Coker under Ga. Code Ann. § 26–2001 (1972), which punishes rape "by death or by imprisonment for life, or by imprisonment for not less than one nor more than 20 years." Ga. Code Ann. § 26–2001 (1972). Rejecting his general plea of insanity, the jury found him guilty of rape, in addition to charges of escape, armed robbery, motor vehicle theft, and kidnapping, which are not at issue here. Pursuant to the bifurcated trial procedure upheld last term in *Gregg v. Georgia*, a separate sentencing proceeding commenced. 428 U.S. at 153. The trial court instructed the jury to consider the following aggravating circumstances: (1) that the rape had been committed by a person with a prior record of conviction for a capital felony; and (2) that the rape had been committed in the course of committing another capital felony, namely, the armed robbery of Allen Carver, Elnita's husband. The trial court also instructed the jury that it need not impose the death penalty. Finding both aggravating circumstances, the jury sentenced Mr. Coker to death by electrocution. The Georgia Supreme Court reviewed Mr. Coker's conviction and sentence and affirmed both. *Coker v. State*, 216 S.E.2d 782, 797 (1975). We granted certiorari on a single claim: that the death penalty for rape violates the Eighth Amendment as incorporated to the states by the Fourteenth Amendment.

II.

We seek guidance in history as we consider whether the death penalty for rape violates the Cruel and Unusual Punishment Clause of the Eighth Amendment. If history is to be our guide, we owe it an unflinching review. In the past, we have peered at the penalty's decay without considering the origin of the rot. Today, we excavate the dilapidated foundation of the death penalty for rape in the United States. Our inspection reveals a history of sex and race discrimination that requires us to tear down this edifice to our country's history of white supremacist patriarchy by invalidating this punishment.

A.

Georgia's rape law, like those across the United States, particularly in the South, descends from a history of sexism and racism that treated women as property and Black men as a threat to white men's property interest in white women's sexuality. The law reflects ingrained misogyny by treating violence against women as unspeakable and life-altering while erecting procedural and societal barriers to prevent women from vindicating their rights to dignity, freedom, and bodily autonomy.

Ancient law treated rape as "the theft of virginity, an embezzlement of [the woman's] fair price on the market." Susan Brownmiller, Against Our Will: Men, Women, and Rape 18 (1975). As a result, early laws tended to define women and the cost of violations against them in terms of their relationships to men. The Code of Hammurabi deemed betrothed virgins who were raped innocent, but married women who were raped were to be "bound and thrown into the river" with the men who raped them. *Id.* at 19. Similarly, Mosaic law treated married women "victimized by rape [as] culpable, adulterous and irrevocably defiled," and prescribed death by stoning as punishment. *Id.* For unmarried women, the consequences depended upon whether they were raped inside or outside the city walls. Inside the walls, the law presumed, a woman who was *really* attacked would have screamed to summon help. Therefore, a woman alleging rape under such circumstances was not a real victim and would be stoned to death. Outside the city walls, the law allowed that no one might hear the woman's screams. In that situation, the man who raped her had to pay the bride price, and the woman had to marry him. *Id.* at 20.[34]

During the reign of English King Henry II in Twelfth century, to bring a prosecution for rape, a woman had to go to the next town and show her injuries, blood, and torn clothes to men there. *Id.* at 26. If the accused claimed innocence, the victim would then be subject to a virginity test by four other women, and if she was found to be a virgin, she would be taken into custody. *Id.* These procedures reflected a strong skepticism of women's rape accusations.

Later English law similarly gave legal force to skepticism of rape complaints. Blackstone, unwilling to state the elements of rape because "they are highly improper to be publicly discussed, except only in a court of justice," nevertheless opined on what made a woman's rape allegation unbelievable. A woman was not to be trusted "if she be of evil fame, and stands unsupported by others; if she concealed the injury

---

[34] These laws made no distinctions between unmarried girls and women, and given marriage ages at the time, many of the victims were likely children.

for any considerable time after she had opportunity to complain; if the place, where the fact was alleged to be committed, was where it was possible she might have been heard, and she made no outcry; these and the like circumstances carry a strong, but not conclusive, presumption that her testimony is false or feigned." 4 William Blackstone, Commentaries, 213–214.

The colonies that would become the United States continued to use rape laws to secure men's interests in women's worth as their husbands' sole sexual property. *See Comment, Forcible and Statutory Rape: An Exploration of the Operation and Objectives of the Consent Standard*, 62 Yale L. J. 55, 72–73 (1952). Early versions of the laws of the Massachusetts Bay Colony based the punishment for rape on the raped woman's status in relation to men, reinforcing husbands' sole control of their wives' sexuality. Capitall Lawes of New England of 1641, 1642. The laws required the death penalty for the rape of a married or "contracted" woman, while the rape of a girl or woman older than 10 years old who was not married or contracted could be punished by death or "some other grievous punishment." *Id.* Further, colonial law made marital rape a legal impossibility because marriage was deemed irrevocable consent, reflecting similar notions of women as their husband's property. *Forcible and Statutory Rape, supra*, at 55 n. 2; *Comment, Rape and Battery Between Husband and Wife*, 6 Stan. L. Rev. 719, 721 (1954). Though the early colonies instituted the death penalty for a wide range of offenses, over time, fewer offenses carried the ultimate punishment. Raymond T. Bye, *Recent History and Present Status of Capital Punishment in the United States*, 17 Am. Inst. Crim. L. & C. 234, 234, (1926). By the early 1900s, the majority of those sentenced to death were sentenced for murder. *Id.* at 244.

Rape prosecutions have also elevated men's concerns about women's chastity over their bodily integrity and their lives. As recently as 1964, the Georgia Supreme Court, composed solely of white men, described the purpose of the state's rape statute as follows: "to guard and protect the mothers of mankind, the cornerstone of civilized society, and the zenith of God's creation, against a crime more horrible than death, which is the forcible sexual invasion of her body, the temple of her soul, thereby soiling for life her purity, the most precious attribute of all mankind." *Sims v. Balkcom*, 136 S.E.2d 766, 769 (Ga. 1964). In the same case, the court strongly implied a woman's "virtue" was more valuable than her life itself. *Id.* ("But any man, who can never know the haunting torment of a pure woman after a brutal man has forcibly raped her, who would arbitrarily classify that crime below murder, would reveal a callous appraisal of the true value of woman's virtue."). The Georgia Supreme Court also described rape in shocking prose that failed to recognize that rape is often accomplished without physical force and that few rapes end in death. *Sims v. Balkcom*, 136 S.E.2d at 769. ("The infinite instances where she has resisted even unto the death the bestial assaults of brutes who were trying to rape her are eloquent and indisputable proof of the inhuman agonies she endures when raped. She has chosen death instead of rape. How can a mere mortal man say the crime of rape upon her was less than death.") *See also* President's Commission on Law Enforcement and the Administration of Justice: The Challenge of Crime in a Free Society 19 (1967) (stating that 25 percent of rape victims were attacked with a deadly weapon and that about 1 percent of rapes ended in homicide).

Despite the Georgia court's proclamation that a woman "is entitled to every legal protection of her body, her decency, her purity and good name" and that "the history of no nation will show the high values of woman's virtue and purity that America has shown," conviction rates suggest that the U.S. tacitly condones rape. *Sims v. Balkcom*, 136 S.E.2d at 769. The Federal Bureau of Investigation reports that rape has the lowest conviction rate of any major crime, with only 28.5 percent found guilty of the offense charged and 36.3 percent of charges acquitted or dismissed. F.B.I. Uniform Crime Reports 1973, 116 tbl. 18 (1974). In some areas of the country, the failure to secure rape convictions is even more extreme: In 1969 in New York City, there were 1,085 arrests for rape and a mere 18 convictions. Lesley Oelsner, *Law of Rape: Because Ladies Lie*, N.Y. Times, May 14, 1972.

This low conviction rate stems from laws that treat women accusers as inherently untrustworthy or mentally ill. Babcock, Freedman, Norton, & Ross, Sex Discrimination and the Law: Causes and Remedies 68 (1975). Though scholars, judges, and laypeople insist that women regularly fabricate rape allegations and hold delusional rape fantasies they are unable to separate from fiction, those beliefs are not borne out. Camille E. LeGrand, *Rape and Rape Laws: Sexism in Society and Law*, 61 Calif. L. Rev. 919, 935–936 (1973), *see also The Rape Corroboration Requirement, supra*, at 1373–1384, Ploscowe, *Sex Offenses: The American Legal Context*, 25 L. & Contemp. Prob. 217, 222 (1960) ("[C]omplaints are too often made of sexual misbehavior that has occurred only in the overripe fantasies of the so-called victims.") In fact, studies show that rape goes underreported. The President's Commission on Law Enforcement and the Administration of Justice in 1967 estimated that three and a half times more forcible rapes occurred than were reported. President's Commission on Law Enforcement and the Administration of Justice: The Challenge of Crime in a Free Society 21 (1967). Other studies have estimated that the actual number of rapes is five to ten times as high. Clark & Lewis, at 40.

Class also plays an important role in the enforcement of rape laws. For instance, Brownmiller notes that historically rape laws tended to protect noblewomen rather than commoners. Brownmiller, *supra*, at 27, 37. Likewise, in the antebellum American South, the insistence that neither rape nor consensual sex across the color line existed largely reflected the reality for plantation owners' wives and daughters, rather than that for lower-class white women. Police determinations that rape complaints are "unfounded" despite corroborating physical evidence still frequently rely on class markers and who will present as a "good victim" in court. *See, e.g.*, Lorenne Clark & Debra Lewis, Rape: The Price of Coercive Sexuality, 27, 36 (1977) ("The victim in this case is 26 years of age, she has been separated from her husband since

1963, she has a 4 year old girl ... she is on welfare, $150.00 a month ... in August of 1969 she was in – Hospital, Psychiatric Ward for three weeks.")

Suspicion of women also makes its way into the courthouse. Distrust of women who make rape accusations has been built into the law. Courts approvingly quote Lord Chief Justice Hale's admonition that rape "is an accusation easily to be made and hard to be proved, and harder to be defended by the party accused, tho never so innocent." *See Davis v. State*, 120 Ga. 433, 435 (Ga. 1904) (citing 1 M. Hale, Pleas of the Crown 635 (1680)). California even enshrines the warning in jury instructions, as do other states that use iterations of the caution that throw doubt on victims' testimony. LeGrand, *supra*, at 932 (quoting Committee on Standard Jury Instructions, Criminal, of the Supreme Court of Los Angeles County, California, California Jury Instructions, Criminal 10.22 at 327 (3rd rev. ed. 1970)).

The victim's word in a rape case is further undermined by the corroboration requirement, which derives from the notion that false accusations pervade the legal system. Seven jurisdictions require corroboration of a victim's testimony to sustain a rape conviction. *Note, The Rape Corroboration Requirement: Repeal Not Reform*, 81 Yale L. J. 1365, 1367 (1972) (hereinafter "*Repeal Not Reform*"). Since rape is defined as between a male perpetrator and a female victim, this has the consequence of placing hurdles on the prosecution of violence against women that do not exist in cases of violence against men.[35] Moreover, there is no reason to believe that female complainants are more likely to fabricate rape charges in the face of the many obstacles to prosecution than any other charge or than male complainants. Georgia's rape law requires corroboration. Had Mrs. Carver been unable to produce injuries, torn clothes, semen, or her husband's testimony had he been away that night, a conviction for Mr. Coker's crime would not have been sustained. Ga. Code Ann. § 26-2001.

Even when they can produce corroborating evidence, some victims are unlikely to secure vindication from the courts. Like the laws of ancient Israel distinguishing between rape victims within and without the city walls, society continues to deem some victims "good" and deserving of protection and others "bad" and undeserving. *See generally* Diana E. H. Russell, The Politics of Rape: The Victim's Perspective 25–43 (1975). Susan Griffin explained the dichotomy in *Rape: The All-American Crime*:

> For the female, civilized behavior means chastity before marriage and faithfulness within it. Chivalrous behavior in the male is supposed to protect chastity from involuntary defilement. The fly in the ointment of this otherwise peaceful system is the fallen woman. She does not behave, and therefore does not deserve protection. Ramparts Mag., Sept. 1971, at 426.

This failure to behave may be admitted in court as a reputation for unchastity and used by the defense to argue that not only was the woman not raped, but that a

---

[35] This gendered treatment of violence is further underscored by the fact that many of the states that require corroboration requirements for rape do not require corroboration to sustain sodomy charges. *Repeal Not Reform, supra*, at 1365.

woman like her is unrapable. *Id.* at 427 ("[A] woman who has had sexual intercourse out of wedlock cannot be raped. Rape is not only a crime against the body, it is a transgression against chastity as defined by men.") This means that women of lesser means, those who engage in sex work, who are divorced, who cohabitate with men outside of marriage, or who commit any number of transgressions against notions of good womanhood find little protection in rape laws. Pamela Lakes Wood, *The Victim in a Forcible Rape Case: A Feminist View*, 11 Am. Crim. L. Rev. 335, 341–342 (1973) (listing rape cases in which juries acquitted based on the victim's "assumption of the risk" through actions like drinking). Racial tropes assign these transgressions to Black women victims almost as a matter of course, leaving them least protected of all. Abbey Lincoln, Who Will Revere The Black Woman? in Black Woman: An Anthology 82 (Toni Cade Bambara, ed.) (1970).

A good victim isn't just chaste, she also fights ferociously to preserve that chastity, her "most precious attribute." If she doesn't, people question whether she was *really* raped. Russell, *supra*, at 42–43 (describing a victim recounting that people told her she "should have resisted more physically"), Griffin, *supra*, at 428 (quoting a police officer asking, "Are you sure your life was in danger and you had no other choice?" of a woman raped with a ten-inch knife to her throat), Wood, *supra*, at 346 (reporting a case in which the jury acquitted because the women did not resist enough or try to escape despite being beaten and emerging from the incident with sizeable bruises). Some jurists even express that they do not believe rape is possible absent extensive injuries. Carol Bohmer & Audrey Blumberg, *Twice Traumatized: The Rape Victim and the Court*, 58 Judicature 391, 398 (1975) (quoting a judge saying "a hostile vagina will not admit a penis"). This puts victims in a precarious position: Fighting back may result in more extreme injuries. Wood, *supra*, at 346. For a victim who did not physically resist, a jury's failure to convict may reinforce her shame and reaffirm the idea that she should have prevented her victimization. *See generally* Russell, *supra*, at 43.

Severe punishments heighten juries' and judges' unwillingness to enter guilty verdicts in rape cases. Though Georgia is the only state that currently punishes the rape of an adult with the death penalty, most other states likewise have severe penalties for rape. These severe penalties result in the same problem noted by this Court with respect to the mandatory death penalty for murder: Juries feel the punishment is out of proportion to the crime, and therefore refuse to convict. *See Furman*, 408 U.S. at 247 (Douglas, J., concurring), 298 (Brennan, J., concurring), 339 (Marshall, J., concurring), *see also* H. Kalven and H. Zeisel, The American Jury, 311–312 (1966). Even some victims, knowing the penalty is death, may be squeamish about reporting their rape. As a result, maintaining severe punishments affords women less, not more, protection from rape.[36]

---

[36] There is also at least some evidence that more severe penalties for rape fail to deter commission of the crime. *See* Barry Schwartz, *The Effect in Philadelphia of Pennsylvania's Increased Penalties for Rape and Attempted Rape*, 59 J. OF CRIM. L. CRIMINOLOGY & POL. SCI. 4, 509 (1968).

The dissent insists that we do a disservice to women by invalidating the death penalty for rape, characterizing rape as "destructive of the human personality." *Infra* at 611–612 (Rehnquist, J., dissenting). Our colleague's view is in some ways understandable. The seriousness of rape as a violation of women's bodily integrity has been so long diminished that it is attractive to underscore the pain and trauma that rape inflicts. But to declare the harm caused "irreparable" sends pernicious messages that survivors of sexual and gender-based violence internalize to disastrous result: that life is not worth living after rape, or that if one survives, it is because she did not resist valiantly enough. Those messages themselves lead to psychological harm and isolation. While many resilient people who are raped overcome these powerful messages, others will feel silenced, shamed, and degraded, will not report to friends, family or police, and they will suffer alone. They may even feel they are not victims at all, because "nice girls don't get raped." Clark & Lewis, *supra*, at 27. The death penalty does nothing to diminish that isolation or the trepidation of reporting and may even exacerbate it through the bifurcated trial process. We should not forget, either, that while some women will testify against strangers, more often, they will testify against someone known to them, which may well heighten barriers to reporting if the punishment is death.

By setting death as the penalty for rape in Georgia while undermining the dignity and equal status of women through special rules applied only to violence against them, the state places women "not on a pedestal, but in a cage." *Weinberger v. Wiesenfeld*, 420 U. S. 636 (1975) (oral argument January 20, 1975, Ruth Bader Ginsburg). The history and present practice of rape law in the United States makes clear that the death penalty for rape does not serve the interests of women, promotes arbitrary enforcement, and undermines the penological purposes it was intended to advance.

B.

In addition to treating women as objects who could be soiled, broken, or valueless as a result of rape, Georgia's rape laws explicitly incorporated enslaved people's status as chattel and, even after Emancipation, continued to treat Black men with a presumption of criminality to police the racial hierarchy and punish interracial relationships. *See generally* Winfield H. Collins, The Truth About Lynching and the Negro in the South: In Which the Author Pleads that the South Be Made Safe for the White Race (1918), *see also Stephen (a slave) v. State*, 11 Ga. 225, 230 (Ga. 1852) ("The crime, from the very nature of it, is calculated to excite indignation in every heart; and when perpetrated by a slave on a free white female of immature mind and body, that indignation becomes greater, and is more difficult to repress."). Prior to the Civil War, Georgia law punished rape by white men with terms of imprisonment of not more than 20 years and attempted rape by white men with not more than five years' imprisonment. Ga. Penal Code of 1816,

§§ 33–34; Ga. Acts of 1816 No. 508 §1. By contrast, enslaved people and free Black men faced a mandatory death sentence for the rape or attempted rape of a free white woman. *Id*.[37]

Though Georgia's legislature enacted a race-neutral statute a year after the abolition of slavery, the Georgia Supreme Court continued to sanction race-based differences in the standard of proof for rape, evincing the continuity of dual systems of justice. In *Dorsey v. State*, the Georgia Supreme Court wrote that a Black man's race could be considered in rape cases to "rebut any presumption that might otherwise arise in favor of the accused that his intention was to obtain the consent of the female, upon failure of which he would abandon his purpose to have sexual intercourse with her." 34 S.E. 135, 136–137 (Ga. 1899). Therefore, though the Georgia death penalty statute was formally race-neutral, evidentiary distinctions and majority white, majority male juries could be counted on to continue to effect the ultimate punishment on Black men while reserving lesser or no punishments for white men. Though *Neal v. Delaware*, 103 U.S. 370, 391 (1881), made it unconstitutional for Black men to be excluded from juries on the basis of their race, Black people have continued to be disproportionately excluded from jury service. Even when explicit references to race gave way, racially coded language describing Black men accused of rape as less than "dog[s]" persisted in the court's opinions. *Sims v. Balkcom*, 136 S.E.2d at 769 (describing "the bestial assault of brutes" and asserting that "[e]ven a cur dog is too humane to do such an outrageous injury to the female").[38]

The histories and ongoing harms of Jane Crow and Jim Crow overlap and multiply for Black women. Pauli Murray, *The Negro Woman in the Quest for Equality*, Speech before the National Council of Negro Women in Washington, D.C (Nov. 1963) (coining the term "Jane Crow"). Enslaved Black women lived outside the bounds of the protection of rape law entirely. Rape by their enslavers or by other enslaved people was no crime at all, and rape by other white men was deemed a trespass. Brownmiller, *supra*, at 162–163. Frances Beal, Double Jeopardy: To Be Black and Female, in The Black Woman: An Anthology, 92 (Toni Cade Bambara, ed.) (1970) (describing the sexual abuse and exploitation of Black women by white colonizers). At the same time, despite permissive standards of proof for rape by Black defendants, Black women raped by Black men were not protected. *Washington v. State*, 75 S.E. 253, 253 (Ga. 1912) (stating that no *Dorsey* charge was required when both people were "of color and there was no evidence as to their social standing"). Moreover, in a study of the death penalty for rape in Florida between 1940 and 1964,

---

[37] It should also be noted that with respect to enslaved people sentenced to death, their only hope for commutation was if the person who enslaved them petitioned the governor. Enslaved people had no right to petition the governor for commutation themselves. GA. ACTS OF 1816 No. 508 §3.

[38] Strikingly, the Georgia Supreme Court's opinion in this case did not once mention the race of the accused or the victim, though the syllabus describes the accused as "an indigent and illiterate negro" and notes that since 1930, Georgia had "executed for rape 58 Negro persons and only 3 White persons." *Sims v. Balkcom*, 136 S.E.2d at 767.

white men received the death penalty for rape of a white woman in six cases (5 percent), while none of the eight white men who raped Black women did. Marvin E. Wolfgang & Marc Riedel, *Race, Judicial Discretion, and the Death Penalty*, 407 Annals Am. Acad. Pol. & Soc. Sci., 119, 125 (1973) (citing Florida Civil Liberties Union, *Rape: Selective Electrocution Based on Race* (1964)). Even today, the burden of failed rape prosecutions likely falls disproportionately on Black women. In Menachem Amir's two-year study of forcible rapes in Philadelphia, of the reported 646 victims and 1,292 accused, 77 percent were offenses between Black men and Black women. Patterns in Forcible Rape 44 (1971).

The death penalty for rape remains steeped in its racial past. Of the 455 men executed for rape between 1930 and 1972, 405 of them – 89.5 percent – were Black men. US Dep't of Just., Bureau of Prisons, Nat'l Prisoner Stats., Bull. No. 45, *Capital Punishment 1930–1968*, 7 (1969). These figures understate the actual racial disparity in punishment for sexual assault and rape by omitting white mobs' extrajudicial lynching of Black men for the rape or sexual assault (real or fabricated) of white women and girls. Nor can these numbers account for racial discrimination at discretionary junctures such as arrest or charging. *See* Partington, *supra*, at 52 (quoting Bullock, *Significance of the Racial Factor in the Length of Prison Sentences*, 52 J. Crim. L., C. & P.S. 411, 412 (1962)) ("Field evidence of racial discrimination in the administration of criminal justice has generally indicated that public officials, under the influence of their prejudices, tend to make decisions that exaggerate Negro criminality.") A study of rape cases in eleven Southern states from 1945 to 1965 revealed that nearly seven times as many Black men were sentenced to death as white men, and Black defendants with white victims were eighteen times more likely to receive the death penalty than any other defendant-victim race combination. Wolfgang & Riedel, *supra*, at 129–130. Not one of the twenty-nine nonracial variables that could explain the racial disparities proved statistically significant. *Wolfgang and Riedel, supra*, at 132. It is no coincidence that our first forays into regulating the death penalty began as interventions in spurious rape prosecutions against Black men and boys in the South. *See e.g., Powell v. Alabama*, 287 U.S. 45 (1932); *Hamilton v. Alabama*, 368 U.S. 52 (1961).

Given these facts, today's case is a strange vehicle for a challenge to the death penalty for rape.[39] Nevertheless, we draw from the information provided by the parties in considering how the statute's history helps us understand its current operation. The State has not offered the total number of rape prosecutions brought since *Furman*. Instead, we know only that the Georgia Supreme Court has reviewed sixty-three cases under the statute, six of which resulted in death sentences and were reviewed

---

[39] This very term, before Mr. Coker petitioned for *certiorari*, two other men, John Eberheart and John Hooks, both Black men convicted of rape and sentenced to death in Georgia, sought *certiorari* before this Court on the same issue that is now before us.

under the procedures mandated by statute and upheld in *Gregg*. Of those six, one death sentence was reversed, leaving five men on Georgia's death row for rape. Three of those men have petitioned us for review of their cases this year. Two out of three of the petitioners are Black men convicted of raping white women. Mr. Coker is far from the penalty's usual victim. Regardless of the man now before us, however, we must not forget those our opinion will most affect.

III.

With the history and the present operation of rape law in mind, we now strike down the death penalty for rape as a violation of the Eighth and Fourteenth Amendments of the U.S. Constitution. In *Gregg*, we held that the Eighth Amendment must be interpreted in light of the "evolving standards of decency that mark the progress of a maturing society" and also that that punishment must comport "with the dignity of man." 428 U.S. at 173. Surely the time has come that a plainly racist punishment that perpetuates women's lesser status under law is far behind our progress.

Our judgment of the evolving standards of decency must be informed by objective factors such as public attitudes as expressed through state legislatures and juries' sentencing decisions. Though our understanding of the meaning of legislation is somewhat obfuscated by the recent upheaval in the capital sentencing arena, the direction of change suggests that the community no longer supports the death penalty for rape. By 1925, only 18 states, the District of Columbia, and the Federal Government authorized the death penalty for rape of an adult. Bye, *supra*, at 241–242. At the time of our decision in *Furman*, three more jurisdictions had abandoned the penalty.

After *Furman* invalidated the nation's capital punishment laws, thirty-five states reinstated the sentence in some form. *Gregg*, 428 U.S. at 173 n. 23. Of those, six enacted statutes that authorized the death penalty for at least some rape cases: Georgia, North Carolina, and Louisiana for rape of an adult woman,[40] and Florida, Mississippi, and Tennessee for rape of a child.[41] North Carolina, Louisiana, and Tennessee's statutes were subsequently invalidated because they imposed mandatory sentences. *See Woodson*, 428 U.S. at 280, *Roberts*, 428 U.S. at 325, *Collins v. State*, 550 S.W.2d 643 (Tenn. 1977). That leaves Georgia, Florida, and Mississippi alone in imposing the death penalty for rape in the United States.

Georgia argues that the rarity of capital rape statutes is not dispositive because of the difficulty facing legislatures after our pronouncements in *Furman*. Eleven of the sixteen states that retained capital rape statutes in 1971 enacted mandatory

---

[40] GA. CODE § 26–2001 (1970); N.C. GEN. STAT. § 14–21 (1969); LA. REV. STAT. ANN. § 14:42 (1950).
[41] FLA. STAT. ANN. § 794.011(2) (1976); MISS. CODE ANN. § 97-3-65 (SUPP. 1976); TENN. CODE ANN. § 39-3702 (1974).

death penalty statutes in response to *Furman*, and those states may have chosen to dispense with the death penalty for rape rather than require it in all cases. This fails to explain, however, why the six states that have reenacted death penalty statutes after *Woodson* and *Roberts* neglected to include rape in their discretionary capital sentencing statutes. On balance, there is a strong and pronounced trend away from the death penalty for rape in this country.

We also consider the jury "a significant and reliable objective index of contemporary values because it is so directly involved" in sentencing decisions. *Gregg*, 428 U.S. at 181. According to the facts before us, at least 9 out of 10 Georgia juries have not imposed a death sentence upon conviction for rape. Of at least equal import is that Georgia juries have chosen so scarcely to impose the penalty, and when they have done so, they have chosen it disproportionately for a disfavored class. In doing so, jurors have revealed that their discretion is not sufficiently bounded by the safeguards we found would promote nonarbitrary application of the death penalty in *Gregg*. Procedural justice without substantive effect betrays our commitment to equal justice under law.

As Justice Douglas recognized in *Furman*, the English Bill of Rights of 1689, on which our Cruel and Unusual Punishment Clause is based, "was concerned primarily with selective or irregular application of harsh penalties," and a punishment is "unusual" if it is racially discriminatory or "imposed under a procedure that gives room for the play of such prejudices." 408 U.S. at 242 (Douglas, J., concurring). Here, there are decades – even centuries – of evidence that the death penalty for rape has continued to give play to prejudice long after formally discriminatory laws were stricken from the registers. Unconstitutional punishments are not only those that are barbarous but also those that are applied "selectively to minorities whose numbers are few, who are outcasts of society, and who are unpopular, but whom society is willing to see suffer though it would not countenance general application of the same penalty across the board." *Id.* at 245. Thereby, the Eighth Amendment incorporates the basic themes of equal protection. *Id.* at 249. We have had past occasion to focus on the death penalty for rape as disproportionately applied to Black men, as two out of the three petitioners in the cases consolidated in *Furman* stood before the Court as Black men convicted of raping white women. *Id.* at 251–253 (Douglas, J., concurring), 363 (Marshall, J., concurring). There is no indication that the racial disparities then before us have been ameliorated. When one considers the disparities based on the race of victims, the unusualness and arbitrariness of the penalty only sharpens.

Today we must also consider whether the death penalty for rape comports with human dignity. As Justice Brennan pointed out in *Furman*, a death sentence is excessive when it "serves no penal purpose more effectively than a less severe punishment." *Furman* at 280. We have held that the penological purposes of the death penalty are deterrence and retribution. *Gregg*, 428 U.S. at 183. Though there is relatively little analysis of the deterrent role of the death penalty for rape, increased penalties have not lowered the crime rates for rape. Barry Schwartz, *The Effect in Philadelphia of Pennsylvania's Increased Penalties for Rape and Attempted Rape*, 59 J. of Crim. L. Criminology & Pol. Sci. 4, 509 (1968).[42] The infrequent imposition of the penalty also suggests that it is unlikely to have a deterrent effect. *Furman*, 408 U.S. at 311–312 (White, J., concurring). In this instance, the death penalty for rape may well encourage, rather than deter, more violent offenses, since there is no additional penalty for a rape-murder beyond that for rape under the Georgia statutory regime. As pertains to retribution, unlike with murder, women who have been raped can go on to lead meaningful, happy lives. Without diminishing the grave harm of rape, declaring that all women's lives will be uniformly bleak and unbearable after rape robs women of strength and agency. The availability of psychological and emotional support is indispensable. The availability of the death penalty is not.

The death penalty for rape is cruel and unusual punishment: arbitrarily applied, excessive, and lacking a penological purpose. The death penalty for rape violates contemporary societal norms by reinforcing presumptions of Black criminality through its disproportionate and arbitrary application to poor Black men. At the same time, the punishment fails to comport with human dignity. Capital rape trials diminish women's place in society by failing to trust their word on an equal footing with men's. Moreover, the punishment fails to make women safer by deterring the commission of rapes or distinguishing between rape and murder. Therefore, the punishment is excessive and lacking a penological purpose.

For these reasons, we invalidate the death penalty for rape and remand for proceedings consistent with this judgment.

---

[42] Likewise, studies of the effect of the death penalty for murder demonstrate no correlation between murder rates and the existence of the death penalty. *Furman*, 480 U.S. at 349 (Marshall, J., concurring).

4

Commentary on *Oliphant v. Suquamish Indian Tribe*

ADAM CREPELLE

The US Supreme Court's decision in *Oliphant v. Suquamish Indian Tribe*[1] is infamous among those who work in federal Indian law and virtually unknown outside the field, despite the fact that the decision provides fertile grounds for exploring critical theoretical and practical issues at the core of the US legal system, including the scope of federal power, the nature and scope of criminal jurisdiction, the role of the writ of habeas corpus, and issues of civil rights, including equal protection, due process, and the rights guaranteed to defendants in criminal cases. Although the Supreme Court's reasoning in *Oliphant* has been much maligned, the court continues to abide by it. In fact, the Supreme Court has extended some of *Oliphant*'s reasoning to tribal civil jurisdiction as well.

The *Oliphant* decision has caused immeasurable harm to Indian tribes and to Indian women in particular, as *Oliphant* divested tribes of criminal jurisdiction over non-Indians who commit crimes within the tribe's territory. The *Oliphant* decision removed the ability of tribal governments to fully protect the people living within its territory. *Oliphant*'s most pernicious consequences are felt by Native women, who suffer sexual assault and domestic violence at more than double the rates of any other US citizens. Indeed, all three branches of the federal government have acknowledged that Indian women are going missing and being murdered at crisis levels.[2]

The *Oliphant* decision was issued in 1978, near the end of a defining decade in federal Indian law and policy. Throughout the history of the United States, federal Indian policy has vacillated wildly. Following World War II, the United States implemented a policy of terminating tribal governments. The United States' aim was to assimilate Indians into the US mainstream. Towards this end, the United States relocated Indians, often coercively, from their rural reservations to major metropolitan areas. In 1953, the United States also extended state criminal law and civil adjudicatory authority over tribes in five states and the Alaska Territory with Public

---

[1] 435 U.S. 191 (1978).
[2] www.whitehouse.gov/briefing-room/presidential-actions/2021/05/04/a-proclamation-on-missing-and-murdered-indigenous-persons-awareness-day-2021/.

Law 83–280. Other states were allowed to assume jurisdiction over the tribes within their borders. Supplanting tribal institutions with state jurisdiction was thought to expedite assimilation; plus, PL 280 came with the added benefit of reducing federal expenditures.

In 1970, President Richard Nixon explicitly disavowed tribal termination in favor of tribal self-determination. Congress embraced tribal self-determination in 1975, when it passed the Indian Self-Determination and Education Assistance Act. Tribes responded to the policy change by asserting their sovereignty, and tribes in Washington State were at the forefront of this movement. Several tribes in Washington began selling cigarettes on their reservations sans state taxes, providing a substantially lower price than off reservation retailers. More significantly, tribes in Washington asserted their treaty fishing rights resulting in the "Fish Wars." A federal district court ruled in favor of the tribes, holding their treaty rights entitled tribal fishermen to half the state's salmon catch in 1974. The Supreme Court subsequently affirmed the district court's ruling in 1979. Consequently, non-Indian angst about tribal sovereignty was running high.[3]

Against this backdrop, enter Mark David Oliphant. Oliphant was a non-Indian resident of the Port Madison Indian Reservation, located across the Puget Sound from Seattle. Oliphant got into a drunken brawl at the Suquamish Indian Tribe's annual Chief Seattle Days celebration. When tribal police responded and attempted to break up the disturbance, Oliphant assaulted the tribal police officer. Oliphant was arrested and was soon out on pretrial release. He retained counsel, who quickly filed a habeas petition in federal court, seeking to quash the tribal criminal charges. While those legal proceedings were pending, Oliphant was a passenger in a car driven by Daniel Belgarde, who engaged tribal police in a high-speed chase on the Port Madison reservation's roadways, which ended when Belgarde crashed into a tribal police car. After Belgarde was arrested and released, he promptly retained the same lawyer as Oliphant. That attorney filed a matching habeas petition on Belgarde's behalf.

Oliphant's and Belgarde's habeas petitions were filed under the Indian Civil Rights Act, which requires tribal governments to respect most of the individual rights guaranteed by the US Constitution.[4] Neither claimed to be innocent. Neither claimed tribal law was unfair; after all, racing on public roadways and punching police officers are illegal just about everywhere. Neither claimed any actual wrongdoing by the tribal court. Instead, Oliphant and Belgarde both claimed the tribal

---

[3] SARAH KRAKOFF, *Mark the Plumber v. Tribal Empire, or Non-Indian Anxiety v. Tribal Sovereignty?: The Story of Oliphant v. Suquamish Indian Tribe*, in INDIAN LAW STORIES 264 (Philip P. Frickey, Carole E. Goldberg & Kevin K. Washburn, eds., 2010).

[4] Unless otherwise stated, remaining legal authorities in this article are collected in, Adam Crepelle, *Tribal Courts, The Violence Against Women Act, and Supplemental Jurisdiction: Expanding Tribal Court Jurisdiction to Improve Public Safety in Indian Country*, 81 MONT. L. REV. 59 (2020) [Crepelle, *Tribal Courts*].

court could not treat them fairly *simply because* they were non-Indians, arguing tribal courts should have no criminal jurisdiction over non-Indians.

The federal district court rejected this argument. The Ninth Circuit did too, citing existing precedent and explaining Indian law's foundational tenet is tribes possess all sovereign powers that have not been explicitly relinquished by the tribe or removed by Congress.[5] The Ninth Circuit said there was no evidence the Suquamish had surrendered this inherent power,[6] nor was there any evidence that Congress had stripped tribes of this power.[7] The Ninth Circuit also pointed out depriving tribes of criminal jurisdiction would contradict Congress's current policy of promoting tribal self-determination.[8]

The Supreme Court disagreed. Virtually every element of the court's analysis has been roundly criticized. The Supreme Court began by asserting the exercise of tribal criminal jurisdiction over non-Indians "is a relatively new phenomenon."[9] This is simply not true. Early treaties between the United States and Indian tribes expressly authorize tribal criminal jurisdiction over non-Indians.[10] There are also accounts of tribes asserting criminal jurisdiction over non-Indians well into the 1800s.[11] After claiming that tribal criminal jurisdiction over non-Indians was "new," the court turned to an 1830 treaty between the Choctaw and the United States.[12] The court never explained why it referenced the Choctaw's treaty rather than the Suquamish's own treaty – which was negotiated 25 years later in entirely different circumstances.[13] In another bizarre move, the Supreme Court bolstered its conclusion by citing a withdrawn opinion from the Solicitor of the Department of Interior and a repudiated 1960 Senate Report.[14]

Oliphant also relied on highly dubious precedent. Only one case in the history of the United States seemed to support the majority's view, and the supporting passage was dicta from an 1878 territorial court.[15] The Supreme Court admitted that the author of the opinion, Isaac Parker, was an infamously bad judge. Worse, the Supreme Court acknowledged "Judge Parker's views as to the ultimate destiny of the Indian people are not in accord with current thinking on the subject."[16] The Supreme Court's opinion also relied on other jurisprudence that was out of step

---

[5] *Oliphant v. Schlie*, 544 F.2d 1007, n.1 (9th Cir. 1976).
[6] *Id.*, at 1010.
[7] *Id.*, at 1010–1012.
[8] *Id.*, at 1013.
[9] *Oliphant v. Suquamish*, 435 U.S. 191, 197 (1978).
[10] Crepelle, Tribal Courts, at 64.
[11] Adam Crepelle, *Lies, Damn Lies, and Federal Indian Law: The Ethics of Citing Racist Precedent in Contemporary Federal Indian Law*, 44 N.Y.U. REV. L. & SOC. CHANGE 529, 562 (2021) [Crepelle, *Lies*].
[12] Oliphant, at 197–199.
[13] Crepelle, *Lies*, at 559.
[14] Oliphant, at n.11 and n.15.
[15] *Id.*, at 199–201.
[16] *Id.*, n.10.

with contemporary notions of racial justice, opinions which describe Indians as "heathens," "savages," and an "unfortunate race."[17]

Aside from its curious legal reasoning, the policy motivations underlying *Oliphant* are suspect. The Supreme Court never claimed a tribal court transgressed the rights of a non-Indian; in fact, the Supreme Court conceded civil rights are adequately protected by the Indian Civil Rights Act.[18] More troubling, the Supreme Court admitted its opinion would likely lead to increased non-Indian crime on reservations.[19] Nonetheless, the Supreme Court forged ahead with its declaration that tribes had no criminal authority to hold non-Indians accountable for crimes committed on reservations.[20] Justice Marshall wrote a three sentence dissent, joined by Chief Justice Burger.[21]

Justice Tatum's new dissent vigorously challenges the majority opinion. After providing the factual background and noting the court's neglect of procedure, Justice Tatum sets forth the fundamental principle of federal Indian law: Tribes retain all sovereign powers not expressly or necessarily relinquished as a result of their dependent status. Justice Tatum then clearly explains criminal law is a core component of sovereignty. Justice Tatum next distinguishes between external and internal sovereignty. She notes tribes have surrendered control over external affairs, like making war with foreign countries, to the United States. However, she explains criminal law has always been deemed an integral part of internal sovereignty. Justice Tatum then emphasizes the Suquamish never relinquished criminal jurisdiction in a treaty. Furthermore, Justice Tatum points out that the majority admits Congress has never stripped tribes of criminal authority over non-Indians. Justice Tatum's dissent follows long-established Indian law precedent to conclude the Suquamish possessed inherent authority to protect their citizens from non-Indian criminals.

Life in Indian country would be much different if Justice Tatum's dissent carried the day. Nowhere would the difference be greater than for Indian women. A 2016 report from the National Institute of Justice found over half Indian women will experience sexual violence during their lifetime.[22] Congress described the level of violence endured by Indian women as "epidemic" in 2010,[23] and President Obama described the level of violence Indian women experience as "an assault on our national conscience that we can no longer ignore."[24] In addition to the high level of

---

[17] Crepelle, *Lies*, at 540.
[18] Oliphant, at 211–212.
[19] *Id.*, at 212.
[20] *Id.*
[21] Oliphant, at 212 (Marshall, J., dissenting).
[22] André B. Rosay, *Violence Against American Indian and Alaska Native Women and Men*, NAT'L INST. OF JUST. J., 09/2016, at 38, 40, www.ncjrs.gov/pdffiles1/nij/249821.pdf.
[23] Tribal Law and Order Act of 2010, Pub. L. No. 111–211, § 202(a)(5)(A-C), 124 Stat. 2262.
[24] Lynn Rosenthal, *The Tribal Law and Order Act of 2010: A Step Forward for Native Women*, PRES. BARACK OBAMA WHITE HOUSE BLOG (July 29, 2010, 5:13 p.m. ET), https://obamawhitehouse.archives.gov/blog/2010/07/29/tribal-law-and-order-act-2010-a-step-forward-native-women [https://perma.cc/78SM-HH2Z].

violence, 97 percent of Indian women report being victimized by a non-Indian[25] – and many rightly point to Oliphant as a significant reason for this disparity. And as grim as these figures are, they likely underrepresent the true level of violence endure: Every single Indian woman on some reservations report being the victim of sexual violence.[26]

Advocates for Native victims of violence have long expressed that *Oliphant* endangers Native women. Congress chipped away at *Oliphant*'s holding in the Violence Against Women Reauthorization Act of 2013 (VAWA). For the first time since 1978, Congress made small allowances for tribal nations to prosecute non-Indians. However, VAWA contains a number of problems which blunt its effectiveness. VAWA addresses only three crimes: dating violence, domestic violence, and violation of a protective order. Even if a non-Indian commits one of these three crimes, the tribe can prosecute only if the non-Indian has one of the specified relationships with the tribe or the victim. The tribe must also provide the defendant with certain procedural safeguards in order to prosecute. These safeguards are more stringent than any other jurisdiction in the United States must meet and are expensive. Many tribes simply cannot afford to implement VAWA. As of 2021, only about twenty-seven of the 574 federally recognized tribes have opted to exercise the "special domestic violence criminal jurisdiction" (SDVCJ) contained in the statute.[27] Even those who do exercise SDVCJ lack the authority to prosecute related crimes, such as battery of children present at the time of the violence or assaults committed against the police who respond to the calls or the guards who work in the tribal jails. VAWA's SDVCJ would be unnecessary if Justice Tatum's dissent prevailed.

Justice Tatum's dissent would have prevented Indian country's jurisdictional quagmire. Who possesses the authority to prosecute a given crime in Indian country – the tribal, federal, or state government – depends on a complex calculus involving the identity of the offender, the identity of the victim, and the nature of the crime. Sorting through this complicated analysis can take years. Plus, if the agency makes an incorrect determination, the case will be tossed for lack of subject matter jurisdiction. Police officers often do not want to deal with these jurisdictional complexities when there are crimes being committed that they can more quickly and easily address. Accordingly, state and federal prosecutors usually ignore Indian country crimes. As a result, Indian country's jurisdictional scheme is routinely exploited by non-Indian criminals, who know they are effectively above the law on reservations.

The Supreme Court's decision in *Oliphant* was based on demonstrably false assumptions and ignored or subverted precedent. It was reached in the absence of any finding – indeed any allegation – that the tribe had violated any defendant's

---

[25] Rosay, at 42.
[26] Sarah Deer, *Sovereignty of the Soul*, 38 SUFFOLK U.L. REV. 455, 456 (2005).
[27] www.ncai.org/tribal-vawa/get-started/currently-implementing-tribes.

civil rights or that such rights were not already adequately protected. It was reached with the explicit acknowledgment that it would lead to an increase in lawlessness in Indian country, a prediction that has sadly come true. Two decades into the twenty-first century, *Oliphant's* declaration that the ability to mete out criminal justice depends on whether a person is an Indian stands as a disgrace to the US legal system.

OLIPHANT V. SUQUAMISH INDIAN TRIBE, 435 U.S. 191 (1978)

JUSTICE MELISSA L. TATUM, DISSENTING

I agree with Justice Marshall and Chief Justice Burger that the majority erred in finding that the Suquamish Tribe lacks criminal jurisdiction to prosecute Petitioners. I write separately to dissent because the majority's decision is not only erroneous, it is the result of an approach that is contrary to precedent, ignores well-established canons of construction, and creates a potentially dangerous environment in Indian country.

I.

The majority's opinion gives short shrift to key facts. A more complete statement of the relevant facts may be found in the opinion of the US Court of Appeals for the Ninth Circuit and in Petitioner's Brief. Drawing on those two sources reveals that both Petitioners, Mark Oliphant and Daniel Belgarde, reside on the Port Madison Reservation. The Port Madison Reservation is located on the opposite side of Puget Sound from Seattle and is under the governance of the Suquamish Indian Tribe.

The Tribe governs the reservation pursuant to the 1855 Treaty of Point Elliott, 12 Stat. 927. The Suquamish Tribe operates pursuant to a constitution adopted in 1964 and approved by the Secretary of the Interior. The tribal government has also enacted a Law and Order Code, which by its terms applies to all persons on the reservation, both Indian and non-Indian.

The tribe holds an annual celebration known as Chief Seattle Days. The festival draws thousands of people. As part of the planning process for the 1973 event, the tribe reached out to area law enforcement departments, including the county and the Western Washington Agency of the Bureau of Indian Affairs, to request assistance. The only assistance received in response to this request was the services of one deputy for one eight hour shift. The tribe was informed that it would have to shoulder the responsibility for providing the necessary law enforcement personnel.

During the celebration, Oliphant became involved in a drunken altercation with another man. Tribal police intervened, and during their attempt to stop the fight, a tribal officer was knocked down. Oliphant was arrested and charged with assault on an officer and resisting arrest. The arrest occurred at 4:30 am on August 19, 1973. Oliphant was arraigned the same day, and although initially held without bond, he was released a few days later on his own recognizance.

On August 23, 1973, before the start of any trial proceedings in tribal court, Oliphant filed a petition with the federal district court seeking a writ of habeas corpus. In his petition Oliphant alleged that the tribal court had no jurisdiction over non-Indians, and that subjecting him to the jurisdiction of the tribal court denied him due process as guaranteed by the United States Constitution. The tribal trial court stayed Oliphant's trial pending resolution of the habeas petition.

In a memorandum opinion and order entered on April 5, 1974, the district court denied Oliphant's petition, finding that Oliphant was subject to the jurisdiction of the tribal court. By a 2-1 vote on August 24, 1976, a divided panel of the Ninth Circuit affirmed the decision of the district court. *Oliphant v. Schlie*, 544 F.2d 1007 (1976). Meanwhile, in the time between the district court's denial of Oliphant's petition and the Ninth Circuit's decision affirming that denial, on October 12, 1974, Petitioner Belgarde was arrested after tribal police chased him for two hours at speeds "immensely exceeding" the posted speed limit. The chase ended when Belgarde crashed into a tribal police car. He was arrested and charged with reckless endangerment and destruction of public property. The police did not arrest either of Belgarde's two companions who were also in the car, one of whom was Mark Oliphant.

Belgarde filed a petition for a writ of habeas corpus on November 6, 1974, alleging, among other things, that the tribal court lacked jurisdiction over him. The federal district court denied his petition, and he appealed September 4, 1975. The parties agreed to stay the appeal pending the outcome of Oliphant's (then) pending appeal. Belgarde joined Oliphant in his petition to this Court seeking a writ of certiorari. This Court granted that petition and consolidated the two cases, despite the lack of a decision from the court of appeals in Belgarde's case. The sole question before this Court is whether tribal courts possess criminal jurisdiction over non-Indians.

II.

Before turning to the merits of the suit, I must first raise a procedural issue not addressed by the majority in its opinion. Both Oliphant and Belgarde filed their petitions for a writ of habeas corpus before their trials started. Since the beginning of this country, the "Great Writ" has been a vehicle for challenging the legality of a person's detention. See *U.S. v. Hayman*, 342 U.S. 205 (1952)(discussing the history of the writ); *see also* 3 Blackstone's Commentaries 129. Over the past two centuries, habeas corpus has become a way for a person to invoke the power of the federal courts to ensure that state court convictions were not obtained in violation of federally guaranteed rights. *Fay v. Noia*, 372 U.S. 391 (1963); *U.S. v. Hayman*, 342 U.S. 205 (1952); *Ex parte Royall*, 117 U.S. 241, 246–247 (1886).

Congress explicitly extended the writ to include review of tribal court decisions as part of the 1968 Indian Civil Rights Act, which declares that the "privilege of the writ of habeas corpus shall be available to any person, in a court of the United States, to test the legality of his detention by order of an Indian tribe." 25 USC §1303. This is the first time this Court has been confronted with a case brought to the federal courts seeking a writ of habeas corpus challenging a tribal court conviction. It is far, however, from the first time this Court has explored the contours of the writ of habeas corpus and the requirements necessary for successfully seeking such a writ.

For almost 100 years, this Court has consistently held that exhaustion of state court remedies is a prerequisite for challenging a state criminal conviction through a petition for a writ of habeas corpus. *Ex parte Royall*, 117 U.S. 241 (1886); *Ex parte Hawk*, 321 U.S. 114 (1944); *Picard v. Connor*, 404 U.S. 270 (1971); *Pitchess v. Davis*, 421 U.S. 482 (1975). The exhaustion requirement's primary purpose is to protect the state courts' role in the enforcement of federal law and prevent disruption of state judicial proceedings. Under our federal system, the federal and state courts are "equally bound to guard and protect rights secured by the Constitution," *Ex parte Royall*, 117 U.S. 241, 251 (1886). *See also Picard v. Connor*, 404 U.S. 270, 275 (1971); *Wilwording v. Swenson*, 404 U.S. 249, 250 (1971). In light of these overlapping duties, the exhaustion requirement is designed to minimize friction between state and federal courts by allowing the state court the first opportunity to address the issue. *Ex parte Royall*, 117 U.S. 241, 251 (1886). Exhaustion not only respects the ability of the original court to decide these issues, it also insures that if and when the issues reach this Court, it will be upon a full record and with the benefit of the lower courts' thinking on the issues. *Darr v. Burford*, 339 U.S. 200, 214–216 (1950).

The same statements about the role of the state courts can be said of tribal courts. *See* American Indian Policy Review Commission, *Final Report to Congress* at 12 (Washington: Government Printing Office 1977) ("AIPRC Final Report"). This Court has repeatedly recognized the role that tribal courts hold in our federal system and recognized their authority over both Indians and non-Indians who reside on the reservation. *Williams v. Lee*, 358 U.S. 217 (1959); *Fisher v. District Court*, 424 U.S. 382 (1976).

While one might try to argue that the writ discussed in §1303 for challenging tribal court convictions differs from the writ discussed in §2254 for challenging state court convictions, such an argument is forestalled by the language and history surrounding §1303. The text of the Indian Civil Rights Act clearly states that "***the*** privilege of ***the*** writ of habeas corpus." (emphasis added). The phrasing of this text, and the role Congress envisioned the writ to play, clearly indicate that Congress was talking about one singular writ – not two distinct writs.

Nor is it relevant that §2254 contains an explicit exhaustion requirement, while §1303 does not. The exhaustion requirement in §2254 was codified in 1944 and declares that an "application for a writ of habeas corpus on behalf of a person in custody pursuant to the judgment of a State court shall not be granted unless it appears that ... the applicant has exhausted the remedies available in the courts of the State." 28 USC §2254(b)(1)(A). The exhaustion doctrine preceded the 1944 statute by decades and, as discussed above, is a requirement developed by this Court as a means of accommodating the potentially conflicting roles of the state and federal courts. As we have previously recognized, it is clear when including the exhaustion requirement as part of §2254, Congress' intent was to codify the common law requirements developed by this Court. *Darr v. Burford*, 339 U.S. 200, 210–211 (1950). A similar exhaustion rule exists for collateral challenges to federal convictions under §2255. *Sanders v U.S.*, 373 U.S. 1 (1963).

While the existence of the writ provides a way to ensure states respect federal law and thereby to ensure the sanctity of our federal union, the operation of the writ "created an area of potential conflict between state and federal courts." *Darr v. Burford*, 339 U.S. 200, 205 (1950). One of the potential areas of conflict is the timing of federal review. Since the purpose of the writ is to protect defendants from being convicted of a crime in violation of federally guaranteed rights, the question arises as to whether the writ "imperatively require(s) the circuit court ... to wrest the petitioner from the custody of the state officers in advance of his trial in the state court." *Ex parte Royall*, 117 U.S. 241, 251 (1886). In considering this question, this Court declared:

> Nor do their circumstances, as detailed in the petitions, suggest any reason why the state court of original jurisdiction may not, without interference upon the part of the courts of the United States, pass upon the question which is raised as to the constitutionality of the statutes under which the appellant is indicted. The circuit court was not at liberty, under the circumstances disclosed, to presume that the decision of the state court would be otherwise than is required by the fundamental law of the land, or that it would disregard the settled principles of constitutional law announced by this court, upon which is clearly conferred the power to decide ultimately and finally all cases arising under the constitution and laws of the United States.

Ex parte Royall, 117 U.S. 241, 252 (1886). *See also* AIPRC Final Report at 212 ("It was not the intent of Congress when it enacted the 1968 Civil Rights Act to make Federal courts general overseers of tribal government. It is extremely important that the principle of exhaustion of tribal remedies be strictly adhered to by the Federal courts ...").

In light of these long-established principles, I see no reason why Petitioners should be excused from exhausting their tribal court remedies before seeking a writ of habeas corpus under §1303.

III.

Over the last 150 years, this Court has repeatedly held that tribal governments are "domestic dependent sovereigns," whose sovereignty was necessarily reduced upon incorporation into the United States. *Cherokee Nation v. Georgia*, 30 U.S. 1 (1831); *Worcester v. Georgia*, 31 U.S. 515 (1832). Much of the existing body of federal Indian law consists of efforts to define what it means to be a domestic dependent sovereign, that is, to determine which portions of tribal sovereignty remain and which portions have been reduced or eliminated. See *Johnson v. M'Intosh*, 21 U.S. 543 (1823); *Cherokee Nation v. Georgia*, 30 U.S. 1 (1831); *Worcester v. Georgia*, 31 U.S. 515 (1832); *Ex parte Crow Dog*, 109 U.S. 556 (1883); *U.S. v. Kagama*, 118 U.S. 375 (1886); *Lone Wolf v. Hitchock*, 187 U.S. 553 (1903); *Williams v. Lee*, 358 U.S. 217 (1959); *Fisher v. District Court*, 424 U.S. 382 (1976); *Moe v. Confederated Salish & Kootenai Tribes*, 425 U.S. 463 (1976).

The key principle that emerges from these cases is summarized by the leading treatise as follows:

> Perhaps the most basic principle of all Indian law ... is the principle that those powers which are lawfully vested in an Indian tribe are not, in general, delegated powers granted by express acts of Congress, but rather inherent powers of a limited sovereignty which has never been extinguished. Each Indian tribe begins its relationship with the Federal Government as a sovereign power, recognized as such in treaty and legislation.

Felix S. Cohen, *Handbook of Federal Indian Law* 122–123 (1941). Our cases also establish a process for answering new questions regarding the boundaries of "domestic dependent sovereign:"

> The whole course of judicial decision on the nature of tribal powers is marked by adherence to three fundamental principles: (1) An Indian tribe possesses, in the first instance, all the powers of any sovereign state. (2) Conquest renders the tribe subject to the legislative power of the United States and, in substance, terminates the external powers of sovereignty of the tribe, e.g., its power to enter into treaties with foreign nations, but does not by itself affect the internal sovereignty of the tribe, i.e., its powers of local self-government. (3) These powers are subject to qualification by treaties and by express legislation of Congress, but, save as thus expressly qualified, full powers of internal sovereignty are vested in the Indian tribes and in their duly constituted organs of government.

Felix S. Cohen, *Handbook of Federal Indian Law* 122–123 (1941). This breaks down into the following steps: (1) Is the power in question one that a sovereign would possess; (2) Is this power one of external sovereignty or internal self-government; (3) Did the tribe cede the power in a treaty; and (4) Has Congress expressly eliminated the power? Each of these questions will be explored in turn.

A. Is the Power in Question One that a Sovereign Would Possess?

The ability of a government to prosecute and punish those who violate its laws is a fundamental aspect of sovereignty. In the words of the Ninth Circuit, "Surely the power to preserve order on the reservation when necessary by punishing those who violate tribal law, is a sine qua non of the sovereignty that the Suquamish originally possessed." *Oliphant v. Schlie*, 544 F.2d 1007, 1009 (1976); *see also* AIPRC Final Report at 99 ("Sovereignty means the authority to govern, to exercise those powers necessary to maintain an orderly society. The powers of the sovereign government are familiar: the power to enact laws; the power to establish court systems; the power to require people to abide by established laws …").

The ability, indeed the obligation, of the sovereign to prosecute crimes is a distinguishing feature of criminal law. In the words of one treatise, "This is the foundation of the criminal law. Where an act has a tendency to injure the public, it is the duty of the state, as the representative of the public, to take such steps as may be necessary to prevent it." Clark & Mikell, *Handbook of Criminal Law* 4 (West 1915). As another leading treatise states, "With crimes, the state itself brings criminal proceedings to protect the public interest …." LaFave & Scott, *Handbook on Criminal Law* 11 (1972). This is why criminal cases are brought by the sovereign and are styled "People v. Defendant" or "The Government v. Defendant." There can thus be no question that prosecuting crimes is a fundamental aspect of sovereignty.

B. *Is this Power One of External Sovereignty or Internal Self-Government?*

External sovereignty, when juxtaposed with internal self-government, has been used to refer to powers such as negotiating treaties with foreign governments or enacting immigration laws. Internal self-government has been used to refer to the power of a sovereign to regulate matters internal to its territory, such as criminal laws, family relations, and education policy. Just as the states surrendered their external sovereignty when they become part of the federal union, so too were tribal governments divested of their external sovereignty. *Cherokee Nation v. Georgia*, 30 U.S. 1 (1831).

The majority misconstrues our precedent on this issue, resulting in it ignoring critical cases and arrogating to itself a power that properly rests in the executive and legislative branches of our federal government. The majority begins this process by quoting out of context language from the lower court's opinion:

> "It must always be remembered that the various Indian tribes were once independent and sovereign nations …." *McClanahan v. Arizona State Tax Comm.*, 411 U.S. 164, 172 (1973), who, though conquered and dependent, retain those powers of autonomous states that are neither inconsistent with their status nor expressly terminated by Congress.

Oliphant v. Schlie, 544 F.2d at 1009. The majority seizes on the phrase "inconsistent with their status" and uses it to embark on an exploration of what it thinks is "implied" or "understood" about whether the ability to criminally prosecute non-Indians is inconsistent with the tribe's status as a domestic dependent sovereign. This approach is not consistent with precedent, nor is it even consistent with the approach used by the court of appeals, despite the fact it purports to borrow from and follow the court of appeals.

Our precedent makes clear that the question of whether a certain power is "inconsistent" with the tribes' status is synonymous with the question "is this power one of external sovereignty"? Powers that are classified as being ones of "external" sovereignty (as opposed to powers of internal self-government) are powers that are "inconsistent with the tribe's status." *Cherokee Nation v. Georgia*, 30 U.S. 1 (1831); *Worcester v. Georgia*, 31 U.S. 515 (1832). A closer look at the Ninth Circuit's opinion reveals that the lower court understood this and structured its approach is accordingly.

As the court of appeals correctly stated, "The proper approach to the question of tribal criminal jurisdiction is to ask 'first, what the original sovereign powers of the tribes were, and, then, how far and in what respects these powers have been limited.'" 544 F.2d at 1009 (quoting *Powers of Indian Tribes*, 55 I.D. 14, 57 (1934)). After concluding that tribal governments originally possessed this power, and that the power was one of internal self-government, the court of appeals then "turn[ed] to the relevant treaties and Congressional acts to see whether any has withdrawn from Suquamish the power to punish Oliphant for a violation of the tribal law and order code." 544 F.2d at 1010. Finding no such cession in a treaty and no Congressional act extinguishing the power, the court of appeals considered "whether the exercise of criminal jurisdiction by the Suquamish in cases such as this one would interfere with or frustrate the policies of the United States." 544 F.2d at 1012.

This last question was not an independent inquiry into whether tribes retain the power to criminally prosecute non-Indians, but rather an examination of whether such a power would conflict with existing provisions of federal law. 544 F.2d at 1012–1013. This is the same inquiry we conduct in questions of federal preemption. See *Sperry v. Florida*, 373 U.S. 379 (1963); *San Diego Unions v. Garmon*, 359 U.S. 236 (1959). Because tribal governments are also subject to federal law, and because this inquiry is not in conflict with our prior cases, it is acceptable to include this question as part of the inquiry into whether tribes retain the power to criminally prosecute non-Indians for crimes committed on the tribe's reservation.

Unlike the court of appeals' approach, however, the majority, in its journey to determine whether tribes possess the ability to criminally prosecute non-Indians, sets off not only for the wrong destination, it takes several wrong turns during its exploration, resulting in its analysis getting lost on a confusing path unguided by precedent. In finding a "shared understanding" that tribes lack criminal jurisdiction over non-Indians to be "implicit" in federal law, the majority approaches criminal jurisdiction as a power that rests on the identity of the offender as being Indian or non-Indian. This approach not only contradicts the conventional understandings of criminal law discussed above, it also contravenes a well-established line of precedent reaching back to our earliest Indian law decisions. That precedent declares that a tribal government is a sovereign government, albeit a domestic dependent sovereign rather than an independent country, and that consequently, a tribal government's authority extends throughout the boundaries of its territory. *Cherokee Nation v. Georgia*, 30 U.S. 1 (1831); *Worcester v. Georgia*, 31 U.S. 515 (1832). We have recognized this power as extending to all persons on the reservation, regardless of whether they are Indian or non-Indian. *See Moe v. Confederated Salish & Kootenai Tribes*, 425 U.S. 463 (1976); *Williams v. Lee*, 358 U.S. 217 (1959); *Worcester v. Georgia*, 31 U.S. 515 (1832). *See also, United States v. Mazurie*, 419 U.S. 544, 557 (1975) ("Cases such as *Worcester* ... and *Kagama* ... establish the proposition that Indian tribes within 'Indian country' are a good deal more than 'private, voluntary organizations ...'").

Furthermore, this Court has consistently held that the status of being "Indian" is a political, not a racial status. *U.S. v. Antelope*, 430 U.S. 641 (1977); *U.S. v Mazurie*, 419 U.S. 544 (1975); *Morton v. Mancari*, 417 U.S. 535 (1974). It follows, then, that the political entity to which an Indian belongs is a government. As discussed above, this Court has consistently recognized that tribal governments possess sovereignty to the extent it has not been ceded in a treaty or extinguished by Congress. A fundamental aspect of sovereignty is the ability to keep the peace, protect its citizens, and punish those who violate the law.

In support of their arguments, both Petitioners and the majority point to the demographics of the Port Madison Reservation to support the conclusion that the Suquamish tribal government lacks authority to prosecute non-Indians. Neither petitioners nor the majority point to any treaty, statute, court decision, or other law demonstrating the relevance of these demographics. We have never held that a government's power diminishes based on the percentage of land owned by nonresidents or the percentage of immigrants who live there. Indeed, we recently rejected such an argument. *Moe v. Confederated Salish & Kootenai Tribes*, 425 U.S. 463, 476 (1976).

Contrary to the majority's analysis, our approach has always been to inquire whether the tribe operates as a government and whether that government has been recognized by the federal government. The Suquamish Tribal government has never ceased to exist. It operates pursuant to a Constitution approved by the Secretary of the Interior and has enacted a Law and Order Code. The tribe is federally recognized, meaning it possesses a government-to-government relationship with the federal government, in accordance with the current federal policy. *See* Richard Nixon, *Special Message to the Congress on Indian Affairs* (July 8, 1970). Consequently, unless ceded by the tribe or extinguished by Congress, the Suquamish Indian Tribe continues to possess its original sovereign powers to prosecute non-Indians who commit crimes on the Port Madison Reservation.

C. Did the Tribe Cede the Power in a Treaty?

The previous two subparts establish that the authority to prosecute non-Indians who commit crimes on the reservation is a sovereign power that is part of a tribe's power of internal self-government. It is thus not necessarily divested by virtue of the tribe's incorporation into the United States. According to precedent, the next step is to determine whether the Suquamish Tribe ceded this aspect of its sovereignty in a treaty. Our precedent also declares that treaties are grants of rights from tribes and anything not ceded is reserved to the tribe. *United States v. Winans*, 198 U.S. 371, 381 (1905). In interpreting the language in a treaty, precedent instructs us to read the language as it would have been understood by the Indians. *Cherokee Nation v. Georgia*, 30 U.S. 1 (1831).

The relevant treaty is the Treaty of Point Elliott, 12 Stat. 927. The only potentially relevant portion of that treaty is found in Article IX, which states, "And the said tribes agree not to shelter or conceal offenders against the laws of the United States, but to deliver them up to the authorities for trial."

That language says nothing that can reasonably be construed to cede the ability of the Suquamish Tribe to prosecute non-Indians who commit crimes within the tribe's territory. Rather, it is more of an extradition agreement, in that the tribe agrees not to "shelter" or "conceal" individuals who have violated federal law. It does not by its terms distinguish between Indian and non-Indian offenders, nor does it speak to violations of tribal law, but rather speaks only to "laws of the United States."

An examination of the history behind the treaty and the substance of the treaty negotiations confirms this interpretation. Federal negotiators presented the tribe with a template for the proposed treaty. That template included, as Article VIII, a provision addressing criminal offenses by or against non-Indians:

> The United States also to indemnify the Indians for horses stolen by the whites.
>
> Citizens of the United States may safely pass through their reserve .... *Injuries committed by whites towards them not to be revenged, but on complaint being made they shall be tried by the Laws of the United States and if convicted the offenders punished.* Injuries by Indians to whites to be in like manner prosecuted and punished according to law.
>
> Every tribe to be responsible for offenses committed by its people or by others in their lands. Chiefs in the first instance to be looked to and required to deliver up criminals at once--to be in return supported in the exercise of their lawful authority by the Government. (emphasis added).

That proposed text is nowhere to be found in the final version of the Treaty, the version ratified by Congress. Indeed, the proposed text is the only provision in the template that was *not* included in the final draft. Although the records of the negotiation contain no explicit indication of why this language was omitted, the only logical conclusion is that the tribe protested and the provision was dropped.

This conclusion is reinforced by a review of other treaties negotiated around the same time, all of which contain the same or equivalent language as was included in Article VIII of the template. The omission of such language distinguishes the Treaty of Point Elliott from these contemporaneous treaties and further points to the inevitable conclusion that the treaty was not merely silent on the issue, but that the tribe actively negotiated to retain that power. Thus, even without our canons of construction, which instruct us to interpret the terms of a treaty as the Indians would have understood them, *Worcester v. Georgia*, 31 U.S. 515, 551–557 (1832), and that treaties are grants of rights from tribes and not reservations of rights to them, *United States v. Winans*, 198 U.S. 371, 381 (1905), all evidence points toward a finding that the Suquamish Indian Tribe retained its sovereign authority to criminally prosecute non-Indians. When those canons are factored into the analysis, the inevitable conclusion is that the Tribe did not cede this authority in the Treaty of Point Elliott.

D. Has Congress Expressly Eliminated the Power?

Our previous decisions do provide that even if a tribe retains a sovereign power, Congress can eliminate that power. Since doing so would abrogate a treaty, however, Congress must clearly indicate its intent to do so. *Lone Wolf v. Hitchcock*, 187 U.S. 553, 566 (1903). Neither Petitioners nor the majority point to any statutory language which satisfies this requirement. Indeed, both Petitioners and the majority look for statutory language which would either confer this power on tribal governments or which declares that tribes retain this sovereign power. Such an approach turns our precedent on its head without explanation or justification.

The majority goes so far as to declare that "While Congress never expressly forbade Indian tribes to impose criminal penalties on non-Indians, we now make express our implicit conclusion of nearly a century ago that Congress consistently believed this to be the necessary result of its repeated legislative actions." In making this declaration, the majority arguably exceeds the powers bestowed upon this Court by the U.S. Constitution. In *Lone Wolf*, this Court declared that "the judiciary cannot question or inquire into the motives of which prompted the enactment of this legislation." *Lone Wolf v. Hitchcock*, 187 U.S. 553, 568 (1903). By looking for unwritten and "implicit" understandings, the majority comes perilously close, and likely even crosses, the boundary between the Court's duty to interpret the language of a statute and its legislative history and the legislature's duty to set federal Indian policy.

This Court has repeatedly declared that Congress, and Congress alone, possesses plenary authority over Indian affairs. AIPRC Final Report at 106–107. The current express policy of both the legislative and executive branches of the federal government is to support tribal self-determination and to work with tribes in a government-to-government relationship. Since the tribe has nowhere ceded this authority (the majority recognizes that "By themselves, these treaty provisions would probably not be sufficient to remove criminal jurisdiction over non-Indians") and Congress has nowhere extinguished it (the majority admits that "Congress never expressly forbade Indian tribes to impose criminal penalties on non-Indians"), the only possible conclusion in light of existing precedent is that the Suquamish Indian Tribe possesses the authority to prosecute non-Indians who commit crimes on its reservation. Indeed, this is the position taken by the Solicitor General in the brief he filed on behalf of the United States as amicus curiae. It is also consistent with the recent comprehensive report on the current status of federal Indian law issued by a Congressionally created commission. In its final report to Congress, the American Indian Policy Review Commission declared that

> ... present law fully and unequivocally supports the conclusion that Indian tribes initially possess all elements of internal sovereignty and that their sovereign attributes can be diminished only by Congress ... These sovereign attributes include such basic governmental powers as ... the power to regulate non-Indian individuals in Indian country. AIPRC Final Report at 102–03.

In addition to its conclusion that tribal governments possess the authority to regulate non-Indian conduct on reservations, the American Indian Policy Review Commission reiterated at numerous points throughout its report that the time was not yet ripe for Congress to enact any legislation restricting that authority, and that significantly more information was needed before Congress undertook such an endeavor, as unilateral action applicable to all tribal governments was not warranted nor was it appropriate:

> This Commission has not proposed any legislative action with regard to the jurisdiction or authority of tribal governments. We have rejected any such effort as being premature and not warranted by any factual evidence. We note that there are some 287 tribal governments within the United States (there are approximately 80,000 state, county and municipal governments) and it is not feasible to attempt to legislatively determine the precise power of each of these governments in one legislative enactment. We also reject the notion that the jurisdictional reach of Indian tribes within Indian country should be limited to their own membership alone. If such a position were adopted it could be truly said that the tribes were mere social clubs, an assembly of property owners, with no more authority than any civic association. This surely was not the result contemplated by the tribes when they entered into treaties with the United States. Nor is it a result to be desired by anyone today - Indian or non-Indian - when the consequences are analyzed. For in many of the areas of Indian country the only workable law enforcement authority present is that of the tribe.
>
> The Commission does not advocate that resolution of jurisdictional conflicts be left solely to the courts. To the contrary, we recommend the state and county governments sit down with the tribal governments and to the extent possible resolve their jurisdictional conflicts to their mutual satisfaction on the basis of mutual respect. To the extent resolution cannot be achieved, then and only then will legislative action by the Congress be appropriate .... AIPRC Final Report at 5.

In the list of its recommendations, the Commission included:

> 8. No legislative action be undertaken by Congress in relation to tribal jurisdiction over non-Indians at this time ....

29. Corrective legislation, if any is needed must be premised on the continued protection of tribal self-government. The scope of the application of the Assimilative Crimes Act must be strictly limited. It must be recognized and accepted the laws of the tribes will not always conform to the laws of States in which their reservation lies. This is the meaning of self-government …. AIPRC Final Report at 14–18.

Given the Commission's charge and the time and attention it spent studying the issues and formulating its recommendations, the fact that the majority of this Court willingly ignores long-established procedural protocols and readily sets aside the foundational Indian law principles created to guide this Court's decision-making, all in order to make the type of sweeping declarations deemed inappropriate by the Commission, is deeply troubling.

IV.

The majority's decision will inevitably lead to a dangerous and untenable situation in Indian country, as the Ninth Circuit recognized in its opinion:

This case well illustrates the need for the jurisdiction here involved … When the Suquamish Indian Tribe planned its annual Chief Seattle Days celebration, the Tribe knew that thousands of people would be congregating in a small area near the tribal traditional encampment grounds for the celebration. A request was made of the local county to provide law enforcement assistance. One deputy was available for approximately one 8-hour period during the entire weekend. The tribe also requested law enforcement assistance from the Bureau of Indian Affairs, Western Washington Agency. They were told that they would have to provide their own law enforcement out of tribal funds and with tribal personnel.

Appellant was arrested at approximately 4:30 A.M. The only law enforcement officers available to deal with the situation were tribal deputies. Without the exercise of jurisdiction by the Tribe and its courts, there could have been no law enforcement whatsoever on the Reservation during this major gathering which clearly created a potentially dangerous situation with regard to law enforcement. Public safety is an underpinning of a political entity. If tribal members cannot protect themselves from offenders, there will be powerful motivation for such tribal members to leave the Reservation, thereby counteracting the express Congressional policy of improving the quality of Reservation life. *Oliphant v. Schlie*, 544 F.2d 1007, 1013 (1976).

It is particularly important to note here that the State of Washington possesses no power to prosecute either Oliphant or Belgarde for their alleged crimes. A state possesses the power to prosecute a non-Indian who commits a crime in Indian country only if the victim of that crime is also non-Indian. *See* Robert N. Clinton, *Criminal Jurisdiction over Indian Lands: A Journey through a Jurisdictional Maze*, 18 Ariz. L. Rev. 503, 570 (1976). A State has more extensive powers only if it is the recipient of a special grant of jurisdiction. Public Law 280 grants such jurisdiction to six states (California, Minnesota, Nebraska, Oregon, Wisconsin, and Alaska), and authorizes other states to assume such jurisdiction. Public Law 83–280, 67 Stat. 588 (1953). Although the State of Washington initially opted in and chose to extend its criminal jurisdiction over the Port Madison reservation, it explicitly retroceded that jurisdiction in 1971 and that retrocession was accepted by the Secretary of the Interior in 1972.

Thus, since the state cannot criminally prosecute either Oliphant or Belgarde, the majority's finding that the tribe lacks jurisdiction results in the federal government being the only government with the authority to prosecute Petitioners for these alleged crimes. As the Ninth Circuit recognized,

> Federal law is not designed to cover the range of conduct normally regulated by local governments. Minor offenses committed by non-Indians within Indian reservations frequently go unpunished and thus unregulated. Federal prosecutors are reluctant to institute federal proceedings against non-Indians for minor offenses in courts in which the dockets are already overcrowded, where litigation will involve burdensome travel to witnesses and investigative personnel, and where the case will most probably result in a small fine or perhaps a suspended sentence. Prosecutors in counties adjoining Indian reservations are reluctant to prosecute non-Indians for minor offenses where limitations on state process within Indian country may make witnesses difficult to obtain, where the jurisdictional division between federal, state and tribal governments over the offense is not clear, and where the peace and dignity of the government affected is not his own but that of the Indian tribe.
>
> Traffic offenses, trespasses, violations of tribal hunting and fishing regulations, disorderly conduct and even petty larcenies and simple assaults committed by non-Indians go unpunished. The dignity of the tribal government suffers in the eyes of Indian and non-Indian alike, and a tendency toward lawless behavior necessarily follows.

Oliphant v. Schlie, 544 F.2d 1007, 1013–1014. As this excerpt makes abundantly clear, it is not difficult to foresee the harm that will result from the lawlessness made inevitable by the majority's decision. Indeed, this case in and of itself already illustrates that harm. Even after the federal district court denied his petition for a writ of habeas corpus, and while still on pretrial release pending his trial in tribal court, Mark Oliphant clearly felt sufficiently confident in the success of his appeal that he continued to flout the authority of the tribal government by being present for, if not an actual participant in, Belgarde's allegedly criminal conduct.

v.

The majority concludes its opinion by quoting from our decision in *Ex parte Crow Dog*, in which we rejected an attempt by the federal government to extend its criminal jurisdiction over Crow Dog, declaring that the federal government was trying to apply its law, by argument and inference only, ... over aliens and strangers; over the members of a community separated by race [and] tradition, ... from the authority and power which seeks to impose upon them the restraints of an external and unknown code ...; which judges them by a standard made by others and not for them .... It tries them not by their peers, nor by the customs of their people, nor the law of their land, but by ... a different race, according to the law of a social state of which they have an imperfect conception ...

Ex parte Crow Dog, 109 U.S. 556, 571 (1883). The majority found "particular guidance" in these considerations, finding that they "speak equally strongly against" allowing tribes to exercise criminal jurisdiction over non-Indians. The majority's assertion, like the rest of its opinion, ignores critically important context and precedent.

In *Crow Dog*, this Court was faced with the question of whether the federal government, a government of limited powers, had the authority to reach into the borders of Indian country, arguably in violation of a treaty, and exercise criminal jurisdiction over an Indian who killed another Indian in Indian country. *Ex parte Crow Dog*, 109 U.S. at 557. We found no such authority because nothing in the constitution or other federal law had given this authority to the federal government and to exercise such authority in violation of a treaty required that Congress clearly express its intent to abrogate that treaty obligation. *Ex parte Crow Dog*, 109 U.S. at 561–572. Thus, not only was federal criminal jurisdiction lacking, to allow the federal government to exercise such authority would violate the due process requirement that mandates an individual must be on notice that his conduct must conform to that government's requirements. *See Musser v. Utah*, 333 U.S. 95 (1948).

In the present case, we are confronted with the question of whether two individuals who reside on a reservation that is under the governance of Suquamish Indian Tribe can commit criminal acts against that government and not be subjected to tribal prosecution for those actions. The majority's use of the quotation from the opinion in *Ex parte Crow Dog* is akin to the defendant's arguments in *United States v. Elliott*, 266 F. Supp. 318 (S.D.N.Y. 1967). In that case, defendant argued that he could not be prosecuted under a federal statute enacted in 1917 that prohibited blowing up a bridge in another country because the federal government had not prosecuted anyone under that statute and therefore he had no notice it was still good law. The federal district court had no trouble dismissing that argument, declaring:

[T]his statute does not penalize conduct which, through a long period of nonenforcement, has acquired the status of customary usage, nor has opprobrium for the act been suddenly revived. Conspiring to destroy a bridge is not, and never has been, permitted by community mores. Defendant would have to know his act was wrong and if consummated a crime .... His surprise at finding the conspiracy an offense ... is naive in the extreme and clearly affords no defense.

Elliott, 266 F. Supp. at 326. As with the defendant in *Elliott*, there can be no doubt that Petitioners in the case at bar should have been on notice that their behavior violated tribal law and that they were subject to criminal prosecution by the tribe. Petitioner Oliphant assaulted a tribal law enforcement officer. Petitioner Belgarde led tribal law enforcement officers on a high speed chase that ended with destruction of tribal government property. I can think of no jurisdiction in this country, indeed, no jurisdiction on this planet, in which such behavior is not a criminal act. To allow these Petitioners to evade the criminal jurisdiction of the government within whose territory they reside and against which government they committed their crimes is without precedent. Indeed it is contrary to precedent, to federal Indian policy, and to common sense.

I therefore dissent.

5

Commentary on *State v. Rusk*

JOANNE SWEENY

The Maryland criminal case of *State v. Rusk* began as a rape trial in 1977 that was unremarkable except for the fact that the defendant was convicted by a jury.[1] The trial had all the hallmarks of a typical rape case: a defendant who testified that the sex was consensual (creating a "he said, she said" narrative), evidence presented that the defendant and the victim were not total strangers (they had met at a bar that night), and a recounting of how many drinks the victim (but not the defendant) had that evening. The conviction surprised the public defender and probably the prosecutor as well.[2] But it was not until the case went up on appeal that it began to carry wider political and social significance.

The issue in *State v. Rusk* was perhaps unique because it did not center on whether the victim consented; on appeal, the defendant admitted that she did not. In fact, he did not appeal his related assault conviction. The issue on appeal was whether he used force or the threat of a force. On appeal, the conviction was reversed 8–5 by an en banc panel[3] with the majority finding legally insufficient evidence "to warrant a conclusion that appellant's words or actions created in the mind of the victim a reasonable fear that if she resisted, he would have harmed her, or that faced with such resistance, he would have used force to overcome it."[4] To come to this decision, the majority downplayed the victim's statements that she was afraid, by linking that fear only to "the look in his eyes," and implied that the "light choking" the victim described "could have been a heavy caress."

The dissent criticized the majority for not only stepping into the jury's role as fact-finder, but also for conflating submission with consent and for ignoring the victim's statements that she was very much afraid that night. The dissent also criticized the state of Maryland's rape laws, which ultimately focused on the victim's

---

[1] 424 A.2d 720 (Md. 1981).
[2] JEANNIE SUK, *"The Look in His Eyes": The Story of State v. Rusk and Rape Reform*, in CRIMINAL LAW STORIES 171, 183 (Donna Coker & Robert Weisberg, eds., 2013).
[3] That the Court of Special Appeals chose to hear the case en banc was unusual in itself and showed how important the judges felt the issue was. *Id.*
[4] *Rusk v. State*, 406 A.2d 624, 628 (Md. Spec. App. 1979), *rev'd*, 424 A.2d 720 (Md. 1981).

resistance (despite resistance not being an element of the crime) instead of the acts of the attacker.[5]

Rape myths abound in *State v. Rusk*. Certainly, these myths are prevalent in the Special Court of Appeals decision (and explicitly called out in the dissent), which essentially ridiculed the victim's fear and reduced a "light choking" to a "heavy caress." The Court of Appeals of Maryland is that state's highest court; its decisions are appealable directly to the Supreme Court of the United States. But even the Maryland Court of Appeals did little to dispel these myths and failed to adequately address the shortcomings in existing rape laws.

State v. Rusk became a lightning rod for the rape law reform movement of the 1970s and 80s. The original conviction was not even reported, but, once the conviction was overturned on appeal, public opinion became sharply divided on the case,[6] particularly because of the judges' emphasis on the victim's lack of resistance to the defendant.[7]

This commentary first summarizes both the Maryland Court of Appeals and the Court of Special Appeals decisions in this case. Next, it explains the state of rape laws in Maryland and nationally in 1977 as well as the feminist critiques of those laws at that time. Using that framework, this commentary then compares the original opinion in *State v. Rusk* to the feminist judgment by Professor Michelle J. Anderson, writing as Justice Anderson.

THE ORIGINAL OPINION

The facts of the case are relatively simple:[8] The victim, known only as "Pat" throughout all the proceedings, met the defendant at a bar, and the defendant appeared to know the friend who accompanied Pat to the bar. The defendant and Pat chatted for a bit, and Pat decided to go home. Rusk asked her for a ride to his house, and she agreed. Before they left the bar, she told him that she was just giving him a ride and not to read anything into it. Once they arrived at his apartment, she left the car running while he asked her repeatedly to go up into the apartment with him. She repeatedly refused, and he eventually took the keys out of the ignition and asked her again to go with him to his apartment. At this point, Pat was frightened.

---

[5] The dissent also cited a myriad of sources that revealed the extent of the rape myths hidden in the majority opinion. *Id.* at 633 (Wilner, J., dissenting).

[6] Rusk's initial conviction was controversial even among the few people who knew about it. For example, the trial judge's clerk was so horrified at the conviction that he took it upon himself to contact a bail bondsman for Rusk. The bondsman was similarly sympathetic to Rusk and contacted a local attorney to take over Rusk's appeal. Even some of the jurors who convicted Rusk changed their minds once he was sentenced and stated that they agreed to convict only because they were hungry and being kept from lunch. Suk, *supra* note 2, at 186.

[7] *Id.* at 191–192.

[8] Of course, Rusk's version of events is different but, because she was appealing his conviction, Pat's version of the events was the only version considered by the courts.

It was one o'clock in the morning, and she was in an unfamiliar neighborhood. She agreed and went into the apartment. She waited in his bedroom, and when he emerged from the bathroom, again asked if she could go home. He said no.

He then partially undressed her and had her remove the rest of her clothes. She asked again if she could go, and he told her no. She finally asked him if he would let her go and not kill her if she let him "do what he wanted." At this point, she was crying, and he began to "lightly choke" her. She asked again if he would let her go if she let him do what he wanted. He said yes, and they had intercourse. Afterwards, Pat asked yet again if she could leave, and Rusk finally gave her her keys, and she left. She reported the assault later that night.

Rusk was convicted by a jury of second-degree rape and assault. He appealed the conviction, and the initial panel of judges ruled 2–1 to affirm the conviction. But, because the dissenting judge certified the opinion for publication, an en banc panel was convened and heard the matter.[9] The panel of thirteen judges reversed the conviction, overturning the jury verdict, in an 8–5 decision. The decision rested on the majority's finding that the victim did not resist the defendant and did not sufficiently fear the defendant to "overcome her attempt to resist or escape."[10] To minimize Pat's statements that she acted out of fear, the majority declared that Rusk's aggressive action of taking her car keys prevented her from escaping in her vehicle but not her ability to seek help on foot. Similarly, the majority appeared to agree with the defense's suggestion at oral argument that the "light choking" was actually a "heavy caress." Either way, the majority found that neither the act, nor the way Rusk looked at Pat, which she took to be threatening, was sufficient to cause her to reasonably fear for her safety.

The dissenting judge agreed with the majority's summary of existing case law but then diverged sharply in his application of that law to the facts. First, the dissent emphasized the deference given to jury verdicts and juries' unique ability to weigh the credibility of the witnesses and other evidence. The dissent then explained that, as the majority failed to acknowledge, "submission is not the equivalent of consent[,]... and ... the real test is whether the assault was committed without the consent and against the will of the prosecuting witness."[11]

The dissent then delved into existing knowledge about the crime of rape and the rape myths[12] that obscure the crime and lead to systemic underreporting and refusal to arrest, prosecute, or convict for that crime. Considering the date of the opinion – 1979 – the dissent is surprisingly knowledgeable about the true nature of sexual assault and the many obstacles victims must overcome before a criminal case will

---

[9] *Id.* at 188.
[10] *Rusk*, 406 A.2d at 626.
[11] *Id.* at 630–631 (Wilmer, J., dissenting).
[12] The dissent actually uses the word "myth," to describe the mistaken believe that police and prosecutors have that women lie about being raped. *Id.* at 635.

be brought to trial. Even at that date, the dissent shows that there was considerable data about who perpetrators were, how rarely cases were prosecuted, and how often women were disbelieved. The passion and empathy evident in the dissent likely made the case much more newsworthy and a source of fuel for feminist activists. It was this public attention that likely convinced the Maryland Court of Appeals to grant *certiorari*.

The Maryland Court of Appeals reversed the intermediate court's decision and reinstated Rusk's conviction, but they did so in a largely procedural manner by focusing on the deference that should be given to a jury verdict.[13] The Court emphasized, for instance, that the jury believed Pat's version of events, particularly the fear she felt.[14] There was also some discussion of the legal underpinnings of the case – most significantly, a repudiation of the requirement of resistance – but there was still a heavily reliance on the lone instance of physical force (the "light choking") to find that the requirements of the statute were met.

As with the Court of Special Appeals' decision, there was a vociferous dissent to the Court of Appeals decision. Most notably, the dissent focused on the victim's lack of resistance and implies she is merely a regretful, though willing, participant.[15]

The conflict between the majority and the dissent, a reversed mirror of the same conflict at the Court of Special Appeals, also echoed the social movement forces that were at work at the time of those decisions: resistance vs. force, submission vs. consent.

RAPE LAW REFORM

State v. Rusk was tried just as rape laws were being reformed across the country, and this movement resulted in the addition of rape shield laws in several states, including Maryland. But the conception of rape as needing an element of force or threat, as well as the victim's resistance to that force or threat, remained. The country had not yet fully embraced the concept of rape being about lack of consent, and, in many places, it still has not done so.

In the 1970s, feminist activists (including the National Organization for Women) and "law-and-order" groups joined forces to pressure legislators to change their rape laws, and they were largely successful.[16] These reform efforts fell into five major categories: "the redefinition of the offense," "the repeal of the spousal exception," "the protection of the victim at trial," "changes in the penalty structure," and "changes in the statutory age."[17]

---

[13] *State v. Rusk*, 424 A.2d 720, 728 (Md. 1981).
[14] *Id.*
[15] *Id.* at 733 (Cole, J., dissenting).
[16] Leigh Bienen, *Rape III – National Developments in Rape Reform Legislation*, 6 WOMEN'S RTS. L. REP. 170, 171 (1980).
[17] *Id.*

As part of the first category, reformers sought to expand the definition of rape to include acts beyond penile–vaginal intercourse, as well as create gradations of rape for different kinds of acts. The Maryland rape law at play in *Rusk* is an example of such reforms. Rusk was convicted of second-degree rape, which has the following elements: "(1) ... vaginal intercourse with another person, (2) by force or threat of force, (3) against the will, and (4) without the consent of the other person."[18] In contrast, first-degree rape largely tracked the common law definition and required the use of a weapon, serious bodily harm to the victim or another, or the threat of imminent harm to the victim or someone known to the victim.[19] The 1976 law also introduced a rape shield law, which was evident in *Rusk*.[20]

Yet, despite these reforms, rape remained (and remains) an extremely underreported crime and a crime that is rife with victim-blaming or disbelief that a crime has actually occurred. A major point of contention during the reform movement of the 1970s was the role of consent vs. resistance. Maryland's reformed rape law contained a requirement of force or threat, which was considered to be progress because it focused on the actions of the perpetrator instead of the resistance of the victim.[21] However, "force" is often confused with the element of consent, as shown in the Special Court of Appeals majority decision in *Rusk*. As the dissent in *Rusk* noted, they are not the same.

Even with an adequate distinction between consent and force, however, consent can be misconstrued to mean lack of resistance so that, without proof that the victim "screamed, fought back, attempted to flee, or demonstrated by her overt behavior that she did not consent,"[22] consent could be inferred. The majority opinion in *Rusk* eliminated this requirement of physical resistance only where the victim's fear was "reasonably grounded," leaving it to the trier of fact to make the determination of where "persuasion ends and force begins."[23] Ultimately, if *Rusk* is seen as a turning point in rape jurisprudence – and it certainly was at the time – it still could have been so much more. Enter Justice Anderson's opinion.

THE FEMINIST JUDGMENT

The first part of Justice Anderson's decision reads as a straightforward analysis of a violent crime. The facts are recited, largely in line with what the original judgment described. In Part V, however, the feminist nature of the opinion truly

---

[18] *Rusk*, 406 A.2d, at 629 (citing Md. Annot. Code art. 27, s 463(a)).
[19] J. William Pitcher, *Legislation: Rape and Other Sexual Offense Law Reform in Maryland – 1976–1977*, 7 Univ. Baltimore L. Rev. 151, 159 (1977).
[20] *Id.* at 156.
[21] Bienen, *supra* note 16, at 181.
[22] *Id.* at 182.
[23] *Rusk*, 424 A.2d at 727.

shines. Notably, the opinion lists every act that Rusk committed that satisfied the "force or threat of force" requirement and notes that each act is sufficient in and of itself.

The revised opinion also tells the tale as a series of intentionally escalating acts committed by Rusk. First, he asked Pat for a ride home, and then, when they arrived, he repeatedly asked Pat to come up to his room in an attempt to wear down her resistance. When she continued to say no, he got physical with Pat by taking her car keys so she could not leave. In so doing, he controlled her only reasonable means of escape from him. Any alternative would have her wandering around at one in the morning in an unfamiliar area, which would open her up to even more danger than the threatening man in her car. Things only got worse when she went into Rusk's apartment; he refused her requests to leave and held on to her car keys so that she was effectively trapped there.

As noted by Justice Anderson's opinion, Rusk then increased his physical pressure on Pat by pulling her to the bed and undressing her. She responded by crying and asking him if he would not kill her if she let him have sex with her. He replied in the affirmative and then "lightly choked" her when she cried again. She finally acquiesced.

This story emphasizes the power that Rusk had over Pat. First, he used social pressure to agree to give him a ride home, and when this kind of pressure stopped producing results, he escalated to physical pressure, culminating in a sexual assault. By telling the story this way, Justice Anderson emphasizes that Pat did not want to have sex with Rusk, and he knew that. Yet, he continued applying every form of pressure he could – first verbal, then physical, culminating in him "lightly choking" her. As Justice Anderson's opinion shows, at every juncture, Rusk intentionally used one kind of force or another to get what he wanted from the terrified woman in front of him.

As Justice Anderson explains, *Rusk* was decided after Maryland passed a rape shield law that prohibits reputation or opinion evidence "relating to a victim's reputation for chastity or abstinence."[24] However, even with such a rape shield law, the original opinion felt the need to describe every alcoholic drink Pat had that evening. Justice Anderson's opinion points out that the Court of Appeals was even more inappropriate: It introduced Pat as a 21-year-old divorcing single mother who left her child for the night to go "bar hopping," a description practically dripping with moral judgment. As for Rusk, we are told nothing of his background, save a brief statement that he and two of his male friends went to the bar to "pick up some ladies." There was certainly no mention of Rusk's prior drug paraphernalia convictions or that he had been diagnosed as having an "anti-social" personality, information that was not revealed until the sentencing hearing.[25]

[24] Md. Code Art. 27, § 461A.
[25] Suk, *supra* note 2, at 184.

And, as noted above, rape myths abound at every level of this case. In his briefs and at oral argument, Rusk painted a picture of a woman who accused him of rape because she regretted her voluntary sexual acts, a trite story that plays into deeply entrenched fears of false claims of rape. This myth – that women often lie about being raped – is a contention that has pernicious resilience despite having been repeatedly debunked by actual research.[26]

On appeal, Rusk abandoned his story that Pat was a willing participant, instead arguing that, though she did not consent, he did not "force" her. And by so doing, Rusk highlighted a second rape myth: that a "real" rapist uses physical force, usually a weapon. This myth was also prevalent in Rusk's sentencing argument that he was "not in fact a real rapist."[27]

This rape myth goes hand in hand with the myth that a woman who does not consent will physically resist her captor. Justice Anderson reminds us the law requires no such resistance to find force in any other kind of violent crime. Instead, *Hazel v. State*,[28] a case that both the Special Court of Appeals and the Court of Appeals relied on, actually added such a requirement to the statute's requirement that force must be present. This requirement inappropriately places the focus of the inquiry on the victim's acts of resistance rather than the defendant's acts of force, thereby placing an additional burden on rape victims.

However, as Justice Anderson's opinion explains, women are routinely advised to *not* fight back, despite the proven efficacy of doing so. Also, Justice Anderson's opinion points out that physical resistance is one of many natural reactions to signs of violence from another person, and it is also a predominantly male response to stress. More recent studies have shown that women are more likely to adopt other responses such as freeze or "tend and befriend."[29] It is no stretch to argue that Pat was operating under these more passive responses to stress.

Resistance is a problematic requirement for just such reasons; it compels the trier of fact to look away from what should be the only consideration: affirmative consent from both sexual partners. By looking at what the victim did to properly communicate a "no," rape jurisprudence falls victim to yet another rape myth: the miscommunication myth. This myth presumes that sexual assaults are simply a misunderstanding, and if a woman would simply say "no" in exactly the right way, her assailant would stop immediately.[30] Rusk's contention that he believed Pat was consenting, a contention he dropped on appeal, is emblematic of this myth.

---

[26] *See, e.g., False Reporting*, National Sexual Violence Resource Center (2012), www.nsvrc.org/sites/default/files/Publications_NSVRC_Overview_False-Reporting.pdf, at 3.

[27] Suk, *supra* note 2, at 184.

[28] 157 A.2d 922, 925 (1960).

[29] Shelley E. Taylor, et al., *Biobehavioral Responses to Stress in Females: Tend-and-Befriend, Not Fight-or-Flight*, 107 PSYCH. R. 411, 421 (2000).

[30] *See, e.g.*, KATE HARDING, ASKING FOR IT 18 (2015).

Justice Anderson's opinion neatly sidesteps this myth by returning the focus on to Rusk's increasingly aggressive acts, instead of what Pat did to communicate her lack of consent. Justice Anderson's express rejection of *Hazel*'s resistance requirement is essential to correct the unfair and often insurmountable burden the resistance requirement places on victims of sexual assault.

Hazel's requirement that the victim's fear be "reasonable" is also extremely problematic and was rightly rejected by Justice Anderson. Such a requirement again improperly places the focus on the victim and their actions during the sexual assault instead of examining the acts of the defendant. A "reasonable fear" requirement likewise places the fact-finder in what may appear to be the shoes of the victim but is instead a place of judgment of their reaction to a frightening situation where the judger has the benefit of hindsight, ample time to weigh the situation, and the removal of any active threat to themselves. In short, there is no way for a trier of fact to actually know what they would do in the victim's shoes unless they had already been in a similar situation, and perhaps not even then. Justice Anderson's opinion, with its focus on how Rusk repeatedly crossed Pat's clearly stated boundaries, therefore places the fact-finder back in its proper role.

CONCLUSION

Of all the good done by Justice Anderson's opinion, perhaps the most striking is how she describes the events of that night – and sexual assault in general – as a question of sexual autonomy and boundaries that were undoubtably crossed. It is the crossing of these boundaries, as Justice Anderson so eloquently puts it, that constitutes the necessary force for sexual assault. In her opinion, Justice Anderson gives Pat a sense of dignity that was stolen from her the night she was assaulted and repeatedly thereafter by a criminal justice system that did everything it could *to* place the blame on her shoulders.

STATE V. RUSK, 424 A.2D 720 (MD. 1981)

JUDGE MICHELLE J. ANDERSON DELIVERED THE OPINION OF THE COURT

This case raises the question of what actions on the part of a defendant are sufficient to prove force in a rape case. For a sufficiency of the evidence claim, the standard of review is "whether, after viewing the evidence in the light most favorable to the prosecution, *any* rational trier of fact could have found the essential elements of the crime beyond a reasonable doubt." *Jackson v. Virginia*, 443 U.S. 307, 319 (1979) (citation omitted). Therefore, we construe the facts of this case in the light most favorable to the trial verdict.

I.

On Sept. 21, 1977, 21-year-old Pat attended her high school reunion. Afterward, she went to a bar with a friend where she met her friend's acquaintance, 31-year-old Edward Rusk. They chatted for a bit. When Pat said she needed to head home because she had to rise early in the morning, Rusk asked, "Would you mind giving me a lift?" Pat reluctantly agreed. On the way to the car, she told Rusk, "I'm just giving a ride home, you know, as a friend, not anything to be, you know, thought of other than a ride."

When Pat and Rusk arrived outside his apartment at about 1 a.m., Pat left her car running and said, "Well, here, you know, you are home." Rusk asked Pat to come inside to his apartment repeatedly. She refused each time. Then Rusk reached over to Pat's car keys in the ignition, turned her car off, and took her keys. Pat testified:

> At that point, I was scared, because he had my car keys. I didn't know what to do. I was someplace I didn't even know where I was. It was in the city. I didn't know whether to run. I really didn't think, at that point, what to do. Now, I know that I should have blown the horn. I should have run. There were a million things I could have done. I was scared at that point, and I didn't do any of them.

What was she scared of? "Him," she testified. What was she scared that he was going to do? "Rape me, but I didn't say that. It was the way he looked at me, and said, 'Come on up, come on up;' and when he took the keys, I knew that was wrong."

Pat reluctantly followed Rusk up to his apartment. He went into the bathroom and, when he emerged, Pat testified, "I asked him if I could leave, that I wanted to go home, and I didn't want to come up. I said, 'Now, I came up. Can I go?'" But Rusk refused to allow her to leave. He turned off the lights and pulled her onto his bed, where he removed her shirt and told her to remove her pants. She complied. Pat testified:

> I was still begging him to please let, you know, let me leave. I said, "you can get a lot of other girls down there, for what you want," and he just kept saying, "no;" and then I was really scared, because I can't describe, you know, what was said. It was more the look in his eyes; and I said, at that point — I didn't know what to say; and I said, "If I do what you want, will you let me go without killing me?" Because I didn't know, at that point, what he was going to do; and I started to cry; and when I did, he put his hands on my throat, and started lightly to choke me; and I said, "If I do what you want, will you let me go?" And he said, yes, and at that time, "I proceeded to do what he wanted me to."

Pat testified that Rusk then "made me perform oral sex, and then sexual intercourse." Afterwards, Pat asked Rusk if she could leave, and he gave her the keys and allowed her to go.

Pat reported that Rusk raped her to Officer Hammett of the Baltimore City Police Department at 3:15 a.m.

A jury heard the testimony of the witnesses, saw the evidence related to the events in question, and convicted Rusk of two crimes:(1) rape in the second degree, and (2) assault. The trial judge sentenced Rusk to 10 years' imprisonment for the rape and five years for the assault, to be served concurrently.

On appeal, the assault conviction stands. Rusk only challenges the rape conviction based on the sufficiency of the evidence to prove the crime. He concedes that Pat did not consent to sex on the instance in question. He argues, however, that the state did not prove force beyond a reasonable doubt.

Sitting en banc, the Court of Special Appeals of Maryland divided sharply. Eight of thirteen judges voted to reverse Rusk's conviction and five dissented. The majority opinion in the Court of Special Appeals decided:

> In all of the victim's testimony we have been unable to see any resistance on her part to the sex acts and certainly can we see no fear as would overcome her attempt to resist or escape as required [by the cases]. Possession of the keys by the accused may have deterred her vehicular escape but hardly a departure seeking help in the rooming house or in the street. We must say that "the way he looked" fails utterly to support the fear required by [the cases].

The majority surmised that Rusk's "light choking" of Pat's neck could have simply been a "heavy caress," and concluded that it did not believe "all the facts and circumstances in the case were sufficient to cause a reasonable fear which overcame her ability to resist. In the absence of any other evidence showing force used by appellant, we find that the evidence was insufficient to convict appellant of rape."

Five judges dissented in the case with "profound conviction," noting, "Law enforcement agencies throughout the country warn women not to resist an attack haphazardly, not to antagonize a potential attacker, but to protect themselves from more serious injury." The dissent concluded, therefore, that Pat acted in a "prudent" fashion by not physically resisting Rusk, and that the issue of force was a factual question for the jury to which appellate judges should defer.

II.

At common law, rape was defined as "the carnal knowledge of a female forcibly and against her will." Nonconsent (the same thing legally as "against her will") and force were the two key elements of the crime. Proof of nonconsent and force historically focused on whether the complainant physically resisted the defendant's advances. If she resisted, she did not consent, the sex was deemed to be "against her will," and the defendant had to overcome her resistance with force. The complainant's resistance was key to both the elements of nonconsent and force.

In the United States, until change began over the last 10 years, the law across the states has generally required the complainant to physically resist the defendant's sexual advances – either with utmost resistance, earnest resistance, or reasonable resistance. Some states required no resistance in their codes, but a complainant's resistance nevertheless was central to proving nonconsent and force in practice. Over the past decade, however, many states have eliminated the formal requirement that a complainant resist her attacker, so the place of victim resistance in rape law is jurisprudentially unclear.

Maryland's definition of rape mirrors the common law. The Maryland Code (1957, 1976 Repl. vol., 1980 Cum. Supp.), Art. 27, § 463(a) (1), provides, in relevant part: "A person is guilty of rape in the second degree if the person engages in vaginal intercourse with another person: (1) By force or threat of force against the will and without the consent of the other person ...."

The Maryland statute contains no requirement of victim resistance, and no requirement of victim fear. Maryland nevertheless imposed such a requirement, not by statute but by judicial opinion. This Court described the kind of resistance required to prove force for rape in *Hazel v. State*, 221 Md. 464, 469, 157 A.2d 922, 925 (1960):

> Force is an essential element of the crime and to justify a conviction, the evidence must warrant a conclusion either that the victim resisted and her resistance was overcome by force or that she was prevented from resisting by threats to her safety. But no particular amount of force, either actual or constructive, is required to constitute rape. Necessarily that fact must depend upon the prevailing circumstances. As in this case force may exist without violence. If the acts and threats of the defendant were reasonably calculated to create in the mind of the victim having regard to the circumstances in which she was placed a real apprehension, due to fear, of imminent bodily harm, serious enough to impair or overcome her will to resist, then such acts and threats are the equivalent of force.

Hazel continued: "Since resistance is necessarily relative, the presence or absence of it must depend on the facts and circumstances in each case. But the real test, which must be recognized in all cases, is whether the assault was committed without the consent and against the will of the prosecuting witness."

III.

In this case, Pat expressed through words and actions opposition to sex repeatedly. Rusk therefore concedes, as he must, that his penetration of her was "against [her] will and without [her] consent." Rusk argues, however, that he did not employ "force or threat of force" against Pat to obtain sex, so his conviction for rape must be overturned.

It was the province of the jury as finder of fact to believe or disbelieve witnesses, to observe their demeanors, and to judge their credibility. The jury in this case heard and saw the evidence firsthand and concluded beyond a reasonable doubt that Rusk obtained sex by force. On appeal, we give great deference to the jury's conclusions.

Jackson, 443 U.S. at 319. In the following analysis, we describe the evidence and its inferences in the light most favorable to the state, assessing Rusk's actions and Pat's responses in roughly chronological order as described in Pat's testimony.

We identify six instances of Rusk's words and actions in this case that provide sufficient, independent and collective evidence for the jury to conclude beyond a reasonable doubt that Rusk obtained sex with Pat "by force or threat of force:" stealing her keys, restraining her liberty, bargaining not to kill her, strangling her, assaulting her, and penetrating her in the face of her clearly expressed nonconsent.

A. *Stealing the Victim's Keys*

Rusk's action to steal Pat's car keys was sufficient evidence for the jury to conclude beyond a reasonable doubt that Rusk obtained sex by force.

On the evening in question, when Pat indicated to Rusk at the bar that she needed to go home, Rusk asked which way she was going. Pat told Rusk the direction she was headed and he asked for a ride. At that point, Pat lacked a socially graceful way to refuse Rusk's request to drop him off at his apartment. The two of them left the bar and walked to her car.

Pat began her solo encounter with Rusk by expressing nonconsent to sex. As they walked to the car, she told Rusk that she was "just giving a ride home, you know, as a friend, not anything to be, you know, thought of other than a ride." She thereby defined a boundary: that she wanted only to be his friend that evening, not his sexual partner. Her words made plain that her willingness to give Rusk a ride home was not also an expression of willingness to engage in sex, and should not be understood by him as an entrée into an intimate encounter. In this first utterance when the parties were alone, therefore, Pat expressed clear opposition to sex with Rusk.

Once she arrived at his apartment, Pat left her keys in the ignition and kept her car running. She told Rusk, "Well, here, you know, you are home." Her statement was a polite way to say that she wanted him to get out of her car so she could call it a night. Leaving her car running indicated, again, that she did not want to visit his apartment or have sex with him. Combined with her verbal nudge to get out of the car, Pat expressed a commitment to the boundary she previously set: that she was not willing to have sex with Rusk.

Nevertheless, Rusk remained in Pat's car and repeatedly asked her to come up to his apartment. She said no each time. His repetitive questions were an attempt to wear her down – to get her to change her mind and come up to his apartment. She stuck to her boundary and again refused his entreaties for additional intimacy. At that time, Pat remained in control of her sexual autonomy.

Rusk understood the sexual boundary Pat set, but he did not wish to respect it. He understood Pat's refusal to come inside, and the concomitant fact that he was not going to be able to obtain sex from her with her consent. Since he was not going to get what he wanted without overcoming Pat's verbal resistance, he decided to wrest control of the situation. He reached over to the driver's side, turned off the ignition of Pat's car, removed her car keys from the ignition, and took them against her will.

Rusk's theft of the keys was significant to Pat. Her keys were of great importance to her freedom. Pat was in an unfamiliar part of the city and had no idea how to get out of the area and return home without her car. Without the keys to her car, she was stranded and afraid, isolated in an unknown place.

His theft of the keys was also significant to Rusk. By turning off her car and seizing them, Rusk made it clear that he was now in charge of the situation and that he was willing to ignore Pat's boundary. After she repeatedly indicated that she would not come up to his apartment, Rusk stole her keys to coerce her to do so. His acts were designed to override her expressed boundary and to obtain sex with her by doing so. Turning off Pat's car without permission and seizing her keys was designed to get Pat to do what she already stated she was not willing to do. It constituted force.

Stealing someone's car keys or blocking other means of escape is a plain method of coercion that can constitute force. When a person expresses that she does not want sex, and an actor then steals their car keys or blocks other means of escape to isolate the person and have sex with them, those actions constitute force in a rape case. When it is clear that the complainant wishes to leave and not have sex with the defendant, and the defendant blocks their means of escape to coerce them into sex, there is actual force.

B. *Restraining the Victim*

Rusk's action to restrain Pat in his apartment was sufficient evidence for the jury to conclude beyond a reasonable doubt that Rusk obtained sex by force.

Pat followed Rusk up to his apartment. Rusk knew that she did not want to be there and that the only reason she came to his apartment was because he coerced her by stealing her keys. When she arrived inside his apartment, Pat testified, "I asked him if I could leave, that I wanted to go home, and I didn't want to come up. I said, 'Now, I came up. Can I go?'" But Rusk refused her requests to exercise autonomy and leave. Pat could not get home without her keys. Rusk controlled the situation.

At that point, Rusk pulled Pat onto his bed and began to remove her clothes. When he asked her to remove her pants, she complied. Pat knew what was coming, but nonetheless pled for her freedom and tried to reason with Rusk. She testified: "I was still begging him to please let, you know, let me leave. I said, 'you can get a lot of other girls down there, for what you want,' and he just kept saying, 'no.'"

Rusk continually denied Pat the ability to leave his apartment. His actions expressed a sense of entitlement to control her. His intentional restraint held her captive in his apartment and forced her to comply. She had already made clear that she did not want to have sex with him. Restraining Pat against her will to get her to do what she already stated she was not willing to do constituted force. Restraining a person's liberty to obtain sex is legally sufficient force.

Moreover, Maryland's common law crime of false imprisonment occurs when a person (without legal authority or justification) intentionally restrains another person's ability to move freely. *Tate v. State*, 32 Md. App. 613, 615, 363 A.2d 622 (1976). Here, Rusk had no legal authority or justification to restrain Pat and his intentional restraint of her constituted false imprisonment, which met the force requirement. When it is clear that the complainant wishes to leave and not have sex with the defendant, and the defendant restrains them to coerce sex, that restraint is actual force.

C. *Bargaining Not to Kill the Victim*

Rusk's bargain not to kill Pat if she had sex with him was sufficient evidence for the jury to conclude beyond a reasonable doubt that Rusk obtained sex by force.

Once Rusk pulled Pat onto his bed and began to remove her clothes, Pat testified that she was afraid of Rusk, afraid he would rape her, and afraid he might even kill her. She became desperate, and made a last ditch effort. She testified:

> I said, at that point — I didn't know what to say; and I said, "If I do what you want, will you let me go without killing me?" Because I didn't know, at that point, what he was going to do; and I started to cry … and I said, "If I do what you want, will you let me go?" And he said, yes, and at that time, "I proceeded to do what he wanted me to."

This moment with its exchange of words is significant. Pat expressed to Rusk that she feared he would or could kill her, a remarkable and specific statement of the threat she felt Rusk posed. She was expressing her belief that her life was at stake – that she was threatened with death. The Maryland rape statute requires "force or threat of force," and the threat of being killed would be a threat of force.

But how can a victim's words and actions constitute a defendant's "force or threat of force"? It is a good question, one that suggests that the force analysis should remain on the defendant's actions. Here, however, it is not Pat's question that constitutes the threat of force. It is Rusk's response to it, given the coercive environment he had already created.

When Pat asked, "If I do what you want, will you let me go without killing me?" Rusk replied "yes." His reply did not disabuse her of the belief that she was under the threat of death. He did not deny the risk she believed he posed, correct her belief as mistaken, nor indicate that he did not intend to hurt her. If you were attempting to have consensual sex with someone and out of the blue they said, "If I do what you want, will you let me go without killing me," you would immediately stop and say, "Whoa, you've got me all wrong: There is no way I would ever hurt you," or something like that. You would try to understand whatever you did to scare them and apologize for it.

Rusk understood what Pat's question meant. She expressed that she believed he was threatening her with death, and Rusk did not disagree. Instead, he confirmed the threat he posed. Rusk had already stolen her keys and restrained her in his apartment. Rusk knew that the bargain not to kill her would mean that he got sex, and he wanted that threat to coerce her into it.

Where a victim asked an assailant, "If I do what you want, will you let me go without killing me?" and the assailant agrees to the bargain to obtain sex, the assailant is agreeing to allow the threat of death to coerce sex. A bargain to submit to sex in exchange for not being killed or physically harmed is a threat of force in a rape case.

D. *Strangling the Victim*

Rusk's action to strangle Pat was sufficient evidence for the jury to conclude beyond a reasonable doubt that Rusk obtained sex by force.

At the critical moment on his bed that evening when Pat asked Rusk not to kill her, Rusk took additional action to force Pat to comply. She testified, "I started to cry; and when I did, he put his hands on my throat, and started lightly to choke me."

Setting aside the adverb *lightly* for a moment, Rusk placed his hands on her neck and began to compress it. This kind of strangulation of the neck blocks blood vessels and can restrict the airway. It can cut off oxygen to the brain and have serious consequences, including unconsciousness and death. Because its consequences are potentially lethal, strangulation is a terrifying act of aggression. As a form of lethal force, strangulation can be a specific and deliberate mechanism to endanger life. Pat testified that the pressure Rusk applied with his hands to her throat in this instance was "light." As such, his strangulation was not likely an attempt to kill her, but simply a warning that he could.

On appeal, Rusk claims that the strangulation may have simply been a "heavy caress." There is no evidence for this claim. The record does not indicates that Pat and Rusk were engaged in mutual acts of intimacy at the moment he put his hands on her neck. Rather, the record indicates that, just before he put his hands around her throat and compressed it, Pat asked him, "If I do what you want, will you let me go without killing me?" and broke into tears. As if to underscore the threat he posed to her life, Rusk "lightly" strangled her. Immediately thereafter, Pat submitted to sex. When strangulation is used to coerce sex, it constitutes actual force in a rape case.

E. *Assaulting the Victim*

Rusk's assault of Pat, which he did not challenge on appeal, was sufficient evidence for the jury to conclude beyond a reasonable doubt that Rusk obtained sex by force. Whether the jury concluded that Rusk assaulted Pat by stealing her keys, restraining her freedom, bargaining not to kill her, strangling her neck, or some combination of thereof, the evidence that allowed the jury to conclude beyond a reasonable doubt that Rusk assaulted Pat also allowed it to conclude that Rusk obtained sex from her by force. Rusk concedes the assault conviction on appeal, which itself constitutes sufficient evidence of force for the rape conviction.

Once Pat drove Rusk to his apartment and she refused to come inside, every action Rusk took was designed to force Pat to submit to sex. From the moment he stole her keys, Rusk acted in a way that expressed the belief that he controlled what happened between them and that he was entitled to have Pat accede to his demands. Rusk engaged in an unwanted pursuit of Pat throughout the evening and then an unwanted intrusion upon her sexual autonomy.

Rusk relentlessly pressured Pat to submit, refusing her every request to leave. He was aware that his behavior was unwanted by Pat and that he was violating her stated boundary. He was aware that his behavior was perceived as bullying and life-threatening. He was aware that his actions intimidated her into sex. Rusk was willing to ignore Pat's expressed desire and violate her expressed boundary. These actions constitute force. After Rusk forced Pat into sex, she again asked him if she could leave his apartment. This time, finally, he agreed, gave her the keys, and let her go. She regained her autonomy only after she submitted to sex.

Force to obtain sex may be expressed as coercion, relentless pressure, bullying, or physical acts to corner, threaten, or harm a victim. Here, all four were present. Rusk obtained sex by stealing Pat's keys, restraining her freedom, agreeing not to kill her, and strangling her. These acts, singly and together, constitute sufficient force.

F. *Penetrating the Victim Without Consent*

Finally, Rusk's sexual penetration of Pat in violation of her clear expressions of nonconsent was also sufficient evidence for the jury to conclude beyond a reasonable doubt that Rusk used force.

Throughout the evening in question, Pat expressed through words and actions her opposition to sex. She expressed nonconsent to sex as she and Rusk walked to the car, once she arrived at his apartment to drop him off, as she left her car running, as she nudged him to leave her car, when she asked to leave his apartment, when she told him she wanted to go home, when she begged him to stop, and when she implored, "If I do what you want, will you let me go without killing me?" At each of these moments, she clearly stated she was not willing to have sex with Rusk.

In spite of Pat's clearly expressed nonconsent, Rusk penetrated her sexually. Penetrating someone in the face of a "no" or a stated sexual boundary forces the complainant to do what she does not want to do. Sexual penetration requires important physical effort intrinsic to the act itself – physical effort that is ordinarily mutual, shared, and welcome by both parties. However, when the physical effort of penetration is inflicted on an unwilling participant who has clearly expressed nonconsent to the act, it becomes force sufficient for rape.

Here, Rusk's sexual penetration of Pat in the face of her clearly expressed nonconsent allowed the jury to conclude beyond a reasonable doubt that Rusk obtained sex from her by force.

IV.

Until the second wave of feminism began to reform rape laws in this country over the last decade, the law has been biased against those who report having been sexually assaulted. It has tended to denigrate sexual autonomy in general, and women's sexual autonomy in particular. Rape cases have involved far too much suspicious scrutiny of a complainant's behavior, with the damning question of whether her behavior on the instance in question suggested that she "asked for it." Traditionally, a rape complainant was presumed to be at fault for the sex that occurred and was often the one, rather than the defendant, who was considered on trial. Police officers, prosecutors, defense attorneys, and judges have engaged in victim-blaming, frequently attributing responsibility for a sexual attack to the victim. Women have been systematically disbelieved and maligned for reporting rape. As a result, only a small percentage of rapes and attempted rapes are reported to authorities; fewer still end in convictions. F.B.I. Uniform Crime Reports (1978), p. 14.

Historically, the law insisted that the sexual proclivities of a woman who alleged that she was raped were relevant to the truth of her allegation. A chaste woman was considered more likely to have resisted a defendant's sexual advances and to have lodged a legitimate claim of rape. By contrast, an unchaste woman was considered more likely to have succumbed willingly to sexual advances and lied about it afterward. *See Humphreys v. State*, 175 A.2d 777, 780 (Md. 1961) ("[T]he general character of the victim as to chastity or lack of chastity is admissible ... in determining whether the act was committed with or without consent"). However, Maryland rejected that idea in 1976 with the passage of a rape shield law, which states: "Evidence relating to a victim's reputation for chastity or abstinence and opinion evidence relating to a victim's chastity or abstinence may not be admitted in a prosecution for" rape and other sexual offenses. Md. Code Art. 27, § 461A. So, a complainant's chastity is generally no longer considered relevant in a rape case.

The Court of Special Appeals majority opinion, however, implied that the complainant here was unchaste. Its decision began by noting:

> The prosecutrix was a twenty-one-year-old mother of a two-year old son. She was separated from her husband but not yet divorced. Leaving her son with her mother, she attended a high school reunion after which she and a female friend, Terry, went bar hopping in the Fells Point area of Baltimore.

The description of the complainant as a married woman who left her child to go "bar hopping" suggested that she may be morally suspect. It suggested that she does not care much about her child or sexual fidelity to her husband, and that she may have been open for a sexual experience on an evening in which she planned to be inebriated. The court thereby suggested that Pat was not to be trusted, probably unchaste, and possibly at fault for any subsequent sex.

The court below continued its suspicious scrutiny of Pat's behavior:

> In all of the victim's testimony we have been unable to see any resistance on her part to the sex acts and certainly can we see no fear as would overcome her attempt to resist or escape as required .... Possession of the keys by the accused may have deterred her vehicular escape but hardly a departure seeking help in the rooming house or in the street. We must say that "the way he looked" fails utterly to support the fear required ....

Here the court described Pat as not only responsible for what happened that evening because she failed to resist, but also possibly crazy for interpreting the environment Rusk placed her in as threatening. The court below concluded that Pat failed to behave correctly on the instance in question and therefore there was no rape. It dismissed as insignificant Rusk's actions of stealing her keys, restraining her in the apartment, bargaining not to kill her, strangling her neck, and assaulting her.

Bias against rape victims occurs not only when courts engage in critical scrutiny of an alleged rape victim's actions and sexual purity. Bias is also evidenced by the unique procedural requirements that rape victims must meet that victims of other crimes need not meet. The resistance requirement itself, for example, does not apply to other crimes that require force. To understand how the resistance requirement disadvantages rape victims as compared to others, one need only review an analogy to robbery.

If a man took a woman to an unfamiliar part of the city, stole her car keys, and told her that he was not going to give them back unless she came up to his apartment where he took $500 from her against her will, it would be clear that he obtained the money by force. The law does not demand that the robbery victim resist to prove force. Likewise, if a man restrained a woman in his apartment, and prohibited her from leaving unless she gave him $1000, it would be clear that he obtained the money by force, whether she physically resisted him or not. If he then demanded $1500 and she asked him, "If I do what you want, will you let me go without killing me?" and he replied, "yes," it would be clear that he obtained the money by force, whether she resisted or not. Finally, if he told her he wanted $2000, strangled her by placing his hands around her neck and applying pressure, and then took $2000 from her, it would be clear that he obtained the money by force, whether she resisted or not. The resistance requirement is not applied in other crimes requiring force.

Unique procedural requirements in rape law, such as the resistance requirement, have, in some jurisdictions, been an explicit part of a statute, and have in others been devised by courts, even where the statute is silent on the matter. In Maryland, we have an example of the latter.

Despite the fact that a requirement of victim resistance does not appear in the Maryland rape statute, more than 20 years ago, this Court in *Hazel* held that a victim's resistance is required to prove force. *Hazel v. State*, 221 Md. 464, 469, 157 A.2d 922, 925 (1960) ("the evidence must warrant a conclusion either that the victim resisted and her resistance was overcome by force or that she was prevented from resisting by threats to her safety"). Moreover, despite the fact that a victim's fear does not appear in the Maryland rape statute, *Hazel* suggested that it is also a crucial part of the force analysis. *Id.* ("If the acts and threats of the defendant were reasonably calculated to create in the mind of the victim having regard to the circumstances in which she was placed a real apprehension, due to fear, of imminent bodily harm, serious enough to impair or overcome her will to resist, then such acts and threats are the equivalent of force.").

The Maryland rape statute requires only that the defendant use "force or threat of force" to obtain sex. However, Maryland caselaw has incongruously focused on the *complainant's* behavior to prove the *defendant's* force. It has required that the victim resist and have a reasonable fear of the situation in order to prove the defendant used force to obtain sex.

As the dissent in the Court of Special Appeals pointed out, however, many authorities have discouraged victims from physically resisting sexual attack. The U.S. Department of Justice has warned, "If you are confronted by a rapist ... you should not immediately try to fight back. Chances are, your attacker has the advantage. Try to stay calm and take stock of the situation." The dissent also cited a pamphlet from a Maryland county police department, similarly warning:

> Extensive research into thousands of rape cases indicates that attempts at self defense, such as screaming, kicking, scratching and use of tear gas devices and other weapons, usually have provoked the rapist into inflicting severe bodily harm on the victim. Since it is unlikely you will be able to overcome the rapist with force, you must think about what he will do if you try and fail. Before you do anything, remember ... IF WHATEVER YOU DO DOES NOT HELP YOU, MAKE SURE THAT IT WILL NOT HARM YOU.

To require a victim to resist a sexual assailant when officials have discouraged resistance and encouraged victims to remain passive is nonsensical and unfair.

We must pause at this point to correct the misapprehension of public safety based on the latest research. We now know that physical resistance to an attempted rape actually decreases a woman's chance of being raped and does not increase her risk of serious bodily injury or death. A 1979 Department of Justice study of almost 40,000 rapes and attempted rapes in 26 American cities has determined that, of the women who physically resisted, more than 80 percent avoided being raped. Of the women who remained passive, only 33 percent avoided being raped. The study also indicated that serious injury requiring medical attention correlated positively with rape completion. We should therefore underscore that victims who fight back against their attackers decrease their chances of being raped, and decrease their risk for serious bodily injury or death. We urge police departments in Maryland and elsewhere to discourage victim passivity in response to sexual attack, and to encourage victims to fight back against sexual assailants.

Our understanding of the crime of rape has evolved over the past two decades, and the doctrine of rape law must evolve with it. Today, we join with many other jurisdictions to reject the legal requirement that a victim resist to prove that the attacker used force. Additionally, although victim resistance is not required to prove an attacker used force, a victim's verbal or physical resistance should be sufficient to show force.

It is unfair to require a victim to act in any specific way when facing a sexual attack. Like all mammals, those facing attack may act in unpredictable ways, which include freezing in fear, fighting back vigorously, crying, or becoming profoundly passive. What the victim says or does has no bearing on what the defendant says or does – the verbal and physical actions that the defendant takes – which should remain the focus of the force analysis.

Additionally, whether the victim's fear of the defendant is reasonable or not has no bearing on what the defendant says or does. Rather than examining the mind of the victim, rape law should focus on the defendant's words and actions to determine if he deployed verbal or physical coercion to force the complainant to submit to sex.

As a result, we reject the notion that a complainant has to resist in some way to prove the defendant used force. We also reject the notion that a complainant's fear of a defendant has to be reasonable to prove the defendant used force. To the extent that *Hazel* required victim resistance or a certain kind of victim fear to prove force, we overrule it.

Still, there is much in *Hazel* to laud. In it, we noted that "no particular amount of force, either actual or constructive, is required to constitute rape," and "force may exist without violence," both of which are undoubtedly true. We also said in *Hazel* that, "the real test, which must be recognized in all cases, is whether the assault was committed without the consent and against the will of the prosecuting witness." We continue to rule that the real test that must be recognized in all rape cases is whether the sex was completed without the complainant's consent. As noted, sexual penetration in the face of a "no" or a stated sexual boundary forces the complainant to do what she does not want to do. A defendant's action to disregard or override a complainant's sexual boundary constitutes force.

Ethical sexual engagement inevitably negotiates both desires and boundaries. At its best, sex includes mutual desire, although this kind of desire is not legally required. However, to protect sexual autonomy, the law does require that one respect one's partner's stated sexual boundaries. In this case, Rusk did not respect Pat's stated sexual boundary and forced sex on her.

We find that the evidence in this case was sufficient for the jury to find beyond a reasonable doubt that Rusk deployed "force or threat of force" against Pat to obtain sex. We therefore reverse the Court of Special Appeals and reinstate Rusk's conviction for second degree rape.

It is so ordered.

6

Commentary on *People v. Wu*

JOHN FELIPE ACEVEDO

Helen Wu was convicted of the second-degree murder of her seven-year-old biological son, Sidney Wu, by strangulation. Helen had been in a relationship with Gary Wu, Sidney's father, for eight years and they were married eight days before the homicide, although Helen believed that Gary only married her because he believed she had money. On the morning of the incident, she had interceded on her son's behalf after Gary struck him for refusing to leave the family's car. Once Gary left for work Sidney confided in his mother that Gary referred to her disparagingly; that the house they lived in belonged to Gary's girlfriend; and that Gary scolded and beat him. This confirmed a warning Helen had received earlier from Gary's mother that Helen should take care of Sidney because Gary would not care for him. Upon hearing this information, she began to have heart palpitations and trouble breathing and decided to kill Sidney and herself. When Gary Wu returned from work, he found both of them nonresponsive and summoned paramedics and the police who determined that Sidney was dead and that Helen had "decreased level of consciousness," and that Helen's injuries, "... were the type of wound which a layperson ... might make in a serious attempt to commit suicide."[1]

At trial the court refused to instruct the jury on the defense of unconsciousness. The defense of unconsciousness is a complete defense and requires acquittal by the jury when the defendant can show that, although they did act, they were at the time not conscious of acting.[2] However, what *Wu* is best known for, and the reason it frequently appears in criminal law casebooks, is for its discussion of the cultural defense.[3] The California Court of Appeal found error in the trial court's refusal to provide instruction on the cultural defense since there was a factual basis for the defense presented at trial.[4] *Wu* provides both a thoroughly developed factual basis

---

[1] *People v. Wu*, 235 Cal.App.3d 614 (1991).
[2] 1 Witkin, Cal. Crim. Law 4th Defenses s.36 (2022).
[3] *See, e.g.*, JOHN KAPLAN, ROBERT WEISBERG & GUYORA BINDER, CRIMINAL LAW: CASES AND MATERIALS 396 (9th ed. 2021).
[4] *People v. Wu*, 235 Cal.App.3d 614 (1991).

and a jury instruction for the cultural defense in a criminal trial. *Wu* is unique because it is the only case in which the cultural defense has been used in conjunction with the defense of automatism or unconsciousness rather than insanity (at the time the defendant acted they "lacked capacity either to appreciate the criminality of his conduct or to conform his conduct to the requirements of law"),[5] duress (the defendant was coerced to act by force or threat of force),[6] or provocation (a partial defense available in homicides when the defendant acted "under the influence of extreme mental or emotional disturbance …").[7]

This commentary proceeds as follows. First, it provides an overview of the cultural defense. Second, it turns to *Wu* and the use of the cultural defense in that case. Third, it discusses Leti Volpp's take on the case in her feminist judgment.

THE "CULTURAL DEFENSE" DEFENSE

The rise of the cultural defense is tied to a multicultural view of society that emerged in the late 1960s as part of the struggle for minority rights in many democracies following World War II and decolonization.[8] Multiculturalism asserts that minority groups "can maintain their distinctive collective identities and practices," from the dominant culture in which they are located.[9] Multiculturalism is the opposite of assimilation, in which immigrants are expected to conform to the norms of the dominant culture.[10] These definitions leave unanswered, "What is culture?" Anthropologists have asserted that culture "denotes an historically transmitted pattern of meanings embodied in symbols, a system of inherited conceptions expressed in symbolic forms by means of which men communicate, perpetuate, and develop their knowledge about and attitudes towards life."[11] Or, culture is an abstraction, a way of life, distinct from society or the "collection of individuals in a community."[12]

Therefore, the cultural defense can be understood to align with multiculturalism because it relies on the continued existence within a dominant culture of definable minority cultures and subcultures. From a defendant's perspective, "you cannot hold them to a standard of behavior without comprehending, from their perspective, what it was they were doing."[13] But, despite popular belief, there is no stand-alone

---

[5] Model Penal Code, s. 4.01 (1985).
[6] *Id.* at s. 2.09.
[7] *Id.* at s. 210.3; *see also* Alison Dundes Renteln, The Cultural Defense 24–36 (2004).
[8] Will Kymlicka, *The Rise and Fall of Multiculturalism? New Debates on Inclusion and Accommodation in Diverse Societies*, 68 Int'l Soc. Sci. J. 133, 136 (2018).
[9] Sarah Song, *Multiculturalism, Revised* in The Stanford Encyclopedia of Philosophy (Edward N. Zalta ed., 2020), https://plato.stanford.edu/entries/multiculturalism/#ClaMul.
[10] *Id.*
[11] Clifford Geertz, The Interpretation of Cultures 89 (1973).
[12] Renteln, *supra* note 7, at 10–11.
[13] Lawrence Rosen, Law as Culture: An Invitation 172–173 (2006).

cultural defense. Instead, the cultural defense is used with existing excuses or justifications to either mitigate the crime by arguing for a lesser included offense or to seek acquittal.[14]

There have been two primary critiques of the cultural defense. First, that culture is often contested even by members of the cultural group.[15] And second, that once introduced by courts there will not be a way to limit its application.[16] To deal with these concerns, some advocates of the cultural defense have proposed a *cultural defense test* to determine if culture is appropriate for inclusion: "1. Is the litigant a member of the ethnic group? 2. Does the group have such a tradition? 3. Was the litigant influenced by the tradition when he or she acted?"[17] Although this test may help to limit when a cultural defense should be allowed to go to the jury in some cases,[18] it also runs the risk of turning cultures into caricatures of themselves. To limit stereotyping, it has been suggested that cultural factors be limited to explaining the defendant's state of mind rather than group behavior or beliefs.[19] This raises a third concern, the ability to link the defendant's mental state with their cultural identity. To address this concern, it has been proposed that the cultural defense not be allowed when the defendant was aware or reasonably should have been aware of the standards of the dominant society.[20] Despite the theoretical controversy about the limits of the cultural defense in practice it is infrequently invoked and rarely successful.

PEOPLE V. WU

At trial the judge allowed testimony by psychiatrists that the defendant was acting in a fugue state, or in a manner in which they are automatically acting without consciousness. In addition, other expert witnesses debated whether she "had the values and motives of a traditional Chinese mother," all of which was presented before the jury. However, the trial judge refused to provide an instruction to the jury on the defense of unconsciousness, or acting in a fugue state, as the defense requested. On appeal the majority's decision, written by Acting Presiding Justice Timlin, held that the failure of the trial court to provide jury instructions on the

---

[14] RENTELN, *supra* note 7, at 24–36.
[15] Id. at 206–207.
[16] *Cultural Defense in the Criminal Law,* 99 HARV. L. REV. 1293, 1308 (1986).
[17] RENTELN, *supra* note 7, at 207.
[18] One obvious concern is the test is limited to cases involving parties who belong to ethnic minorities, though there is no logical reason why the cultural defense may not be similarly appropriate for say, a religious minority. For example, in a case involving a Mormon defendant, or Orthodox defendant, there may be some circumstances where the defendant's Mormon or Orthodox upbringing may be relevant.
[19] Leti Volpp, *(Mis)identifying Culture: Asian Women and the "Cultural Defense,"* 17 HARV. WOMEN'S L. J. 57, 58 (1994).
[20] James M. Dono van, *Delimiting the Culture Defense,* 26 QUINNIPIAC L. REV. 109, 138 (2007).

defense of unconsciousness was reversable error when there was a factual basis for the defense presented at trial.[21] Although the majority could have reached its conclusion to reverse the trial court without discussing the use of cultural evidence, it chose to reach the issue because there was no existing precedent to guide trial courts in California.

The defense of unconsciousness, "applies to persons who are not conscious of acting but who perform acts while asleep or while suffering from a delirium of fever, or because of an attack of [psychomotor] epilepsy, a blow to the head ... or any similar cause."[22] The defense does not require complete incapability of movement, merely that the "subject acts without awareness."[23] The majority rejected the State's argument, "... that there was no evidence of unconsciousness 'deserving of the jury's consideration' to justify giving the instruction."[24] The State based its argument on Wu's testimony that she knew she had killed her son Sidney. Notwithstanding the State's argument, the majority found that there was sufficient evidence presented at trial that a reasonable jury could conclude that the defendant acted in an unconscious state. Indeed, Wu's testimony was that she had no memory of the act. Further, expert testimony was presented at trial that indicated Wu acted in a "fugue or dissociated state, i.e., a state in which she acted without conscious awareness during the strangulation."[25] Because there was evidence to support an unconsciousness defense, it was reversable error not to provide instruction on the defense of unconsciousness.[26]

Although a new trial was ordered based on the trial court's failure to provide jury instructions on the defense of unconsciousness, the majority also addressed the issue of cultural evidence in order to guide the lower court at retrial. However, the majority did not seek to define culture, but simply found that the cultural evidence presented at trial meant that the jury should be instructed, "that it may consider evidence of defendant's cultural background in determining the existence or nonexistence of the relevant mental states."[27] The requested instruction stated, "You have received evidence of defendant's cultural background and the relationship of her culture to her mental state. You may, but are not required to, consider that the [sic] evidence in determining the presence or absence of the essential mental states of the crimes defined in these instructions, or in determining any other issue in this case."[28] That is, the issue of culture either explained the source of preexisting stress, which led to the unconsciousness or explained why Sidney's comments to her could

---

[21] Wu, 235 Cal.App.3d, at 614.
[22] Id.
[23] Id. at 873–874.
[24] Id. at 873.
[25] Id. at 879.
[26] Id.
[27] Id. at 887.
[28] Id. at 879 (quoting jury instruction. Correction in original).

have "constituted 'sufficient provocation' to cause the defendant to kill Sidney in a 'heat of passion.'"[29]

The majority was not persuaded by the State's objection to the instruction based on the admission of contradictory evidence about the defendant's culture. Some of the experts had testified that she was acting with the "values and motives" of a traditional Chinese mother, while other experts asserted that Chinese culture did not encourage filicide. The majority noted that it is the duty of the jury to sort through conflicting evidence. In addition, the majority held that the instruction did not focus the attention of the jury on a particular witness, and that the defendant was not trying to assert that she was unaware of "the general body of laws regulating society."[30] Finally, the majority noted that existing jury instructions told the jury that "evidence of defendant's cultural background may be considered by the jury in relation to certain elements of the crime with which she was changed or lesser included offenses."[31] Culture in *Wu* was therefore not being offered as a total defense, but rather as a factor to mitigate the defendant's mental state to a lesser included offense.

FEMINIST JUDGMENT

The deployment of cultural defense has proven to be problematic for many feminists for two primary reasons. First, it often leads to a stereotyping of women's roles in society.[32] And, second, it has been used by defendants to justify their violence against women.[33] The feminist opinion of Professor Leti Volpp, concurring as Judge Volpp, addresses both of these problems while focusing its critique on the overt stereotyping that can occur in the description of cultures and especially women's roles in a culture. As with the majority's opinion, Volpp bases her decision on a close reading of the factual and expert witness testimonies. Volpp also adds to the facts by culling additional information from the record on appeal.

Volpp notes that the majority opinion flows from the presumption that it is possible to provide a singular definition of what a "traditional Chinese mother" or "traditional Chinese woman" is. The State and defense both relied on a stereotype of women's roles in Chinese culture rather than acknowledging that although culture can be a strong influence on a person's actions, it does not determine them. Culture provides the cosmology through which an individual sees the world – indeed a culture creates the very categories through which a person understands the world – but this does not justify a stereotype of a culture.[34] Volpp uses a broader understanding

---

[29] *Id.* at 884.
[30] *Id.* at 881.
[31] *Id.*
[32] Volpp, *supra* note 19, at 58–59.
[33] *See, e.g.*, Alice J. Gallin, *The Cultural Defense: Undermining the Policies Against Domestic Violence*, 35 B. C. L. Rev. 723, 273–274 (1994).
[34] Rosen, *supra* note 13, at 3–4.

of the role of culture to argue that culture can be used to determine the defendant's mental state without reference to stereotypes. In fact, Volpp calls for the cultural defense to not be used as an all or nothing defense, but rather as part of the evidence a jury hears to understand the actions of the defendant. It is on par with other background evidence juries are routinely permitted to consider.

By arguing for the admission of culture as it relates to a particular defendant, Volpp's approach presents a compromise on the admission of cultural defense into criminal law. She answers the critics who have called for the barring of cultural defenses out of fear that they will be used broadly to justify violence against women and children. Instead she offers a narrower use of the defense that focuses on the intersectionality of traits possessed by each defendant and each victim.[35] She also addresses critics who argue that the government often overreacts to the outcomes of cultural practices, especially regarding the disciplining of children, while at the same time disregarding the cultural beliefs at the root of the defendant's actions.[36] Volpp's approach would allow juries to take into account a defendant's culture without diminishing protections for women and children and more importantly without reducing the culture to a caricature. The inclusion of cultural information in criminal cases will continue to be controversial as cultures shift and "assert their right to follow their traditions."[37] But, just because it may be difficult or contested does not mean that cultural testimony should be excluded. In fact, by not including cultural testimony, the court would be cultivating disregard for the minority defendant's mental state.[38]

There is an aspect of *People v. Helen Wu* that Volpp does not address, but is worthy of discussion, especially from a feminist perspective. Although *Wu* is known for its analysis of the cultural defense, it also contained a troubling analysis of the defense of unconsciousness. The expert testimony that Wu fell into a fugue state because of "heat of passion or emotional status, under such a strong stress,"[39] fits with the stereotype of the hysterical woman suffering from neurosis because of sexual desires.[40] Although hysteria is no longer an official diagnosis, the image of women overreacting in the realm of sexuality or love is embedded in the dominant hetero-normative masculine culture and on full display in the way society discusses women, which is reflected in the portrait of Wu in the opinion.[41] In addition, the expert psychological

---

[35] See generally Gallin, *supra* note 33.
[36] RENTELN, *supra* note 7, at 55–57.
[37] *Id.* at 212.
[38] Deepa Das Acevedo, *Unbundling Freedom in the Sharing Economy*, 91 S. CAL. L. REV. 793, 797 (2018) (internal citations omitted).
[39] *Wu*, 235 Cal.App.3d, at 875.
[40] Carroll Smith-Rosenberg, *The Hysterical Woman: Sex Roles and Role Conflict in 19th Century America*, 39 SOC. RES. 652, 653 (1972).
[41] DOMINIK ZECHNER, *The Phantom Erection: Freud's Dora and Hysteria's Unreadablities*, in PERFORMING HYSTERIA: IMAGES AND IMAGINATIONS OF HYSTERIA 89 (Johanna Braun ed., 2020).

testimony in *Wu* fully displayed the continued taint of Freudian notions of women and sex.[42] It would be wise for future courts to question whether they are falling into this stereotype of the hysterical, fainting woman when they discuss issues such as female unconsciousness.

There is one final thing to note: what happened to Helen Wu. As an initial matter, it is worth mentioning the California Supreme Court declined to review the case on the merits and ordered the opinion depublished, but left in place the order for a new trial with the instructions requested by the defendant.[43] In California, a depublished opinion "must not be cited or relied on by a court or a party in any other action."[44] Wu's attorney, Gary Scherotter, believes it was the cultural aspects of the decision that led to the depublication.[45] On retrial Wu was found guilty of voluntary manslaughter, which suggests the second jury took culture into account as a mitigating factor. If the jury had relied on the defense of unconsciousness or automatism, then it would have acquitted her.[46]

PEOPLE V. WU, 235 CAL. APP. 3D 614 (CAL. CT. APP. 1991)

JUDGE LETI VOLPP, CONCURRING

Helen Wu was convicted of the second degree murder of her son. The question presented in this case is whether, in refusing to give two instructions that she requested, one related to the defense of unconsciousness, and the other related to her cultural background and its possible impact on her state of mind, the trial court committed prejudicial error. I agree with the majority's conclusion in this case that the trial court erred in failing to give both instructions. I write separately to express concerns about the majority opinion's dependence upon the characterization of Helen Wu as a "traditional Chinese woman," and to offer additional clarification to courts on the admission of cultural evidence.

I begin with a recitation of facts upon which the requested instructions were predicated, that draw upon the majority opinion and from the record on appeal. When the issue is whether it is error to give an improper instruction, on appeal "we must assume that the jury might have believed the evidence upon which the instruction favorable to the losing party was predicated, and that if the correct instruction had been given upon that subject the jury might have rendered a verdict in favor of the

---

[42] MICHAEL FOUCAULT, MADNESS AND CIVILIZATION: A HISTORY OF INSANITY IN THE AGE OF REASON 136–158 (1965) (describing the evolution of the idea of hysteria in psychology).
[43] RENTELN, *supra* note 7, at 37.
[44] 8 CA R.CT. 8.1115(a) (2017).
[45] RENTELN, *supra* note 7, 37 (citing personal communication with Gary Scherotter).
[46] *Id.* at 36–37.

losing party." (*Henderson v. Harnischfeger Corp.*, 12 Cal.3d 663, 674 (1974)). What immediately follows is the evidence which the jury might have found credible and upon which the defendant's requested instructions were predicated.

I.

Helen Wu (Helen) was born in 1943 near Shanghai, China. When she was 19 years old, she moved to Macau. She married and had a daughter in 1965. After eight years of marriage, she and her husband divorced. Helen worked at a greyhound racetrack, writing statistics for the races and for newspapers. In the mid-1970s she was engaged to a man who developed lung cancer, who then died. That man's sister, Nancy Chung (Nancy), became Helen's close friend and confidante. According to Nancy, her brother made her promise to help Helen because Helen was kind, moral and too trusting.

Helen had met Gary Wu (Gary), the son of one her friends, in 1963. In 1973 Gary moved to the United States, and married a woman named Susanna Ku (Susanna). He opened several restaurants in the Palm Springs area.

In late-1978 Helen began receiving letters from Gary, who told Helen that he was unhappy in his marriage and that Susanna was unable to have children. When Gary returned to Hong Kong in 1979, he called Helen. He said he was getting a divorce, and asked Helen to come to the U.S. and marry him. They spent one night together in Macau and a second night in Hong Kong, and talked about Helen coming to the U.S. Gary expressed the wish that Helen could have a baby with him. They opened a joint bank account into which Gary deposited $6,000; Gary subsequently sent Helen $20,000 more so she could apply for a visa to come to the United States.

In 1979, Helen came to the U.S. on a three-month visitor's visa. Gary met her at the airport, hugged and kissed her, and during the drive to Palm Springs told her that his divorce proceedings would be completed soon, and that she should trust him and that he would definitely marry her. At first Helen stayed in Yucca Valley with Gary's mother. Two months later she moved into an apartment in Palm Springs where Gary would visit her. At his request, Helen had brought $15,000 of the money he had sent her, which was deposited into a joint account in Palm Springs. In 1980 Helen became pregnant. She was in poor health during and after her pregnancy, and felt ashamed that she remained unmarried while she was pregnant. She obtained a six-month extension on her visa, but it eventually expired. Meanwhile, Gary and Susanna were divorced, but Gary did not share this with Helen.

Gary and Helen's son Sidney was born on November 14, 1980. Depressed, Helen cried all the time. She told Gary that she wanted to return to Macau, expecting that he would ask her to stay. Instead, he told her to go back and regain her health. Gary suggested that she bring Sidney with her to Macau but she refused, fearing that she and Sidney would be humiliated because she was not married and Sidney was illegitimate. Gary said that if Helen stayed in Macau that he would bring Sidney to visit her every year. He gave Helen $20,000, which she placed in their joint account in Macau and never spent; he told her he would send money every month if he was able.

When Helen returned to Macau she did not tell anyone about Sidney other than her friend Nancy. After about one year of ill health she began working. Gary called once a month to talk about Sidney and they exchanged letters. He indicated it would be easier for him to sponsor Helen for a visa after he naturalized as a U.S. citizen. Helen never asked him about his divorcing Susanna, since she assumed that once he did he would apply for her to return to the U.S. She thought it was better that Sidney was living in a family with two parents and did not try to gain custody of Sidney while she waited for Gary to get divorced.

In 1981 Helen wrote Gary and asked him to bring Sidney for a visit. When Gary said they could only come for the summer, she wrote back and said that she wanted Sidney to stay, and that if he could not stay, it would be much harder after he left, and maybe it would be better for Sidney not to come. In 1984, Gary resumed his relationship with his ex-wife, Susanna. That year he asked Helen to come visit the U.S., but she did not want to go unless she and Gary were getting married so that she and Sidney would have dignity and status. By 1986, Gary had stopped writing and sharing information about Sidney with Helen. Gary and Susanna separated again in 1986, at which point Gary told Sidney that Helen was actually his mother.

In 1987 Gary arranged to meet Helen when he was in Hong Kong and told Helen that Sidney had not wanted to come on the trip. He indicated he needed money for his business so Helen gave him $21,500 from their joint back account; they then parted ways. Gary said nothing about bringing Helen back to the U.S., which upset Helen so much she wanted to die after he left.

When she learned that Gary was planning another trip to Hong Kong, she wrote and said that if he brought Sidney she could help him with a loan. Gary called her immediately and agreed to bring Sidney on the trip. Since Helen did not have the money, she arranged to borrow it from Nancy.

In January 1988, Gary brought Sidney, who was then seven years old, to visit Helen in Hong Kong. Before meeting, Helen borrowed $100,000 from Nancy. She showed the cash to Gary as well as a receipt for a certificate of deposit of a million Hong Kong dollars which had also been loaned to Helen by Nancy. Gary smiled and hugged and kissed her. He invited Helen to stay in the hotel but she thought it was only because of the money, and refused. On this visit Sidney called Helen "Mommy."

One evening during the visit they had dinner with Nancy. Gary proposed to Helen that they get married, which Helen thought was a way for him to obtain the money she had borrowed from Nancy. She was frightened of what would happen when he realized that it was not her money. After dinner she returned to her friend Nancy's house, and tried to commit suicide by jumping out of the window, but was restrained by Nancy, Nancy's daughter and a servant.

According to Nancy, Gary on this visit suggested that if Nancy invested money in his restaurant business, he could sponsor her for U.S. citizenship. Nancy declined, saying she did not know anything about the restaurant business. Gary then said there was another way to help her become a U.S. citizen, and said he could marry her. When Nancy asked, "What about Helen?" Gary indicated that he could first marry Nancy and later marry Helen. He wrote Nancy a letter suggesting they get married, and then called to see if she had received the letter. Nancy denied she had received it, but she had in fact received and saved it, and produced it at trial. She spared Helen the knowledge that Gary had proposed to her.

During the next year Helen worked at a school and at the dog racing track. She sometimes traveled with Nancy, who would pay their expenses. Helen wanted to see Sidney but did not know if Gary was still married to Susanna and did not want to upset Sidney's life. She bought Sidney gifts, but did not send them, not wanting to disrupt his life.

In June 1989, Helen wrote Gary and said that she did not know if he regarded her as his wife; he referred to her as such when they were with Sidney and during telephone conversations. In the letter, she told Gary that she might be in the United States on a vacation trip with Nancy, and that she would decide if she could stay there after seeing Sidney. In August 1989 she called Gary from Las Vegas. Hearing that Gary's mother was terminally ill, Helen came to Palm Springs to visit. Gary's mother told Helen that when she died that Helen should take Sidney because Gary would not take good care of him. One of Gary's cousins said the same to Helen.

Toward the end of August, Gary told Helen that they were going to Las Vegas; when she said she did not want to, he said it was important as "she was the main character" because they were going to be married. They married at midnight on September 1. Gary asked Helen not to tell anyone about the marriage because he feared that Susanna would demand more money from him. On the marriage application Helen saw that Gary had been divorced in 1980. On September 5, they went to Los Angeles to consult an attorney about immigration law. Helen, following the marriage and consultation, was still of the opinion that Gary had married her because of his belief that she had a lot of money. During the drive home from Los Angeles, this belief was reinforced by Gary's comments. Helen told Gary that she wanted to stay in the U.S. because Sidney wanted her to stay. Gary said that she was listening to Sidney too much and that she needed to return to Hong Kong to retrieve more money from the bank. When Helen asked if he had married her for her money, he responded that until she produced the money, she had no right to speak. Helen asked Gary whether the marriage was not worthwhile simply for the purpose of legitimizing Sidney, and Gary replied that many people could give him children. Helen told Gary he would be sorry. She later explained that remark meant that she was thinking about killing herself.

After the trip to the lawyer, Helen asked Gary to get her a plane ticket for September 16 so that she could return to Macau. She asked him to let her have ten more days of happiness with her son and to not let Sidney know she was leaving. Gary asked if Helen was going to get the money, which made her very angry; she gave him $6,300 she had brought with her from Macau.

On September 9, the day of the incident in question, Helen and Sidney had lunch with Gary's sister, who told Helen that she should take Sidney away because Gary only cared about money and not his relatives. She warned Helen that after Gary's mother died, Sidney would be miserable and treated like trash. Later that day, Helen interceded on Sidney's behalf when Gary twice hit Sidney when Sidney would not get out of the family car.

In the evening, Helen and Sidney played and talked. Sidney told Helen that Gary said she was "psychotic" and "very troublesome." He then told Helen that the house they lived in belonged to a woman named Rosemary and that Rosemary was actually Gary's girlfriend. He also told her that Gary made him get up early so Gary could take Rosemary's daughters to school in the morning and if he did not get up, Gary would scold and beat him. He said Gary loved Rosemary more than him.

Helen thought about what she had been told by Gary's mother, sister and cousin about how Gary treated Sidney and how she needed to take care of him. She felt pain and palpitations in her heart. She told Sidney she wanted to die. He clung to her neck and cried. She then left the bedroom, and cut the cord off a window blind. She returned to the bedroom and strangled Sidney with the cord. She then wrote a note to Gary which said "now this air is vented. I can die with no regret." She then attempted to strangle herself, failed, went to the kitchen and slashed her left wrist with a knife, and then returned to the bedroom and lay down next to Sidney on the bed, having first placed a wastepaper basket under her wrist to catch the blood so that the floor would not be dirtied.

Dr. Michael Mostyn, the doctor who saw Helen when she was taken to the emergency room, testified that she had cut the veins in her wrist, but not the arteries, which are normally deeper beneath the surface than the veins, and that venous bleeding, if not irritated or prevented from clotting with the use of hot water, would stop, and that in his opinion a person who had simply slashed their veins, rather than their arteries, would not die. He also testified that this fact was not common knowledge to the "man on the street."

Dr. Saul Faerstein, a physician specializing in psychiatry, testified after reviewing pictures of the wounds on defendant's wrists, that they did not appear to have been inflicted by a "malingerer," but were the type of wound which a layperson, particularly one who was agitated, severely depressed, or confused, might make in a serious attempt to commit suicide.

Nancy testified that two days after Sidney's death, she received a telephone call from Gary, who was fishing for information about how Helen had accumulated the money he believed she possessed. Nancy evaded his questions, and then Gary told her that Helen had strangled Sidney and "committed suicide," but that Helen had been saved. While in custody awaiting trial on murder charges (Cal. Pen. Code,

§ 187), Helen was put on suicide-watch and tried to commit suicide. She later told the jury "I just want to die. I don't want to bother and trouble anyone." Following a trial by jury, Helen was convicted of second degree murder and sentenced to 15 years in prison.

II.

The defense raises two issues on appeal relating to the trial court's failure to give requested instructions, one regarding the defense theory that Helen was unconscious at the time she strangled her son, and the other regarding whether the jury could consider Helen's cultural background in assessing her mental state. As previously noted, I agree with the majority's conclusion that the trial court erred in failing to give the requested instructions. That said, I write separately to comment on the majority's reliance on possible stereotypes, and because I think additional clarification on the admission of cultural evidence is warranted.

The prosecution argued at trial that Helen killed Sidney because of vengeful anger at Gary, which theory the majority describes as a "Medea-like gesture." The reference, of course, is to Euripides' Greek tragedy *Medea*, which tells the story of a mother who ruthlessly kills her sons in order to take revenge on a husband who has betrayed her. *See* Euripides, Medea and Other Plays (Philip Vellacott trans., 1963). In contrast, the defense's theory was that Helen had intended to leave the world together with Sidney so she could take care of him in an afterlife. That the prosecution and the defense offered dueling narratives of what unfolded is not remarkable – that is the nature of our current adversarial system. What does bear noting is the majority's description of these theories. The majority describes these dueling narratives as follows: the facts presented at trial "did vary considerably as to whether defendant had 'motherly' feelings toward the victim, her son, *whether she was a 'traditional' Chinese woman*, and, based on the above-noted factors, whether the motive for his death was a desire for revenge against Sidney's father or guilt over having not taken good care of the child and fear that he would be ill-treated in the future." (emphasis added). In describing the case in this way, the majority both replicates the Manichean duality of the defense and prosecution and reifies two particular stereotypes of Asian women: the passive "lotus blossom" and the devious "dragon lady." *See* Renee Tajima, Lotus Blossoms Don't Bleed: Images of Asian Women, in Making Waves: An Anthology of Writing by and about Asian Women (1989). As archetypes, these flattened depictions do not reflect the complexity of human behavior. Logically, for example, one might simultaneously feel mixed motives: both motherly feelings and a desire for revenge. The reliance on such stereotypes is my first concern.

My second concern is to provide future guidance to trial courts as to how to handle assertions of a cultural defense. To situate my guidance, a portion of the arguments surrounding the requested instruction, the trial court's ruling, and the decision of the majority bear repeating. At trial, defense counsel requested an instruction pinpointing the defense theory of the case. Specifically, counsel requested the following instruction:

> You have received evidence of defendant's cultural background and the relationship of her culture to her mental state. You may, but are not required to, consider that the [sic] evidence in determining the presence or absence of the essential mental states of the crimes defined in these instructions, or in determining any other issue in this case.

The prosecutor objected to this instruction on the ground that it was not a pattern California Jury Instructions – Criminal (CALJIC) instruction: There is "no guidance in the appellate courts ... on the issue of cultural jury instructions or cultural defense" and "it's real touchy, in a major case, to be messing around with non-pattern jury instructions. People smarter than myself have put together all the pattern jury instructions. I think they have covered every conceivable type of crime, certainly in this case they have, and I don't think that we need to be giving the jury extra instructions."

In addition, the prosecutor expressed concern that there was no appellate law on the subject of instructions on "cultural defenses," and that "the problem, apparently, to me, is that the jury has heard evidence about that, and whether we called it cultural defense, I don't know, but they certainly have heard the word 'culture' probably a thousand times in this trial; maybe not a thousand, but hundreds."

The trial court took the matter under submission and then rejected the instruction, expressing the concern that the instruction placed the court's "stamp of approval on [the defendant's] actions in the United States, which would have been acceptable in China." Although defendant's attorney specifically pointed out that there was no evidence to support the court's idea that Helen's actions would have been acceptable in China, and that the instruction merely told the jury that it could either consider or not consider the evidence of cultural background in determining defendant's mental state at the time of the crime, the trial court refused, saying "the Court would be saying to the jury that you may disregard the other instructions I am giving you and apply a cultural defense to this and I don't think I can do that."

On appeal, the People do not contend that the instruction should not have been given because there was no established appellate law on such an instruction. Rather, the People contend that failure to give the requested instruction was not error for five reasons: (1) defendant's defense as to mental states was sufficiently covered by the other instructions given; (2) "[n]either an awareness of the obligation to act within the general body of laws regulating society nor acting despite such awareness is included within the definition of malice required for murder," citing Penal Code section 188; (3) the evidence that defendant had the values and motives of a traditional Chinese mother was contradicted by other evidence; (4) the prosecution's expert noted that nothing in Chinese culture or religion encouraged filicide; and (5) the instruction essentially directed "the jury's attention to particular testimony for its consideration in determining a reasonable doubt on a disputed factual issue."

The majority in this case dismisses all five points of the People's argument, a result with which I agree. As to point (1), the majority correctly indicates that it is error to refuse to give an instruction requested by a defendant which "directs attention to evidence from which a reasonable doubt of his guilt could be engendered." *People v. Sears*, 2 Cal.3d 180, 190, 84 Cal.Rptr. 711, 465 P.2d 847(1970). Simply pointing out that the jury may consider evidence of her cultural background in determining the presence or absence of the relevant mental states should have been given.

As to point (2), the majority surmises that the People must be attempting to argue that the instruction requested by defendant was an inaccurate statement of the law. But, as the majority notes, "we fail to see how it relates to the instruction requested by defendant. Defendant did not present evidence that she was unaware of the general body of laws regulating society, or that she had acted with or without regard to such general rules of behavior. In fact, during closing argument, her attorney specifically stated that he was asking the jury to apply only the laws of the state of California to the facts of defendant's case. But he did argue that she was, at the time of the killing, in a highly overwrought emotional state, and that her emotional state could be explained by reference to the effect of her cultural background on her perception of the circumstances leading up to and immediately preceding the strangulation." Again, we see the majority here correctly assessing that cultural background may shape an individual's perception of circumstances.

The majority dismisses the People's point (4) concerning the prosecution's expert who noted that nothing in Chinese culture or religion encouraged filicide, by pointing to the "well-accepted principle of law" that "the fact that there may be a conflict in the evidence in no way obviates the need to give an otherwise appropriate jury instruction; it is, after all, the jury's duty to sort through such conflicting evidence." I will return to the use of experts who testify about "Chinese culture or religion" later in my concurrence.

My issue is with how the majority responds to the People's point (3), which is that the jury should not be invited to consider Helen's cultural background because there was evidence contradicting that "defendant had the values and motives of a traditional Chinese mother." In answering this argument, the majority repeats the claim that a conflict in the evidence does not render a requested jury instruction inappropriate. This is correct, of course. My issue is that the majority does not question the presumption that one can identify a "traditional Chinese mother" or a "traditional Chinese woman." In fact, the majority's opinion begins with the following sentence: "A jury convicted defendant, a traditional Chinese woman, of the second degree murder of her son." This presumption also appears in the majority's response to People's point (5), stating that the instruction appropriately "directed the jury's attention to conflicting evidence related to the defendant's theory that her mental state at the time of the killing had been affected by her cultural background and to the prosecution's theory that, in fact, defendant was not a traditional Chinese woman, had not been affected by the relevant cultural influences, and had, instead, been motivated by a desire for revenge against Sidney's father rather than by a mother's love."

Yet what is a "traditional Chinese mother" or a "traditional Chinese woman"? Setting aside the possible futility of such a question – would we ever attempt to define a "traditional American mother" or a "traditional American woman?" – both parties and the majority opinion presume that a "traditional Chinese woman" will have motherly feelings, among other characteristics. The prosecution pointed to Helen's previous divorce, her careers as hotel manager and racetrack statistician, her firm disbelief in religion, her independence and mobility, and her displays of temper as evidence that Helen was not a "traditional Chinese mother" or "traditional Chinese woman." In making this argument, the prosecution equated a "traditional Chinese mother" or "traditional Chinese woman" with what the People called a "stereotypically passive and submissive Chinese woman bound by Chinese culture and religion." Put differently, because aspects of Helen's life did not fit this characterization, she could not be "a traditional Chinese mother."

But this reduces culture – or certain cultures – to stereotype. Beyond that, it raises the likelihood that an inquiry into a defendant's culture can transform instead into a box-checking test concerning the defendant's identity within her cultural group. The inquiry as to cultural evidence then becomes whether a defendant fits into a particular identity, rather than an inquiry about her behavior. If Helen could not meet the threshold test of showing that she fit into the category "traditional Chinese mother" or "traditional Chinese woman," she would not receive the benefit of the jury instruction as to cultural information that might help explain her actions. Again, this threshold test relies on a stereotype of Chinese (or Asian) women as the self-sacrificing woman and mother, the passive and submissive "lotus blossom." As the People suggest, if Helen falls out of that stereotype, any information about her cultural background is not only unpersuasive, it is irrelevant. If Helen is not a "traditional Chinese mother" or woman, according to the People, she can only be understood as a vengeful Medea, an archetype from Greek tragedy that fuses in this case with the stereotype of the deceitful Asian "dragon lady." While it may be tempting to rely upon such mental shortcuts, we must be wary of repeating this practice when it comes to determining who is, and who is not, entitled to a particular defense.

III.

The majority also held that that the jury could consider evidence of defendant's cultural background in determining the presence or absence of the "essential mental states of the crimes defined in these instructions, or in determining any other issue in this case." The essential mental states at issue here were (1) premeditation and deliberation, (2) malice aforethought, and (3) specific intent to kill. I agree with the majority that the cultural background evidence was plainly pertinent to certain mental states, which are elements of the charged offense.

First, the evidence of defendant's cultural background was clearly relevant to the issue of premeditation and deliberation: in the language of the majority, was Helen planning to take revenge upon Gary in a deliberate and premeditated "Medea-like gesture," or was this killing a result of Helen learning from Sidney what his life was actually like with his father, filtering this knowledge through her cultural background, and responding by attempting parent-child suicide? Perhaps even more obviously, the evidence of defendant's cultural background was also relevant to the issue of whether the defendant acted with malice aforethought, or instead acted in the heat of passion, which would reduce an intentional killing to voluntary manslaughter. Specifically, the series of events recounted in the Facts section above provided the opportunity for the jury to conclude that Helen, after learning of her husband's deceptions and considering what that meant for her and her son based on her cultural background, was acting in the "heat of passion" when she killed her son.

These observations are bolstered by the testimony of experts on transcultural psychology who believed that Helen's emotional state was intertwined with, and explainable by reference to, her cultural background, as the majority also concludes. Testimony was given by three experts: Ching-piao Chien, a board-certified psychiatrist with a specialty in the treatment of depressive disorders and transcultural psychiatry; Terry Sai-Wah Gock, a clinical psychologist with an expertise in suicidology; and Juris Draguns, a clinical psychologist and editor of the *Journal of Cross-Cultural Psychology*. Drs. Gock and Chien spent several hours interviewing the defendant.

Dr. Chien was asked about the significance of the "depression in [defendant's] thought processes" on her decision to strangle Sidney; he testified:

> A: It was very – in my expertise as a transcultural psychiatry, in my familiarity, with my familiarity with the Chinese culture translate and from the information interview I obtain from Helen, she thought she was doing that out from the mother's love, mother's responsibility to bring a child together with her when she realized that there was no hope for her or a way for her to survive in this country or in this earth.
>
> Q: Well, are you telling us that the death of Sidney was her act of love?
>
> A: Yes. It's a mother's altruism. This may be very difficult for the Westerner to understand because I have dealt with many other so-called children who are sent to me from the children bureau. Children can be easily taken away from the mother in our agencies' mind. Social worker, when they discovered child abuse case or whatever case, children can be easily taken away from the parents.

But in the Asian culture when the mother commits suicide and leave the children alone, usually they'll be considered to be a totally irresponsible behavior, and the mother will usually worry what would happen if she died, 'Who is going to take care of the children? Anybody [sic—nobody] can supply the real love that mother could provide,' so and so.

Dr. Terry Gock, a clinical psychologist who interviewed defendant for a total of nine and a half hours in three interview sessions testified that on the day Sidney was killed, defendant was experiencing a very high level of emotional turmoil, i.e., an emotional crisis, which he described as "when our, when our feelings are so conflicting, so confused and so, so distressful that we, that we don't perhaps know exactly how to plan a course of action, plan a solution in the most rational way." He stated that in his opinion, defendant's cultural background was very intertwined with her emotional state on the evening of the killing. Specifically, Dr. Gock testified:

> A: [It is] very difficult to divorce ourselves from our culture and act in a totally culturally different way. And so, you know, she in many ways is a product of her past experiences, including her culture. And also when she experience certain things, like some of the information that she, that she got from her son that evening, it was, it was very distressful for her. And in some sense the kind of alternatives that she, if you would perhaps, you know, it's not as rational as an alternative that the only way she saw out was perhaps—you know, maybe that's the best word is the way she saw how to get out of that situation was quite culturally determined .... And then in terms of what are some of the alternatives then for her. In—perhaps in this country, even with a traditional woman may, may see other options. But in her culture, in her own mind, there are no other options but to, for her at that time, but to kill herself and take the son along with her so that they could sort of step over to the next world where she could devote herself, all of herself to the caring of the son, caring of Sidney.
>
> Q: Was that the motive for killing him?
>
> A: Motive, if you will, yes.
>
> Q: What was her purpose?
>
> A: Her purpose is to, is that she, is, in many ways is, is a benevolent one. It's a positive one where she believed – and this, this sounds sort of implausible to some, some of us whose, who are raised in another culture. That what she believed was that she was not exactly killing but, through death, both of them would be reunited in the next world where she could provide the kind of caring that Sidney did not get in this world.

There was also testimony from Professor Juris G. Draguns, a clinical psychologist and an expert in the area of cross-cultural psychology. He discussed, among other things, a "classical sociological study of suicide" which contained information about suicide and filicide, noting that the study's author described the situation of killing oneself and one's child as follows:

She's talking then about American mothers for the most part in Chicago in the 1920's. These mothers apparently did not yet regard their infant children as separate personalities with an independent right to live but, rather, as part of themselves, sharing their troubles, and to be taken on with them into death:

Except in extreme ends to which it leads, this attitude of interpreting the interests and attitudes of another, in terms of one's own interest, is not abnormal nor even unusual. In cases in which this attitude leads to murder before a suicide, the person committing the murder does not regard himself as doing anything criminal or even wrong. He is moved by love, pity, sympathy. He is removing someone from the wicked world before the wickedness has touched him. He's doing kindness by removing the other from suffering, which he has endured and which, therefore, the other also endures or will in time encounter.

And this, I believe, very much fits the mental state in the psychological situation of Mrs. Wu at the time when she took Sidney's life and attempted to take her own.

Examining this testimony, all three psychological experts sought to convey the idea that Helen killed Sidney not in order to punish Gary, but out of her love for Sidney, her feeling of failure as a mother, and her desire to be with her son in another life. All three experts attested to the way that Helen's past experiences growing up and living in Chinese cultural communities shaped her perceptions and reactions. Professor Draguns' testimony, in providing a transhistorical and cross-cultural comparison, additionally provided insight into Helen's possible motivations without requiring she prove her identity as a "traditional Chinese woman." She could believe she was killing her child to end suffering, similar to other mothers experiencing turmoil, as described in the Chicago study.

IV.

This provides an opportunity to provide some clarification on the admission of cultural evidence. Although many refer to the term "cultural defense," there is no separate formal defense. Rather, defendants may offer evidence regarding cultural background as relevant to a traditional defense. Cultural evidence can also be offered as a mitigating factor during plea negotiations or at sentencing.

In recent years, the question whether the criminal law should recognize cultural differences has drawn increasing attention. Three cases where cultural evidence has been admitted have been highly publicized: *People v. Kimura* (No. A-091133, Santa Monica Super. Ct. Nov. 21, 1985) (unpublished decision), where a Japanese immigrant woman, learning of her husband's infidelity, attempted parent-child suicide but was rescued while her children drowned; *People v. Dong Lu Chen* (No. 87-7774, N.Y. Super. Ct. Mar. 21, 1989) (unpublished decision), where a Chinese immigrant husband bludgeoned his wife to death after she informed him she was having an affair; and the case of *People v. Moua* (Cal. Super. Ct. Feb. 17, 1985) (unpublished decision), where a Hmong immigrant man engaged in "marriage by kidnapping."

A controversy has ensued. Some argue that cultural evidence should be admitted given this country's commitment to cultural pluralism and to individualized justice. See Note, *The Cultural Defense in the Criminal Law*, 99 Harv. L. Rev. 1293 (1986). Others argue that cultural evidence is irrelevant: ignorance of the law is no excuse; whether a practice is lawful or illegal in another cultural context is immaterial; and admitting cultural evidence forestalls the necessary assimilation of immigrants. See Julia P. Sams, *The Availability of the "Cultural Defense" as an Exclude for Criminal Behavior*, 16 Ga. J. Int'l. & Comp. L.J. 335 (1986).

In considering these two points of view, it is important to understand that the admission of cultural evidence seems to arise only in cases involving immigrant defendants, particularly immigrants of color. Perhaps this is because immigrants are presumed to be motivated by cultural backgrounds while the culture of majority community members is often not visible. For example, that the heat of passion defense has traditionally excused men for killing their wives who commit adultery is viewed as independent of culture, when common sense would tell us otherwise. More recently, courts have permitted defendants who engage in anti-gay violence to claim what is called a "homosexual panic" defense, see *Developments in the Law – Sexual Orientation and the Law*, 102 Harv. L. Rev. 1519, 1542–46 (1989), which undoubtedly is cultural as well. In a sense, every defense is a cultural defense. However, in the case of a recent immigrant, it is often argued that allowing any defense that turns on cultural differences constitutes special treatment. But when a jury and a defendant are from the same community, jurors already understand the defendant's cultural background. When they are not, jurors may miss important information. If a jury is to consider the reasonableness of the beliefs and acts of a person in the defendant's situation, a defendant's cultural background is surely relevant to this inquiry and will help combat endemic racism or other stereotyping which can shape the perception of a defendant's mental state as incomprehensible.

Yet what is meant by "cultural background"? The culture of immigrant defendants is often presented as static, as is evident in this instant case whereby Helen Wu is asked to show she is a "traditional Chinese woman" or "traditional Chinese mother." By static, I mean unchanging over time. A more accurate way to consider culture is that it is dynamic, and fluid. Cultural identities undergo constant transformation. Culture is also not monolithic. Culture is experienced differently, as shaped by age, gender, class, race, sexuality, etc., and culture is also contested within communities. Again, an analogy may be useful. Is there such a thing as a "traditional American mother" or "traditional American woman"? Does this traditional American mother live in rural community, or the suburbs? Or is she a city dweller? Does she work outside the home? Is she white, or Asian, or Latina, or Black, or Native American? Is she middle class? Does she have to be? If there is a so called "traditional American mother," does the description fit the vast majority of American mothers, or just a small minority? And if the latter, is the definition even useful? I raise these rhetorical questions to caution against the use of experts who present evidence about culture writ large, such as the prosecution's expert, Dr. Eugene Hanson, who testified about a uniform and unspecified "Chinese culture" that did not encourage "filicide." More pertinent would be the testimony of experts who consider an individual defendant's particular location and how specific cultural experiences shaped that defendant's experiences, facilitated by personal interviews between the experts and the defendant, as occurred with Drs. Chien and Gock. In addition, trial courts should remember that, while culture is often stripped of politics and material concerns, a defendant's cultural background consists not only of what are depicted as insular and time-honored traditions but by factors such as a person's access to social support networks, or economic resources.

Given some of the cases that have received publicity, it should be noted that tensions have arisen between those who presume that admitting cultural evidence condones violence against women and those who think that admitting cultural evidence is necessary in fairness to defendants from minority communities. See Marianne Yen, *Refusal to Jail Immigrant Who Killed Wife Stirs Outrage*, Washington Post, April 10, 1989. Certainly the claim that admitting cultural evidence condones violence against women has little applicability to Helen Wu's case, where she was the one who resorted to violence. Beyond this, the equation of "immigrant culture" with "violence against women" assumes that immigrant culture is monolithically patriarchal and that the cultural evidence admitted for immigrant communities will inevitably hurt women. Such an assumption is apparent in the following quotation from Brooklyn District Attorney Elizabeth Holtzman, speaking about the case *People v. Dong Lu Chen*: "There may be barbaric customs in various parts of the world, but that cannot excuse criminal conduct here." *Id.* Yet the assumption that admitting cultural evidence is necessarily negative for women reflects the belief that non-U.S. culture is necessarily more sexist than the culture of U.S. law, belied by the longstanding provocation defense in cases of adultery. We should thus think of cultural evidence as not inevitably furthering sexism. Sexism is, frankly, a universal feature of all cultures, including that of U.S. law.

At the same time, we must recognize that in recent cases, such as that of *People v. Dong Lu Chen*, the cultural evidence presented by an anthropological expert relied upon stereotypes about Chinese culture condoning male violence against women, leading to a shockingly lenient sentence of probation. The recent coining of the term "intersectionality" to refer to the interplay of racism and sexism in the experiences of women of color provides us with a useful analytical tool in responding to this kind of case. See Kimberlé Crenshaw, *Demarginalizing the Intersection of Race and Sex: A Black Feminist Critique of Antidiscrimination Doctrine, Feminist Theory, and Antiracist Politics*, 1989 U. Chi. Legal F. 139. The theory of intersectionality reminds us that any invocation of "Chinese culture" in a case involving male violence against women must consider how "Chinese culture" might be experienced differently by Chinese men and Chinese women, and also advises us that claims to culture are contested.

The difficult issues raised by the admission of cultural evidence requires rejecting an all-or-nothing approach that either precludes all cultural evidence, or admits it without considering to what extent the evidence presented is made up of reductive stereotypes. Information about a defendant's culture should not be reduced to stereotypes about a community, but should address the individual's location in her community, that community's history, and how the individual's cultural location shaped her perceptions. Cultural evidence can be challenged as irrelevant if it is based on stereotypes with little basis in reality, and testimony to demonstrate how particular cultural norms are contested within communities can also be offered into evidence. Here, if the prosecution had sought to dispute the notion that there can be a "traditional Chinese woman," rather than accepted the notion and fought the inclusion of Helen Wu within that category by pointing to various examples of her agency, the prosecution's attempt to dispute the defense theory of the case might have had a more successful outcome.

7

Commentary on *Winnebago Tribe of Nebraska v. Bigfire*

ANN E. TWEEDY

Writing in 1997, US Supreme Court Justice Sandra Day O'Connor reminded us that "[t]oday, in the United States, we have three types of sovereign entities – the Federal government, the States, and the Indian tribes."[1] *Winnebago Tribe of Nebraska v. Bigfire* is the first tribal court decision in the Feminist Judgments series. Because tribal cases are rarely mentioned in criminal law textbooks, the unique intersection between tribal law and feminism has not sufficiently been explored. As of 2022, there are over 570 federally recognized Tribal Nations in the United States and it is estimated that approximately 300 have fully functioning tribal courts. Tribal Nations predate the creation of the United States by at least 20,000 years.[2] While many tribal courts have adopted Anglo-American norms and practices, most tribal codes encourage or mandate that the tribal judiciary apply tribal common law and traditional principles in their decisions. The Winnebago Tribe (located in Nebraska) reestablished a contemporary tribal court in 1986.[3]

The Supreme Court of the Winnebago Tribe issued its decision in *Winnebago Tribe of Nebraska v. Bigfire* in 1998, upholding the statutory rape convictions of two males, both of whom, although minors, were significantly older than their female victims.[4] A third case, which was very similar to the other two, was also addressed in the opinion, but this third case, *Winnebago Tribe v. L.W.*, was dismissed due to a double jeopardy bar.[5] Because the case itself is difficult to locate (published only in the Indian Law Reporter), we have included the case in full as an appendix to this chapter.

---

[1] Sandra Day O' Conner, *Lessons from the Third Sovereign: Indian Tribal Courts*, 33 TULSA L. REV. 1, 1 (1997).
[2] Matthew R. Bennet et al, *Evidence of humans in North America during the Last Glacial Maximum*, 373 SCIENCE 1528 (2021)(describing human footprints dating to about 23,000 to 21,000 years ago in New Mexico).
[3] www.winnebagotribe.com/index.php/government/tribal-court.
[4] *Winnebago Tribe v. Bigfire*, 25 Ind. L. Rep. 6229 (Winnebago S. Ct., Sept. 11, 1998).
[5] *Id.* at 6234.

THE LOWER COURT DECISIONS IN THE THREE CASES

In the lower court, the Winnebago Tribal Court, the three cases had been decided individually, with Hon. Heidi Drobnick ruling on the case against Mr. Bigfire and Hon. Barbara Kueny ruling on the other two cases, one of which was against C.L. and the other of which was against L.W.[6] While the Tribal Court decision in the *L.W.* case is not entirely clear as to what arguments were made by the defendant, the defendants in *Bigfire* and *C.L.* argued in the Tribal Court that they were denied equal protection based on sex in violation of the Winnebago Constitution because the females with whom they had had sexual relations were not charged.[7] All of the defendants raised the equal protection argument on appeal, framing it in the appellate court as a selective prosecution claim.[8]

The facts of the case against Mr. Bigfire are by far the most developed in the published opinions. At 17 and a half years of age, Mr. Bigfire was alleged to have had nonconsensual sexual relations with a female who was 12 years old. He was initially charged with first-degree sexual assault under Winnebago Criminal Code § 3-418(1)(A) and (B).[9] First-degree sexual assault is a Class I offense, and § 3-418(1)(A) and (B) apply where:

> [a]ny person ... subjects another person to sexual penetration; and
> A. Overcomes the victim by force, threat of force, express or implied, coercion, or deception; [or]
> B. Knew or should have known that the victim was mentally or physically incapable of resisting or appraising the nature of his/her conduct ....[10]

Although the Tribal Court noted that "ample evidence" in the case indicated that "force or coercion was present,"[11] the charge of first-degree sexual assault was reduced to a second degree charge under Winnebago Tribal Criminal Code § 3-419(1)(C) "in response to the female's inability to testify at trial."[12] Section 3-419(1)(C) defines second degree sexual assault as the act of "subject[ing] an unemancipated minor to sexual penetration ..."[13]

---

[6] *Winnebago Tribe v Bigfire*, 24 Ind. L. Rptr. 6232 (Winnebago Tr. Ct., June 19, 1997); *Winnebago Tribe v. Levering*, 25 Ind. L. Rptr. 6022 (Winnebago Tr. Ct., Sept. 4, 1997); *Winnebago v. Whitewater*, 25 Ind. L. Rptr. 6022 (Winnebago Tr. Ct., Sept. 4, 1997).

[7] *Bigfire*, 24 Ind. L. Rptr 6233; *Whitewater*, 25 Ind. L. Rptr. at 6022; *Levering*, 25 Ind. L. Rptr. at 6022.

[8] *Bigfire*, 25 Ind. L. Rep. at 6229.

[9] *Id.* 6233.

[10] Winnebago Tribal Criminal Code § 3-418 (2015). The legislative history notes indicate that this section was passed in 1986 and amended in 1989 and thus it would have been in its present form in 1997 when Mr. Bigfire was charged.

[11] *Bigfire*, 24 Ind. L. Rptr. at 6239.

[12] *Id.* at 6233.

[13] Winnebago Tribal Criminal Code § 3-419(C) (2015). As with § 3-418, the legislative history notes for § 3-419 indicate that the section was passed in 1986 and amended in 1989 and thus it would have been in its present form in 1997 when Mr. Bigfire was charged.

After a thorough constitutional analysis, the Tribal Court in *Bigfire* ultimately rejected the defendant's equal protection challenge under the Winnebago Constitution. The evidence as to the defendant's use of force against the victim appeared to be determinative, with the Tribal Court noting that "[t]here seems to be little to be gained and huge detriments both physiologically and in law enforcement in charging victims of violent sexual assault with criminal sanctions."[14]

In the case of *L.W.*, the 17-year-old defendant was also charged with second degree sexual assault, and the victim, who was 12 and three-quarters, was not charged.[15] The Tribal Court held a bench trial and acquitted L.W. on the grounds that, by using the terms "subject," Winnebago Tribal Criminal Code § 3-419(1)(C) requires a defendant to bring the victim under his or her "control or dominion" and that there was "no fact in evidence that suggest[ed] that the defendant exercised control, dominion, or threat thereof" over the victim.[16] The Tribe appealed but, at oral argument, "indicated a willingness to withdraw its appeal of L.W.'s acquittal to avoid subjecting the defendant to double jeopardy in violation of Article IV, Section 3(c) of the Winnebago Constitution."[17]

In the case of *C.L.*, a 15-year-old male was charged with second degree sexual assault of a 13-year-old victim, who was not charged.[18] The Tribal Court dismissed the case on equal protection grounds in response to a pretrial motion to dismiss.[19] The Tribal Court noted that it was aware of four other cases involving alleged violations of § 3-419(C) and that, in all of them, only the males were charged.[20] The Tribal Court concluded, in light of the gender neutral language of § 3-419(C), that prosecution of only males was a violation of equal protection.[21]

The Tribal Court in both *C.L.* and *Bigfire*, discussed traditional tribal approaches to sexual crimes, evidence that is analyzed prominently in Justice Deer's concurrence in part and concurrence in the judgment.[22] This evidence was discussed briefly in *C.L.*, and the Tribal Court in that case used it to support its conclusion that the prosecution of only males for sexual assault violated equal protection.[23] The *C.L.* Court noted that "[t]raditionally, a sexual encounter, whether forced or not, outside of marriage was dealt with in a severe and punishing manner" and concluded that "[t]ribal tradition imposed punishment on both genders for sexual

---

[14] *Bigfire*, 24 Ind. L. Rptr. at 6239.
[15] *Whitewater*, 25 Ind. L. Rptr. at 6022; *Bigfire*, 25 Ind. L. Rptr. at 6229.
[16] *Id.*
[17] *Bigfire*, 25 Ind. L. Rptr. at 6229.
[18] *Id*; *Levering*, 25 Ind. L. Rptr. at 6022.
[19] *Bigfire*, 25 Ind. L. Rptr. at 6229; *Levering*, 25 Ind. L. Rptr. at 6022.
[20] *Levering*, 25 Ind. L. Rptr. at 6022; *Bigfire*, 25 Ind. L. Rptr. at 6229.
[21] *Levering*, 25 Ind. L. Rptr. at 6022.
[22] *Id.*; *Bigfire*, 25 Ind. L. Rptr. at 6229; *see also* Justice Deer's concurrence in part and concurrence in the judgment at 33–39 & n. 5.
[23] *Levering*, 25 Ind. L. Rptr. at 6022.

misconduct."[24] The Tribal Court in C.L. thus relied on traditional evidence to support its conclusion that Winnebago law regarding statutory rape should be applied equally to both sexes.

Although it seems extremely likely, it is not entirely clear whether the Tribal Court in both *Bigfire* and *C.L.* was relying on exactly the same evidence as to traditional punishments for sexual crimes. Rather than the abbreviated assessment of the evidence that we see in *C.L.*, the Tribal Court in *Bigfire* reproduces in full the evidence on traditional views on rape that it solicited from Cultural Preservation Officer and Tribal Historian David Lee Smith. After analyzing the evidence and noting that both men and women were punished harshly for rape but that "[m]en were treated more harshly for the same type of crime," the Tribal Court in *Bigfire* concludes that "[t]he parties have not provided enough information at this point to make a determination whether gender distinctions are appropriate under Winnebago laws."[25] Thus, although the Tribal Court in *Bigfire* (unlike the Tribal Court in *C.L.*) seems to see the traditional evidence as potentially justifying differential treatment of the sexes in the statutory rape context, the traditional evidence does not appear to have been a basis of the Tribal Court's holding that Mr. Bigfire's equal protection rights had not been violated. Instead, the evidence as to Mr. Bigfire's use of force appears to have been determinative for the lower court.

Nonetheless, this evidence, reproduced in full in footnote 92 of Justice Deer's concurrence in part and concurrence in the judgment, is jarring and disturbing, especially given the importance of tribal custom and tradition as a tool to interpret tribal law. The evidence concerns the roles of husbands and wives, punishment for such crimes as adultery, mourning rituals, and punishments for theft, incest, and rape. Capital punishment, violent beatings, banishment, and violent disfigurement are among the traditional punishments detailed in the Moral Laws.[26]

THE WINNEBAGO SUPREME COURT DECISION

The Winnebago Supreme Court ultimately upheld the conviction of Mr. Bigfire and reversed the dismissal of C.L.'s sexual assault charge. It also determined that, because of the double jeopardy bar in the Winnebago Constitution and By-Laws, it lacked jurisdiction over the Tribe's appeal of L.W.'s acquittal and over L.W.'s cross-appeal, and, accordingly, it dismissed that case.[27] The Winnebago Supreme Court first explained that because any potential claims for violation of the equal protection guarantee of the Indian Civil Rights Act[28] had not been exhausted, C.L.'s and

---

[24] *Id.*
[25] *Bigfire*, 25 Ind. L. Rptr. at 6239.
[26] *Id.*
[27] *Id.* at 6234.
[28] 25 U.S.C. § 1302(a)(8).

Mr. Bigfire's equal protection challenges were properly understood to have been brought solely under the Winnebago Constitution.[29]

The Winnebago Supreme Court then proceeded to evaluate what approach to use to evaluate the gender discrimination claims under the Winnebago Constitution. After acknowledging that the US Supreme Court utilizes intermediate scrutiny for gender-based classifications, the Winnebago Supreme Court rejected that approach in favor of strict scrutiny because of the seriousness of gender discrimination.[30] However, it went on to note that "in determining what constitutes a compelling governmental interest, this Court must always look to the preservation of tribal culture, traditions, and sovereignty and to the promotion of the health and welfare of tribal members as the most compelling reasons for the formation and operation of tribal government."[31] Thus, it determined that "[o]nly invidious and irrational discriminations and disparities in governmental treatment unsupported by tribal law, customs, and usages [would] be struck down under the equal protection provisions of the Winnebago Constitution."[32]

The Winnebago Supreme Court then proceeded to examine whether the defendants were similarly situated to the alleged female victims whom, the defendants argued, also should have been charged.[33] Due to the age differences between the alleged victims and the defendants, the Court expressed "grave doubt[]" about whether they were similarly situated.[34] However, because the Tribe had not argued that they were not similarly situated as a result of the age differences, the Court proceeded with the equal protection analysis as though the similarly situated requirement had been met.[35] The Court then noted that the number of cases (three) was arguably too small to rule out mere coincidence and demonstrate discriminatory effect.[36] The Court further highlighted the lack of any evidence of discriminatory intent beyond the "slight inferences" that could be drawn from the Tribe's prosecution of three males, concluding that "[a[bsent such a clear showing of discriminatory effect and purpose the defendants' constitutional claims must fail."[37]

Despite its rejection of the defendants' claims of sex discrimination, the Court turned to the question of whether the Tribe had demonstrated a compelling tribal

---

[29] *Bigfire*, 25 Ind. L. Rptr. at 6230.
[30] *Id.* at 6231.
[31] *Id.* The Majority's analysis at this point in the decision appears to exemplify the hierarchical relationship between tribal sovereignty and gender that Winnebago feminist Reyna Ramirez objects to. Reyna Ramirez, *Race, Tribal Nation, and Gender: A Native Feminist Approach to Belonging*, 7 MERIDIANS 22, 23 (2007). Justice Deer, by focusing on the stringent standards for selective prosecution, exercises judicial restraint and avoids the need to make unnecessary (and potentially problematic) pronouncements on whether individual rights could ever take precedence over tribal custom and tradition.
[32] *Bigfire*, 25 Ind. L. Rptr. at 6231.
[33] *Id.*
[34] *Id.*
[35] *Id.*
[36] *Id.*
[37] *Bigfire*, 25 Ind. L. Rptr. at 6232.

interest to justify making gender-based decisions in deciding who to prosecute for statutory rape. The Tribe argued that any differential treatment was justified because "underage sexual activity has different physiological, psychological, and economic consequences for young men and women," including pregnancy.[38] The Court noted that it had to "consider those claimed [Tribal] interests in the context of tribal custom and traditions."[39]

The Winnebago Supreme Court then applauded the fact that Chief Judge Drobnick in the *Bigfire* case below had independently consulted an expert on traditional gender roles in the context of sexual misconduct.[40] It viewed the evidence of custom and tradition as demonstrating that "gender differences were commonly drawn for the punishment of sexual misconduct because of the natural biological differences ... between the sexes," and it interpreted Chief Judge Drobnick's opinion as relying on the evidence.[41] The Winnebago Supreme Court found no need to independently solicit additional expert testimony, noting that all sources seemed to agree that "Ho-Chunk[42] tradition recognizes and *respects* different roles for males and females," particularly in the context of sexual misconduct.[43] It pointed to anthropologist Paul Radin's work describing differing gender roles of men and women in marriage and additionally set out the testimony of one of the judges on the Winnebago Supreme Court, who was from a related tribe (the Ho-Chunk Nation). She explained that the differing cultural gender roles for men and women did not elicit any "feeling of inequality" for her.[44]

Based on what the court saw as a confluence of authoritative sources on Winnebago tradition, the Winnebago Supreme Court then concluded both that the strict scrutiny standard had been satisfied because the gender distinctions at issue were traditional and lacked "pejorative or discriminatory implications" and that the distinctions therefore furthered the "compelling governmental interest of preserving tribal traditions and culture."[45] The court further explained that Winnebago tradition appeared to accord males the duty of protecting females, and remarked that its decision was supported by *Michael M. for Superior Court*, a United States Supreme Court that upheld a statutory rape law that solely applied to male conduct.[46]

---

[38] Id.
[39] Id.
[40] Id.
[41] Id.
[42] Ho-Chunk is the traditional name for the Winnebago people.
[43] *Bigfire*, 25 Ind. L. Rptr. at 6232. "Ho-Chunk" is a more traditional term for the people comprising the Winnebago Tribe, and it also can be used to refer to members of the related Ho-Chunk Nation. *See, e.g.*, Renya K. Ramirez, *Henry Roe Cloud: A Granddaughter's Native Feminist Biographical Account*, 24 WICAZO SA REVIEW 77, 79 (2009).
[44] *Bigfire*, 25 Ind. L. Rptr. at 6232.
[45] Id. at 6233.
[46] Id. (citing *Michael M. v. Superior Court*, 450 U.S. 464 (1981)). *Michael M.* has been criticized by some feminists as paternalistic, *see, e.g.*, MARTHA CHAMALLAS, INTRODUCTION TO FEMINIST LEGAL

The Winnebago Supreme Court then qualified its decision in two respects. First, it noted that it was not saying that all gender discrimination would be upheld against equal protection challenges based on the tribal constitution, explaining that "invidious gender discrimination practiced by the Tribe against members of either sex that cannot be supported by tribal custom or practice or any other compelling governmental interest" would be struck down.[47] Second, it explained that the tribal ordinance at issue was gender neutral, which appeared to reflect the current policy of the Tribal Council.[48] It then proposed that a clear and unambiguous showing of selective prosecution of males only may well violate the statute, given its gender neutral character, although it concluded that that claim had not been asserted in the case at bar nor had the necessary showing been demonstrated, given the small number of prosecutions at issue in the case.[49]

The Winnebago Supreme Court's decision is somewhat paradoxical in that it adopts the strict scrutiny standard from US constitutional jurisprudence to evaluate alleged equal protection violations based on sex under the Tribe's constitution and yet it quickly determines that no violation of equal protection occurred because tribal culture and tradition support gender differentiated punishment of sex crimes.[50] The court further explains that traditional gender differentiations in tribal culture relating to sexual conduct are "without pejorative or discriminatory implications" and that they therefore "must be sustained as involving the compelling tribal governmental interest of preserving tribal traditions and culture."[51]

One scholar questioned the court's concomitant adoption of strict scrutiny and its determination that culturally rooted gender distinctions relating to sexual conduct demonstrate a compelling tribal interest, seeming to suggest that construing culturally rooted gender differences as a compelling tribal interest drains the strict scrutiny standard of its force.[52] However, this scholar's criticism, while containing some valid points, is overstated in that he did not look at the *Bigfire* opinion holistically and instead ignored parts of the court's analysis that qualified the deference to traditional gender roles.[53] Indeed, as noted above, the *Bigfire* Court suggests that it may well arrive at a different result in a situation where an alleged perpetrator

---

THEORY 81 (3rd. ed. 2013), and Justice Deer's focus on the insufficiency of evidence for a selective prosecution claim and on age differences between those charged and their female victims provides a more satisfactory analysis from a feminist standpoint.

[47] *Bigfire*, 25 Ind. L. Rptr. at 6233.
[48] *Id.* at 6232–6233.
[49] *Id.* at 6233.
[50] *Id.* at 6232–6233.
[51] *Id.* at 6233.
[52] Mark D. Rosen, *Multiple Authoritative Interpreters of Quasiconstitutional Federal Law: of Tribal Courts and the Indian Civil Rights Act*, 69 FORDHAM L. REV. 479, 542–544 (2000).
[53] *See* Ann E. Tweedy, *Sex Discrimination Under Tribal Law*, 36 WM. MITCHELL L. REV. 392, 413–415 (2010).

could show a larger number of prosecutions of only males in violation of the policy of the Tribe's gender-neutral statutory rape law.[54] It further expressed "grave doubts" about whether the defendants and victims in *Bigfire* were similarly situated (which would be required to prevail on a federal equal protection claim) because the defendants were significantly older (and thus more mature) than the victims.[55] Finally, it emphasized that the claim was brought under the tribal constitution, rather than the Indian Civil Rights Act (ICRA), which is a federal statute that requires tribes to protect individual rights like due process and equal protection.[56] The court understandably exclaimed that "[w]hat is tribally appropriate under Ho-Chunk tradition and customary law certainly was not rendered illegal and unconstitutional by the Tribe's own constitution!"[57] Thus, it is possible that future defendants who bring forth more persuasive evidence (in terms of the number of times only males were prosecuted) may sway the majority in an ICRA case, as opposed to a constitutional case (although tribal custom and tradition also play a role in ICRA analyses).[58]

While the original opinion in *Bigfire* was adequate and, as Justice Deer explains in her partial concurrence, appears to have come to the correct result, especially in light of the age gap between the victims and the defendants, there are certainly parts of the opinion that would benefit from further development, and Justice Deer's concurrence in part and concurrence in the judgment fills in those gaps and adds to the development of tribal law jurisprudence in the important area of statutory rape and sex crimes more generally.

First, Justice Deer fittingly addresses the selective prosecution question, which is the heart of defendants' claim, at the outset. Second, she provides crucial guidance on how tribal courts should apply tribal custom and tradition to the questions before them. Third, she elucidates the power dynamics at play in the case. Finally, she supplies context, missing from the majority opinion, on the ways in which sexual assault has been used as a tool of colonialism in an attempt to destroy tribal cultures.

Because, as further explained below, protecting tribal cultures is necessary to protecting the well-being of Native women and because Justice Deer's guidance on judicial use of culture and tradition helps preserve the unique cultural aspects of tribal courts, Justice Deer's opinion furthers a feminist goal. Additionally, her conception of sexual assault as a *sui generis* crime recognizes the long history of sexual crimes' being used as a tool to dominate women and their use, in the context of colonialism, as a genocidal tool.[59] Finally, especially given the significant age differences between

---

[54] *Bigfire*, 25 Ind. L. Rep. at 6231, 6233–6234. The Court noted that the basis for such a claim would be statutory, rather than constitutional. *Id.* at 6234.
[55] *Id.* at 6231.
[56] *Id.* at 6230; 25 U.S.C. § 1302.
[57] *Bigfire*, 25 Ind. L. Rep. at 6233.
[58] *See* Tweedy, *supra* note 53, at 408, 413–414.
[59] *See, e.g.*, Melissa Farley et al., *Garden of Truth: The Prostitution and Trafficking of Native Women in Minnesota*, at 12 (2011), available at www.niwrc.org/sites/default/files/images/resource/Garden-of-Truth.pdf; ANGEL MAE HINZO, VOICING ACROSS SPACE: SUBVERTING COLONIAL STRUCTURES IN

the male perpetrators and the female victims and the fact that force appears to have been used in at least one of the cases, Justice Deer's fleshing out of the selective prosecution framework in order to provide additional scaffolding for the majority's equal protection analysis helps support the welfare of vulnerable victims of sexual assault.[60] Assuming these are Native victims of sexual assault, which is likely accurate in light of the defendants' arguments that the alleged victims should have been charged by the Tribe as well,[61] their sense of exploitation would have been undoubtedly magnified by the longstanding historical use of sexual assault as a tool of colonialism.[62]

SELECTIVE PROSECUTION

The majority mentions that the defendants have alleged selective prosecution but, rather than addressing the requirements for showing selective prosecution, the Justices in the majority focus their analysis on equal protection generally.[63] This is unfortunate because, as Justice Deer explains, at least in the federal context, selective prosecution is an extremely difficult claim to prove.[64] A large sample size is required to make the showing, and the defendant must also show that those who were not prosecuted were similarly situated.[65] As Justice Deer rightly emphasizes, there is no need for the Winnebago Supreme Court to incorporate federal standards into its own law, but, in light of the majority's use of a federal standard of scrutiny in the equal protection context, the federal standards for selective prosecution do warrant discussion. Justice Deer also identifies aspects of tribal justice systems that may require tweaking of the federal standard if it were to be used as persuasive authority, such as the fact that tribal prosecutors tend to be more closely linked to the community than state or federal prosecutors and that they generally have smaller caseloads.

Given the stringency of the federal standard and its potential use as persuasive authority in tribal courts, the very small sample size of four prosecutions presented by the defendants, and the significant age difference between the three male defendants in the case and the female victims (which tends to suggest that the defendants

---

Ho-Chunk/Winnebago Tribal History 40–42 (Dissertation, UC Davis 2016); Reyna Ramirez, *Race, Tribal Nation, and Gender: A Native Feminist Approach to Belonging*, 7 Meridians 22, 27 (2007).

[60] *See, e.g.*, Martha Chamallas, Introduction to Feminist Legal Theory 82 (3rd ed. 2013) (discussing feminist approaches to statutory rape).

[61] Tribes generally only have criminal jurisdiction over Native American defendants, and this rule was in place at the time that the Winnebago Supreme Court decided *Bigfire*. *Oliphant v. Suquamish Indian Tribe*, 435 US 191 (1978) (1978); 25 U.S.C. §1301(2). Today, there is a limited exception under the Violence Against Women Act, but tribes have to have certain measures in place in order to exercise this jurisdiction. 25 U.S.C. § 1304.

[62] *See, e.g.*, Sarah Deer, *Decolonizing Rape Law: A Native Feminist Synthesis of Safety and Sovereignty*, 24 Wicazo Sa Review 149, 150–151 (2009).

[63] *Bigfire*, 25 Ind. L. Rep. at 6229, 6231.

[64] Prosecutorial Misconduct § 4:11 (2nd ed. 2020).

[65] *Id.*

and victims were not similarly situated), the majority's decision to not focus on the selective prosecution aspect of the claims constitutes a missed opportunity to easily dispose of the case. Justice Deer's discussion of the federal standards for selective prosecution and the unique role of tribal prosecutors in tribal communities adds an important dimension to the Winnebago Tribal Supreme Court's decision. Her opinion on this issue will thus be helpful to tribal judges and justices who find themselves wrestling with similar claims in the future.

Justice Deer's delineation of the stringent federal standards for selective prosecution also furthers protection of Indigenous girls in the context of the facts before the court in *Bigfire* and in similar factual scenarios. As Justice Deer explains, allusions to force reverberate throughout the Winnebago Tribal Supreme Court opinion and are a central focus of the lower court opinion in *Bigfire*. Because "Native women and girls are two and a half times more likely to be raped than any other demographic … and are twice as likely as all other women to be victims of violence,"[66] analysis of the stringent federal standards for selective prosecution furthers protection of the female victims of the statutory rapes at issue in the case. At least one of the victims appears to have been forcibly raped, and the youth of all three victims combined with the age gaps between them and the alleged perpetrators demonstrates a strong likelihood of exploitation. Even putting aside the issue of force, analyzing (and possibly imposing) stringent standards for claims of selective prosecution in the context of this case furthers the protection of adolescent girls (here 12 and 13 year olds) from predation by older teenagers. Moreover, by focusing on the stringent standards required to prove selective prosecution as well as on the age differences between the defendants and victims, Justice Deer's approach avoids relying on the US Supreme Court case of *Michael M. v. Superior Court*, a case in which it was held that biological gender differences justified treating girls and boys differently in the statutory rape context and which was criticized by many feminists as paternalistic.[67] Justice Deer's approach, which exemplifies judicial restraint, also has the benefit of leaving for another day resolution of thorny disagreements among Indigenous feminists as to the relative importance of tribal sovereignty and individual rights.[68]

THE ROLE OF TRIBAL CUSTOM AND TRADITION

Perhaps the most significant contribution of Justice Deer's concurrence in part and concurrence in the judgment is the methodology she proposes for courts to incorporate information about tribal custom and tradition in their legal analyses. Tribal

---

[66] Susan Filan, *Epidemic Hiding in Plain Sight*, 57-ARIZ. ATT'Y 44 (July/Aug. 2021).

[67] *See Bigfire*, 25 Ind. L. Rptr. at 6233 (citing *Michael M. v. Superior Court*, 450 U.S. 464 (1981)); MARTHA CHAMALLAS, INTRODUCTION TO FEMINIST LEGAL THEORY 81 (3rd ed. 2013) (discussing feminist reactions to the *Michael M.* case).

[68] *See supra* note 31 and discussion of the approaches of Eva Petoskey and Renya Ramirez, *infra*, at 142–43.

custom and tradition should be central to such analyses, but the approaches of tribal courts in incorporating it are widely variable and the information, which may be primarily reflected in oral histories, can be difficult to obtain.

As explained above, in the lower court decision in *Bigfire*, Chief Judge Drobnick sought information on tribal culture and tradition in the context of gender roles and sexual misconduct from a tribal elder and historian after the parties failed to provide any briefing to the court on such issues.[69] The information provided to the court, reproduced in footnote 92 of Justice Deer's concurrence in part and concurrence in the judgment, was not solely focused on traditional punishments for rape and sexual intercourse with underage victims, but more expansively addresses property rights in cases of divorce and violent punishments for infidelity that differed by gender (as well as punishments for rape and intercourse with underage victims). While little context is given and we do not know in what period the punishments were applied, the extreme character and brutality of some of the punishments demonstrate that they would not comport with community standards for humane treatment of guilty persons today. Justice Deer wisely points out that American culture is not in any way bound by traditional European punishments like drawing and quartering and that neither should tribes be bound by such traditional punishments (nor should we be surprised that they existed, when violence was so integral a part of Western culture in earlier times as well).

But where does this leave tribal courts, given their need to explicitly incorporate tribal custom and tradition into their decisions in order to be respectful and nurturing of tribal cultures (rather than destructively exerting an assimilative force by borrowing too much from state and federal law)? Justice Deer importantly recognizes that "[s]ociety evolves, laws evolve, and customs evolve." It is particularly crucial to recognize this fact in the tribal law context, given the dominant culture's frequent demand that Native cultures, if recognized at all, behave in romanticized ways that are reflective of cultural frameworks (or perceived frameworks) from the distant past.[70] At the same time, however, given that rights such as equal protection are meant to protect vulnerable classes of persons from society at large, custom and tradition have to be distinguished from a simple snapshot of current public opinion.[71] Justice Deer provides

---

[69] *Winnebago Tribe of Nebraska v. Bigfire*, 24 Ind. L. Rptr. 6232, 6239 (Winnebago Tr. Ct., June 19, 1997), aff'd 25 Ind. L. Rep. 6229 (Sept. 11, 1998).

[70] See, e.g., Kathryn E. Fort, *The Vanishing Indian Returns: Tribes, Popular Originalism, and the Supreme Court*, 57 ST. LOUIS U. L. J. 297, 309–310 (2013); *see also Lac du Flambeau Indians v. Stop Treaty Abuse*, 781 F. Supp. 1385 (W.D. Wis. 1992).

[71] See, e.g., *Pablo v. Ak-Chin Indian Community*, Special Master's Report, No. CV-2015-00024-CO (Ak-Chin Indian Community Court Oct. 20, 2017), at 24–26, 28, available at https://turtletalk.files .wordpress.com/2017/10/redacted-special-master-report.pdf. While reliance on rights has been criticized by male critical legal studies theorists, some intersectional feminists, such as Patricia Smith, emphasize the symbolic power that rights have for disenfranchised groups. MARTHA CHAMALLAS, INTRODUCTION TO FEMINIST LEGAL THEORY 83 (3rd ed. 2013) (discussing Patricia Smith's views relating to the importance of rights).

us with a much-needed methodology when she adjures us to "separate traditional *principles* from traditional *actions*." Justice Deer then distills a number of principles from the information provided to the lower court, explaining that the most relevant for this case is that "age difference in rape cases was relevant."

The majority opinion briefly mentioned the information on tribal culture and tradition[72] received by the lower court without explaining its content. It instead focused more on the work of a non-Native anthropologist for information on traditional Ho-Chunk (or Winnebago) gender roles and the need to respect women, as well as incorporating some information on tribal culture received from one of the three Justices deciding the case, who was a member of a related tribe.[73] The evidence of tribal custom and tradition that the majority of the Winnebago Supreme Court relies on relates to spousal relations and gender roles generally; given that it does not directly pertain to rape or sexual misconduct, the majority's conclusion that the Tribe has a compelling interest in maintaining differing gender roles that is furthered by prosecuting solely males for statutory rape does seem somewhat tenuous. Justice Deer's approach of facing the information on traditional punishments received in the lower court head-on, distilling principles from it, and then identifying the most relevant principle based on the factual situation before the court provides a more intellectually satisfying result and importantly offers guidance for future tribal courts as to how to undertake the core task of incorporating tribal custom and tradition into their decision-making.

Justice Deer's proposed methodology is a feminist framework because it is sovereignty-supporting and Indigenous feminists like Eva Petoskey have explained the need to preserve tribal sovereignty in the face of potential incursions from federal law (even when the federal law supports the rights of female tribal members). In Eva Petoskey's words, "I don't really have a life without the sovereignty of the tribe."[74] Eva Petoskey's view of tribal sovereignty as taking precedence over individual gender-based rights is common among Indigenous feminists, although it has been criticized by some. For example, Winnebago feminist Reyna Ramirez argues that race, tribal nation, and gender "should be non-hierarchically linked as categories of analysis" both to further an understanding of oppression and to understand the "full potential of ... liberation ...."[75] Importantly, however, Ramirez and Petoskey, along

---

[72] "Tribal custom and tradition" is widely discussed in the tribal law context and is often relied upon as a basis for tribes to depart from federal court interpretations of US constitutional rights in interpreting similarly worded rights under the Indian Civil Rights Act or, as in this case, tribal constitutional rights. See 1 COHEN'S HANDBOOK OF FEDERAL INDIAN LAW § 4.05 (2019); Ann E. Tweedy, *Tribal Laws & Same-Sex Marriage: Theory, Process, and Content*, 46 COLUM. HUM. RTS. L. REV. 104, 148–149 (2015).

[73] *Bigfire*, 25 Ind. L. Rep. at 6232–6233.

[74] GLORIA VALENCIA-WEBER, RINA SWENTZELL, & EVA PETOSKEY, *40 Years of the Indian Civil Rights Act: Indigenous Women's Reflections in* INDIAN CIVIL RIGHTS ACT AT FORTY 39, 49 (2012).

[75] Reyna Ramirez, *Race, Tribal Nation, and Gender: A Native Feminist Approach to Belonging*, 7 MERIDIANS 22, 23 (2007). Ramirez sees Indigenous feminism as sharing some commonalities with

with many other Native feminists, are in agreement that furthering tribal cultures and the sovereignty necessary to sustain them is a feminist project – they differ as to whether tribal sovereignty should take precedence over gender-based rights or, instead, whether they should be understood as being on the same plane.[76] In forging a path for tribal courts to integrate custom and tradition into their decisions in a way that is compatible with their contemporary norms, Justice Deer buttresses tribes' ability to safeguard and maintain their unique cultural aspects. In this way, she furthers the survival of Native women.

AGE DIFFERENCES AND SUBSTANTIVE EQUALITY

The majority acknowledged the potential importance of age and the related issues of maturity and power dynamics in its opinion but chose not to rely on them because of the parties' concession that the unprosecuted females were similarly situated to the male defendants.[77] As Justice Deer recognizes, however, the age differences between those prosecuted and those not prosecuted are rightly understood to be an integral part of the case. (Additionally, as described in the lower court decision in *Bigfire*, there are also strong allegations of force in at least one of the cases, although Mr. Bigfire argued on appeal that that evidence was not before the jury.)[78] All of the defendants in *Bigfire* were 17 or 15, while the females were 12 or 13.[79] Furthermore, the previously mentioned critique of the majority decision seemed to treat equal protection as simply an anticlassification principle,[80] a conception that tends to be in tension with tribal justice systems' focus on substantive justice as well as with feminist approaches that seek to further equality for women as a group.[81] Focusing on the age differences between the victims and perpetrators and resulting effects on the power dynamic between them is more in tune with an antisubordination conception of equal protection, under which distinctions between groups are permissible to redress past wrongs and to further substantive equality.[82]

---

other intersectional feminisms, although she also discusses the somewhat distinct focus on tribal sovereignty among Native feminists. *Id.* at 24, 31, 32.

[76] Reyna Ramirez, *Race, Tribal Nation, and Gender: A Native Feminist Approach to Belonging*, 7 MERIDIANS 22, 24, 33–34 (2007).

[77] *Bigfire*, 25 Ind. L. Rep. at 6231.

[78] *Bigfire*, 24 Ind. L. Rptr. at 6233, 6239; *Bigfire*, 25 Ind. L. Rep. at 6229.

[79] *Id.* at 6229.

[80] Rosen, *supra* note 52, at 542–544; Reva B. Siegel, *Equality Talk: Antisubordination and Anticlassification Values in Constitutional Struggles over Brown*, 117 HARV. L. REV. 1470, 1472–1473, 1476 (2004).

[81] *See, e.g.*, ROBERT ANDERSON ET AL., AMERICAN INDIAN LAW: CASES & COMMENTARY 582–583 (4th ed. 2020) (quoting *Sage v. Lodge Grass School* Dist. No. 27 (Crow Ct. App. 1986)); Deborah Brake, *The Struggle for Sex Equality in Sport and the Theory Behind Title IX*, 34 U. MICH. J. L. REFORM 13, 27–28 (2001).

[82] *See* Siegel, *supra* note 80, at 1472–1473, 1476; Brake *supra* note 81, at 27–28. Indeed, other tribes have passed laws that require a minimum age difference between the perpetrator and victim. *See, e.g.*, SQUAXIN IS. TRIBAL CODE 9.12.715.

Additionally, since the *Bigfire* case was decided by the Winnebago Supreme Court, more ethnohistorical information about the Winnebago Tribe and its Ho-Chunk culture has been brought to light, much of which highlights aspects of Winnebago culture that were more egalitarian with respect to gender than was the dominant American culture at the time.[83] While my lack of expertise in the area of Ho-Chunk culture makes me hesitant to draw conclusions about it, this additional information may suggest that upholding the prosecutions in light of the age differences between the victims and the perpetrators is a more culturally sound approach than basing the decision on the cultural salience of gender differences broadly defined.

SEXUAL ASSAULT AS A *SUI GENERIS* CRIME

Justice Deer recommends that sexual assault be treated as a sui generis crime (or a crime unlike any other) in the legal system in order to take into account "the broader picture of the crime of sexual assault and the history of abuse on reservations and in boarding schools." She further recommends, given federal limitations on tribal sentencing authority, that the Tribe think creatively in crafting punishments that are culturally appropriate and that meet the needs of victims.

Highlighting the importance of sexual assault in light of its brutal use as a tool of colonialism is vitally important and supports the substantive equality of women. Angel Mae Hinzo, for example documents how settlers' attacks on the Winnebago to appropriate their lands during the nineteenth century were frequently coupled with sexual violence against Winnebago women.[84] These acts of violence led to military resistance on the part of the Tribe, which in turn led to the Tribe's being characterized as hostile, a characterization which was then used to excuse further incursions on their land rights.[85] As Justice Deer's scholarship has demonstrated, the historic use of sexual assault as a tool of colonialism increases the trauma and weight of each contemporary act of sexual assault.[86] Accordingly, it is proper – and it centers the experiences of Native women–to recognize the grave harms wrought by sexual assault in the tribal justice system and to consider it a sui generis crime.

At the same time, it is appropriate, as Justice Deer advocates, to recognize that boys and men may also be victims of sexual assault. Indeed, one of the most recent tribal jurisdiction cases to come before the US Supreme Court involved a

---

[83] *See, e.g.*, ANGEL MAE HINZO, VOICING ACROSS SPACE: SUBVERTING COLONIAL STRUCTURES IN HO-CHUNK/WINNEBAGO TRIBAL HISTORY 21, 34–35, 39, 44 (Dissertation, UC Davis 2016); Renya K. Ramirez, *Henry Roe Cloud: A Granddaughter's Native Feminist Biographical Account*, 24 WICAZO SA REVIEW 77, 93–95 (2009).
[84] *Id.* at 40–42.
[85] *Id.*
[86] *See, e.g.*, Sarah Deer, *Decolonizing Rape Law: A Native Feminist Synthesis of Safety and Sovereignty*, 24 WICAZO SA REVIEW 149, 150–151 (2009).

non-Native's sexual molestation of a boy who was a Mississippi Choctaw member.[87] In addition to the other gaps it would create, having a sex-based statutory rape law would also cause unnecessary problems for transgender and nonbinary victims who could similarly be viewed as unprotected by such laws. The move to protect all vulnerable groups from sexual assault is consistent with a broad feminist approach, rooted in antisubordination.

CONCLUSION

Justice Deer's concurrence in part and concurrence in the judgment highlights the difficulty of proving selective prosecution, an issue that received insufficient attention in the majority opinion. Perhaps most importantly, she provides a roadmap for tribal courts as to how to incorporate tribal custom and tradition, thus significantly advancing jurisprudence in this area. She also highlights the age and power differences between the perpetrators and victims, which support the justice of upholding these prosecutions. Finally, she recenters the fact that this case is ultimately about sex crimes and reminds us of the importance to tribes of effectively addressing such crimes, in part because of their intertwinement with colonialism. Her opinion springs from an antisubordination conception of feminism and from a recognition that safeguarding tribes' uniqueness and ever-evolving cultures is a feminist project.

WINNEBAGO TRIBE OF NEBRASKA V. BIGFIRE, 25 IND. L. REP. 6229 (WINNEBAGO S. CT. 1998)

JUSTICE SARAH DEER, CONCURRING IN PART AND CONCURRENCE IN THE JUDGMENT

This is a case of first impression for the Winnebago Supreme Court with significant implications for the future of this Court's equal protection analysis. The subject matter, too, is grave. Although Native people have known for generations that sexual abuse is a problem in our communities, only recently has there been national dialogue on the significant number of crime victims in Indian country. Thus, there are two weighty issues in front of the Court, requiring the utmost care and concern. The Winnebago Tribe is a contemporary, living government with independent sovereign powers that predate the United States government. Principles articulated in this case strike at the very heart of tribal existence – safety, health, and the well-being of children.

---

[87] *Dolgencorp v. Mississippi Choctaw Tribe of Indians*, 746 F.3d 167, 169 (5th Cir. 2014), *aff'd* by an equally divided court, 136 S. Ct. 2159 (2016).

This court is asked to interpret the equal protection clause in the Winnebago Constitution found in Article IV, §3 (h):

> The Winnebago Tribe of Nebraska in exercising its powers of self government shall not ... [d]eny to any person within its jurisdiction the equal protection of its laws or deprive any person of liberty or property without due process of law.

This Court has consolidated three separate criminal cases from the lower courts which all ask the same constitutional question – namely, is it a violation of the Winnebago Constitution for a tribal prosecutor charge males, but not females, for statutory rape?

Here, each defendant was charged with violating WTC Title 3, §3-419(C), which reads: "Any person who subjects an unemancipated minor to sexual penetrations is guilty of sexual assault in the second degree." The language of the statute appears to be gender-neutral, but on closer look it would be very difficult to charge females with this offense because of the penetration requirement. In the cases at bar, the tribal prosecutor filed charges against the male defendants but not the female minors. The three defendants in these cases argue that the statutory rape code in the Winnebago Criminal Code should be applied equally to both young men and young women.

Defendant Hugh Bigfire was 17 ½ years old when he had sexual intercourse with a 12-year-old girl in 1996. The tribal prosecutor charged Mr. Bigfire, but not the 12-year-old. Defendant L.W. was 17 years old when he had sexual intercourse with a 12-year-old girl in 1997. Again, the tribal prosecutor charged L.W. with sexual assault but not the 12-year-old. Defendant C.L. was 15 years old when he had sexual intercourse with a 13-year old girl in 1996. He was charged with sexual assault, but not the 13-year-old girl.

Two Winnebago trial court judges came to opposite conclusions in these cases.

Presiding Judge Drobnick considered the equal protection arguments of Defendant Bigfire and issued her opinion on June 19, 1997. She wrote an extensive decision, ultimately denying Bigfire's motion to dismiss. The Honorable Barbara Kueny oversaw the cases involving L.W. and C.L. and issued her opinions on September 4, 1997. She concluded that the tribal prosecutor impermissibly filed charges against the male defendants, but not the female minors, and granted their motions to dismiss pursuant to the equal protection clause in the Winnebago constitution.

I agree with the Court's ultimate conclusion that it does not violate the Winnebago Constitution for a tribal prosecutor to use her discretion in applying the statutory rape statutes to the older, male minors in cases such as those consolidated here before the Court. I also endorse the majority's conclusion that this Court is not bound by federal or state law.

I write separately with regards to four specific issues.

(1) The equal protection claim could have been quickly disposed of based on the power of prosecutorial discretion;
(2) Reliance on a "strict scrutiny" standard to gender discrimination matters is inconsistent with Winnebago common law and may have undesirable outcomes in future cases;
(3) Judge Drobnick's decision, while noteworthy in its depth, included within her opinion a document entitled "Moral Laws of the Ho-Chunk" (hereinafter *Moral Laws*) that solicited from a Winnebago elder and historian regarding how gendered issues may have been dealt with in the past. The lower court's use of the *Moral Laws* raises troubling questions about developing contemporary tribal law norms based on culture and tradition; and
(4) Finally, I seek to underscore how sexually based crimes raise important issues in our communities that may not be anticipated by the Anglo-American system. For this reason, I offer some commentary on issues regarding sexual assault that may arise in the future.

I. PROSECUTORIAL DISCRETION

I wholeheartedly support the majority's findings and conclusions that this Court is not bound by the constitutional interpretations of federal courts with regard to the United States Constitution. However, to the extent that we rely on Anglo-American law as persuasive or informative, this case could have been resolved on much simpler grounds – namely, that the prosecutor exercise of discretion was entirely lawful.

In this case, we have consolidated three cases in which teenaged male minors were charged with sex offenses but their purported sexual partners (much younger female minors) were not likewise charged. Both Judge Drobnick and the majority provide several cogent responses to the defense's contention that the prosecution of only the older male minors was unlawful, but I would dismiss the claims based solely on the basis of prosecutor's exercise of discretion was proper. There is no evidence in the record to suggest a tendency or trend of only prosecuting males for status offenses beyond these three instances.[88]

To the extent that Anglo-American law is *persuasive* to tribal courts, there is a clear directive from the United States Supreme Court as how to resolve claims of selective prosecution in *United States v. Armstrong*, 517 U.S. 456 (1996) which held that to succeed in a case for selective prosecution, the defendant must establish that the Government declined to prosecute similarly situated suspects.

---

[88] If such evidence exists, then the issue should be addressed through the equal protection framework described below in Section II.

Tribal prosecutors, who have much smaller caseloads than a typical federal prosecutor, must make difficult decisions within a small community where everyone ordinarily knows each other. The government in this case has less than 2,000 citizens who reside on approximately 28,000 acres of land. Tribal prosecutors are uniquely positioned to understand crime on the reservation. Tribal prosecutors have a limited budget and must prioritize their efforts based upon importance to the Tribe. Neither the Winnebago code nor common practice suggests that prosecutors must justify each discretionary decision in light of their ongoing commitments and dynamic docket load.

II. STANDARD OF REVIEW

I disagree with the majority's hasty application of strict scrutiny standards to allegations of gender discrimination arising out of the Winnebago Tribe Constitution. I believe it is antithetical to other common law principles in Winnebago legal traditions as presented in Judge Drobnick's analysis. The majority argues that the Winnebago constitution requires the highest judicial scrutiny anticipated in Anglo-American law, but it does not provide sufficient justification for the application of this standard. Both Judge Drobnick and the majority go to great lengths to explain that Winnebago common law does allow for important distinctions between men and women. As such, the strict scrutiny standard may be in conflict with Winnebago common law.

As noted by the majority, judicial reliance on so-called standards of review are neither required by the text of the United States Constitution nor have they become part of the Winnebago constitutional canon. Indeed, the idea of using the "heightened scrutiny" did not exist in Anglo-American law until the famous footnote 4 in *Carolene Products* in 1938, just 50 years ago. 304 U.S. 144 (1938). The Winnebago Court is relatively young, and is still early in its development of constitutional jurisprudence. Since the various different standards of scrutiny (rational, intermediate, and strict – along with other derivations) have proved challenging, if not arbitrary, in their application in federal courts, this Court is not obliged to use them.

Indeed, application of strict scrutiny as understood by Anglo-American law might undercut some very important issues of fairness and equality. It is clear from the record that Winnebago people can, and do, recognize gender as an important facet to be considered in assessing legal obligations and remedies. These distinctions emanate from the epistemology and cosmology of the Winnebago people and do not carry the stigma of gender discrimination found in the history of United States law. Here, the majority acknowledges that "Ho-Chunk tradition recognizes and respects different roles for males and females in the Winnebago Tribe ..." and "... [G]ender role differentiation and gender differences in legal or customary treatment related to those roles are natural and expected." It is puzzling, then, that the majority claims that gender discrimination is subject to the highest level of scrutiny, which would require this Court to apply strict scrutiny all forms of gender differentiation. If the Court applies a strict scrutiny standard in future cases, these important aspects of gender differences from Winnebago common law may be struck down by the use of the Anglo-American standard of strict scrutiny.

The majority does note that this case may be better characterized as a question of age discrimination rather than gender discrimination. The prosecutor used her discretion to charge older, mature teenage males who had sexual intercourse with 12-year-olds.

In the Anglo-American system, age is rarely characterized as a suspect class and allegations of age discrimination is usually evaluated using a rational basis test.[89] These defendants were all older than the victims. Thus, the principles of age discrimination can help to guide interpretation of the Winnebago Tribe's equal protection clause. In Anglo-American law, age discrimination is typically given "rational-basis" review. Such a standard would provide more flexibility for the Winnebago to consider acts of culturally based gender discrimination.

III. MORAL LAWS OF THE HO-CHUNK

According to the Winnebago Tribal Code, "no conduct constitutes an offense unless so declared by this Code, or by any other Tribal resolution or ordinance or Code provision or by federal law."[90] Thus, unwritten common law cannot create crimes that are not enumerated in the code itself. However, this provision does not preclude the tribal court from relying on common law to analyze the Winnebago Constitution. Indeed, the use of common law is required by the Winnebago tribal code. In Sec. 1-109 of the Winnebago Tribal Code, Winnebago courts are instructed to "apply the Tribal Constitution, and the provisions of all statutory law hereto or hereafter adopted by the Tribe. In matters not covered by Tribal statute, the Court *shall* apply traditional Tribal customs and usages, which shall be called the common law."[91] The last decade has seen a dramatic rise in tribal courts engaged in revitalizing and strengthening tribal customs and traditions. It is critical that we carefully consider, for example, what types of customs are appropriate for the Winnebago's contemporary day-to-day governance.

I concur with my colleagues that the Judge Drobnick properly sought out information regarding the gendered customs and traditions of the Winnebago people to help her answer the equal protection question in this case. Indeed, WTC 1-109 the Court is given permission to "request the advice of counselors and Tribal elders familiar with it." Future practitioners in Winnebago courts should expect that the

---

[89] *See, e.g., Massachusetts Bd. of Retirement v. Murgia*, 427 US 307 (1976); *Vance v. Bradley*, 440 US 93 (1979); and *Gregory v. Ashcroft*, 501 US 452 (1991).
[90] WTC Sec. 3-105 (TCR 86-79).
[91] Emphasis added.

Court will carefully review this type of information as we consider the codification of tribal common law in our future opinions.

In this case, Judge Drobnick asked the Tribe's Cultural Preservation Officer and Tribal Historian (well-respected Winnebago elder David Lee Smith) to provide clarity as to tribal tradition or culture regarding sexual assault and the expected behavior of minors. He provided the Court with a copy of a document entitled *Moral Laws of the Ho-Chunk (1660)* (hereinafter *Moral Laws*) to the lower court. While the majority did not directly mention the substance of the *Moral Laws* provided by Mr. Smith in this case, it is an important matter that this Court may need to address in the future.

In short, the *Moral Laws* cited by Judge Drobnick include descriptions of antiquated actions that have no place in contemporary laws of tribal nations today.[92]

---

[92] This is the full excerpt published by the lower court in the *Bigfire* case. It is entitled *Moral Laws of the Ho-Chunk (1660)*, authored by Tribal Historian and elder, David Lee Smith:

> The Winnebago married their wives in order to remain with them throughout life. If a man quit his wife, everything the man had would be hers. But when the man could prove on his side that she had been unfaithful to him, either before or since he had left her, he could take another wife without anyone being able to rouse objection. The man then did not have to give anything to his unfaithful wife. The law also stated that the man can cut the unfaithful wife's nose in half to mark her as an unfaithful wife. Her relatives could not do anything. Shame was the work (sic) everyone understood.
>
> If a woman bore children that did not belong to her husband, the children were left out in the elements to die. The woman was then exiled from the village. If a woman bore children out of wedlock, both her and her offspring had to leave the village.
>
> The rules against marriage within the clans or gens were strictly enforced. If a man married within his clan, he would be exiled after he was beaten by his clansmen and probably killed away from the village. Both men and women shared equally in the profit if they sold anything.
>
> The children would always live with their mother until the boys were ready to be married. If the husband died, the wife could not married (sic) again unless she mourned for four years. She could marry again only if their mother-in-law gave her permission. When her four years of widowhood had expired, and if she strictly observed the requirements of her mourning, her sister-in-laws dressed her in new garments and combed her hair. She was now free to court and marry anyone she wanted.
>
> When the wife dies, the husband observed his mourning. He did not weep, but made presents to the parents of his deceased wife. The man was not permitted to marry until after four years of mourning. If either the man or woman did not follow the rule, they were exiled from the village.
>
> If a man or woman stole from another, she or he had to pay restitution for twice the cost of the stolen object. If a youth stole or threatened anyone in the village, his clansmen would beat him. If a youth did not show respect for the elders, he or she would be given away to relatives, or forced to stay in the wilderness for two months.
>
> Incest was punishable by death. A man or woman could never marry into their clans. In Ho-Chunk culture, a fifth cousin was still included as family. If a man raped a young woman who was at least 13 or above in age, he was killed. If a man raped a child and killed that child, he was tortured to death by his own clansmen. If a man raped an older woman, he was put to death. If an older woman raped a younger boy, she was forced to run the gauntlet and then exiled. If a woman beat her husband, she was beat by his sisters and near woman relatives. If a man beat his wife, the wife could throw his personal belongings out of her house. The house was hers. If the man forced his way back in her house, he was beaten by his clansmen. If he did it a third time, he was exiled. If he did it a fourth time, he was killed. If an older woman accused her husband of raping her, she was forced to walk on hot stone to prove she did not lie.

Identifying key principles of common law is part of the judicial function, but suggesting that outdated practices of disfigurement, corporal punishment and execution should guide our common law development is to misunderstand the role of cultural information in the legal process.

The majority did not clearly endorse the *Moral Laws* and but did reference them (only for the age difference question) also relied on observations made by a non-Native anthropologist who studied the Winnebago people and published *The Winnebago Indian* in 1923 (Paul Radin) as well as personal knowledge of the Court's only Ho-Chunk justice, Justice Hunter. Radin observed that young Ho-Chunk men were warned about the consequences of abusing women, which included that "you will really be killing yourself by such behavior." In my view, the majority should have addressed the *Moral Laws* head-on to avoid future reliance on the passage and to set forth specific directions on how Winnebago common law can be identified, applied, and evolve.

As a non-Winnebago justice, I have no ability to assess the *validity* of the information in the *Moral Laws*.[93] Thus, I will tread lightly on this matter only to raise questions of contemporary application. I approach the passage as a person who interprets legal texts – not as a Winnebago person. The record does not provide the complete context under which the *Moral Laws* were solicited, written, and received. It is not clear whether the passage is connected to the year 1660 in some way. It is not clear whether this passage reflects a society that had been forced to convert to Christianity at some point and took on the trappings of Western patriarchy. The *Moral Laws* are also internally inconsistent – it describes actions of brutal corporal punishment, torture, and execution. Yet the final line reads "A man considered women and children sacred. He was put here by the Creator to protect them. If he did not, he would suffer forever in the bad Spirit World." However, the rest of the *Moral Laws* describe acts that do not connote sacredness or respect. For example, out-of-wedlock children were left in the elements to die. Youth who engaged in theft were subject to a beating by clan elders. Reconciling the entirety of the report with this last line is difficult, if not impossible. Moreover, the inclusion of this document in the record may do further harm by perpetuating stereotypes of Native people as savage, uncivilized, and violent.

Herein lies the problem for many tribal courts – how to distinguish descriptions of historical actions from foundational principles of tribal common law to be applied in today's courts. If the *Moral Laws* were to be literally relied upon in sentencing, for example, this Court may be asked to order violence from the bench, including beatings, torture, and executions. Suppose that this Court was asked to interpret an ambiguous tribal domestic violence statute in the future. Relying on the *Moral Laws* would be a different sort of exercise. For example, if a man were accused of slashing his wife's nose after discovering infidelity, he might raise a cultural defense

---

    A man considered women and children sacred. He was put here by the Creator to protect them. If he did not, he would suffer forever in the bad Spirit World.

[93] The Winnebago Tribal Council has the authority to appoint judges that are not Winnebago citizens. WTC Sec. 1–204 (1986).

based on the *Moral Laws*. The Anglo-American criminal justice system is not bound by traditional punishments such as being drawn and quartered or the violation of due process in the Salem Witch Trials. Society evolves, laws evolve, and customs evolve. Not every action steeped in "tradition" should be considered binding on contemporary Winnebago courts. Again, I do not take issue with the accuracy of the information, but the *Moral Laws* likely describes a very different time and place.

Regardless of its year of origin, the *Moral Laws* use the *past* tense (e.g., The Winnebago *married* their wives, the children *would* always live with their mother, if a youth *stole* or *threatened* anyone, etc.). Thus, the text more likely refers to practices of the past. Without further context, it is unclear whether these references are to distant or recent past. We must make an effort to separate traditional *principles* from traditional *actions*.

There are some principles that can still be helpful in a contemporary setting. In my opinion, there are potentially five useful common law *principles* that can be gleaned from the *Moral Laws*:

(1) Life-long monogamy was a preferred form of marriage and parenting;
(2) Intra-clan marriage was heavily discouraged;
(3) All genders were expected to mourn their spouse for a specific period of time before remarrying;
(4) Theft was punished by ordering restitution;
(5) Rape was a serious offense, especially in cases where an older man or woman raped a younger person or child, and was punished severely; and
(6) A home and household goods were the property of women.

Some of these principles are also found in Anglo-American law (such as the laws prohibiting theft and rape). Other principles are not consistent with Anglo-American law, such as women's sole ownership of household property. While some might see this process of gleaning principles from antiquated laws as a method of sanitizing the substance of the *Moral Laws*, I can think of no other way to apply the information in the contemporary setting. This is not an attempt to erase history; this is an effort to ensure that Winnebago laws are appropriate for the times.

In the case at bar, the relevant principle would be #5. The *Moral Laws* make it clear that that the age difference in rape cases was relevant. The specific language talks about a man raping a child or a young woman, and an older woman raping a young boy. Therefore, the prosecutor is charging the defendants properly under tribal statute and tribal common law principles.

IV. SEXUAL ASSAULT AND WINNEBAGO LAW

I write this section to set forth my opinion that the issue of sexual assault deserves special consideration in tribal law – that Winnebago sexual assault law be interpreted in a way that will be more responsive than the Anglo-American system. In this instance, I would propose that sexual assault be treated as a *sui generis* crime. That is, sexual assault is a crime unlike any other. This Court should approach and consider the application of sex crimes like rape and abuse, which are particularly egregious crimes and require unique analysis within sovereign tribal nations. Understanding the context of sexual assault against Native children by using analysis that takes into account the broader picture of the crime of sexual assault and the history of abuse on reservations and in boarding schools.

The Winnebago Tribal Code offers the following useful legislative intent for sexual assault cases:

> It is the intent of the Winnebago Tribe of Nebraska to enact laws dealing with sexual assault and related criminal sexual offenses which will protect the dignity of the victim at all stages of judicial process, which will insure that the alleged offender in a criminal sexual offense case have preserved the constitutionally guaranteed due process of law procedures, and which will establish a system of investigation, prosecution, punishment, and rehabilitation for the welfare and benefit of the residents of this reservation as such system is employed in the area of criminal sexual offenses.[94]

Although the federal government has authority to prosecute crimes on the Winnebago Reservation committed by Indians pursuant to the Major Crimes Act (18 U.S.C. §1153), preliminary statistics tell us that federal prosecutors decline over 80 percent of Indian country cases that come to their attention.[95] As such, tribal courts may be the only option for punishing sexual abuse committed against Native children. Per binding federal law, the maximum penalty that can be imposed for any offense in tribal court is one-year and/or a $5,000 fine.[96] This penalty may be insufficient in the eyes of many, who are used to seeing sexual abuse crimes garnering lengthier sentences in the Anglo-American legal world. However, there is no federal prohibition on developing or revitalizing other sanctions that are consistent with tribal law. The Winnebago Tribe would be well within its power to assign more culturally appropriate sentences consistent with the needs of contemporary victims.

Returning to the issue of gender, I submit that sexual abuse laws should be interpreted as gender-neutral whenever the statutes allow. Boys are subjected to sexual abuse just as girls are. Consider a case from the 1980s on the Hopi reservation, wherein one non-Native elementary school teacher molested at least 142 male students over 8 years.[97] While sexual abuse is sometimes thought of as a crime primarily experienced

---

[94] WTC Sec. 3-416 (1986).
[95] United States Comm'n on Civil Rights, Indian Tribes: A Continuing Quest for Survival 154–55 (1981).
[96] Indian Civil Rights Act (1968).
[97] John R. Shafer & Blaine D. McIlwaine, *Investigating Child Sexual Abuse in the American Indian Community*, 16 Am. Indian Quarterly 157, 163 (1992). The name of the perpetrator was John Boone and he is now serving a life sentence in federal prison.

by girls and women, Winnebago boys should receive the same protection of the law as do girls. The current Winnebago sexual assault statutes allow this court to ensure that both male and female victims are protected by the law. The prosecutor, however, may use her discretion to determine how to expend time and resources.

The laws that were ultimately used in this case may be appropriately classified as "statutory rape" laws, meant to prohibit minors from engaging in sexual activities, even if they give consent. The Winnebago Tribal Code does not have a separate age of consent law. Instead, it prohibits subjecting "an unemancipated minor to sexual penetration." (WTC Sec. 3-419(1)(C)), which essentially makes the age of consent 18. The subtext throughout the record suggests that these cases may have involved overt acts of violence or coercion, but the prosecutor was unable to secure testimony from the victims. This is not uncommon. Particularly in small communities, victims may be unwilling or unable to testify due to fear, shame, and embarrassment. Using Subsection 3-419(1)((C)) requires the tribal prosecutor to simply prove that sexual penetration took place, and does not need to rely on victim testimony regarding other details of the event(s).

While statutes are the province of the tribal legislature, the Winnebago courts are tasked with interpretation and application of the laws to particular human actions. Sexual abuse and domestic assault are threats to the sovereignty of the Tribe just as a rapists are threats to the self-determination of individual victims. This court has a solemn responsibility of interpreting the laws faithfully with these tenets in mind.

Ultimately, the majority came to the correct conclusion – the Winnebago equal protection clause does not prohibit tribal prosecutors from charging men in sexual assault cases even if the statute itself is gender-neutral. My primary reason for this concurrence is to critique the strict scrutiny standard and the *Moral Laws* as referenced in the lower court.

APPENDIX

SUPREME COURT OF THE WINNEBAGO TRIBE OF NEBRASKA WINNEBAGO TRIBE OF NEBRASKA V. HUGH BIG FIRE, ET AL. NOS. 97-03, 97-04 AND 97-05 (SEPT.11, 1998) 25 INDIAN L. REP. 6229 (1998)

SUMMARY

In consolidated actions in which the defendants assert an equal protection challenge to gender neutrality in the application of tribal criminal law addressing sexual assault, the Supreme Court of the Winnebago Tribe of Nebraska holds that the tribal constitution and by-laws permit the Tribe to differentiate in prosecutions for violation of the tribal code based on gender.

FULL TEXT

Before CLINTON, Chief Justice, HUNTER and BOTSFORD, Associate Justices

PERCURIAM

This matter came before the Court on April 8, 1998, for oral argument. The matter involves a consolidated appeal of three cases involving the prosecution by the Winnebago Tribe of three males under the age of 18. All three cases were prosecuted under Winnebago Tribal Code (WTC) Section 3-419(1)(C) which is a second degree sexual assault statute.[98] The three males were prosecuted for having sexual relations with females who were under age 18 also. The females were not prosecuted. On appeal, the three defendants argue that their prosecutions under WTC § 3-419(1)(C) constitute impermissible selective prosecution, and as such are violations of the equal protection guarantee of Article IV, Section 3(h) of the Winnebago Constitution, as amended in Amendment X, Section 3(h), effective June 23, 1983.[99]

In *Winnebago Tribe v. Bigfire*, SC 97-03 (CR 96-487 below, reported at 24 Indian L. Rep. 6232 (1997)), the appellant Bigfire, then 17 years old, had sexual relations with a 12-year-old girl in August 1996. Mr. Bigfire was charged and tried as an adult. At oral argument, counsel for Mr. Bigfire informed this Court that a motion to move the prosecution to juvenile court had been overruled. Mr. Bigfire originally was charged with first degree sexual assault under WTC § 3-419(1)(A) and (B), but the charge was reduced to second degree sexual assault because the 12-year-old girl was unavailable to testify at trial.[100] Appellant Bigfire made a motion to dismiss on the matter below. The motion was denied. On February 27, 1997, following a jury trial, Chief Judge Heidi A. Drobnick entered a judgment of conviction which found Mr. Bigfire guilty of second degree sexual assault. In her February 26, 1998, order denying the motion to dismiss, Judge Drobnick stated, "The evidence showed that this was not a consensual sexual encounter." On appeal, Mr. Bigfire asserts that the jury never made such a finding. Appellant Bigfire appealed both the order denying his motion to dismiss and the judgment of conviction.

The facts in *Winnebago Tribe v. L.W*, SC 97-04 (JD 97-087 [25 Indian L. Rep. 6022] below) are quite similar. In this case, it is again undisputed that the 17-year-old

---

[98] Winnebago Tribal Code Section 3–419(1)(C) provides "Any person who subjects another person to sexual contact and … (C) Any person who subjects an unemancipated minor to sexual penetration is guilty of sexual assault in the second degree."

[99] As Amended, Article IV, Section 3(h) of the Winnebago Constitution states: "The Winnebago Tribe of Nebraska in exercising its powers of self-government, shall not: … (h) deny to any person within its jurisdiction the equal protection of its laws …"

[100] Winnebago Tribal Code Section 3–419(1)(A) and (B) provides: "Any person who subjects another person to sexual contact and (A) Overcomes the victim by force, threat of force, express or implied, coercion or deception; or (B) Knew or should have known that the victim was physically or mentally incapable of resisting or appraising the nature of his/her conduct is guilty of second degree sexual assault."

defendant L.W. had sexual relations with a 12-year-old girl. The incident occurred on January 21, 1997 and the defendant L.W. was charged with second degree sexual assault. The 12-year-old girl was not charged. The defendant L.W. made a motion to dismiss on constitutional grounds.111e motion to dismiss was denied.

On July 3, 1997 a bench trial was conducted. L.W. was found not guilty after the trial. In a September 3, 1997 order, the Honorable Barbara Kueny opined that the word "subject" in WTC Section 3-419(1)(C) means "to bring under control or dominion." Judge Kueny ruled that there was no evidence that the defendant "exercised control, dominion, or threat thereof over the victim"; consequently, she found the defendant, L.W., not guilty.

The Tribe appealed the Judge's interpretation of the second degree sexual assault statute and the defendant L.W. appealed the denial of the pretrial motion to dismiss. However, at oral argument, the Tribe indicated a willingness to withdraw its appeal of L.W.'s acquittal to avoid subjecting the defendant to double jeopardy, in violation of Article IV, Section 3(c) of the Winnebago Constitution. That provision states: "The Winnebago Tribe of Nebraska in exercising its powers of self-government shall not: ... (c) subject any person for the same offense to be twice put in jeopardy."

In the third case, *Winnebago Tribe v. CL.*, SC 97-05 (JD 97-016 [25 Indian L. Rep. 6022] below), a 15-year-old male was charged with second degree sexual assault of a 13-year-old girl. The fact that the two minors engaged in sexual relations on July 4, 1996, is not in dispute. Again, only the male was charged with violating WTC § 3-419(1)(C). In this case, however, the defendant C.L.'s pretrial motion to dismiss on constitutional grounds was granted on September 4, 1997, by the Honorable Barbara Kueny. The order struck the count based on WTC Section 3-419(1)(C) from the complaint to uphold C.L.'s right to equal protection. The opinion cited the four prosecutions under the statute in which only the males had been charged. The Tribe appealed that order granting the motion to dismiss.

On January 16, 1998, this Court granted a joint motion to consolidate the appeals of the three cases. All three cases raised the issue of the constitutionality of the prosecution of only males and not females under WTC Section 3-419(1)(C).

To decide the question of whether WTC Section 3-419(1)(C) violates the equal protection guarantee of the Winnebago Constitution, this Court must address the following issues: (1) What law applies to the interpretation of the equal protection clause of the Winnebago Tribal Constitution? (2) What is the standard this Court should use in evaluating alleged violations of the equal protection guarantee of the Winnebago Constitution? (3) What is the result of applying that standard in this case?

The parties agree that the second degree sexual assault statute is gender-neutral on its face. The defendants below, Bigfire, L.W. and C.L., argue that the fact that only males were charged and prosecuted in these cases indicates impermissible selective prosecution, denying them of their equal protection rights under Article IV. Section

3(h) of the Winnebago Constitution. When asked at oral argument, their counsel was clear that they made no claim at trial or on appeal under the Indian Civil Rights Act of 1968. 25 U.S.C. §§ 1301-03. They therefore failed to exhaust any tribal remedies with respect to these federal claims. The defendants' argument is based primarily on the assertion that the purpose of WTC Section 3-419(1)(C) is to prevent sexual relations between minors; selective prosecution of males only is discriminatory and does not further the Tribe's purpose. Another argument advanced by the defendants is that upon the showing of the discriminatory effect of selective prosecution of a law. The burden shifts to the Tribe to prove a nondiscriminatory purpose. Finally, the defendants argue that the equal protection guarantee of the Winnebago Constitution legally supersedes and displaces any tribal custom of the Ho-Chunk people of the Winnebago Tribe of Nebraska that may have involved treating male and female sexual offenders differently.

On the other hand, the Tribe argues that its prosecution of only the males in these cases is permissible gender discrimination because one of the purposes of WTC Section 3-419(1)(C) is the prevention of pregnancy in female minors. The Tribe argues that to require prosecution of both parties in all cases of sexual relations between minors would have a chilling effect on prosecutorial discretion and would interfere with the prosecution of eases since the two minors generally are the only witnesses to the crime. Finally, the Tribe argues that the equal protection guarantee in the Winnebago Constitution does not necessarily require an identical application of the law based upon the complex dynamics of these cases.

The appeals were consolidated by order of this Court and all parties were represented by counsel. Briefs were filed by all sides and the matter and oral argument was heard at the Hamline University School of Law on April 9, 1998. On being questioned about the double jeopardy implications of its appeal in *Winnebago Tribe of Nebraska v. L.W.*, SC 97-04, counsel for the Tribe indicated a willingness to withdraw the appeal at oral argument, noting, however, that he would like to have the issue it raised decided by this Court. This Court will address the priority of the appeal in the *L.W.* case as the final aspect of this decision.

DECISION

What Law Applies to the Interpretation of the Equal Protection Clause of the Winnebago Tribal Constitution?

This case presents a question of first impression for this Court. Article IV, Section 3(h) of the Winnebago Constitution guarantees some measure of equal protection of the laws to tribal members, reservation residents, and other persons with whom the tribal government deals. Although the language is virtually identical to the language of the federal Indian Civil Rights Act of 1968, 25 U.S.C. § 1302 and similar language in the United States Constitution's guarantee found in the Fourteenth

Amendment, this Court is not bound to apply federal or state law to this question. It is solely a question of the interpretation of tribal law. Just as a state court may interpret provisions of an identically worded state constitution to mean something different and more protective than a similar federal constitutional guarantee, so a tribal court is free to interpret the tribal constitution independently of the meaning afforded similar language in federal law. This independence is not only a logical result of the sovereignty of the tribe as a separate political community within the United States, but also a necessary option to protect the separate and different cultural heritage of the tribe and to adapt the meaning of legal concepts derived from Anglo-American roots to the unique cultural context of communal tribal life. It is only with such sensitive adaptation of such legal concepts to the precise tribal community served by tribal law that such legal concepts will take on true meaning and provide real and meaningful legal protections.

This Court does not mean to discount, however the importance of the federal Indian Civil Rights Act of 1968 for tribal court systems. While tribal law need not provide identical guarantees to that afforded by this federal law, all tribal courts must be mindful that providing less guarantees than required by this federal statute can result in federal court review of the tribal decision in any tribal juvenile or criminal cases resulting in detention under the writ of habeas corpus remedy afforded in the Act by 25 U.S.C. 1303. The Winnebago Tribe of Nebraska, however, did not specifically adopt the Indian Civil Rights Act as the basis for the provision of civil rights protections to its constituents and this Court is not bound by that Act in interpreting the Winnebago Constitution.

The Winnebago Tribal Code, Section 1-109 requires this Court to apply the tribal Constitution and tribal laws in its decision-making. If tribal statutes do not address the matter, this Court is specifically directed by that provision to apply traditional tribal customs and usages. If the tribal constitutions. Tribal statutes or common law fail to address the issue, only then is this Court free to apply "any laws of the United States or any state therein." Winnebago Tribal Code, Section 1-109.

The defendants are certainly correct that the people of the Winnebago Tribe of Nebraska through the adoption of their Constitution and By-Laws and any amendments thereto or through the laws enacted by their duly elected Tribal Council have the power to change, alter, or abandon tribal customs and traditions and to make their newly adopted rules the applicable law. Indeed, in requiring the Winnebago tribal courts to apply written tribal law in preference to tribal customs and traditions, WTC § 109 makes this point perfectly clear. The harder problem, of course, is when will the adoption of a new written tribal positive law, either in the form of a constitutional provision or a tribal code provision, be found to displace prior tribal customs and usages. Like most tribes, the Winnebago Tribe of Nebraska agreed to removal from their ancestral homelands and to the acceptance of new reservation lands precisely to preserve their separate cultural and political identity as a people. Therefore, while it is true that the people of the Winnebago Tribe of Nebraska can directly through constitutional amendment or indirectly by tribal ordinance alter their tribal traditions and customs, they should not be found to have done so unless they do so explicitly or unless the new positive law creates such an irreconcilable conflict with tribal traditions and customary law that the two cannot conceivably be harmonized and coexist. Otherwise all tribal written law, including both the Constitution and By-Laws of the Winnebago Tribe of Nebraska and its amendments and the Winnebago Tribal Code, should be interpreted against the backdrop of and in harmony with evolving tribal custom and tradition.

This Court therefore will apply the law of the Winnebago Tribal Constitution in an interpretation consistent with the sovereign status of this Nation. Insofar as the Winnebago Tribal Constitution is unclear or vague as to meaning or interpretation of any of its provisions, this Court can and will look to tribal law, customs, and usages to provide background for and illuminate the meaning of such constitutional provisions.

What Is the Standard That This Court Should Use in Evaluating Alleged Violations of the Equal Protection Guarantee of the Winnebago Constitution?

The question of what standard that this Court should apply to this issue is a difficult one. On one hand, it could be simple to look to the standards applied to gender discrimination case in federal constitutional cases or the federal cases involving the Indian Civil Rights Act. An adoption of the federal standards would be allowable if there were not the requirement that this Court first look within the tribal system in its application of laws.

In addition, blind adoption of federal standards as tribal law without any effort to look to tribal standards poses the obvious question of why the establishment of tribal court and legal systems was necessary if all the tribal court system does is merely parrot the law and procedure applied in the Anglo-American court systems. Thus, it is necessary that this Court attempt to fashion a standard for determining equal protection issues that may be analogous to federal or state standards but which also draws upon rich cultural, social, and political heritage of the Winnebago Tribe of Nebraska. Only by the creation of such tribally unique standards will tribal courts realize the full potential of being legal systems within tribal sovereigns.

The standard which this Court will utilize is to first analogize to the federal standard. First we must ask if there are two similarly situated people who have been treated differently under the law and was that treatment based on some suspect or quasi-suspect classification such as race or, as claimed here, gender?"[101] The second question is whether the statute has been applied in a way which has a discriminatory effect based on such a classification and is motivated by a discriminatory purpose. Third, if discriminatory effect and motive are found. The burden shifts to the Tribe

---

[101] The question of whether or not the statute is gender-neutral on its face is not at issue as the parties agree that it is gender-neutral on its face.

to demonstrate a compelling governmental interest for any perceived disparity in treatment. It is worth noting that this last standard must be applied very carefully in a manner that is consistent with the laws, customs and traditions of the Winnebago Tribe of Nebraska. In this sense, this Court therefore departs in two ways from the laws applied by federal courts to resolve gender discrimination cases. First, rather than applying intermediate scrutiny to gender discrimination as directed by the United States Supreme Court for federal constitutional claims, *see e.g. Frontiero v. Richarson*, 411 U.S. 677 (1973), *Craig v. Boren*, 429 U.S. 190 (1976), this Court takes gender discrimination quite seriously and applies the highest level of scrutiny to such claims-strict scrutiny. Accordingly, a compelling governmental interest, not merely an important governmental interest, must be found and the discrimination must be essential to furthering that interest. Second, in determining what constitutes a compelling governmental interest, this Court must always look to the preservation of tribal culture, traditions, and sovereignty and to the promotion of the health and welfare of tribal members as the most compelling reasons for the formation and operation of tribal government. Accordingly, a compelling justification for a gender or other differentiation can be found in the rich culture, history and traditions of the Winnebago Tribe. Only invidious and irrational discriminations and disparities in governmental treatment unsupported by tribal law, customs, and usages therefore will be struck down under the equal protection provisions of the Winnebago Constitution.

What Is the Result of Applying the Announced Standard to These Cases?

In applying the above-mentioned standard to these cases, this Court will address the standards separately.

Are Two Similarly-Situated People Treated Differently by the Tribe in Each Case Based on a Suspect or Quasi-Suspect Classification?

Both parties seem to agree that the first question clearly can be answered in the affirmative. In the three cases presented on appeal, the facts are not in dispute. In all three cases, three underage males were prosecuted under the statute for having sex with three females. In all three cases, three underage females were not prosecuted under the statute even though by its terms both parties engaged in an underage, consensual sexual encounter violating the statute. The facts therefore provide a substantial basis for believing that the parties to the alleged sexual encounters were treated differently by the Tribe *on the basis of their gender*, a suspect classification.

On the record in this case, however, there is significant room for doubt as to whether the disparity of treatment resulted from the parties' gender. In addition to gender another consistent theme runs through the three prosecutions that form the universe from which the defense in these cases claims discriminatory selective prosecution-the older, perhaps sexually more mature, teenager was always charged. Indeed, it is possible that the prosecutor made his decision based on sexual maturity or age, nonsuspect classifications, rather than on the basis of gender. The fact that it was a *boy* who was the perceived sexual aggressor in each case may have been coincidental to the fact that in each case the perceived sexual aggressor was the older, more sexually mature minor. Had the Tribe made such a claim, this Court might have been tempted to rule that the defense failed to carry its initial burden of showing that the disparity in treatment was based solely on gender, since it could equally well have been the product of a judgment about age or sexual maturity. Since the Tribe made no such claim before his Court, however, the Court is reluctant to rest its decision solely on this grounds and will proceed with its analysis as if the defense had satisfied the first part of this standard of review, even though it has grave doubts as to the matter.

Has the Statute Been Applied in a Way Which Has a Discriminatory Effect and Is Motivated by a Discriminatory Purpose?

In reviewing the cases on appeal, it is difficult to consider three cases in which the three males have been charged and not the three females as having a significant discriminatory effect. Since the number of cases prosecuted is so few, it can be considered a result of coincidence rather than discriminatory effect. As noted above, it may also be a result of judgments about age or sexual maturity. Perhaps the next fact pattern to present itself will be a 17-year-old female and a 12-year-old male. In that fact pattern, the prosecutor indicated at oral argument that he would probably prosecute the female, suggesting that age or sexual maturity, not gender was the motivating purpose and that in a larger universe of cases no discriminatory effect would be demonstrable.

Nevertheless, even assuming that the limited class of three cases do rise to the level of discriminatory effect, is that compounded with a motivation that demonstrates a discriminatory purpose? There is simply no evidence in this record beyond the slight inferences that can be drawn from this limited class of three cases of an intent on the part of the Tribe or the prosecutor to discriminate against the accused on the basis of their gender. Absent such a clear showing of discriminatory effect and purpose the defendants' constitutional claims must fail.

Can the Tribe Demonstrate a Compelling Governmental Interest Supporting a Gender Distinction in the Prosecution of Second Degree Sexual Assault Cases Involving Minors?

The Tribe argues, among other things, that biological differences related to sexual maturity and pregnancy among teenagers Justify making prosecutorial decisions based on the gender (as well as age) of the underage minor. They focus on the fact that the charge involves sexual conduct, rather than say a robbery or burglary, and that gender is relevant to the issue of sex since underage sexual activity has different physiological, psychological, and economic consequences for young men and women, not the least of which is pregnancy (Tribe's Brief at pp. 19-23). Reduced to its barest level, the argument seems to be that since only women can become pregnant and therefore often suffer more harm from underage sexual activity than men. A prosecutor is justified in this narrow area of sexual activity in drawing gender based classifications to further the compelling governmental interest in preventing the unwanted harms of underage sexual activity to minors, including teenage pregnancies which have devastating economic, cultural, and social impacts on young Winnebago women. The Tribe also all too briefly refers to the traditional roles of men and women and the differences in the culture and history of the Winnebago Tribe in treatment of the sexes on matters relating to procreation as a further justification for its alleged gender based prosecution policy in second degree sexual assault cases involving underage sex (Tribe's Brief at p. 7).

The defendants argue that the Tribe's purported purpose of preventing pregnancy is simply not true since the statute is gender neutral on its face. Ignoring the fact that a statute may have multiple purposes, the defendants argue that the gender neutrality of the statute demonstrates that prevention of pregnancy was not *the* governmental interest that the Winnebago Tribal Council sought to further by adopting the second degree sexual assault statute prohibiting underage sex. They argue further that treating females differently due to greater risks of physical or psychological injury to them is to enshrine archaic stereotypes into the laws of the Winnebago Tribe (Defendants' Brief at p. 12 and p. 16).

To review the Tribe's asserted claims of a compelling governmental interest, it is essential to consider those claimed interests in the context of tribal custom and traditions. The archaic gender stereotypes and remnant of patriarchy denounced by the defendants are stereotypes and roles historically created and sanctioned (and now denounced) by the Anglo-American legal system, not by native cultures. This Court must consider whether the use of different roles based on gender, particularly in areas of sex and procreation, is of a similar discriminatory patriarchal nature when employed within the Winnebago Tribe, a political and cultural community with an entirely distinct history and tradition from that of the Euro-American legal communities.

To that end, as noted above, this Court and all Winnebago tribal courts are permitted by law and must consider tribal common law. Indeed, since the parties failed to present any evidence on tribal custom and tradition, in her decision in the *Bigfire* case below, Chief Judge Drobnick properly consulted an expert in tribal custom and tradition, Mr. David Lee Smith, the Cultural Preservation Officer and Tribal Historian of the Tribe, as she was authorized to do by WTC § 1-109. Indeed, this Court applauds her initiative in this matter and her efforts to conform her decision-making to tribal custom and tradition. Based on his report, she found that under traditional Winnebago customary law, gender differences commonly were drawn for the punishment of offenses related to sexual misconduct because of the natural biological differences in this area between the sexes, the different consequences of misconduct for men and women, and different roles ascribed by the tribal tradition to men and women (without creating any hierarchy or cross-gender disrespect).

While this Court similarly is authorized by WTC § 1-109 to independently consult tribal counselors or elders regarding tribal traditions and customary law, it felt no additional need to do so since all sources it consulted on this matter seem to agree on the point made by the report of the Tribe's Cultural Preservation Officer. The objective sources and observers all seem to agree that Ho-Chunk tradition recognizes *and respects* different roles for males and females in the Winnebago Tribe and, particularly, tolerates and encourages different responses to sexual misconduct for men and women.

In addition to the report of the Tribe's Cultural Preservation Officer set forth in full in the lower court opinion in *Bigfire*, other sources all point to traditional Ho-Chunk recognition of and respect for gender differences in matters of tribal life. Paul Radin, a noted anthropologist/ethnologist, wrote the classic western ethnographic work on Ho-Chunk culture, *The Winnebago Tribe*, in 1923. Although this work may be questioned as to some areas, much of his work is a detailed accounting of the customs and traditions of the Winnebago people. Much of what he recorded was verbatim records of what tribal informants told him about Winnebago culture and traditions. In his chapter on a System of Education, he quotes the teachings of a tribal member who said:

> My son, never abuse your wife. The women are sacred. If you abuse your wife and make her life miserable, you will die early. Our grandmother, the earth, is a woman, and in mistreating your wife you will be mistreating her. Most assuredly will you be abusing our grandmother if you act thus. And as it is she that is taking care of us you will really be killing yourself by such behavior. Radin at p. 122.

This quotation nicely summarizes Ho-Chunk thinking on gender relationships. Gender differences constitute a natural part of life. Indeed, the Earth, the Grandmother who gives life, is female. Thus, gender role differentiation and gender differences in legal or customary treatment related to those roles are natural and expected. In Ho-Chunk culture, therefore, gender differences or disparities in treatment do not signal hierarchy, lack of respect or invidious discrimination, but, rather, are a respected and natural part of life. They are, indeed, part of the way that the Winnebago world view brings meaning to life.

In short, the role of the women was seen by Ho-Chunk communities in a context that is not analogous to the roles of females in the Anglo-American cultures. Thus, it is not accurate to attribute the archaic stereotypes of the Anglo-American cultures to the Winnebago Tribe's culture.

The accounts collected by Paul Radin are indicative of the oral teachings to young people. Another section included this instruction:

> My daughters, if at any time you get married, never let your husband ask for a thing twice. Do it as soon as he asks you. If your husband's folks ever ask their children for something when you are present, assume that they had asked it of you. If there is anything to be done, do not wait till (sic) you are asked to do it, but do it immediately. If you act in this way then they will say that your parents taught you well. My son, if you find nothing else to do, take an ax and chop down a tree. It will become useful someday. Then take a gun and go out hunting and try to get game for your family. Radin at p. 132.

The only female member of this court is Ho-Chunk, although enrolled at the Ho-Chunk Nation of Wisconsin, rather than the Winnebago Tribe of Nebraska. She reports to this Court that Radin's accounts and those of the Tribe's Cultural Preservation Officer are not so vastly different than what young people may be told today by tribal elders. Specifically, she indicated:

> Although I am enrolled as a Ho-Chunk (formerly Wisconsin Winnebago). I consider myself to have been raised with some core values of the Winnebago. Thus, I personally view my role in terms of gender to be vastly different dependent on whether I am in an anglo/European setting or whether I am in a Winnebago tribal setting. The roles are not interchangeable nor are the values of the roles equally interpretative.[102] For example, I would not ask my husband, my brother or any male relative to rise and speak for me in role as an attorney or as an employee in the anglo/European systems. My non-Indian counterparts would be aghast at such archaic and stereotypical behavior. In fact, I would find it inappropriate in that setting. However, I have no hesitation nor feeling of inequality if I ask my husband, my brother or another male relative to speak for me in a Winnebago setting. In fact, I am proud to act in a manner that is consistent with my tribal mores and values as having been brought up properly by my family.

Can such contrasting customs and cultural traditions be analyzed under a single western legal standard? Does gender differentiation always mean the same thing as must the determination for determining whether illegal gender discrimination has occurred take account of the cultural context in which the question is asked. In this Court's view, the standard must attempt to combine what is necessary from both contexts. Since the legal concept of equal protection of the laws is an Anglo-American

---

[102] As I have taught Native American Law to many non-Indian students over the years, I have found it difficult to explain this simple notion to them as we study one case in particular which considers the membership of the tribe based on whether or not the parent is the mother or the father. It is difficult for non-Indians to grasp the concept of gender stereotypes and patriarchal hierarchies are not universal among nations and that legal gender differentiation therefore is not universally thought to be discriminatory or pejorative.

legal concept, this Court must look in part to the current American legal tradition to find that any *unjustified* gender differentiation drawn by the Tribe would violate the Tribe's constitutional guarantee of equal protection of the laws found in Article IV, Section 3(h) of the Constitution and By-Laws of the Winnebago Tribe of Nebraska, as amended. But this analysis must stop short of simply applying another standard to a different cultural system with a unique legal tradition without adjustments for or taking any account of that which is unique in that system. Accordingly, this Court finds that in applying the strict scrutiny standard it has announced for gender classifications, it must recognize that traditional differentiations, commonly accepted and practiced by the Tribe without pejorative or discriminatory implications, such as gender distinctions related to sexual conduct, must be sustained as involving the compelling tribal governmental interest of preserving tribal traditions and culture. What is tribally appropriate under Ho-Chunk tradition and customary law certainly was not rendered illegal and unconstitutional by the Tribe's own constitution!

In the context of these cases, it certainly was appropriate within a tribal legal system to apply tribal laws on second degree sexual abuse only to older males who had committed the crime and to make them more accountable. This Court's research into and understanding of Ho-Chunk tradition and customary law suggests that within the Winnebago culture, the male clearly is assigned the obligation of protecting the women.

The areas of sexual misconduct and domestic abuse were specifically singled out as areas in which the Winnebago tradition and customary law assigned roles and responsibilities based on gender. Thus, even if a discriminatory effect and motivation could be shown clearly by the defendants in these cases (which the Court doubts given the limited universe of cases and the prosecutor's explanation of his prosecution policy), the Tribe has a compelling governmental interest based on tribal traditions and usages for such gender differentiation in the area of sexual misconduct. Accordingly, the equal protection claims of the defendants in *Bigfire* and *C.L.* must fail.

While not bound by federal law in this appeal, this Court notes that any federal court hearing like appeals from federal or state prosecution decisions would probably arrive at a like conclusion, albeit by a very different process of analysis. In *Michael M. v. Superior Court*, 450 U.S. 464 (1981), the United States Supreme Court upheld against equal protection attack a state statutory rape statute (covering essentially the same conduct as WTC § 3-419(J)(C)) that by its terms applied only to males. It indicated that in areas of sexual misconduct gender classification was constitutionally permissible. The defendants in these cases creatively argue that since the Tribe adopted a gender neutral statutory rape statute, rather than one that was expressly gender selective, *Michael M.* is not analogous. Were federal constitutional decisions on this question binding on this Court, which they are not on a question of tribal law, this Court would be hard pressed to accept the defendants' argument. Reading the record in this case as favorably to the defendants as one can, the most that it shows is that the Tribe through selective prosecution accomplished *de facto* (i.e., by its behavior) precisely what the United States Constitution, according to *Michael M.* permits it to accomplish *de jure* (i.e., by express legal provision). We fail to see how that distinction could be constitutionally determinative.

While this Court finds that any gender differentiation that might actually have been employed on the facts of these cases would not violate the equal protection guarantees of Article IV, Section 3(h) of the Constitution and By-Laws of the Winnebago Tribe of Nebraska, it offers two important observations on the scope and meaning of its holding. First, this Court is not holding that since Winnebago customs recognize and sanction gender differentiation in some contexts, any and all gender discriminations are therefore legal under Winnebago law. Clearly, invidious gender discrimination practiced by the Tribe against members of either sex that cannot be supported by tribal custom or practice or any other compelling governmental interest will be struck down by the Winnebago courts as violating the Tribe's constitutional guarantees of equal protection of the laws. For example, should the Winnebago Tribal Council improvidently adopt a totally hypothetical tribal ordinance that assigned tribal enrollment through the mother's lineage, a Winnebago tribal court presumably would look quite unfavorably on such an ordinance as unsupported by any tribal custom or tradition (since Winnebago clan membership traditionally descends through the father's line) and irrationally discriminating on the basis of their gender. Second, while this Court holds that the Constitution and By-Laws of the Winnebago Tribe of Nebraska *permits* the Tribe to differentiate in prosecutions for violation of W T C § 3-419(1)(C) based on gender, that holding does not indicate that the tribal prosecutor should do so. In adopting a sexual abuse ordinance that was gender neutral, the Tribal Council plainly adopted a current tribal policy of furthering gender neutrality in this area as much as possible. Were a tribal prosecutor to adopt a policy of consistently making gender based prosecution decisions under this statute (a showing not made on the scanty record in this case), the tribal prosecutor clearly would be improperly substituting his judgment for that of the Tribal Council. If such a pattern of behavior were clearly and unambiguously shown, the Winnebago tribal courts might be prepared to enforce the policy adopted by the Tribal Council to reign in such a lawless pattern of prosecutorial misconduct. No such claim has been made, however, in this case and no clear and unambiguous showing has been made of such a pattern. All this Court is holding is that if such a pattern were shown it would not violate the Tribe's constitutional guarantee of equal protection of the laws, even though it might violate the policies underlying the gender-neutral language of WTC §3-419(1)(C). While the criminal defendants argue that the adoption of WTC § 3-419(1)(C) as a gender neutral statute overturns tribal tradition and renders selective prosecution based on gender unconstitutional, this Court cannot accept that argument. The gender neutrality of section 3-419(1)(C) merely reflects *current* tribal policy. It does not purport to and cannot overturn the Constitution and By-Laws of the Winnebago Tribe. Which *permits* (but does not require) such traditional gender differentiation in areas of sexual misconduct.

Whether This Court Has Jurisdiction over the L.W. Case

The Tribe appealed the L. W. case in part to secure review of the tribal court's interpretation of WTC § 3-419(1)(C) as requiring that the victim be brought under the dominion and control of the accused and the accused cross-appealed the denial of his motion to dismiss. Based in part on the trial judge's interpretation of WTC § 3-419(1)(C), however, L.W. was acquitted following trial. When asked at oral argument whether overturning the acquittal could result in double jeopardy in violation of Article IV, Section 3(c) of the Winnebago Constitution and By-Laws, as amended, the tribal prosecutor candidly conceded that it would, and, accordingly, indicated a willingness to drop the appeal. Since any new prosecution of L.W. for violation of section 3-419(1)(C) would violate his tribal constitutional protections against double jeopardy, this Court clearly lacks jurisdiction over the cross-appeals in the L. W. case and the appeal must be dismissed in conformity with the tribal prosecutor's acknowledgment at oral argument.

CONCLUSION

Based on the foregoing, the decision of the tribal court in *Bigfire*, SC 97-03, is affirmed. The Tribe did not violate the civil rights of the defendant by prosecuting him alone on this matter. The Tribe's appeal in L. W., SC 97-04, must be and hereby is dismissed without objection by the Tribe. Finally, the decision of the tribal court in *CL.*, SC 97-05, must be and hereby is reversed.

Egi Heskekjen
It is so ordered.

8

Commentary on *Commonwealth v. Blache*

MARIE-AMÉLIE GEORGE

It is all but axiomatic that the gravamen of sexual assault is nonconsent, rather than force or violence. The law, however, does not always reflect that principle, particularly when alcohol is involved. Courts have struggled to resolve how intoxicated a person must be before they are incapable of consenting, at which point any sexual intercourse will establish the *actus reus* of rape. Even more contested is the *mens rea* requirement, with jurisdictions divided on whether defendants must know about the victim's incapacity to consent before they are liable for sexual assault. Fueling these arguments is a broader debate over rape law and policy: whether criminal law should be punishing the *actus reus* of nonconsensual sex or the blameworthy *mens rea* of the perpetrator. In *Commonwealth v. Blache*, the Massachusetts Supreme Judicial Court indicated that criminal law was primarily concerned with punishing bad actors who meant to cause the victim harm.[1] The rewritten feminist judgment, on the other hand, emphasizes that victims suffer regardless of the perpetrator's intent. The opinions thus come to different outcomes because they define the harm of rape in fundamentally different ways.

Consent is complicated when one or both parties are intoxicated. Most jurisdictions have specific provisions that criminalize sexual intercourse with a heavily intoxicated victim when the perpetrator surreptitiously provided the intoxicant.[2] The more difficult cases involve those where victims are voluntarily intoxicated, meaning they consumed drugs or alcohol of their own free will. This scenario is all too common, particularly since alcohol has become a primary means of facilitating social interactions.[3] Sexual assault between people who know each other, often called acquaintance or date rape, is the most common form of rape;[4] a large

---

[1] 880 N.E.2d 736, 738–739 (Mass. 2008).
[2] Patricia J. Falk, *Rape by Drugs: A Statutory Overview and Proposals for Reform*, 44 ARIZ. L. REV. 131, 192 (2002).
[3] JENNIFER S. HIRSCH & SHAMUS KHAN, SEXUAL CITIZENS: A LANDMARK STUDY OF SEX, POWER, AND ASSAULT ON CAMPUS 83 (2020).
[4] Jeffrey S. Jones, *Comparison of Sexual Assaults by Strangers Versus Known Assailants in a Community-Based Population*, 22 AM. J. EMERGENCY MED. 454, 454 (2004).

percentage these types of sexual assaults occur when the victim is heavily intoxicated.[5] Just as victims are more likely to be assaulted when they have consumed drugs or alcohol, so too are perpetrators more likely to commit assault when they are inebriated.[6]

When a victim is intoxicated, defendants are typically charged under prohibitions on sexual intercourse with an incapacitated person.[7] Intoxication thus becomes analogous to unconsciousness, sleep, or illness, all of which render the victim incapable of consenting. Of course, intoxication and nonconsent are not synonyms; alcohol consumption can give rise to welcomed, mutually desired sexual encounters.[8] Intoxication creates a spectrum that ranges from impairment in cognitive functioning to complete unconsciousness. Courts have struggled to pinpoint where incapacitation, and therefore the *actus reus* of rape, is situated on that scale.[9] Part of the challenge is that the boundary between intoxication and incapacitation is often blurry, and the point in time when a victim crosses the threshold from one to the other can be impossible to identify. The most common test that courts use is that a person must be so incapacitated as to be unable to appraise or control their conduct.[10] Some jurisdictions apply a similar framework, requiring that the victim be unable to understand "the nature and consequences" of the sexual act.[11] However, other states focus on the victim's inability to resist the sexual assault.[12]

The *mens rea* requirement is even more complex and controversial. A minority of jurisdictions impose strict liability on defendants, but most states permit mistake of fact defenses.[13] In these latter jurisdictions, a defendant either must have known or reasonably should have known that the victim was so intoxicated as to be incapable of consenting.[14] Mistakes of fact can enter a case in one of two ways: a defendant's reasonable mistake as to the victim's ability to consent may be an element the prosecution needs to disprove or it may be an affirmative defense for the defendant to raise.[15]

Feminist scholars have critiqued mistake of fact defenses in sexual assault cases in part because they turn attention away from the harm of nonconsensual sex and instead focus the inquiry on the blameworthiness of the defendant. Additionally, these defenses tend to allow juries to hear about and consider a victim's sexual

---

[5] Michal Buchhandler-Raphael, *The Conundrum of Voluntary Intoxication and Sex*, 82 BROOK. L. REV. 1031, 1032 (2017).
[6] HIRSCH & KHAN, *supra* note 3, at 61.
[7] Buchhandler-Raphael, *supra* note 5, at 1033.
[8] *Id.* at 1037.
[9] *Id.* at 1058–1059.
[10] Falk, *supra* note 2, at 195–196.
[11] Samar A. Shams, *Rape*, 3 GEO. J. GENDER & L. 609 (2002).
[12] Falk, *supra* note 2, at 195–196.
[13] Kit Kinports, *Rape and Force: The Forgotten Mens Rea*, 4 BUFF. CRIM. L. REV. 755, 758 (2001).
[14] Marlene A. Attardo, *Defense of Mistake of Fact as to Victim's Consent in Rape Prosecution*, 102 A.L.R.5th 447 (2002).
[15] Falk, *supra* note 2, at 162.

history. Although rape shield laws generally prohibit defendants from introducing evidence of their victim's sexual past, legislators and judges alike have carved out exceptions for a defendant with a reasonable, yet mistaken belief, concerning the victim's consent.[16] Both of these criticisms of the mistake of fact defense point to a singular problem: The defense undermines the purpose of sexual assault statutes, which is to protect individuals from unwanted sexual activity.[17]

THE ORIGINAL OPINION

Before *Commonwealth v. Blache*, Massachusetts did not allow juries to consider a defendant's mistake as to consent. Instead, defendants were strictly liable when they engaged in sexual intercourse with a complainant who was incapable of consenting. The *Blache* decision thus transformed the jurisdiction from a strict liability to a negligence regime when a victim is voluntarily intoxicated.

The facts of *Blache*, like many sexual assault cases, are deeply troubling. The defendant, a police officer, responded to the scene of an accident, where he met the extremely inebriated complainant. Not only had the complainant driven her car into a fence, but her behavior during the forty-five minutes that the defendant drafted his report ranged from outlandish to offensive.[18] The complainant licked the patrol car windows, pulled down her pants and urinated on the street, and grabbed the defendant's genitals.[19] After the defendant drove the complainant home, they engaged in what the defendant claimed was consensual sexual intercourse.[20] The complainant, for her part, dialed 911.[21] A toxicology expert calculated that, at the time of the assault, the complainant's blood alcohol level would have been more than two to three times higher than the legal limit to drive.[22]

A jury convicted the defendant of rape, but Massachusetts Supreme Judicial Court reversed that decision because of problems with two of the instructions. The first related to the *actus reus* requirement. The judge had informed the jury that a person was incapable of consenting if her level of intoxication rendered her "wholly insensible."[23] On appeal, the court ruled that this instruction insufficiently distinguished between mere intoxication and incapacity, as it was "a matter of common knowledge that there are many levels of intoxication."[24] In a companion case

---

[16] Michelle J. Anderson, *From Chastity Requirement to Sexuality License: Sexual Consent and a New Rape Shield Law*, 70 GEO. WASH. L. REV. 51, 110 (2002).
[17] Falk, *supra* note 2, at 199.
[18] *Com. v. Blache*, 880 N.E.2d 736, 738–739 (Mass. 2008).
[19] *Id.* at 739.
[20] *Id.*
[21] *Id.* at 740.
[22] *Id.*
[23] *Id.*
[24] *Id.* at 742.

decided the same day, *Commonwealth v. Urban*, the court emphasized "that an extreme degree of intoxication is required before the incapacity rule will apply."[25] As a result, in *Blache*, the court held that incapacity was only relevant when "the complainant's physical or mental condition was so impaired [due to her intoxication] that she could not give consent."[26] In doing so, it rejected the defendant's argument that a complainant had to be nearly unconscious, and therefore unable to communicate her lack of consent, to qualify as incapacitated.[27]

The second error was that the trial judge did not provide an instruction concerning the defendant's possible mistake of fact as to the complainant's incapacity. At the time of the decision, Massachusetts was an outlier among the states by not allowing defendants to argue mistake of fact.[28] In a previous case, *Commonwealth v. Lopez*, the Massachusetts Supreme Judicial Court had rejected the mistake of fact defense because, unlike other jurisdictions, Massachusetts defined rape as a general intent crime.[29] Since the prosecution needed to prove only that the defendant engaged in sexual intercourse by force and that the victim did not consent to the activity, the defendant's state of mind as to the victim's consent was irrelevant as a matter of law.[30] In most other jurisdictions, intent was an element of the crime, and therefore a mistake of fact could negate liability. The *Lopez* Court also expressed concern that permitting the defense might result in victims having to resist the crimes with force to communicate an unqualified lack of consent.[31] Consequently, the defense could "eviscerate the long-standing rule in this Commonwealth that victims need not use any force to resist an attack."[32]

The Massachusetts Supreme Judicial Court changed course in *Blache*, permitting mistake of fact defenses in cases involving a voluntarily intoxicated victim. In doing so, it aligned itself with most states, which permit defendants to raise this defense. The court reasoned that, since the only force required in these situations was that necessary for penetration, incapacity cases turned on the victim's consent.[33] Where the victim was voluntarily intoxicated, defendants had a greater likelihood of making a mistake as to the complainant's capacity to consent.[34] The court thus imposed an additional burden on the prosecution, holding that the Commonwealth must prove that "the defendant knew or reasonably should have known that the complainant's condition rendered her incapable of consenting to the sexual act."[35]

---

[25] *Com. v. Urban*, 880 N.E.2d 753, 758 (Mass. 2008).
[26] *Blache*, 880 N.E.2d at 746–747.
[27] *Id.* at 742.
[28] Attardo, *supra* note 14.
[29] 745 N.E.2d 961, 965–966 (Mass. 2001).
[30] *Id.*
[31] *Id.* at 967.
[32] *Id.*
[33] *Blache*, 880 N.E.2d at 744.
[34] *Id.*
[35] *Id.* at 745.

Blache therefore made mistake of fact an element of the crime, rather than an affirmative defense. The court was quick to emphasize that mistake of fact only applied to cases in which a victim was voluntarily intoxicated and that it continued to reject the defense in rape cases more generally.[36] By limiting mistake of fact defenses to voluntary intoxication cases, the court introduced an inconsistency in Massachusetts rape law.

THE FEMINIST JUDGMENT

In the rewritten opinion, Professor Ben McJunkin affirms the defendant's conviction. Unlike the original opinion, he maintains strict liability as the *means rea* for cases in which a victim is voluntarily intoxicated, rather than the negligence standard the *Blache* Court adopted. Thus, rather than emphasizing the potential risk to unwitting defendants, the rewritten opinion reinforces that criminal law should be concerned with the harm of nonconsensual sex.

McJunkin follows much of the same reasoning as the original decision, particularly that mistake of fact defenses in rape cases are inappropriate as a matter of statutory interpretation and judicial precedent. However, he comes to a different conclusion from the original opinion because of his answer to the policy question associated with the mistake of fact defense. As the rewritten opinion recognizes, the most persuasive argument for the mistake of fact defense is "the increased likelihood of punishing honest mistakes." Where this concern tipped the scales for the *Blache* Court in favor of permitting the mistake of fact defense, the feminist judgment proceeds in the opposite direction. As McJunkin argues, although delineating the boundary between intoxication and incapacity is not an easy task, "there is wisdom in requiring defendants to walk that line at their own peril." According to McJunkin, the question for the court was whether the risk of nonconsensual intercourse should be borne by the sexual aggressor or the impaired party. The original decision put the burden on the complainant; the rewritten opinion shifts the onus onto the defendant.

Debates over how to define consent in cases involving voluntarily intoxicated victims are continuing, particularly given that the focus of sexual assault reform has shifted to college campuses where alcohol is a prominent feature of many social activities.[37] The rewritten opinion thus provides a framework that is as important today as it was when the Massachusetts Court decided *Blache*. As McJunkin emphasizes, consent is not in the eyes of the beholder. Rather, consent is an essential fact that individuals must secure before a sexual encounter. The feminist judgment thus enshrines consent as the touchstone of the law, thereby ensuring that rape laws protect all victims of nonconsensual sexual intercourse.

---

[36] *Id.* at 748.
[37] Aya Gruber, *Consent Confusion*, 38 Cardozo L. Rev. 415 (2016).

COMMONWEALTH V. BLACHE, 880 N.E.2D 736 (MASS. 2008)

JUSTICE BEN A. MCJUNKIN DELIVERED THE OPINION OF THE COURT

It has been more than two decades since our own Justice Frederick L. Brown, of the Massachusetts Appeals Court, famously proclaimed that there is "no social utility in establishing a rule defining non-consensual intercourse on the basis of the subjective (and quite likely wishful) view of the more aggressive player in the sexual encounter." *Commonwealth v. Lefkowitz*, 20 Mass. App. Ct. 513, 521 (1985) (Brown, J., concurring). That perspective has been, and continues to be, the prevailing legal view in Massachusetts. Accordingly, our rape law has never allowed a mistake-of-fact defense with respect to the element of sexual consent.

The defendant here, a Methuen Police Department officer convicted by a jury of raping a woman who was in his protective custody due to her level of intoxication, implores us to adopt a new perspective. He argues that his subjective perceptions of his victim's intoxication should excuse the harm he imposed by engaging in sexual intercourse with someone physically incapable of consenting. This we decline to do, just as this Court has declined every similar entreaty, in every context made, since 1642.

We took this appeal, along with a companion case, *Commonwealth v. Urban*, 450 Mass. 608 (2008), to clarify the current state of rape law in the Commonwealth. For the reasons explained below, the judgment of the Appeals Court is affirmed.

I.

A.

Just before 2 a.m. on the morning of August 18, 2000, the Methuen Police Department received a 911 call from David MacRae. MacRae was requesting police assistance to remove an unwanted and very intoxicated female guest from his home. The department dispatched Officer David Blache, the defendant, to respond to the call.

When the defendant arrived on the scene, MacRae briefly advised him of the situation. MacRae had spent the evening drinking with the complainant,[38] MacRae's friend, Allan Castro, and the complainant's coworker, Deborah Foss. MacRae and the complainant had been dating for about a week at the time. Over the course of the night, the foursome traversed the city, finding their way into various bars in both Haverhill and Lawrence, including a biker bar and a blues club. At each venue, the complainant consumed several drinks. She would later testify that, in addition to

---

[38] In accordance with the longstanding practice of this Court, the complainant remains anonymous.

drinking "a lot" that evening, she had also smoked marijuana and ingested the anti-anxiety medication Klonopin. At the final drinking establishment, the complainant became belligerent, made a scene, and picked fights with other patrons. As the group left that bar, shortly before closing, the complainant was argumentative, had difficulty walking, and fell twice. Foss helped to stabilize the complainant until they reached McRae's car. Because the complainant was too inebriated to drive, McRae drove the complainant to his home while Castro used the complainant's keys to ensure that her car followed.

Once at MacRae's home, the complainant continued acting out aggressively. She told MacRae that she did not like him, and that she only wanted him for sex. When MacRae suggested that she needed sleep and should leave, the complainant began hitting and kicking him. MacRae threatened to call the police, but the complainant stated that she would falsely tell the police that MacRae had been hitting her. About forty-five minutes after they had arrived at MacRae's, the complainant grabbed her keys and attempted to drive home. She instead drove into a fence and then backed into MacRae's house with her vehicle. It was at this point that MacRae took her keys and called to request police assistance, informing the dispatcher that the complainant was "way beyond drunk" and that he wanted her removed from the premises.

Due to her intoxicated state, the complainant has only intermittent memories of the evening. While waiting for the police to arrive, she had apparently "passed out" in MacRae's bedroom. When she awoke, the defendant was already on the scene. The complainant approached the defendant and initially informed him that MacRae had punched her. The defendant did not observe any indications that this might be true, and he testified later that he believed she was lying. Witnesses testified that the complainant appeared to still be drunk and was slurring her speech.

The defendant concluded that the complainant was obviously in no condition to drive. He arranged for a tow truck to transport the complainant's car while he collected information for the accident report. According to testimony from MacRae, Castro, the defendant, the tow truck driver, and a passenger in the tow truck, the complainant made numerous sexual advances toward the defendant during this period. Among other things, the complainant attempted to kiss the defendant, attempted to grab his crotch on several occasions, and asked him numerous times if he would like to have sex with her. The defendant repeatedly rejected the complainant's overtures, proclaiming to those on the scene that he had a wife and kids.

At some point, the complainant pulled down her pants and began urinating in the street in front of MacRae's house. The defendant stopped her, asked her to pull her pants up, gave her a napkin, and instructed her to go urinate in the woods. When the complainant returned, she complained of being cold. The defendant offered her a seat in the front seat of his cruiser. There, she activated the car's lights and siren. When the defendant told her to stop, she again pulled down her pants to expose her genitals. At some point, the complainant lifted her shirt and licked the inside of the cruiser window.

Because the complainant did not have money for a cab, the defendant called his department to request permission to drive her home. The Methuen Police Department has a policy requiring two officers present when transporting an individual. The commanding officer, however, gave the defendant permission to drive the complainant home unaccompanied. The officer reminded the defendant to report his mileage when he returned the complainant home, a departmental policy intended to ensure that such trips do not involve any detours. While the defendant was on the phone with the department, the complainant again activated the cruiser's lights and removed her pants while in the police vehicle. The defendant finished his call and eventually moved the complainant to the cruiser's back seat, even as she persisted in making additional sexual advances toward him. The defendant, with the complainant in the back seat, left MacRae's house about forty-five minutes after he had arrived.

It is at this point that accounts of the evening diverge. On direct appeal from a criminal conviction, we must view the evidence in the light most favorable to the Commonwealth. *Commonwealth v. Latimore*, 378 Mass. 671, 676–77 (1979). We therefore recite the facts that the jury could have found, reserving some details for later discussion. According to the complainant, she remembers complying with the defendant's request at MacRae's house that she move to the back seat. She has no further memory until the defendant parked the cruiser next to a dumpster in an unfamiliar parking lot. At this point, the defendant opened the back-seat door behind the driver's side, pulled down the complainant's pants, unzipped his own, and vaginally raped her. She remembers saying more than three times that she did not want to have sex. She tried to kick the partition separating the front and back seats, as well as to kick the defendant, yet she was unable to get out from under him. When the defendant later drove her home, he warned her that the police have a "code of silence" and that nobody would believe her if she were to report the attack.[39]

Although she does not remember any of them, the complainant appears to have made at least four phone calls from her home after the defendant left. Castro testified that he answered two calls from the complainant at MacRae's house, each about thirty minutes after the defendant and complainant had departed. On the first call, the complainant reportedly said, "Tell Dave [MacRae] thanks for the best fuck of my life," and then hung up. In a second call, a few minutes later, she said, "Tell Dave I'm going to go for the whole rape thing," and hung up. At 3:26 a.m., the Haverhill Police Department received a tearful 911 call from the complainant

---

[39] By contrast, the defendant's testimony – which the jury was not required to credit – was that he drove the complainant home, walked her to her front door, and unlocked it for her. He claims to have returned to his cruiser and radioed in his mileage, per protocol. However, he testified that he then returned to the complainant's home and asked to use her restroom. According to the defendant, when he exited the restroom, the complainant was already fully naked. He claims that they embraced, that the complainant voluntarily performed oral sex on him, and that they had consensual intercourse on her couch. He testified that he was inside her home for about five minutes.

reporting that she was raped. The complainant then called 911 a second time, thirteen minutes later, to ask whether officers were coming.

Officer Penny Durand was dispatched to the victim's home, along with another officer. Officer Durand testified that the complainant was quite upset and appeared to still be intoxicated during this encounter. After speaking with the complainant, the officers convinced her to go to the hospital to have a rape kit performed. A hospital nurse similarly described the complainant as agitated, upset, and distraught, yet alert as to person, place, and time. The nurse recorded the complainant's blood-alcohol content (BAC) as 0.14 percent at 7:30 a.m. Marijuana was also detected in her blood. Another doctor estimated that the complainant's BAC at the time of intercourse would have been between 0.176 and 0.240 percent, which would cause confusion, disorientation, imbalance, impaired perception, loss of judgment, lethargy, memory loss, and slurred speech. The Massachusetts State Police Crime Lab determined that the defendant was the source of sperm found on the complainant's vaginal swab. The zipper area of the defendant's pants also tested positive for semen. No sperm was found in the oral swab, and semen was not detected in the rear seat of the police cruiser.

B.

The defendant was indicted for one count of rape, in violation of Mass. G.L. c. 265, § 22(b) (1). Following a jury trial that spanned 10 days, the jurors returned a verdict of guilty and the defendant was sentenced to a term of 8–10 years in state prison. Several incidents during the course of the trial are relevant to the defendant's appeal.

On the second day of trial, the Commonwealth's attorney informed the court that a news article about the case had appeared in the *Lawrence Eagle Tribune*. The article contained factual errors, including stating that the defendant was facing three counts of rape, rather than one. The trial judge questioned the jury and learned that one juror had read the article the night before. The judge conducted two colloquies with the juror at sidebar, first inquiring whether the juror had gleaned any information from the article that had not yet been presented at trial and then instructing the juror regarding the factual inaccuracies in the article. Having concluded that the juror's impartiality had not been compromised, the judge instructed the entire jury that the defendant was facing only a single count of rape, and they should not factor extraneous information into their deliberations.

During closing arguments, the prosecutor emphasized that the defendant had violated his duty as a sworn police officer. In particular, the prosecutor made the following statements:

> This is really a very simple case. This is a case about a police officer who was on duty, who was responding to a call. And he had a duty, a duty to protect the public,

in this case a duty to protect a vulnerable young woman who was highly intoxicated and behaving out of control. He abused the power of his position. He violated his duty by having forcible sexual intercourse with her against her will. And, members of the jury, this is a lot more than a dereliction of duty. This is a crime because it was by force and it was against her will.

The defense did not object to this argument at the time.

The trial judge then instructed the jury regarding rape, including an instruction on incapacity to consent. That instruction informed the jury that a person may be so intoxicated that they are "wholly insensible so as to be incapable of consenting." The defense also requested that the trial judge instruct the jurors on the possibility that the defendant made a reasonable mistake of fact about whether the complainant had consented. Because Massachusetts courts have never recognized a mistake-of-consent defense to rape, the trial court refused the instruction.

During deliberations, the jury submitted a question to the judge asking to clarify the definition of "wholly insensible." Over the defendant's objection, the judge instructed the jury to "apply your collective understanding of what those words mean in our ordinary discourse and … with some discussion among yourselves, decide the meaning of those words. Each word by itself is plain and are words that are used in ordinary discourse, and I cannot give you any further legal definition or clarification."

On direct appeal, the defendant raised three claims of error. The Appeals Court rejected each of the defendant's claims and affirmed his conviction in an unpublished summary memorandum, pursuant to its Rule 1:28.

II.

The defendant's central claim of error concerns the jury's instructions. In accordance with Massachusetts law, the jury was instructed that a person may be rendered incapable of consenting due to excessive intoxication. The defendant now claims that the jury should also have been instructed to consider his subjective perceptions about whether the complainant was incapable of consenting. To be clear, there can be little doubt that the defendant was aware of the complainant's intoxication. Rather, he claims to have been mistaken about whether the complainant was in fact *so intoxicated* as to be legally incapacitated.

The defendant concedes that our rape law has never permitted such an instruction. His own brief admits that, under the current law, "any perception (reasonable, honest, or otherwise) of a defendant as to a purported victim's consent is irrelevant to a rape prosecution." He nevertheless calls for a change in our law. He points to "an abundance of evidence regarding equivocal conduct" by the complainant on the night in question from which he claims to have drawn the erroneous inference that she was not incapacitated. Moreover, defense counsel stressed at oral argument that our most recent opinion rejecting a similar mistake-of-consent defense in a different context may have left the door open for subsequent judicial reform. *See Commonwealth v. Lopez*, 433 Mass. 722 (2001) (rejecting a mistake-of-consent defense in cases of forcible rape).

Today, we take the take the opportunity to close any door that we may have left open. We see myriad reasons for rejecting a mistake-of-consent defense in cases of a complainant's incapacity, just as we do in cases of forceable rape.

A.

Apart from recognizing that the harm of rape can befall any person, Massachusetts's rape law remains largely unchanged from the days of Hale and Blackstone. *See generally* 1 Hale P. C. 628; 4 Bl. Com. 210. Our earliest rape law statute was passed in 1642. *Commonwealth v. Burke*, 105 Mass. 376, 380 (1870). It punished carnal copulation of a woman by force and against her will. *Id.* The current statutory incarnation of our law similarly defines rape as sexual intercourse compelled by force and against the complainant's will. G.L. c. 265, § 22(b).

The requirement that intercourse be "against the will" of the complainant merely reflects that the sexual act must be nonconsensual. *See Burke*, 105 Mass. at 377 ("The earlier and more weighty authorities show that the words 'against her will,' in the standard definitions, mean exactly the same thing as 'without her consent;' and that the distinction between these phrases, as applied to this crime, which has been suggested in some modern books, is unfounded."). Importantly, under our law, nonconsent describes an objective state of affairs. *Commonwealth v. Lopez*, 433 Mass. 722, 727 (2001). "The simple question, expressed in the briefest form, is, Was the [complainant] willing or unwilling?" *Burke*, 105 Mass. at 377. This is so because rape law, since its earliest days, has been a general intent crime. *Id.* (citing David P. Bryden, *Redefining Rape*, 3 Buff. Crim. L. Rev. 317, 325 (2000) ("At common law, rape was a 'general intent' crime; the requite intention was merely to perform the sexual act, rather than have nonconsensual intercourse.")). Although the Commonwealth must prove that the complainant's nonconsent is "honest and real," it is not obligated to prove that the defendant knew or intended that the sexual intercourse would be without consent. *Commonwealth v. Cordeiro*, 401 Mass. 843, 851 n. 11 (1988).

Accordingly, Massachusetts has never recognized a mistake-of-consent defense to rape. A mistake of fact can operate as a defense to a crime only when it negates the existence of a material mental element of the offense. *See* Model Penal Code § 2.04(1) (1) (1985). Because our statute does not require the defendant to have any mental state with respect to the element of nonconsent, a defendant's beliefs about a complainant's consent are necessarily legally irrelevant. *See, e.g., Ascolillo*, 4105 Mass. at 465 ("We have never suggested that 'in order to establish the crime of rape the Commonwealth must prove in every case not only that the defendant intended intercourse but also that he did not act pursuant to an honest and reasonable belief that the victim consented.'" (quoting *Commonwealth v. Grant*, 391 Mass. 645, 651 (1984))).

B.

Recently, in *Commonwealth v. Lopez*, we again declined a defendant's invitation to overturn our prior decisions and to create a mistake-of-consent defense. In so doing, however, we acknowledged that our rejection of the defense places Massachusetts among a small, but significant, minority of states. 433 Mass. at 732. And our opinion there was ultimately a narrow one. Given the specific factual context, we announced only that the case "does not persuade us that we should recognize a mistake of fact as to consent as a defense to rape in *all* cases." *Id.* at 732 (emphasis in original). Indeed, we explicitly preserved the opportunity to reconsider the mistake-of-consent defense in subsequent cases. *See id.* ("Whether such a defense might, in some circumstances, be appropriate is a difficult question that we may consider on a future case where a defendant's claim of reasonable mistake of fact is at least arguably supported by the evidence.").

We nevertheless found in *Lopez* that our longstanding rule continued to be supported by the weight of reasons. First, we explained that recognizing a mistake-of-consent defense in cases of incapacity would inappropriately encroach on a legislative prerogative. *Id.* at 730. Second, we expressed our concern that a mistake-of-consent defense might resurrect the outmoded requirement that a complainant resist her attacker. *Lopez*, 433 Mass. at 729. Lastly, we noted that good-faith mistakes as to consent seemed implausible in cases where the sexual intercourse was compelled by force or threats of force. *Id.* at 729.

Those same reasons continue to support our rejection of the mistake-of-consent defense in the context of a complainant's incapacity due to intoxication. The defendant's attempts to distinguish forcible rape from the rape of an incapacitated person are both unwise and unavailing.

1.

To start, we once again emphasize that adopting an affirmative defense, such as mistake-of-consent, is essentially a legislative function. Our rape law expresses in no uncertain terms that sexual intercourse with an incapacitated person is prohibited. G.L. c. 265, § 22. It does not provide for a mistake-of-consent defense. Most states that recognize such a defense have adopted it through express legislation. *Id.* at 730 (citing Alaska, Colorado, Oregon, New Jersey, and Texas as examples). Yet the legislature of this Commonwealth has consistently declined to adopt the defense, even while updating our rape law statute in other ways. The most recent revision to G.L. c. 265, § 22 came not a decade ago – well after many of this Court's most prominent decisions declining to recognize a mistake-of-consent defense. *See, e.g.*,

Grant, 391 Mass. at 650; *Ascolillo*, 405 Mass. at 463; *Cordeiro*, 410 Mass. at 851 n. 11. It has long been the view of this Court that legislative inaction under such circumstances should be treated as legislative support for the existing judicial interpretation. *Nichols v. Vaughan*, 217 Mass. 548, 551 (1914).

Moreover, recognizing a mistake-of-consent defense in cases of incapacity presents particularly vexing challenges to the administration of justice that further counsel in favor of awaiting legislative intervention. Determining the precise point at which intoxication becomes so overwhelming as to render a complainant incapable of consenting is already a challenging factual inquiry for a judge or jury. A mistake-of-consent defense would compound that challenge. It would require a factfinder to divine the particular inferences that a defendant may or may not have made about the complainant's level of intoxication, frequently without any direct testimony from the defendant on the matter. With such a defense so easily raised, the Commonwealth could not be confident bringing a prosecution unless the fact of incapacitation (not just intoxication) was so obvious that no reasonable person could have mistakenly believed otherwise. The practical result is that we would effectively make the defendant's mental state with respect to nonconsent an element of the Commonwealth's case. This would be a dramatic change to the unbroken history of our rape law, which has never required such proof. *Cf. id.* at 727 ("Historically, the relevant inquiry has been limited to consent in fact, and no *mens rea* or knowledge as to the lack of consent has ever been required."). And we fear that, in so doing, we would further deter prosecutions for rape, a crime which is already widely under-reported and under-prosecuted. *See Commonwealth v. King*, 445 Mass. 217, 237 n.18 (2005) (detailing the widespread under-reporting of rape).

Under our precedent, this conclusion alone forecloses the defendant's challenge. *See Com. v. Miller*, 385 Mass. 521, 525 (1982) (a request to adopt a mistake defense in rape cases "should be addressed to the Legislature"). We nevertheless proceed in our opinion so as to underscore the weighty interests at stake in this question beyond separation-of-powers concerns.

2.

As we explained in *Lopez*, to recognize a mistake-of-consent defense risks rolling back an important evolution in our rape law regarding how we evaluate the resistance offered by a complainant. For too long, our rape law required that a complainant respond to an attack in a prescribed manner – including by offering physical or verbal resistance to her attacker – in order to support a finding of nonconsent. *See Commonwealth v. Sherry*, 386 Mass. 682, 688 (1982) (citing *Commonwealth v. McDonald*, 110 Mass. 405, 406 (1872)). This is no longer the case. Indeed, if extraneous force or threats are used to compel sexual intercourse, that force alone now suffices to establish nonconsent. *See Lefkowitz*, 20 Mass. App. Ct. at 519. No further showing is required by the Commonwealth. *Id.* On the other hand, where nonconsent is established by the complainant's incapacity to consent – for example, unconsciousness, sleep, illness, or intoxication – the element of force is satisfied merely by proof of "such force as was necessary to accomplish" the act of sexual intercourse itself. *Burke*, 105 Mass. at 380–381. A defendant need not overcome, and a complainant need not offer, any resistance whatsoever.

The move away from a resistance requirement in rape law is a product of two separate commitments. The first is to take seriously complainants' accounts of the varied human responses to unwelcome sexual violation. *See generally* Michelle J. Anderson, *Negotiating Sex*, 78 So. Cal. L. Rev. 1401, 1414–1421 (2005) (detailing fundamental problems with evaluating legal consent by reference to the complainant's behavior, whether the absence of resistance or the presence of affirmative permission). The second commitment is to refocus our rape law on punishing the harm caused by the defendant rather than judging the propriety of the complainant's behavior. Rape law's historical ties to criminal prohibitions on adultery and fornication have for too long clouded the inquiry into a defendant's culpability with social attitudes stigmatizing female sexuality. *See* Anne M. Coughlin, *Sex and Guilt*, 84 Va. L. Rev. 1, 45 (1998) ("Though our system no longer punishes anyone directly for fornication or adultery, the substantive elements of rape still are calibrated so as to require women to prove – as a condition for convicting the men who violated their interest in sexual self-determination – that they should not be held responsible for one of those offenses.").

We fear that a mistake-of-consent defense in cases of incapacity, which shifts the central factual inquiry from whether the complainant was in fact "wholly insensible so as to be incapable of consenting" to whether the defendant *believed* that the complainant was wholly insensible, would once again center the factual inquiry on the complainant's outward conduct toward the defendant. It would require a factfinder to scrutinize the words, actions, and strategic choices of complainants who are not on trial in order to assess the reasonableness of a defendant's belief. *Cf. Commonwealth v. Bailey*, 370 Mass. 388, 394 (1976) (noting the "common observation, supported by some empirical data, [that] juries tend toward considerable and perhaps inordinate skepticism in rape cases, above all where there is a suggestion of willingness or acquiescence on the part of the victim"). We are particularly mindful that such an inquiry will be made against a social backdrop in which men have historically and routinely misinterpreted women's actions as expressing desire when none is present. *See* Anderson, *supra*, at 1406. As a result, a mistake-of-consent defense could have the unfortunate effect of reinstating a *de facto* requirement that a complainant actively resist a sexual aggressor in order to defeat an inference that the defendant made an honest and reasonable mistake as to consent. This would be an especially unfair requirement in cases of incapacity, where criminalization is itself premised on circumstances that render a vulnerable complainant particularly unable or unlikely to resist. A mistake-of-consent defense is therefore simply incompatible with the progress our rape law jurisprudence has made to combat historically entrenched misogyny. *See* Lefkowitz, 20 Mass. App. Ct. at 521 n.1 (Brown, J., concurring) ("Old cultural patterns – no matter how entrenched – must adapt to developing concepts of equality." (quoting Alan Deshowitz, *New Rape Laws Needed*, Boston Herald American (June 24, 1985), at 19, col. 1)).

3.

The most persuasive argument for crafting a separate rule for cases of incapacity is the increased likelihood of punishing honest mistakes. In *Lopez*, we satisfied ourselves that proof of extraneous force in rape cases would necessarily "negate any possible mistake as to consent." *Lopez*, 433 Mass. at 729. In cases of incapacity, however, such extraneous force is not required. *Burke*, 105 Mass. at 380–381. We therefore must reckon with the reality that some defendants will genuinely misapprehend whether an intoxicated partner possesses the capacity to consent. We are not persuaded, however, that the costs of such mistakes must, as a rule, be borne by the impaired party rather than the mistaken one.

Massachusetts has a long history of so-called "strict liability" criminal prohibitions.[40] *See, e.g., Commonwealth v. Mixer*, 207 Mass. 141, 142–143 (1910) (collecting cases from Nineteenth and Twentieth centuries). Such prohibitions elevate the protection of potential victims above law's traditional commitment to punish only conscious wrongdoing. *See Commonwealth v. Miller*, 385 Mass. 521, 524 (1982) ("[The] existence of a *mens rea* is the rule of, rather than the exception to, the principles of Anglo-American criminal jurisprudence." (quoting *Dennis v. United States*, 341 U.S. 494, 500 (1951))). The goal of such prohibitions is not to identify and punish the most blameworthy conduct, but to protect vulnerable members of society from harm. *Commonwealth v. Raymond*, 97 Mass. 567, 569 (1867) ("[Strict liability] is the general rule where acts which are not mala in se are made *mala prohibita* from motives of public policy, and not because of their moral turpitude or the criminal intent with which they are committed.").

Given its justifications, strict liability is particularly appropriate when two circumstances are present. First, strict liability is best applied to conduct that is inherently risky. Rather than criminalizing only the culpable infliction of harm, strict liability prohibitions criminalize conduct that "create[s] the danger or probability of it which the law seeks to minimize." *Morissette v. United States*, 342 U.S. 246, 255–256 (1952). Second, strict liability is especially justified where vulnerable parties lack the capacity to protect themselves from harm. When a person is in a state of extreme vulnerability – for example, due to intoxication – it is the proper role of the criminal

---

[40] We have previously eschewed the characterization of our rape law as a strict-liability crime. *Lopez*, 433 Mass. at 728. Traditionally, the label of "strict liability" has denoted crimes which contain no *mens rea* element whatsoever. By contrast, since the earliest days of our Commonwealth, rape has been a general intent crime. *Burke*, 105 Mass. at 377. Nevertheless, it may fairly be said that the *element* of nonconsent is one of strict liability, in that it requires no independent *mens rea*.

law to intervene as a substitute for self-preservation. *Cf.* Martha Albertson Fineman, *The Vulnerable Subject: Anchoring Equality in the Human Condition*, 20 Yale J. L. & Feminism 13 (2008) ("One promising theoretical potential of making vulnerability central in an analysis of equality is that attention to the situation of the vulnerable individual leads us to redirect focus onto the societal institutions that are created in response to individual vulnerability.") Indeed, the United States Supreme Court has upheld strict-liability crimes as consistent with due process on precisely this justification. *See, e.g., United States v. Balint*, 258 U.S. 250 (1922); *United States v. Dotterweich*, 320 U.S. 277 (1943).

We should not conflate the presence of strict liability with the absence of culpability, however. A strict liability prohibition imposes an unqualified duty on individuals to avoid inflicting harm on others. *Mixer*, 207 Mass. at 142 ("In the interest of the public the burden is placed upon the actor of ascertaining at his peril whether his deed is within the prohibition of any criminal statute.") By saying that a duty is "unqualified," we mean that the obligation it imposes does not waiver with circumstance and may not be traded off to advance other interests. *See generally*, Immanuel Kant, Groundwork of the Metaphysics of Morals 31 (Mary Gregor, trans. 1997) (1785). An unqualified duty to avoid inflicting harm requires that a person take all necessary steps to avoid harm – even steps that may be viewed as overprotective or unreasonably costly. *Cf. Mixer*, 207 Mass. at 147 (explaining that the imposition of strict liability criminal responsibility requires a person "to obtain such knowledge as may protect him" or refrain from conduct at issue). One who proceeds with a risky course of conduct in the face of a strict-liability duty is made to internalize responsibility for the consequences of their voluntary acts.[41]

Sexual intercourse with an intoxicated partner necessarily carries inherent risks. Even when both welcomed and consensual, intercourse carries substantial risks, including physical injury, psychological and emotional trauma, disease, and pregnancy. *See generally* Robin West, *The Harms of Consensual Sex*, in The Philosophy of Sex 317, 319 (5th ed. 2008); *Cf. Michael M. v. Superior Court*, 450 U.S. 464, 470–472 (1981) (highlighting the "physical, emotional and psychological consequences of sexual activity"). Not only are these risks exacerbated when a participant is intoxicated, but intoxication creates the additional risk that one or more parties will lack the capacity to consent to sex. Sexual intercourse with an incapacitated partner is itself an additional, egregious form of harm – the violation of one's sexual autonomy and bodily integrity.

---

[41] Doubtless any well-skilled lawyer can craft a hypothetical purporting to depict a person who is entirely unaware that their incapacitated sexual partner is even the slightest bit intoxicated. But such contrivances are more at home in the classroom than in the courtroom. As an empirical matter, proof sufficient to satisfy a factfinder that a complainant was incapacitated beyond a reasonable doubt will almost invariably provide evidence from which a reasonable person should recognize that capacity to consent is at least *potentially* lacking. As a moral matter, we question whether such obliviousness to the condition of one's sexual partner should ever be legitimated by a factfinder as "reasonable."

Further, intoxication that rises to the level of incapacity can leave people especially vulnerable to unwelcome sexual intrusions. *See Burke*, 105 Mass. at 381 ("If it were otherwise, any woman in a state of utter stupefaction, whether caused by drunkenness, sudden disease, the blow of a third person, or drugs which she had been persuaded to take even by the defendant himself, would be unprotected from personal dishonor.") When a person is highly intoxicated, or otherwise impaired, the law does not accept their outward expressions of putative consent – acquiescence, willingness, or even desire – as valid. *See Commonwealth v. Therrien*, 383 Mass. 529, 538 (1981) (nonconsent is a factual question for the jury notwithstanding complainant's particular words). It does so because such outward manifestations may not reflect genuine expressions of sexual autonomy and may be tainted by cognitive impairments and coercive external pressures or circumstances. Because the risks of intoxicated sexual intercourse are borne precisely by those rendered most vulnerable by the intoxication, a strict-liability duty is appropriate.

Certainly, there is no shortage of culpability here. The defendant was clearly aware that the complainant was heavily intoxicated and extremely vulnerable, regardless of which account of the evening the jury credited. The defendant was called to MacRae's home on a report of an intoxicated person who refused to leave. He arrived to an accident scene and a "passed out" complainant. At some point, he took protective custody of the complainant to ensure that she made it home safely. In the process, he had to assist her in using the bathroom, repeatedly instruct her to clothe herself, and restrain her in the backseat of his cruiser to suppress her impulses to play with the cruiser's lights and siren. By his own testimony, the defendant had to unlock the complainant's door in order for her to make it safely inside. By proceeding with sexual intercourse under these circumstances, the defendant voluntarily risked harm to a vulnerable party in pursuit of his own sexual gratification.

In our view, the question before us thus resolves to whether the complainant must suffer the harm of nonconsensual intercourse without recourse or whether the defendant must internalize the consequences of risks he voluntarily imposed. While delineating the boundary between mere intoxication and legal incapacity may not be an easy task, there is wisdom in requiring defendants to walk that line at their own peril. For the foregoing reasons, we yet again reject the invitation to adopt a mistake-of-consent defense in Massachusetts rape law.

III.

The defendant next claims that the complainant in this case was insufficiently intoxicated to warrant an incapacity instruction in the first instance. He argues that a complainant should not be considered incapacitated unless she "was rendered unconscious or nearly so, and was temporarily incapable of making any decisions regarding sexual activity." He implies that such incapacity should be measured by the complainant's physical inability to communicate nonconsent to the defendant, "verbally, physically, or otherwise."

A.

The defendant's proposed standard turns on too narrow a reading of our precedents, most notably, *Commonwealth v. Burke*. *Burke* involved a defendant charged with aiding in the rape of an extremely intoxicated woman. In holding that our rape laws extended to sexual intercourse with a person intoxicated to the point of incapacitation, the *Burke* Court alternatingly described the complainant as "wholly insensible," *id.* at 380, in a state of "utter stupefaction," *id.* at 381, and (arguably) in a "state of unconsciousness," *id.* at 379.[42] However, *Burke* never explicitly limited the scope of incapacitation to those who are "unconscious or nearly so." Instead, that Court held that the legal incapacity to consent applied when someone had been rendered "wholly insensible *so as to be incapable of consenting.*" *Id.* at 380. (emphasis added). The latter part of this phrase contextualizes the former to provide the relevant guidance.

Numerous Massachusetts cases have underscored that unconsciousness is not the touchstone for incapacity. *See, e.g., Commonwealth v. Helfant*, 398 Mass. 214, 217, 221 (1986) (finding complainant unable to consent where she had been injected with Valium, was "in a fog," and felt as if she had "about ten drinks"); *Commonwealth v. Ascolillo*, 405 Mass. 456, 464, 541 (1989) (holding incapacity instruction proper where victim testified she was forcibly raped while awake but under influence of alcohol and cocaine; defendant testified victim was "pretty high" and even may have overdosed); *Commonwealth v. Simcock*, 31 Mass. App. Ct. 184, 195 (1991) (holding incapacity instruction proper where "there was at least some evidentiary basis for the suggestion that the victim might have been severely affected [by alcohol and prior head injury] so as to lack control" even though "the evidence fell short of suggesting the victim was in a state of stupefaction or unconsciousness"). *See also Urban*, 450 Mass. (holding incapacity instruction proper where complainant was "not unconscious" but had become "really drunk," "light-headed," "drowsy," and remembered "few things" about the evening).

A case like the one before us highlights the troubling consequences of the defendant's attempt to define incapacity by the physical ability to communicate

---

[42] The only reference to "unconsciousness" in the *Burke* opinion comes from the following sentence: "The later decisions have established the rule in England that unlawful and forcible connection with a woman in a state of unconsciousness at the time, whether that state has been produced by the act of the prisoner or not, is presumed to be without her consent, and is rape." 105 Mass. at 379. We think it unlikely that the *Burke* Court intended this reference to describe the state of the complainant's inebriation in the case before it, rather than to merely summarize the law of England. We nevertheless include it, charitably, as evidence in support of the defendant's proposed standard, which fails for reasons unrelated to the precise wording used by the *Burke* Court.

nonconsent. The jury heard testimony that, at MacRae's home, the complainant behaved in a sexually forward manner, characterized by the prosecutor as "exceptionally aggressive." Among other things, the complainant repeatedly attempted to touch the defendant's crotch, attempted to kiss him, explicitly requested that he have sex with her, and removed her clothes to expose her genitals. A reasonable jury could easily have interpreted the complainant's overtly sexual behavior a supporting the abundance of testimony that she was heavily intoxicated, perhaps to the point of being insensible. The complainant herself testified that she was only intermittently aware of her surroundings and remembers only fragments of the evening. Three Commonwealth witnesses to this behavior testified that they perceived the complainant as "very intoxicated," "very drunk," and "pretty well drunk." Counterintuitively, however, the defendant would have us hold – as a matter of law – that this evidence proves the complainant's capacity to consent. Under the defendant's proposal, the relevant inquiry reduces to whether a complainant was physically capable of stringing together words and actions that outwardly communicated a preference for sexual intercourse. The defendant would foreclose the factfinder from assessing whether those outward manifestations are in fact themselves evidence of a level of intoxication that incapacitated the complainant.

The defendant's proposed standard fundamentally misunderstands the reasons for rape law's protection of incapacitated persons. Legal incapacity to consent recognizes that certain conditions – e.g., intoxication, unconsciousness, sleep, and cognitive impairments – render an individual particularly unable to protect themselves from the harms of unwelcome sexual intercourse. As such, it does not protect only those who are physically unable to express their nonconsent in ways they might have otherwise. It also protects those who may be more easily pressured, deceived, or manipulated into outwardly expressing putative consent. Their actions in such a state may not reflect their true preferences and may be influenced by an inability to perceive and process relevant information in the present moment. For this reason, our criminal laws intervene to protect especially vulnerable individuals from those who would be inclined to exploit those vulnerabilities. *Cf.* Fineman, *supra*, at 13.

B.

Given the foregoing, a jury instruction on incapacity to consent was warranted. Such an instruction is appropriate so long as there is any reasonable view of the evidence that would support a finding of incapacity to consent beyond a reasonable doubt. *See Commonwealth v. Colon*, 449 Mass. 207, 220 (2007). Here, the jury heard testimony from multiple witnesses, including the complainant, describing her ingestion of at least three different intoxicants and behavior consistent with extreme levels of intoxication. When admitted to the hospital, many hours after her last drink, the complainant's blood alcohol content was still 0.14, a level high enough to justify protective police custody.[43] Medical evidence introduced at trial extrapolated that her blood-alcohol content would have been between 0.176 and 0.24 at the time of intercourse. Based on this evidence, along with the copious testimony describing the complainant's behavior throughout the night, a reasonable jury could have concluded that the complainant had been so intoxicated as to be incapable of consenting.

We also find no error in then language of the particular incapacity instruction given in this case. The jury instructions regarding capacity to consent were as follows:

> So, for example, if [the complainant's] condition as a result of being intoxicated or unconscious or asleep is such that she is wholly insensible so as to be incapable of consenting, then the Commonwealth need only prove that amount of force which was necessary to accomplish the natural or unnatural sexual intercourse.
>
> ...
>
> Now, there was some evidence presented in this case regarding the consumption of alcohol and marijuana and Klonopin by [the complainant] before the alleged incident occurred. You may take into consideration any evidence you find credible on the issue of her sobriety in assessing her ability to consent under such circumstances.

This instruction is a nearly verbatim restatement of the *Burke* standard, discussed *supra*.

Admittedly, the phrase "wholly insensible" is somewhat ambiguous. For this reason, the defendant claims that the trial judge committed reversable error by not elaborating on the meaning of that phrase when the jurors requested clarification. Even standing alone, however, we believe that "wholly insensible" is no more ambiguous than other relevant legal terms, including "force" and "consent," which do not require elaboration. The phrase consists of words that remain in everyday use and have generally understood definitions and applications. The trial judge thus correctly advised the jury to apply their "collective understanding of what those words mean." Moreover, that phrase is situated as part of a larger instruction that provides relevant context. The jury was instructed to determine whether "as a result of being intoxicated or unconscious or asleep," the complainant was "wholly insensible so as to be incapable of consenting." We think such context sufficiently clarified the nature of the inquiry for the jury. Had the trial judge attempted to elaborate upon the phrase, or to provide examples drawn from other cases as the defendant suggests would have been appropriate, he would have run the risk of inappropriately

---

[43] Massachusetts General Laws ch. 111B, § 8 gives police officers the authority to place intoxicated individuals into protective custody for the purpose of assisting them to their residence. Under this statute, blood alcohol content of 0.10 or higher is presumptive evidence of intoxication to the point of incapacitation.

narrowing its possible applications or of tainting the jury by informing them about other factual situations not before them.

IV.

We Can Summarily Dispense with the Defendant's Remaining Claims of Error.

The defendant claims to have been prejudiced by the fact that a juror was exposed to an erroneous external news item about the case. But a juror's exposure to extraneous information does not necessarily warrant dismissal. *See Commonwealth v. Gregory*, 401 Mass. 437, 444 (1988). When exposure occurs, a judge should "conduct a voir dire of jurors to ascertain the extent of their exposure and to assess its prejudicial effect." *Commonwealth v. Francis*, 432 Mass. 353, 369–370 (2000). That is precisely what the trial judge in this case did. The resulting conversations with the impacted juror revealed that the news article had imparted little new information, and that the juror believed he could remain impartial despite the exposure. It is not an abuse of discretion for a judge to rely on a juror's assurances that they can remain impartial. *Gregory*, 401 Mass. at 444. The judge also properly issued a curative instruction to both the individual juror and to the jury as a whole. *See Francis*, 432 Mass. at 370.

Nor did the prosecutor's comments at closing improperly shift the burden onto the defendant. *See Commonwealth v. Amirault*, 404 Mass. 221, 240 (1989) ("A prosecutor cannot ... make statements that shift the burden of proof from the Commonwealth to the defendant."). The prosecutor twice stated that the defendant had violated his duty as a police officer to "protect the public" and to "protect a vulnerable young woman." We do not see how these comments by the prosecutor could have impermissibly shifted the burden of proof to the defendant. First, we find it a permissible characterization of the evidence to suggest that an on-duty police officer committing rape has violated his public duties. Second, the prosecutor also made clear that "this is a lot more than a dereliction of duty. This is a crime, because it was by force and it was against her will." The prosecutor thus plainly stated that the relevant inquiry is whether the Commonwealth had proven the specific elements of the crime of rape. Lastly, as our foregoing discussion in Part II.B.3 makes clear, we view the criminal law as establishing enforceable duties toward others, particularly in cases dealing with the law's protection of vulnerable parties. Consequently, we find nothing prejudicial about invoking the language of duties to explain the particular culpability of a defendant in a case like this one.

Finding no errors, the judgment of the Appeals Court is affirmed.

So ordered.

PART II

Gender on Trial

9

Commentary on *State v. Williams*

KIM HAI PEARSON

From popular literature to reality crime television shows, the trope of children taken from home by nefarious forces threads its way through culture, time, and geographic space. Sometimes, the children are taken by magical beings (fairies, demons, Baba Yaga, goblins, pied pipers, etc.) and other times, ordinary sinister figures or organizations are responsible for the theft of children (the Magisterium, the Shop, the Island, etc.). One might think the meaning of this story is to warn parents that the everyday reality is one in which they cannot assume that their children will remain in their communities and survive childhood. Perhaps the prevalence of taken children stories is connected to the need for an external explanation for the violence against children committed by those closest to them within the community. Perhaps the stories are a cautionary tale to parents that someone is watching and judging them.

What is it to face the existential dread of losing a child? What is it for entire populations to live, surrounded by the absence of thousands of children who were tracked down, in some cases after attempts by family members to hide them, and whisked away – because of their group identity and their way of life being framed as a danger to those children? The insidious and deep roots of eradication efforts of Native populations made by the US government did not cease but were transformed into assimilation plans that involved removing children from their communities and erasing their culture, language, traditions, and spiritual beliefs. Efforts by the United States to stamp out Native populations through assimilation began in the 1800s.[1] Mass takings of Native children in the United States during the mid to late 1870s were prompted in 1878 with the founding of off-reservation boarding schools by Richard H. Pratt.[2] Pratt experimented with "ideological conversion" while supervising imprisoned

---

[1] Charla Bear, *American Boarding Schools Still Haunt Many*, NPR (May 12, 2008), available at www.npr.org/templates/story/story.php?storyId=16516865 (last visited Jan. 1, 2022) (referring to the Indian Civilization Act of 1918 as a herald of assimilation efforts).

[2] Andrea Smith, *Indigenous People and Boarding Schools: A Comparative Study*, prepared for the Secretariat of the United Nations Permanent Forum on Indigenous Issues, 3–7 (2008) E/C.19/2009/CRP.1.

Native individuals.[3] In the United States, boarding school practices[4] led to thousands of Native children lost, unaccounted for, dead, or continuing to live with trauma. For nearly a century, various government and church-run boarding schools housed Native and Indigenous children throughout the United States and Canada.[5] In 1928, the Meriam Report[6] detailed the shortcomings of Native communities in a 900+ page report made by US government officials. The report described the problem with boarding schools, however they continued to flourish throughout the twentieth century, although but are no longer explicit assimilationist.

Even as tribal children were no longer forced or coerced to attend boarding schools as part of the assimilationist project, state power increased over Native families as states delivered social services to families pushed into reservations. The power states began to exercise over Native families stemmed from problems like, not acknowledging differences between Native and non-Native children, "social workers routinely mis[taking] poverty for neglect," and mistaking intergenerational child placements (children raised by grandparents) for neglect – empowering state actors to again remove Native children from their homes.[7] From the 1950s through the 1970s, around one-quarter or more of all Native children were taken from their families.[8] Congressional hearings throughout the 1970s, preceding the passage of the Indian Child Welfare Act, revealed mass removals and around 85 percent of placements with non-Native families.

From 1958–1967 the Bureau of Indian Affairs (BIA) contracted with the Child Welfare League of America to run the Indian Adoption Project. The goal of the project was "increasing the adoption of Indian children by non-Indian families."[9] Although the Adoption Project closed in 1967, it placed about "250 additional Indian children into adoptive homes ... to 'rescue' Indian children from their families and culture."[10] Given this history, it was no wonder that Native families were terrified of losing their children to officials and agencies that were purportedly providing assistance freely to them.

---

[3] Andrea A. Curcio, *Civil Claims for Uncivilized Acts: Filing Suit Against the Government for American Indian Board School Abuses*, 45 HASTINGS RACE & POV. L. J. 54–55 (2006).

[4] *See, e.g.*, DENISE K. LAJIMODIERE, *American Indian Boarding Schools in the United States: A Brief History and Legacy*, in INST. FOR THE STUDY OF HUM. RTS. COLUMBIA U., INDIGENOUS PEOPLES' ACCESS TO JUSTICE, INCLUDING TRUTH AND RECONCILIATION PROCESSES (2015) available at https://doi.org/10.7916/D8GT5M1F (last visited Jan. 4, 2022) (selected legal history of assimilation efforts by the US government and qualitative research gathered from survivors of boarding schools).

[5] Smith, *supra* note 2, at 3, 7.

[6] The Meriam Report, referred to by technical director Lewis Meriam's name, was commissioned by the Department of the Interior. Inst. for Gov't Research, The Problem of Indian Administration (1928), available at https://files.eric.ed.gov/fulltext/ED087573.pdf (last visited Jan. 1, 2022).

[7] ALICE HEARST, CHILDREN AND THE POLITICS OF CULTURAL BELONGING 116–117 (2012).

[8] *Id.*, at 118 (citing the 1977 study by the Association of American Indian Affairs); *see also* STEPHEN L. PEVAR, THE RIGHTS OF INDIANS AND TRIBES 291 (4th ed. 2012).

[9] HEARST, *supra* note 7 (also noting that the race-matching policies in place were not observed for Native children).

[10] HEARST, *supra* note 7, at 117.

Systemic child removal also flourished in Canada. Beginning in 1846 the Canadian government "officially committed to boarding schools." An 1878 report by Nicolas F. Davin, a member of Parliament, urged Canadian leaders to copy the US boarding schools founded by Pratt as exemplars for Canadian "residential schools."[11] In 2008 the Canadian government settled a class action lawsuit related to the boarding schools. The government response included a formal apology by Prime Minster Stephen Harper that occurred nine days after the Canadian government convened a Truth and Reconciliation Commission.[12] On May 27, 2021, 215 unmarked graves of First Nation children were discovered on the grounds of a Canadian boarding school. For nearly a century, various government and church-run boarding schools housed Native and Indigenous children throughout the United States and Canada.[13] Within a short time of the Canadian grave discoveries, the United States began its own reckoning with boarding school deaths.[14] The grim reality of the children's graves is a reminder that state and religious organizations have taken over 150,000 Indigenous children from their families in Canada.[15] Estimates about the number of Native children in the United States removed from their families is not definitively known. Between "1879 and the late 1960s" about 100,000 Native children "passed through" boarding schools.[16] Although many of the children were taken in the 1800s, giving rise to the impression that the graves in Canada (and possible sites in the United States) are from an earlier, less enlightened time, most of the 376 boarding schools in the United States were closed within recent memory.[17] The ongoing removal, injury, and death of Native children for generations, is nothing less than extermination efforts over time without cessation. Judges rarely acknowledge the impact that intergenerational trauma from such an experience on everyday parenting decisions might have. Instead, the courts typically focused their inquiry on whether the parents

---

[11] *Id.*, at 7–10.
[12] Centennial College, *Truth and Reconciliation Commission of Canada*, OUR STORIES (2018) hosted on Pressbooks, available at https://ecampusontario.pressbooks.pub/indigstudies/chapter/truth-and-reconciliation-commission-of-canada/ (last visited Jan. 4, 2022).
[13] Smith, *supra* note 2, at 3,7.
[14] Frank X. Mullen, *Stewart Indian School's 200 Unmarked Graves*, RENO NEWS & REVIEW (Aug. 15, 2021), available at https://reno.newsreview.com/2021/08/15/stewart-indian-schools-200-unmarked-graves/ (last visited Jan. 1, 2022); *see also*, Secretary Haaland announces federal Indian boarding school initiative, U.S. Dep't of the Interior (June 22, 2021), available at www.doi.gov/pressreleases/secretary-haaland-announces-federal-indian-boarding-school-initiative (last visited Jan. 4, 2022); Deb Haaland, *My Grandparents Were Stolen from Their Homes as Children*, THE WASHINGTON POST, June 11, 2021.
[15] Susan Montoya Bryan, *US to review Native American boarding schools' dark history*, THE ASSOCIATED PRESS, June 22, 2021, available at https://abcnews.go.com/Politics/wireStory/us-official-address-legacy-indigenous-boarding-schools-78413721 (last visited Jan. 1, 2022) (reporting that "by 1926, more than 80% of Indigenous children were attending boarding schools ... run by the federal government or religious organizations").
[16] Natalie Pate, Capi Lynn, & Dianne Lugo, *Chemawa Indian School Families Seek Answers, Healing through Federal Investigation*, SALEM STATESMAN JOURNAL (Oct. 25, 2021).
[17] *Id.*

should be criminally liable and punished for a reasonable decision with a bare hint that the parents were making decisions amid unreasonable conditions.

THE ORIGINAL DECISION

On May 3, 1971, the Court of Appeals of Washington, Division One, Panel One affirmed the trial court's manslaughter conviction of a mother and stepfather who failed to meet the "ordinary caution" standard for not obtaining medical care for their 17-month-old child who presented with a fever and toothache. Ultimately, their baby died from gangrene. The trial and appellate courts framed the parents' decision to delay medical care absent socio-historical context. They were behaving as many parents do when a child of that age is teething; they treated the fever with aspirin and monitored the child's fever. It is unclear whether the *Williams* opinion signals that parents should seek medical care for children in such situations but these *particular* parents were inherently unable to meet the "ordinary caution" standard because of their "ignorance." Another possibility is that punishment and deterrence (not reformation) are the dual purposes of criminal law applied in cases of a child's death by accident or misfortune.

The *Williams* Court noted that it would take the extraordinary step of invoking "independent examination of the evidence to determine whether it substantially supports the court's express finding[s]" related to proximate cause of death and when the duty to seek care obtained. The court deployed physician testimony to speak about the point at which the child's condition would have been noticeably bad enough to prompt professional help. The physician testified that the parents would have smelled the child's gangrenous tooth between September 1 and September 5, 1968. The parents testified they were aware of the smell, but that their fears of child removal intensified because of the child's sickness and dishevelled appearance. The parents could not have known that the decisions they made would result in the child's death.

The court's hint that the child's gangrenous tooth could not be identified by its odor implies that the house and child are malodorous to such a degree that the parents could not smell the gangrene. The judge mentions the aspirin the mother dosed the child with more than once, perhaps to hint at repugnance for traditional Native medical practices. Or the aspirin is mentioned to hint at the inadequacy of dosing with aspirin instead of taking the child to the doctor. The parents note that by the time they realized the child was not recovering with aspirin, they were afraid that appearing at the medical clinic with a sick, sweaty child would trigger child removal. Hemmed in at every turn, making all parenting decisions fraught with the possibility of losing that child, it is little wonder that the parents had the ability to make any choice at all regarding the baby.

THE REWRITTEN OPINION

Although the state law in place at the time *Williams* was decided is no longer valid, *Williams* continues to be used in numerous Criminal Law casebooks. Professor

Addie Rolnick, writing as Justice Addie C. Rolnick, interrogates the purpose and value of teaching *Williams* by parsing out the ways in which the court (and contemporary readers) overlay stereotypical narratives about Natives onto people in court proceedings. For example, courts apply a patriarchal, colonialist frame of reference in determining when a parent fails to exercise "ordinary caution" in family law proceedings.

This commentary situates Rolnick's rewritten opinion in the quiet before the explosion of postcolonial thought, civil rights advocacy, and second-wave feminism on to the stage of American political thought; without empirical evidence or statistics about child removals. The original court did not acknowledge or rely on the parents' knowledge of child removal or consider their fear of removal as a reasonable factor when determining whether a fever and toothache were serious enough to outweigh the risk of child removal.

Rolnick uses the lenses of postcolonial thought, emerging second-wave feminism, and critical theory to lay bare the rhetorical sleight of hand the court performs when it simultaneously finds that parents are not held to the standard of medical professionals and that they should have known (though it was not reasonable to expect laypeople to know a toothache could lead to death), meaning that the court's decision reduces down to the parents not having a legal defence or excuse for not seeking medical care. Justice Rolnick's rewrite (1) counters the negative stereotypes used by the court when referring to the "ignorant" Native parents by making them cognizable to the court as parents and credible authorities about the state of their child's well-being; (2) complicates the "reasonably prudent man" standard by giving voice and authority to historically oppressed and marginalized people; and (3) anticipates how centuries of child removal require a nuanced approach to Native parents.

The threat of child removal was probably more than an idle thought for the parents in *Williams*. There is evidence now that, when the child was ill, Native communities were keenly aware that their children being taken en masse and were resorting to drastic measures to protect them - in some cases hiding their children. Whether or not they knew how many children were being taking across the country at the time, the parents in *Williams* only needed one story to explain their fear: they personally knew a relative who lost a child. It was not until the mid to late 1970s that empirical evidence of harmful practices of state child welfare officials was gathered and made public.[18] *State v. Williams*, was heard on the brink of exposés about state child welfare practices and their close connection to the history of trauma and child loss in boarding schools, so the parents and the court did not have the benefit of public knowledge about how many Native children were taken from their families as an explanation for the parents' reticence in seeking medical care. Rolnick sheds

---

[18] *See, e.g.*, Francis P. Prucha, Documents of United States Indian Policy, Task Force Four: Federal, State, and Tribal Jurisdiction (1975); U.S. Gov't Printing Office, Final report to the American Indian Policy Review Commission (1976).

light on the unnecessarily tragic consequences of being unable to see and recognize other individuals as fully realized, comprehensible people. Rolnick exposes the court's preferences by taking seriously the parents' experience and capacity to make reasonable decisions considering their awareness about their status within the community and the relative powerlessness they have vis-à-vis the state.

Even if members of the *Williams* court had been unaware of the massive, slow-moving, efforts to eradicate Natives through assimilation beginning in the late 1800s, the court could have used reasoning that would have rendered a different decision. Rolnick suggests that the court's refusal to see and recognize Native identity as equal to and not lesser than those in the legal and medical fields, led the court to compound the tragic loss of a child and signal to the community that Native parents were inherently ignorant, possibly bad actors, and unreasonable in their reticence to trust the state.

Despite broken-hearted parents and community tragedy, the judge was in no way legally required to affirm a conviction for involuntary manslaughter. The rich, varied, and dynamic civil rights, anti-colonialism, and feminist movements of the 1960s and early 1970s could have provided the Court with a moral, compassionate, and legally justifiable basis to give credence to the parents' reality. Such a decision could have provided expressive value to other vulnerable, marginalized families by signaling that courts can see litigants as fully realized human beings who are capable of loving and raising their children.

For example, the judge could have given the parents the benefit of an already existing presumption that grounds US family law – the presumption that parents act in the best interests of the child. From *Meyer* and *Pierce* to *Troxel* and *DeShaney*,[19] there is, for positive[20] and negative[21] childhood outcomes, the baseline presumption is that parents care for their children and act in their children's best interests. The fact that the judge and the lower court determined the parents guilty in the original case – despite meeting the existing standard for excusing homicide – "committed by accident or misfortune in doing any lawful act by lawful means, with ordinary caution and without any lawful intent" strongly suggests that the court believed *Williams* parents were behaving outside the bounds of ordinary caution.

The opinion provides justifications for separating children from their birth communities by evoking negative stereotypes about Native families, including hints

---

[19] *Meyer v. Nebraska*, 262 U.S. 390 (1923); *Pierce v. Society of Sisters*, 268 U.S. 510 (1925); *Troxel v. Granville*, 530 U.S. 57 (2000); *DeShaney v. Winnebago County*, 489 U.S. 189 (1989).

[20] *Meyer* and *Pierce* solidified parental rights as compared to state's rights to dictate learning a language besides English in school and the ability to opt out of public school in favor of parochial school. See, Barbara Bennett Woodhouse, "*Who Owns the Child?*": *Meyer and Pierce and the Child as Property*, 33 W&M L. REV. 996 (1992).

[21] In *DeShaney*, a parent struck his four-year-old child so severely that the child succumbed to a life-threatening coma; the United States is one of a few countries among highly developed countries that allows parents to use corporal discipline with their children.

about incompetent parenting, nonhygienic homes, malnourishment, financially insecure adults, and skepticism that odor was undetected. There is plenty of evidence that vulnerable, marginalized groups have their parental rights precariously balanced on their decision-making without direction from the state or a safety net, private or public. Parental decisions as seemingly trivial as taking a child to the doctor for a slight fever to wondering when a child is "sick enough" to warrant seeking medical help, can be accompanied with the risk of losing a child to the state and/or to illness.

For parents of low socio-economic class, without formal education, and little family support, judges can find myriad reasons, valid or pretextual, for removing their children. In *Williams*, the absence of the parents' voices is filled with the judge's inability to imagine the effects of living with ongoing, generational trauma and fear that their children will be taken from them. Records of the parents' full identities and their statements in court are lost to history. Their erasure is highlighted and explored in Rolnick's rewrite. Treating the parents as reasonable and changing the nature of reasonableness by crediting the parents with the authority to make decisions based on a storytelling and oral tradition counters the judge's erasure of the Native family. Rolnick does the work of seeing and hearing the voices of the Other using critical theory that was available at the time of the opinion. At the time the case was heard, postcolonial thinkers,[22] civil rights advances in the United States, and second-wave feminist[23] writers had done and were doing the work of political activism and advocacy. Use of these sources could have created an opinion that acknowledged the fully realized humanity of the parents. The reality of their grief for the child, not because they were convicted of a crime, but because they loved and lost a child could have informed the Court's application of law to the parents' situation. Ultimately, there was a failure of imagination. The judge's inability to entertain the probability that the parents would have made a different decision *if they had known* the child would die and that their fears of the state removing the child were informed and real. Instead, the judge seems to have had a static, idealized, mainstream version of parenting that the *Williams* parents could never meet.

By the time *Williams* was heard, the French Feminist movement sparked second-wave feminism in the United States. Feminist ideas could have informed the Court's view of itself in relation to the parents in *Williams*. Rolnick's approach to the parents' situation suggests that the law itself could be interpreted and shaped to take the parents' living situation and identity into account. Rolnick calls attention to

---

[22] *See, e.g.*, FRANTZ FANON, THE WRETCHED OF THE EARTH (1961) and BLACK SKIN, WHITE MASKS (1967) (creating the postcolonial theory that the European "Self" can only exist in relation to the "Other" because the Self is subject, and the Other is object).

[23] *See, e.g.*, SIMONE DE BEAUVOIR, THE SECOND SEX (1949) (trans. to English 1965); BETTY FRIEDAN, THE FEMININE MYSTIQUE (1963); KATE MILLETT, SEXUAL POLITICS (1969); MONIQUE WITTIG, LES GUÉRILLÈRES (1969) (trans. to English 1971).

the parents' identity as Native being a proxy for incompetent parenting, reminiscent of the moral, proto-social scientific judgments passed by the US government about Native living conditions, family ordering, and cultural practices. Without the critique Rolnick offers, *Williams* offers ambiguous lessons in modern law school classrooms; the manslaughter law in Washington state is no longer in effect, leaving the Court's characterization of the Native parents as ignorant and unreasonable intact. Rolnick's rewrite replaces the court's conflation of "Indianness" and ignorance by folding in awareness of the parents' layered identities as young adults, frightened community members, and understandably suspicious, hesitant participants in the US legal system.

STATE V. WILLIAMS, 4 WASH. APP. 908 (MAY 3, 1971)

JUDGE ADDIE C. ROLNICK DELIVERED THE OPINION OF THE COURT

Losing a child is unfathomable, lifelong pain. For a parent who believes they could have prevented the loss, this pain is compounded by guilt and regret This case presents the question of whether such emotional and psychological burdens are sufficient punishment for a child's accidental death, or whether criminal liability is also appropriate.

The lower court in this case chose to punish ordinary parents for decisions they made about how best to care for and protect their child. Those decisions – about whether and when to take the child to a doctor for what appeared to be a simple toothache – were within the bounds of typical parental decision-making. Tragically, they turned out to be wrong decisions; the child in this case died from complications resulting from an infected tooth. In convicting the parents of manslaughter, the lower court failed to take context into account in assessing what constitutes the reasonable actions of a parent. Specifically, the court undervalued the knowledge of Indian families and communities and over-punished everyday decision-making in the context of parenting, a traditionally feminized activity.

In our view, in the case of an accidental death resulting from a parent's mistake, the common law rule of criminal negligence is likely the correct one: Criminal liability is inappropriate unless, considering the parent's knowledge of the circumstances, that parent made a choice that deviates grossly from what a reasonably prudent parent would do. Civil liability or child welfare intervention to protect other children may be premised on a different standard, but no penological purpose is served by punishing parents for a mistake if they made a thoughtful decision under the circumstances and chose an action that was within the broad range of typical behavior, even if a court looking backward can second-guess the decision. However, because we are interpreting a statute that uses the term "ordinary caution" and the lower court relied on our interpretation of the same law in other cases as imposing manslaughter liability for ordinary (civil) negligence, we defer to the legislature to determine which standard is appropriate. Therefore, on review we apply the lower court's ordinary negligence standard to the specific facts of this case. Even under that standard, we hold that the appellants were not negligent, a manslaughter conviction is incorrect as a matter of law..

I. FACTS & PROCEDURAL HISTORY

Most of the facts are not in contention. William Joseph Tabafunda (Billy), a 17-month-old child, died on September 12, 1968, a result of what initially seemed to be a toothache but developed into an infection, gangrene, and eventually pneumonia. His mother, Bernice Williams, and his stepfather, Walter Williams, both Indians,[24] noticed that Billy seemed sick; they initially thought the discomfort was from teething, or that he had a simple toothache. They treated his discomfort with aspirin. According to the testimony of Dr. Gale Wilson, the autopsy surgeon, Billy died because his abscessed tooth developed into an infection, became gangrenous, restricted Billy's ability to eat, and led to malnutrition that lowered his resistance to infection. Billy then developed pneumonia, which caused his death.

According to Dr. Wilson, the baby's condition lasted for approximately two weeks (beginning around August 30) until his death on September 12. Both parents were aware that Billy was ill two weeks before his death. Dr. Wilson testified that the tooth infection would likely have caused a "considerable" temperature, swelling within 48 hours (around September 1), and red and purple discoloration within three to four days (around September 2-3). Within the second week, the appellants noticed that Billy's cheek was discolored and had a "peculiar odor." Dr. Wilson testified that the odor was one "generally associated with gangrene" and "would have been present for a week to possibly ten days before his death." (According to this estimate, the odor would have been present between September 2 and September 5. Dr. Wilson also testified that Billy's condition likely became irreversible after September 5, 1968.

When the baby's condition did not improve, around September 5, his parents talked about taking him to the doctor. They were aware that medical help was available and there is no suggestion that they were financially or physically unable to take him to the doctor. They were afraid to do so, however, because they thought a doctor might see the discoloration on Billy's cheek, suspect them of abusing Billy,

---

[24] The appellants are identified as Indian on the initial paperwork, so we use the same term here. The appellants' brief characterizes both parents as Indians and names Walter Williams' tribe as "Sheshont." This may be an error or misspelling, as we are unable to identify an American Indian tribe by that name. The record indicates that both parents and their families identify as Indians. We do not question this conclusion, but we note that the record lacks detailed information about either parent's tribe or the Indian community in which they lived. Subsequent research indicates that Walter Williams was descended from the Tseshaht First Nation in Canada, which may be the genesis of the misspelling. See note 33.

and report them to a child welfare agency, and that Billy would be taken away from them. They testified that a relative had a child taken away. They also did not understand that Billy's condition was life-threatening.

On January 13, 1969, the Honorable Theodore S. Turner, presiding in Dept. No. 2 of the Superior Court of Washington, convicted Bernice and Walter Williams of Manslaughter. Judge Turner entered findings of fact and conclusions of law on March 10, 1969. Judge Turner found that the appellants had a duty to provide food, clothing, and medical attention to their child, that although they were "aware that William Joseph Tabafunda was ill during the period September 1, 1968 to September 12, 1968," they were "ignorant" and "did not realize how sick the baby was. They thought the baby had a toothache and no layman regards a toothache as dangerous to life. They loved the baby and gave it aspirin in hopes of improving its condition." Turner Order (Mar. 10, 1969), at 2. Regarding the parents' negligence, Judge Turner set forth the following findings of fact:

> They did not take the baby to a Doctor because of fear that the Welfare Department would take the baby away from them. They knew that medical help was available because of previous experience. They had no excuse that the law will recognize for not taking the baby to a Doctor.
>
> The defendants ... were negligent in not seeking medical attention for William Joseph Tabafunda.
>
> [A]s a proximate result of this negligence, William Joseph Tabafunda died.

Id. (emphasis added). Judge Turner specifically concluded that their negligence "did not amount to gross negligence or willful or wanton conduct" but did amount to "simple negligence." *Id.*, at 3. He found them guilty of manslaughter. *Id.*, at 4. Bernice and Walter Williams were each sentenced to three years' probation. A notice of appeal was filed April 24, 1969.

The appellants do not contest the superior court's findings of fact but on appeal they challenge the court's legal conclusion that they are guilty of manslaughter. We note, however, that the italicized language, while set forth as a factual finding, is also part of the court's legal conclusion. *See Kane v. Klos*, 50 Wash.2d 778, 778 (1957). Thus, we review de novo whether the appellants' failure to take the baby to the doctor when they were not aware that his illness was potentially deadly amounted to negligence and whether the failure proximately caused the baby's death.

First, we address the mental state required for criminal liability in this case. Specifically, we discuss the difference between ordinary negligence, which we have held is required for manslaughter in Washington, and criminal negligence, which is required in most jurisdictions. While we hold that only ordinary negligence is required, we express doubts about its propriety in parental neglect cases and urge the legislature to reconsider its applicability in those cases. Second, because liability in this case is based on an omission, we consider the scope of the duty of parents to provide medical care to their children and what actions might constitute a breach of that duty. Third, we consider the element of causation. Causation is part of the actus reus element: In homicide law, an act is only criminal if it causes a death. A parent's failure to take their child to a doctor can only be said to cause the child's death if the doctor could have intervened to save the child. Our review of medical testimony about causation thus helps narrow the window of time in which the parents' act might have been culpable; once Billy was so ill that no doctor could have saved him, the parents' act (failure to take him in) cannot be said to have caused his death. Finally, we examine the parents' actions and decisions during the relevant window of time in context to determine whether they were negligent. This requires that we assess the parents' subjective knowledge of the risk of death and their subjective decision not to seek medical care against an objective benchmark. Because we find that Walter and Bernice Williams' actions – including their assessment of their child's condition, their efforts to provide relief, and their decision about whether and when to seek medical care – were within the realm of what a reasonably prudent parent would do when faced with similar knowledge and circumstances, we reverse their convictions.

II. MANSLAUGHTER AND ORDINARY NEGLIGENCE

We have previously interpreted our manslaughter statutes to require only ordinary negligence, as opposed to the higher standard required by most states of criminal negligence, wantonness, or recklessness. *State v. Hedges*, 8 Wn.2d 652, 666 (1941) (noting that manslaughter statutes premised on ordinary negligence "are rare" but so interpreting Washington's statute). Our criminal code defines manslaughter as a homicide committed "[i]n any case other than those specific in sections 2392, 2393 and 2394" and "not being excusable or justifiable." Rem. Rev. State. §2395. Sections 2392, 2393, and 2394 define first degree murder, second degree murder, and killing in the course of a duel. Rem. Rev. Stat. § 2404 provides, "Homicide is excusable when committed by accident or misfortune in doing any lawful act by lawful means, with ordinary caution and without any unlawful intent."

In *Hedges*, we directly addressed the question of whether manslaughter in Washington requires only ordinary negligence, or whether it requires the kind of criminal negligence required to make a killing criminal at common law. We acknowledged that there were few, if any, cases raising this exact issue. In one manslaughter case, the court characterized the appellants' conduct as "grossly negligent," but we held that the court's description of that conduct did not establish a rule applicable in a case that raised the question of liability for ordinary negligence. *Hedges*, at 663 (*citing State v. Karsunky*, 197 Wash. 87 (1938)). We found instructive a Wisconsin case involving a defendant driving an automobile that collided with a truck. Interpreting a statute worded similarly to Washington's, the Wisconsin court upheld a conviction based on a jury instruction about ordinary negligence. *Clements v. State*, 176 Wis. 289, 185 N.W. 209, 212, 218 (1921).

Imposing criminal liability based on ordinary negligence in manslaughter cases involving normal daily activities, such as parenting, represents a stark departure from the common law. An ordinary negligence standard is more commonly used in cases involving the operation of a motor vehicle, gun, or other dangerous instrumentality. *See Hedges*, at 667 (noting that most second degree assault statutes require "intent or wilful assault" [sic] but second degree assault in the course of hunting was strict liability); *People v. Wilson*, 193 Cal. 512 (1924) (describing criminal liability based on ordinary negligence in motor vehicle cases "even though [it] does not amount to a wanton or reckless disregard of human safety or life" where "a person is doing anything dangerous in itself, or has charge of anything dangerous in its use" and contrasting those cases with other homicide prosecutions). In the present case, the State also relies on RCW 26.020.030, which codifies the common law duty to care for children. That statute imposes criminal penalties on anyone who "wilfully [sic] omits, without lawful excuse, to furnish ... medical attendance for his or her children" and makes such crime a felony if the child is under the age of sixteen. We agree with the appellants that willfulness as used in the statute suggests that more than ordinary negligence is required to establish a criminal violation.

However, the Washington legislature has not spoken on the issue since our previous opinions grounding manslaughter liability on ordinary negligence. We decline at this time to overturn our own precedent, especially when it is not necessary to reach a decision in this case. We therefore accept the superior court's interpretation of the law as requiring only ordinary negligence and turn now to the question of whether the Williams' conduct amounted to negligence under that standard.

III. ACTUS REUS BY OMISSION: DUTY AND BREACH

Potential liability herein is based on an omission. The State has not alleged that Billy died as a result of any positive action on the part of either parent. This is not a case of abuse or intentional harm. Neither the autopsy nor previous medical examinations raised suspicions of abuse. It is undisputed that both parents "had always demonstrated great love for their children." Normally, the criminal law imposes no obligation to aid others, so failure to take action to save another person from death caused by an illness would not be criminal. However, an omission may be criminal where a person had a duty to act. As Billy's natural parent, Bernice Williams had a legal duty to ensure that he was safe and healthy, including obtaining necessary medical care. *See People v. Pierson*, 176 N.Y. 201 (1903). By acting as a parent, Walter Williams assumed the same obligation to care for Billy.

As noted above, this common law parental duty is codified in RCW 26.20.030(1), which provides for criminal punishment of any person who "willfully omits, without lawful excuse, to furnish necessary medical attendance for his or her child." Willfully in criminal statutes means intentionally, not inadvertently. *State v. Spino*, 61 Wash. 2d 246, 249 (1963). In the context of failure to provide financial support to a child, we have more specifically held that a prima facie case of willfulness is established by "a failure on the part of a physically or vocationally able parent to furnish the requisites of support," a presumption that can be rebutted by evidence that the appellant had a "lawful excuse, including a physical, vocational or economic incapacity." *State v. Russell*, 73 Wash. 2d 903, 908 (1968). A similar inquiry applies in cases of failure to provide medical care. Thus, we consider whether the appellants were able to provide care and whether they had a lawful excuse for failing to do so. It is undisputed that the appellants had the means to access medical care for Billy. The question whether they had a lawful excuse is subsumed by our *mens rea* analysis. In our discussion of *mens rea*, we also address whether the appellants knew of the need for medical care because one cannot willfully omit to provide medical care if one does not know such care is needed.

IV. CAUSATION

We must also consider causation because it narrows the time period during which the appellants could be criminally liable for failing to act. The superior court relied on Dr. Wilson's testimony to determine that the appellants' failure to take Billy to a doctor caused his death. In so doing, the superior court necessarily focused on the appellant's failure during the period between when Billy first became sick and when it would have been too late to save him. Any failure to seek medical care after that would not have legally caused Billy's death if his life could not have been saved by that care. Given Dr. Wilson's testimony that Billy's condition would have been irreversible as of September 5, 1968, the relevant period is from September 1 to September 5, 1968. During this window, Billy would have lived but for his parents' failure to take him to the doctor.[25] A similar issue was addressed by the Maryland Supreme Court in *Craig v. State*, 220 Md. 590, 598–599 (1959). The court there held that the parents' negligence would be the proximate cause of their child's death from pneumonia only if the evidence showed they were culpably negligent during the period when medical care could have averted death. The crucial inquiry, then, is whether the appellants' decision not to seek medical care during this period was negligently made.

V. NEGLIGENCE

The State must establish that, during this critical period, the appellants acted with the requisite culpability in failing to take Billy to the doctor. The superior court held that liability requires acting with ordinary negligence, and we have adopted

---

[25] Although the malnutrition and pneumonia are intervening causes, they follow from the initial infection and are not bizarre outcomes, and thus the lack of medical care is still a proximate, or legal, cause of death, not just an actual cause. *See State v. Richardson*, 197 Wash. 157, 164–165 (1938).

that standard for purposes of this opinion. Thus, if the state can establish beyond a reasonable doubt that a reasonable parent would have been aware that Billy needed medical attention and would have brought him to the doctor before September 5, the appellants would be guilty of manslaughter.

The reasonable parent is not the ideal parent, but also not merely the typical parent. Typicality, of course, matters to some degree because as parenting norms change and medical advancements are made, the expectation about what constitutes reasonable care may shift as well. *See Pierson, supra* (discussing legal duty to provide medical care as a product of advancement in medical care). However, reasonableness is not a measure of what most parents do, empirically, but rather a measure of what a prudent parent can be expected to do, normatively. This standard requires acting as prudently as a typical parent who is not mistake-prone, especially oblivious, or uncaring would have acted.

Here, we believe that the reasonably prudent parent of a sick child is someone who is attentive to the child's condition, weighs the need for additional medical intervention, and when not obtaining such intervention, ensures that the child's condition will be monitored. A reasonably prudent parent is not a parent with specialized medical knowledge.[26] This is important because a negligence inquiry asks whether a reasonable parent *should have* known that their child was at risk of death, even if, like the parents in this case, they did not. In terms of the decision whether and when to seek care, a reasonably prudent parent is not one who ignores their child's illness or displays a willingness to risk their child's life in order not to be inconvenienced.

A. *Risk of Death*

It is undisputed that the Williamses did not at any time realize Billy's condition was life-threatening. Billy's death was the result of an infection that began as a regular toothache; the infection gradually become more serious until it caused irreversible damage. The first part of our negligence inquiry, then, must focus on whether the appellants *should have known* Billy's condition was life threatening during the period when medical intervention would have saved his life. If a reasonably prudent parent would have known their child was in mortal danger, the decision not to seek medical care where it was available may give rise to criminal liability, no matter the parents' subjective beliefs or reasoning. See, e.g., *Craig v. State*, 220 Md. 590 (1959) (religious beliefs would not be a lawful excuse for a parent's failure to provide necessary medical care where neglect proximately caused death); but see Robert L. Trescher and Thomas N. O'Neill,

---

[26] If we were confronted with the question of what a reasonable doctor would have done after examining Billy, we might expect that, as a result of specialized medical training, the doctor should have known the seriousness of Billy's condition and the possibility of lethal complications.

Jr., *Medical Care for Dependent Children: Manslaughter Liability of the Christian Scientist*, 109 U. Penn. L. Rev. 203, 211 (1960) (finding that "no single doctrine" has emerged regarding manslaughter liability for parents who refuse medical care because of a belief in faith healing); *Id.* (citing a Pennsylvania court's dismissal of an indictment against a father who used faith healing to treat his child's diabetes in *Commonwealth v. Cornelius*, No. 105, April Sessions, 1956. Philadelphia County (Pa.) Quar. Sess., Nov. 5, 1958).

Dr. Wilson testified that medical intervention in the final week before Billy's death would have come too late to save his life. In the period before this, between September 1 and September 5, the evidence showed that Billy was fussy, had difficulty keeping his food down, and had a swollen cheek.[27] All of these symptoms are consistent with a painful toothache, which the appellants treated with aspirin to reduce the swelling. Walter Williams also testified that he had heard dentists will not pull a tooth while it is swollen, which influenced the appellants' decision to wait for the swelling to go down before visiting the dentist. Another warning sign of the seriousness of Billy's condition would have been the odor produced once gangrene set in. Regarding this, Dr. Wilson estimated that discoloration and odor associated with gangrene would have been detectable "a week to possibly ten days" prior to death. The appellants, however, stated that they noticed a strange odor a week before his death. This admission is consistent with the conservative end of Dr. Wilson's estimated time frame, and it is therefore inappropriate to adopt his broadest possible estimate when determining the legally significant window of time. Even assuming that the odor would have put a reasonably prudent parent on notice of the risk of death, by the time the odor was detectable, Billy's condition was irreversible.

We decline to adopt a standard that requires a reasonable parent to correctly guess at exactly when a minor medical condition becomes life threatening, especially where, as here, the potential danger results from a series of biological responses to the initial condition. Doing so would mean that parents could be prosecuted for failing to recognize rare and unanticipated conditions, complications resulting from underlying conditions, and minor wounds that progress rapidly to serious infections. We do not believe that the appellants' failure to comprehend the risk of death between September 1 and September 5 was negligent.

We note that prosecutions of parents for failure to obtain medical care for the children arise most commonly in faith healing cases. Those cases do not directly apply here because they involve parents' willful refusal to obtain medical care that they knew was advised. Unlike in the present case, parent defendants in faith healing cases do not argue that they failed to realize the gravity of the child's condition or

---

[27] The State's brief asserts that there were "fly eggs in his hair," but no evidence in the record or language in the opinion below supports that assertion.

the risk of death. Rather, they defend their choice not to pursue medical care even though they recognize a grave risk of death.[28]

B. *Decision to Intervene*

The second part of our *mens rea* inquiry must focus on whether, in light of their assessment of his condition, the appellants' failure to seek the advice of a medical professional was negligent. When deciding whether to take a sick child to the doctor, responses of reasonably prudent parents will vary widely. Most parents know that children get sick a lot and most of those sicknesses do not require a doctor visit. Some take children to the doctor at the first sign of illness, knowing that the visit may be unnecessary. Others wait until it is clear that a doctor is needed. There are many reasons why a reasonable parent might wait. Some fear a child is more likely to get sick from germs spread at a doctor's office than from germs at home. Other parents have difficulty scheduling visits, obtaining transportation, or getting time off work. Bringing a sick child to the doctor is also not the only way to treat them; parents employ a range of remedies to help children feel better and sometimes even to help the underlying condition. For example, a parent whose child has a sore throat may reasonably wait and treat the throat with saltwater rinses and anti-inflammatories.[29]

Here, it is undisputed that the appellants took steps to monitor, care for, and treat Billy as they watched his condition, and that they weighed the decision whether and when to seek medical care against a serious, founded concern about losing their child. Hindsight

---

[28] *Compare State v. Sanford*, 99 Me. 441 (1905) (suggesting that a parent who resorted to prayer in lieu of medical attention pursuant to a bona fide belief in its efficacy would not be guilty of manslaughter) *with People v. Pierson*, 176 N.Y. 201 (1903) (reaching opposite conclusion); *People v. Arnold*, 66 Cal. 2d 438, 442 (1967) (manslaughter conviction appropriate where mother "realized at this time that [her child] was gravely ill, since the girl could not walk unassisted, could not retain liquids fed her, could not normally excrete bodily waste, and was losing weight [and] Defendant, although aware that [her child] might die, did not obtain a doctor for her because of defendant's religious convictions against using medical assistance").

[29] The faith healing cases are instructive here to the extent they address the range of decisions and responses that might be considered reasonable and how the reasonableness standard attends to developments over time and to specific contexts. "The test to be applied is whether an ordinarily prudent person, solicitous for the welfare of his child and anxious to promote its recovery, would deem it necessary to call in a physician. The fact that the parents omitted to call a physician because they believed in divine healing, to be obtained by prayer, and did not believe in physicians, is no defense; nor is the statute unconstitutional in its application to such persons." *In re Hudson*, 13 Wash. 2d 673, 696 (1942). Summarizing these cases, Cawley suggests that modern courts, especially when construing statutes, will impose liability. C. C. Cawley, *Criminal Liability in Faith Healing*, 39 MINN. L. REV. 48, 57 (1954). However, Trescher and O'Neill argue that, at least in some communities, widespread legislative and community recognition of certain faith healing practices mean that a decision to forgo medical care based on a sincerely held religious belief may no longer be the basis for a manslaughter conviction. Trescher and O'Neill, *supra* at 217. If this argument is correct, we note that any healing practices based on Indian religious beliefs should be accorded the same consideration. That question is not at issue here because the parents do not argue that they chose to use religious healing instead of seeking medical care.

is tricky, and what is important for purposes of liability is what the parents knew at the time and whether they acted in a reasonably prudent manner in light of that knowledge, not whether they could reasonably have made a different decision or whether facts that later came to light might have changed their decision. In this case, the parents' decision met the standard of a reasonably prudent parent, even though in hindsight we (and they) know that they could have saved Billy's life by making a different one.

Our cases have recognized that reasonableness does not require a correct assessment of available information. For example, we have recognized that a person who kills an innocent person in self-defense is not a murderer as long as the assessment of the situation was reasonable given all of the circumstances. *See State v. Tribett*, 74 Wash. 125, 130 (1913) (approving the trial court's instruction: "Men when threatened with danger are obliged to judge from appearances and to determine therefrom in the light of all the circumstances the actual state of the surroundings, and in such cases if they act upon reasonable and honest convictions, induced by reasonable evidence under all the circumstances, they will not be held responsible criminally for a mistake as to the extent of the actual danger."); *State v. Stockhammer*, 34 Wash. 362, 268 (1904) (quoting 1 Bishop's New Criminal Law, § 305) ("'If, in the language not uncommon in the cases, one has reasonable cause to believe the existence of facts which will justify a killing,-or, in terms more nicely in accord with the principles on which the rule is founded, if without fault or carelessness he does believe them,-he is legally guiltless of the homicide, though he mistook the facts, and so the life of an innocent person is unfortunately extinguished.' So that it will be seen that, if a person acted without reason, he would not be acting without fault or carelessness."). Applying this test to the Williamses, it is clear that they mistook the facts regarding the severity of their son's illness "without fault or carelessness." Instead, the superior court effectively applied a higher standard of reasonableness to parental decision-making by substituting its own retrospective assessment where the parents' assessment that their son was not in mortal danger later turned out to be incorrect.

C. *Contextualizing the Reasonable Person Standard*

The difference in how the trial court assessed reasonableness here compared to self-defense and provocation cases is troubling because the latter areas developed specifically around the idea of a reasonable *man, see, e.g., People v. Rush*, 180 Cal.App.2d 885 (1960) (using standard of a "reasonable man" to deny self-defense instruction to woman despite her argument that a woman in her situation could have believed she was in imminent danger), whereas the legal role of parent has been more closely associated with women. By applying a higher standard of reasonableness to parenting decisions that result in deaths than to decisions about the intentional use of deadly force that result in death, the law accords more deference to decisions made in scenarios closely associated with men than it does to decisions made in scenarios traditionally associated with women.

To be sure, an assessment of reasonableness in either situation should take both men and women into account and should apply when there are both male and female appellants (as here). However, legal equality between the sexes also requires that female-associated roles be treated similarly under the law. In our context, that means that the reasonable parent should not be held to a higher standard of behavior compared to a reasonable defensive killer. The fair standard is whether the appellants made a reasonable assessment of the need for medical intervention, not whether they made a correct one.

Although the "reasonable person" standard refers to the ordinary person, we have recognized that context is important. In *Hedges*, we described the applicable legal standard as the "failure to perform such lawful act with usual and ordinary care as the great mass of mankind exercise under the same or similar circumstances." *Hedges*, at 8 Wash. 2d at 665. In *Tribett*, the appellant killed a streetcar operator and the court allowed testimony about the appellant's knowledge regarding whether the specific streetcar line had a reputation for violence, stating that the appellant "had a right to act upon all he knew-the threats of the parties, their failure to leave the car at a point where their conduct indicated they had intended to leave, the reputation of the line for lawlessness, his knowledge of that fact if he had such knowledge, the hour of the night, the darkness, the isolation at the end of the line, the failure of the parties to leave the car at the end of the line, and the circumstance that they remained upon the car while it passed on the Y in order to reverse and return to the city." 74 Wash. at 130. *See also State v. Churchill*, 52 Wash. 210, 100 P. 309, 219 (1909); *State v. Lewis*, 6 Wn. App. 38, 41 (1971); *State v. Ellis*, 30 Wash. 369, 374 (1902). This standard considers what an ordinary person would have done in the same situation and with the same knowledge.

According to appellants' testimony, they monitored Billy closely during the time he was ill, debating whether to take him to the hospital. They were prepared to take him to the hospital if required, but they were concerned about what might happen when they arrived. As the superior court found, they were afraid that the Welfare Department would take the baby away. The parents testified that they feared the doctor would report them and that a cousin had lost a child this way. Bernice Williams testified that she was "so scared" of losing Billy and that they hoped to take him in once the swelling went down. Here, the parents were weighing a serious concern related to the safety of their child, not simply trying to avoid a trivial inconvenience.

The district court did not inquire further about the appellants' fear, dismissing it as "no excuse that the law will recognize." However, the appellants' fear that their child would be taken is a rational one based on circumstances that should be considered in a court's assessment of reasonableness. The circumstances it arises from require further elaboration here. The appellants testified that their fear was rooted in the experiences of other parents in their community and even in their own families. They testified that Walter Williams' cousin had a child taken away by welfare authorities under similar circumstances.

Their fears are consistent with the concerns expressed by Indian parents in other cities about child welfare workers taking their children. According to a survey conducted by the Association of American Indian Affairs this year, 25–35 percent of all Indian children are separated from their families by child welfare authorities. In Washington, Indian children face an adoption rate 19 percent greater than non-Indian children and a foster care rate ten times greater. The League of Women Voters of Minnesota recently released a report focused on the American Indian population in Minneapolis. The report recounts an interview with a social worker who said that child welfare workers in Minneapolis seem to believe that "Indians don't deserve to be parents" and that Indian children are taken and separated from their siblings, and Indian parental rights eventually terminated, with great frequency. League of Women Voters of Minnesota, Indians in Minnesota (Jan. 1, 1971). *See also* Dorothy M. Jones, *Child Welfare Problems in an Alaskan Native Village*, 43 Social Service Review 297, 300 (1969) (noting that 19 of 28 children who were involved with the child welfare system from one Alaska Native village were removed from the village entirely and only six of those children were ever returned; also documenting the reluctance of community members to seek social services out of fear that children would be taken away). At least one Indian tribal government, the Devil's Lake Sioux Tribe, has enacted a resolution prohibiting state child welfare workers from removing children from the reservation.

The Williamses' fear was based on the belief that child welfare workers are more likely to make unwarranted accusations of neglect against Indian parents and to remove their children permanently. Although comparative statistics on the rate of child removals and adoptions are difficult to find, we note that the U.S. Bureau of Indian Affairs partnered with the Child Welfare League of America from 1958–1967 to pursue the Indian Adoption Project, a partnership with the explicit goal of facilitating the permanent adoption of Indian children.[30] At least 276 Indian children were placed for adoption through this partnership. These efforts were concentrated on children in fifteen states, including Washington. Most of the children were adopted into non-Indian homes in the Eastern or Southern United States.[31] At least one local publication demonstrates that this project has been promoted in the Seattle area Indian community.[32] The project's founders view adoption to be a favorable outcome for Indian children because they believe white adoptive homes are economically and culturally superior to the children's reservation communities.

---

[30] *See* Arnold Lyslo, Adoptive Placement of American Indian Children with Non-Indian Families, Part I: The Indian Project, 40 CHILD WELFARE 4 (1961).
[31] U.S. Dep't of the Interior, Bureau of Indian Affairs, Press Release: Indian Adoption Project Increases Momentum (Apr. 18, 1967).
[32] The American Indian Women's Service League, Inc., Indian Center News (Sep. 1969).

Indian parents, though, may have concerns about child welfare and adoption based on their experiences with past governmental policies that removed children from Indian communities. From the late 1800s through the early 1900s, federal agents placed Indian children in U.S. government-run educational institutions with the goal of assimilating the children and severing ties between them and their tribal communities. A 1934 report assessing this policy experiment noted that "education for the Indian in the past has proceeded largely on the theory that it is necessary to remove the Indian child as far as possible from his home environment" and called this approach "largely ineffective." Lewis Meriam, The Problem of Indian Administration 346, 9 (1934). *See also* Gerard Littman, *Alcoholism, Illness, and Social Pathology Among American Indians in Transition*, 60 Am. J. of Pub. Health 1769, 1775 (1970) (describing the negative effects of government efforts to "alienate Indians from their own culture"). Indian people also regard this experiment as harmful, and it has engendered mistrust by Indian parents of governmental services for children. See Richard M. Ross, *Cultural Integrity and American Indian Education*, 11 Ariz. L. Rev. 641, 660–665 (1969).

Whatever one concludes about the desirability of placing Indian children with white adoptive families, whether one believes child welfare removals of Indian children are warranted, or even whether one believes that the Williamses' concern was misplaced, it is clear from the appellants' testimony and reports from other communities that such a fear is common among Indian parents. It is also clear that the fear, in general, appears to be grounded in the experiences of parents who have lost children and in the knowledge that the federal government has pursued a strategy of removing Indian children from their families and communities. This fear, informed by the Williamses' personal knowledge and the collective knowledge of their community, was an important part of the context in which the Williamses made their decisions about how to treat Billy's toothache and how best to keep him safe. It was an error for the district court to disregard this fear completely when assessing the reasonableness of the appellants' decision.

The Williamses clearly perceived a danger that their child would be taken. That perception, whether or not it is ultimately correct, is reasonable in light of their knowledge of the experiences of their relatives and the documented experiences of Indian parents generally. *See* Trescher and O'Neill, *supra* at 203 ("as a belief becomes widespread and held by a substantial segment of society, it becomes easier to accept that belief as reasonable"). While many non-Indian parents might not face the possibility that a simple doctor visit would result in the permanent loss of a child, the Williamses' knowledge of and fear about this possibility is important in assessing the reasonableness of their conduct "under the circumstances."

In holding that the reasonable person standard is contextual, we must be careful not to traffic in stereotypes. The appellants' own brief describes Walter Williams as "a 24-year old full-blooded ... Indian with a sixth grade education whose occupation is solely that of laborer and whose only previous criminal involvement with the law was for being drunk" and Bernice Williams as "a twenty-year old part Indian with an eleventh grade education and no criminal record."[33]

We are concerned that the description of the parents as Indian and uneducated, together with the mention of Walter Williams' previous criminal history "for being drunk," invoke pervasive negative stereotypes about Indian people. The superior court's findings of fact refer to the parents as "ignorant" when describing their failure to realize that Billy's condition was life threatening. Lack of formal education alone is not a factor that should affect our evaluation of parental decision-making, as parenting is not only the province of the well-educated and the ability to care for and protect a child does not depend on formal schooling. It is clear that the Williamses understood that Billy was sick and that something was wrong with his tooth.

Fairness requires that we apply a uniform standard of reasonableness that is sensitive to circumstances where those circumstances are relevant to the case. Here, the appellants' knowledge of and experience with the possibility of child welfare removal is relevant to their decision, and their identity as Indian parents is relevant to the extent it is connected to the risk of removal and their awareness of it. A circumstance-specific standard, however, does not justify stereotyping them as ignorant and implying that Indian parents fall short of the reasonable parent standard just by virtue of being Indians.[34] This is exactly the kind of stereotyping that may lead to unnecessary child welfare removal of the kind the appellants feared, and it should not be imported into our criminal jurisprudence.

---

[33] Research using obituaries, official documents, and genealogical records, sources not available to the court at the time, indicates that both Walter Lloyd Williams and Bernice Jean (Tabafunda) Williams were descended from Indigenous communities located in an area of the Pacific Northwest that is now part of Canada. Walter Williams was from the Port Alberni Reserve, located on Vancouver Island, B.C. Port Alberni is home to the ćišaaʔatḥ or Tseshaht First Nation, part of the Nuu-chah-nulth or Nootka people. It seems likely that "Sheshont" was a mispronunciation of Tseshaht, rather than, as many commentators have surmised, Shoshone. *See, e.g.*, Paul H. Robinson, Would You Convict? Seventeen Cases that Challenged the Law (2001).

Until 1973, Port Alberni was home to a residential school whose survivors have described being abused. *See* Johnathan Chang and Meghna Chakrabarti, *Stories from Canada's Indigenous Residential School Survivors*, WBUR (Jul. 28, 2021), available at www.wbur.org/onpoint/2021/07/28/stories-from-survivors-of-canadas-indigenous-residential-schools. Bernice Williams' mother, Virginia Tabafunda, from DeRoche, British Columbia. Ancestry records suggest she was of Leq'á:mel and Nooksak descent. She attended the Kamloops residential school, where the remains of 215 children were discovered in mass graves in 2021. *See id.*; Associated Press, *215 Bodies Found at Residential School in Canada*, Indian Country Today (May 29, 2021). The Williamses lived on Vashon Island at the time of their arrest and trial, but Bernice Williams and members of her extended families were longtime residents of Bainbridge Island. Both islands are in the Puget Sound, near Seattle, a few hundred miles south of the Williamses' communities of origin.

[34] The parents' relative youth may affect how we evaluate the reasonableness of their actions; we might think of the reasonable young and inexperienced parent. However, Bernice had already raised another child and both parents were aware of the child's illness.

VI. CONCLUSION

Of course, a parent might be negligent, perhaps even criminally negligent, in failing to care for or protect a child. For example, a parent who is aware their child is being subjected to serious physical abuse by another parent and fails to intervene or make the child safe where they are capable of doing so may not be parenting in a reasonably prudent manner. A parent who inflicts serious physical injury on their child and then fails to seek medical care is not exercising reasonable prudence. *Compare State v. Parmenter*, 74 Wash. 2d 343, 351 (1968). A parent who ignores and fails to monitor a sick child because of an alcohol or drug addiction is also not parenting in a reasonably prudent manner. A parent who knows their child needs urgent medical attention but does not take the child to the doctor because they need to attend a party is not exercising reasonable prudence. Nor would reasonable prudence encompass a parent who reasonably worries about their child being taken away but also knows that the child is in mortal danger and so effectively chooses the child's death over their removal.

In contrast, Walter and Bernice Williams' decision not to bring their son to the doctor during the period of time when medical care could have saved his life was not negligent. Their parenting, including their assessment of Billy's condition, their caretaking, and their decision to delay medical treatment under the circumstances, especially where they had reason to fear that Billy might be taken from them, are consistent with what a reasonably prudent parent would have done under similar circumstances.[35] The decision of the superior court is reversed and the convictions vacated.

VII. INVITATION TO RECONSIDER THE ORDINARY NEGLIGENCE STANDARD

We have decided this case according to our precedents, which interpret Washington law as imposing manslaughter liability based on ordinary negligence. Even under this standard, which is lower than the criminal negligence standard that governs most manslaughter prosecutions, the appellants' convictions must be vacated. We urge the legislature, however, to reconsider our criminal statutes as interpreted in *Hedges*. In assessing the criminal liability of a parent for an omission resulting in the accidental death of a child, we believe that criminal negligence is likely the more correct standard.

Criminal punishment seeks to deter wrongdoing, achieve retribution against people who choose to break the law, or rehabilitate or incapacitate offenders. None of these purposes are served by punishing a parent whose well-intentioned decisions about how best to care for their child turn out to be mistaken. The criminal negligence standard usually applied to manslaughter recognizes this by limiting criminal

---

[35] We agree with the superior court that it certainly does not amount to gross negligence.

liability to those cases where an appellant's behavior diverges so grossly from that of an ordinary person that it is considered morally culpable, thus making retribution appropriate, and raising the possibility that future carelessness might arguably be deterred. While a lower standard may be appropriate for a limited class of cases, such as those involving the operation of dangerous instrumentalities, it is illogical to extend it to parental decision-making.

As we noted in *Hedges*, the Wisconsin legislature amended the statute shortly thereafter to require criminal negligence. *Hedges*, 8 Wn.2d at 666 (*citing State v. Whatley*, 210 Wis. 157 (1932) and *Bussard v. State*, 233 Wis. 11 (1939)). It did so after manslaughter convictions based on ordinary negligence were "severely criticised as attaching too arduous a consequence to acts and omissions of mere inadvertence." See *State v. Whatley*, 210 Wis. 157, 245 N.W. 93, 95 (1932). We urge the legislature to carefully consider the correct standard for parental manslaughter liability before we are faced with another case to which it must be applied.

10

Commentary on *State v. Walden*

LISA R. AVALOS

When *State v. Walden* was decided in 1982, the problem of family violence was just beginning to garner significant attention in the United States and abroad. In 1980, Dr. Lenore Walker published *The Battered Woman*, which laid out the theory of battered women's syndrome and described the cycle of violence that many women endured in their homes.[1] In 1984, the state of New York created a Task Force on Women in the Courts with the goal of examining and eliminating gender bias in the court system.[2] In the late 1980s, further research was published examining the cycle of violence in the home, the experiences of battered women and children, and how a lack of understanding of these dynamics were leading to problematic convictions of battered women who killed their abusers.[3] The United Nations did not begin focusing serious attention on domestic violence against women and children until 1985, and they did not publish their first resource manual on the problem until 1993.[4]

These developments were emerging as *Walden* was decided but were not yet widely known or accepted. *Walden* considered whether a mother could be found culpable as an accomplice when she was present, but did not participate in, a beating that her boyfriend administered to her one-year-old infant. The North Carolina Supreme Court approached this task without the benefits of the nascent domestic violence literature and the attention that research drew to the cycle of violence and the influence that abusers have over their victims. As such, the court never asked whether the mother was a victim of domestic violence herself. But the court went even further than this omission, also overlooking the basic *mens rea* requirements of the criminal law, allowing the mother to be convicted without any proof of her

---

[1] LENORE WALKER, THE BATTERED WOMAN (1980).
[2] LAWYER'S MANUAL ON DOMESTIC VIOLENCE, 20 (Mary Rothwell Davis, Dorchen A. Leidholdt & Charlotte A. Watson, eds.) (6th ed. 2015).
[3] *See, e.g.*, ANGELA BROWNE, WHEN BATTERED WOMEN KILL (1987) and JULIE BLACKMAN, INTIMATE VIOLENCE: A STUDY OF INJUSTICE (1989).
[4] United Nations, *Strategies for Confronting Domestic Violence: A Resource Manual* (1993), https://unodc.org/pdf/youthnet/tools_strategy_english_domestic_violence.pdf.

intent to assist in the commission of a crime. *State v. Walden* demonstrates the need to take into account the gendered dynamics of crimes such as domestic violence and child abuse.

THE ORIGINAL OPINION

Aleen Estes Walden lived with a roommate and her five young children. She was divorced from the children's father and was in a relationship with George Hoskins. On December 9, 1979, police were summoned to Walden's apartment after a neighbor heard the sounds of a young child screaming over a sustained period of time. Police quickly determined that Hoskins had severely beaten one of Walden's children, one-year-old Lamont Walden, with a deadly weapon – a leather belt with a metal buckle. A social worker took Lamont to a hospital, and medical personnel determined that he had lost about a third of his blood. The infant remained hospitalized for a week.

Aleen Walden was present in the apartment while Hoskins administered this beating. She did not participate in the beating, but she also did nothing to stop Hoskins. The evidence showed that she "responded to her son's anguished cries by telling him to hush."[5]

Hoskins was found guilty of assault with a deadly weapon in a separate proceeding, and he served 20 years in prison for this and other crimes against children.[6] But Hoskins' culpability did not put the matter to rest. The state proceeded against Walden on the theory that she aided and abetted Hoskins' beating. A jury convicted Walden of assault with a deadly weapon inflicting serious bodily injury on Lamont Walden. She served approximately two-and-a-half years in prison, despite the fact that she did not administer a single blow to the child.[7]

On appeal, the question before the Court was whether a mother could be found guilty of assault on a theory of aiding and abetting solely on the basis that she was present when her child was assaulted but failed to take reasonable steps to prevent the assault.[8] Walden argued that the jury instructions were erroneous because they allowed her to be convicted for failing to interfere with or attempt to prevent the commission of a felony.[9] She argued that a conviction for aiding and abetting

---

[5] *State v. Walden*, 280 S.E.2d 505, 508 (N.C. Ct. App.).
[6] North Carolina Prison (DOC) Arrest Records for Inmate George J. Hoskins, available at www.ncinmatesearch.org/NC_DPS.html.
[7] North Carolina State Prison Inmate Details for Aleen Walden, available at www.ncinmatesearch .org/NC_DPS.html; *State v. Walden*, 293 S.E.2d 780, 780 (N.C. 1982). Aleen Walden had beaten her children on prior occasions, but her behavior toward them was not an issue in the case on appeal. *State v. Walden*, 280 S.E.2d 505, 508, 509 (N.C. Ct. App. 1981). She had been indicted for misdemeanor child abuse in relation to Lamont Walden, but that charge was later dismissed. *State v. Walden*, 293 S.E.2d 780, 788 (N.C. 1982).
[8] *State v. Walden*, 293 S.E.2d 780, 782 (N.C. 1982).
[9] Id. at 784.

required an affirmative act by the defendant which demonstrated either her assistance with or encouragement of the commission of the crime, or indicating her approval and willingness to assist.[10]

The North Carolina Supreme Court disagreed, noting that a parent has an affirmative duty to protect her child. The Court found that a parent who fails in the duty to take all steps reasonably possible to protect her child has, by her omission, exhibited her "consent and contribution to the crime being committed."[11] The Court also held that it was proper for the trial court to allow a jury instruction indicating that Walden could be guilty of assault with a deadly weapon upon a theory of aiding and abetting, "solely on the ground that the defendant was present when her child was brutally beaten by Hoskins but failed to take all steps reasonable to prevent the attack or otherwise protect the child from injury."[12]

The Court was satisfied that Walden's failure to protect her child constituted consent to and encouragement of the commission of the crime charged, such that Walden was properly found to have aided and abetted Hoskins. Accordingly, the Court found no error in the jury instructions and upheld Walden's conviction.

IMPLICATIONS OF THE ORIGINAL OPINION

Aldeen Walden was not prosecuted because her individual actions gave rise to criminal liability; she was prosecuted because the omission doctrine was combined with a theory of accomplice liability in order to produce this result. In reaching its conclusion, the North Carolina Supreme Court equated a parent's failure to meet her affirmative duty to protect her child – an omission – with aiding and abetting a crime. Because Walden failed to protect her child, the Court reasoned, she aided and abetted Hoskins. But is such a failure tantamount to aiding and abetting? Where was the *mens rea* requirement for aiding and abetting in the Court's decision? The Court was silent on this point.

The opinion was also disturbingly silent in other respects. Although the Court noted that a parent does not have a legal duty to place herself in danger of death or great bodily harm in coming to the aid of her children,[13] it did not consider whether Walden faced any such danger in not coming to Lamont's aid. This was despite evidence in the record that Hoskins "exerted a strong influence over her,"[14] which causes one to wonder how strong that influence was and whether it was the product of violence. A related concern is that Walden's "hush" instruction to the baby was open to multiple interpretations. It could indicate support for Hoskins' beating, but

---

[10] *Id.* at 784.
[11] *Id.* at 787.
[12] *Id.*
[13] *Id.* at 786.
[14] *State v. Walden*, 280 S.E.2d 505, 508 (N.C. Ct. App.).

it could also be Walden's attempt to quiet the child and thereby reduce the chance of Hoskins escalating his assault.

The Court did not probe these questions. Rather, its silence on these matters set a disturbing precedent for similar cases involving poorly understood family violence dynamics. The opinion conveyed an assumption that Walden could have acted without endangering either herself or her children. Its silence also communicated the view that questions about any constraints on Walden's agency were unimportant and did not need to be asked. These oversights have had lasting effects. Since it was decided, *Walden* has frequently been cited for the proposition that parents can be held liable when someone else abuses their child.[15]

THE FEMINIST JUDGMENT

Writing for the majority, Professor Sarah L. Swan, writing as Justice Swan, forefronts these critical issues that were neglected in the original opinion, and calls attention to the gendered policy implications that deserve the Court's attention. She first rejects the notion that presence plus failed duty equals guilt, and instead shines a spotlight on the *mens rea* requirement eclipsed in the original opinion. Swan notes that problematic jury instructions allowed Walden to be convicted on either of two theories. One of these theories would have been legally sufficient, Swan explains, but the other was not.

Swan first notes the *valid* basis for a guilty verdict: Silent presence *can* be a basis to infer that the defendant intended to aid or abet a crime under circumstances where the perpetrator was known to her *and* she communicated her intention to offer assistance to the perpetrator. North Carolina law allows this communication to be inferred through circumstantial evidence indicating that knowing assistance has occurred. The court is entitled to consider such evidence as the relationship between the parties, the defendant's motive, and the defendant's conduct before and after the crime. In this context, Swan writes, the fact-finder would be entitled to weigh the defendant's failure to fulfill her duty to protect her child as one consideration that could indicate the defendant's intention to support and encourage the perpetrator's actions. Swan finds that the jury's verdict would stand if it rested on the basis that Walden's failure to protect her child was indicative of her intent to assist Hoskins' beating of Lamont, and that her silence was her way of conveying her support to Hoskins.

Swan points out, however, that the jury instructions also allowed a guilty verdict to rest on a distinct, and legally insufficient, theory. Specifically, the jury was instructed to convict if they determined that Walden "was present with the

---

[15] Michelle S. Jacobs, *Requiring Battered Women Die: Murder Liability for Mothers Under Failure to Protect Statutes*, 88 J. OF CRIMINAL LAW AND CRIMINOLOGY (1998) 579, 615.

reasonable opportunity and duty to prevent the crime and failed to take reasonable steps to do so."[16] This instruction lacks any explicit requirement of the scienter for aiding and abetting and accordingly would require Walden's conviction without any proof that she satisfied the *mens rea* requirement for the crime. For that reason, Swan finds the jury instructions erroneous, and Walden entitled to a new trial.

The feminist judgment also makes a significant contribution by articulating policy reasons why it is critical for courts to strictly adhere to *mens rea* requirements in cases where mothers are accused of inflicting abuse on their children. Among these, Swan notes that the gendered dynamics of domestic violence, where mothers may also be victims of the men who are abusing their children, can play a key role in shaping the women's responses, and courts must be sensitive to these dynamics in administering justice. Similarly, Swan also points out that racial bias has permeated how authorities respond to allegations of child abuse and neglect, with the result that children of color have, at times, been removed from their families on grounds that may have more to do with cultural or class bias than with actual abuse or neglect. A strict adherence to *mens rea* requirements can help to ensure that courts do not perpetuate discriminatory race and gender biases.

CONCLUSION

If Swan's opinion had carried the day in 1982, Walden would have been granted a new trial. She may still have been found guilty, but only if the jury determined that she *knowingly* advised, instigated, encouraged, or aided Hoskins in committing the assault. By preserving the *mens rea* requirement, the correct jury instruction would have created space for the jury to consider whether, in contrast to knowingly rendering aid, Walden instead remained silent in an effort to avoid antagonizing Hoskins further and to thus prevent an escalation of the violence that Hoskins was inflicting on Lamont.

The jury, therefore, would have been obligated to consider whether Walden's actions were those of an aider and abettor, or whether they were the actions of a mother who was doing as much as she could to protect her child in a context of domestic violence. Put simply, the Court would have had to confront the difficult questions about domestic violence and child abuse that were not considered by the original Court. The jury would have been tasked with analyzing the gendered dynamics between Walden and Hoskins, probing whether Walden was also a victim of Hoskins' abuse and whether she may have been trying to protect her children from him as best she could.

---

[16] *State v. Walden*, 293 S.E.2d at 784.

STATE OF NORTH CAROLINA V. ALEEN ESTES WALDEN, 293 S.E. 2D 780 (1982)

JUSTICE SARAH L. SWAN DELIVERED THE OPINION OF THE COURT

This appeal raises the following question: may a mother be found guilty of aiding and abetting the assault of her child on the sole basis that she had a duty to protect and was present when her child was assaulted yet failed to act? We answer this question in the negative. Criminal complicity requires a *mens rea* of knowingly aiding. Presence and duty may be relevant factors for establishing this *mens rea*, but the standard of knowingly aiding requires the prosecution to establish, to a standard of beyond a reasonable doubt, that the defendant was in fact subjectively aware or believed that she was assisting. In this case, the jury was instructed that it was possible to convict the defendant solely because she was present during the assault, owed a duty to protect the victim, and failed to assist. This is an incorrect statement of North Carolina law, and the trial verdict must thus be overturned and a new trial ordered.

I.

On the evening of December 8, 1979, the neighbor of the defendant Aleen Estes Walden heard what he understood to be the sounds of a child crying and being beaten coming from Aleen Walden's apartment. The following morning, December 9, 1979, that same neighbor again heard the sounds of a small child screaming and crying while being beaten, as well as a "popping" sound. Those sounds continued for approximately 60 to 90 minutes, prompting the neighbor to alert the police.

Officer D.A. Weingarten of the Raleigh Police Department responded and arrived at the apartment building later that morning. Officer Weingarten spoke to the neighbor, and then proceeded to Walden's apartment. The officer knocked at the door and Aleen Walden's roommate, Miss Devine, opened the door and allowed the officer inside. Officer Weingarten stayed for only a few minutes and left with the purpose of obtaining a search warrant. He returned to the apartment a short time later with the warrant. Inside the apartment, he observed Miss Devine again, along with Aleen Walden, her boyfriend George ("Bishop") Hoskins, and five small children. All of the children had obvious cuts and bruises. One-year-old Lamont Walden had red marks on his chest, a swollen lip, bruises on his legs and back, and other bruises, scarring, and cuts. Lamont was taken to hospital, where he was examined by Dr. David L. Ingram, a pediatric specialist and child medical examiner. Dr. Ingram confirmed that there were bruises, skin breaks, and purple marks on Lamont's body. Tests showed that there was also blood in Lamont's urine which resulted in the loss of a substantial quantity of blood (nearly one-third of his total blood volume, according to Dr. Ingram) and required that Lamont be given a blood transfusion. Dr. Ingram testified that in his expert opinion the marks on Lamont were caused by hard blows to the body occurring less than a week prior to his examination.

The other children were examined by social worker Annette McCullers. The children told her that Bishop Hoskins had beaten Lamont that morning, and that the defendant had been present but did not otherwise participate in the beating.

Relying on a theory of aiding and abetting, the defendant Aleen Walden was indicted as follows on April 28, 1980:

> The Jurors for the State Upon Their Oath Present that on or about the 9th day of December 1979, in Wake County Aleen Estes Walden unlawfully and willfully and feloniously assault Lamont Walden, age one year, with a certain deadly weapon, to wit: a leather belt with a metal buckle, inflicting serious bodily injuries, not resulting in death, upon the said Lamont Walden, to wit: numerous cuts and bruises causing severe blood loss and requiring hospitalization.

At trial, three of the children (10-year-old Roderick Walden, eight-year-old Stephen Walden, and seven-year-old Derrick Walden) testified that on the morning of December 9, 1979, Bishop Hoskins hit their brother Lamont with a belt repeatedly over an extended period of time while their mother was in the room, but that she did not say or do anything to interfere. As summarized by the Court of Appeals, evidence at trial further showed that the defendant "was very 'close' to Hoskins, the perpetrator of the assault, and that he exerted a strong influence over her [...] that Hoskins had beaten defendant's children in her presence before, that in the instant case he beat Lamont for an extended period of time, that during this assault defendant had responded to her son's anguished cries by telling him to 'hush,' and that defendant had beaten her children in the past with a lamp cord in Hoskin's presence."[17]

The defendant's evidence regarding the events of December 9, 1979, differed drastically from that of her children. According to her, the child's father, James Walden, appeared at the apartment unexpectedly that morning and administered the beating to Lamont. The defendant also testified that when James Walden appeared at the apartment and began beating Lamont, she tried to stop him but he struck her in the face causing injury.

The jury did not accept the defendant's evidence. The jury found that the defendant aided and abetted Hoskins in the commission of the assault on Lamont, and the defendant was sentenced to 5–10 years' imprisonment.

---

[17] These prior incidents are not part of the indictment, but, as the Court of Appeals found, "are relevant to show defendant's state of mind and her support to the perpetrator."

II.

In the charge to the jury, the trial judge instructed the jury that it could find aiding and abetting on two possible bases:

> It is the duty of a parent to protect their children and to do whatever may be reasonably necessary for their care and their safety. A parent has a duty to protect their children and cannot stand passively by and refuse to do so when it is reasonably within their power to protect their children. A parent is bound to provide such reasonable care as necessary, under the circumstances facing them at the particular time. However, a parent is not required to do the impossible or the unreasonable in caring for their children. Now, a person is not guilty of a crime merely because she is present at the scene. To be guilty she must aid or actively encourage the person committing the crime, or in some way communicate to this person her intention to assist in its commission; or that she is present with the reasonable opportunity and duty to prevent the crime and fails to take reasonable steps to do so. So I charge you that if you find from the evidence beyond a reasonable doubt, that on or about December 9th, 1979, Bishop Hoskins committed assault with a deadly weapon inflicting serious injury on Lamont Walden, that is that Bishop Hoskins intentionally hit Lamont Walden with a belt and that the belt was a deadly weapon, thereby inflicting serious injury upon Lamont Walden; and that the defendant was present at the time the crime was committed and did nothing and that in so doing the defendant knowingly advised, instigated, encouraged or aided Bishop Hoskins to commit that crime; or that she was present with the reasonable opportunity and duty to prevent the crime and failed to take reasonable steps to do so; it would be your duty to return a verdict of guilty of assault with a deadly weapon, inflicting serious injury.

Thus, according to this charge, the first basis upon which the jury could convict the defendant was that the defendant "was present at the time the crime was committed and did nothing and that in so doing the defendant knowingly advised, instigated, encouraged or aided Bishop Hoskins to commit that crime." Alternatively, the jury could convict if the defendant "was present with the reasonable opportunity and duty to prevent the crime and failed to take reasonable steps to do so." While the first stated basis for convicting is indeed a correct statement of North Carolina law, the second is not. Because of this erroneous jury charge, the trial verdict must be overturned.

III.

The first portion of the impugned jury instruction – which states that a defendant who is present and does nothing to oppose a crime may be found guilty of aiding and abetting, if through that presence and inaction, the defendant knowingly advised, instigated, encouraged or aided the principal – is correct. But the subsequent statement that a conviction can follow from a bare finding that the defendant "was present with the reasonable opportunity and duty to prevent the crime and failed to take reasonable steps to do so" is not. Circumstances like presence and inaction can create an inference that the defendant has knowingly aided or encouraged the principal, but *they need not do so*, and establishing presence and inaction is not equivalent to establishing the *mens rea* of knowing aid.

North Carolina courts have long confirmed the general rule that presence by itself is not usually a sufficient basis for aiding and abetting liability. As this Court declared in *State v. Hildreth*, 31 N.C. (9 Iredell) 440, 44 (1849), "one who is present and sees that a felony is about to be committed and does in no manner interfere, does not thereby participate in the felony committed." Rather, "[i]t is necessary, in order to have that effect, that he should do or say something showing his consent to the felonious purpose and contributing to its execution, as an aider and abettor." Similarly, in *State v. Birchfield*, 235 N.C. 410 (1952), this Court noted again that "[t]he mere presence of a person at the scene of a crime at the time of its commission does not make him a principal in the second degree, and this is so even though he makes no effort to prevent the crime, or even though he may silently approve of the crime, or even though he may secretly intend to assist the perpetrator in the commission of the crime in case his aid becomes necessary to its consummation."

But even though mere presence *alone* is not a sufficient basis for a finding of liability, a prosecutor may nevertheless be able to establish that a defendant knowingly advised, instigated, encouraged or aided the principal *through* that presence by introducing additional circumstantial evidence. For example, as the Court of Appeals noted, "a well-known exception to the rule that a bystander may not be convicted for her mere presence at the crime scene is stated thus: 'When the bystander is a friend of the perpetrator and knows that his presence will be regarded by the perpetrator as an encouragement and protection, presence alone may be regarded as encouraging.'" *State v. Jarell*, 141 N.C. 722, 725 (1906).

If the state can show that "the defendant was present, actually or constructively, with the intent to aid the perpetrator in the commission of the offense should his assistance become necessary and that such intent was communicated to the actual perpetrator," that can constitute sufficient evidence of aiding and abetting. *State v. Rankin*, 284 N.C. 219 (1973). This communication of intent to aid need not be by "express words of the defendant, but may be inferred from his actions and from his relation to the actual perpetrator." *Id.* So, presence and inaction can *help* establish the *mens rea*, but it is imperative that the jury actually find that the defendant has knowingly aided or encouraged the crime, meaning that she was subjectively aware or believed that she was assisting.

In other words, silent presence is not *in and of itself* enough to ground criminal liability, but silent presence along with other circumstantial evidence of a defendant's *mens rea* can support an inference that knowing assistance has taken place. *State v. Redfern*, 246 N.C. 293, 297 (1957). Other circumstantial evidence that may help to establish the requisite *mens rea*, as the Court of Appeals noted, can include "the relationship between the parties, any motive the defendant may have had to assist, and the defendant's conduct before and after the crime." *State v. Birchfield*, 235 N.C. 410 (1952).

Moreover, another circumstantial factor which may combine with silent presence to establish that the defendant knowingly aided or encouraged the crime is the existence of a duty. As the judge stated in the jury charge, parents in North Carolina have an affirmative legal duty to provide for their minor children. G.S. 14-316.1 (a) provides that "any parent ... to a child under 16 years of age who fails to exercise reasonable diligence in the care, protection, or control of such child ... shall be guilty of a misdemeanor." This duty includes a duty to affirmatively aid one's child when that child is in peril. Such a duty is and has always been inherent in the duty of parents to provide for the safety and welfare of their children, which duty has long been recognized by the common law and by statute. See *In Re TenHoopen*, 202 N.C. 223 (1932). This duty has also been recognized in other jurisdictions. See *Commonwealth v. Howard*, 265 Pa. Super. 535, 538 (1979) and *Palmer v. State*, 223 Md. 341, 343 (1960).

In this case, both parties knew the assault victim was the defendant's son. The jury could infer from this mutual knowledge that the defendant knew that Bishop Hoskins would view her refusal to perform her parental duty to protect her child as indicative of her support and encouragement of his actions. In other words, the fact that the defendant failed to perform her parental duty here was relevant as one circumstance, among many, that the jury could consider in determining the issue of whether defendant knew that her presence would be regarded by the perpetrator as encouragement or support.

Here, as the Court of Appeals noted, the defendant's parental duty and "the totality of the circumstances" could "warrant[] the inference by the jury that defendant knew her silent presence during the abuse would be regarded by her boyfriend Hoskins as encouragement and support." The evidence indicates that the defendant was very "close" to Hoskins, that "she had witnessed prior beatings by Hoskins (indicating that she was aware of the severity of his treatment of the children); that she had never interfered in the past; that she had herself beaten the children in Hoskins' presence; and that she lied and instructed her children to lie and conceal Hoskins' complicity in the assault." If the conviction rested solely on the basis that the jury had inferred the *mens rea* of knowingly aiding from the surrounding circumstances, the verdict would stand and there would be no valid basis for appeal. However, the jury was also told that they could convict if the prosecution showed only that the defendant was present during the assault, owed a duty to protect the victim, and failed to act. Because this instruction omits the *mens rea* requirement of knowing aid, this is an incorrect statement of law.

IV.

The trial verdict must be overturned because of the shortcomings of the instruction regarding this alternative basis for conviction. This portion of the jury charge likely led the jury to believe that the defendant could be convicted of assault with a deadly weapon as a principal in the second degree on the sole basis that she was present at the time of the assault and failed to exercise her duty to protect her child, *regardless* of whether she knowingly advised, instigated, encouraged or aided Hoskins to commit the crime.

This is an incorrect statement of law. It omits the required *mens rea* for complicity. In essence, this charge asserts that presence, plus a duty, plus no reasonable steps to perform that duty, constitutes aiding and abetting. Missing from this charge is an explicit requirement of the scienter for aiding and abetting (i.e. intending or knowingly aiding). While presence can be a basis to infer knowledge that the crime is occurring, aiding and abetting requires that the defendant know not only that the crime is occurring but that *they are encouraging or aiding it through their presence*. The jury charge in this case suggests that there is no need for a prosecutor to prove that the defendant knowingly advised, instigated, encouraged or aided the crime, and that presence, duty, and inaction can be a substitute for this showing.

The charge is thus incorrect. Although presence usually indicates knowledge of what is occurring, to convict on the basis of aiding and abetting the prosecutor must show, to a standard of beyond a reasonable doubt, that the defendant knowingly aided the principal. Knowing a crime is being committed and knowingly aiding it are not equivalent, and the existence of a duty to protect does not make them so. It is perfectly possible for a person to be present and to fail to take reasonable steps to fulfill their duty to protect, without meeting the standard of "knowingly aiding." For instance, a mother may fervently wish that her husband or boyfriend would not beat her child, yet stand quietly by perhaps so as not to enrage her husband further and risk increased abuse of the child. And the principal may well know that she is standing by on this basis. The heart of aiding and abetting remains as articulated by Judge Learned Hand in *United States v. Peoni*, 100 F.2d 401, 402 (2d Cir. 1938): aiding and abetting requires a defendant to "in some sense associate himself with the venture, that he participate in it as in something that he wishes to bring about, [and] that he seek by his action to make it succeed." Depending on the facts of the case, silent presence while owing a duty to rescue may allow a jury to infer that the standard of knowing aid has been met, but the inquiry does not end by merely showing presence, a duty to protect, and a failure to take reasonable steps to meet that duty.

Strict adherence to doctrinal elements, most specifically *mens rea* requirements, is particularly important in cases like this, where mothers are accused of aiding and abetting abuse inflicted on their children. There are four main reasons for this.

First, the facts of these cases are often difficult to read, and the brutality and violence experienced in these children's lives and by their small bodies regularly triggers emotions of abhorrence, repugnance, and retribution. These in turn may trigger a desire to blame anyone in the immediate vicinity of the abuse, who will often be the mother.

Mothers play a valuable societal role through performing childcare labor, and it is all too easy to blame them when their children suffer abuse. Obviously, sometimes this blame is well-founded. For instance, in Palmer v. State, a 1960 case from the Maryland Court of Appeals, 18-year-old Barbara Ann Palmer was convicted of manslaughter, after her boyfriend, Edward P. McCue beat her one year old child to death. McCue had repeatedly and viciously beat the child, prompting neighbors to attempt to intervene or offer assistance at various points. The defendant rebuffed these attempts. Her evidence at trial was that her child was "ornery and stubborn," and that her boyfriend's "discipline" of the child was reasonable – including when he bit the child on both her buttocks hard enough to leave marks visible days after. Maryland imposed a statutory duty on parents for the "support, care, nurture, welfare and education" of their children, and under Maryland law, "where the defendant owed to a deceased person a specific legal duty, but failed to perform the same, and death resulted to the deceased because of the nonperformance of the duty, (at least under circumstances where the failure to perform constituted gross and wanton negligence) the defendant is guilty of involuntary manslaughter." Palmer was charged with and convicted of involuntary manslaughter, and the Maryland Court of Appeals held that the mother had engaged in gross and criminal negligence by permitting and "in fact compelling" the child to remain in a highly dangerous environment, and affirmatively trying to prevent the child's removal from the danger when neighbors attempted to intercede. Although the mother's young age perhaps warrants some sympathy, criminal culpability could fairly be found in such a case.

Other cases, though, show that juries can be too quick to blame mothers, and illustrate that prosecutors must be held to their burdens of proof to avoid legal slippages in this fraught area. In *State v. McLaughlin*, 42 Or. App. 215 (1979), for example, a mother was indicted for child neglect after her husband beat their infant son to death while she was running a quick errand returning bottles to a store. The husband had a "history of bad temper and violence," including spanking her older daughters and physically striking the defendant on two occasions, but he had never before displayed anger directed at the baby. Nevertheless, at trial, the jury convicted the defendant of child neglect. The appellate court, though, noted that there was insufficient basis for this conviction, and the case should never have gone to the jury at all.

Second, another important policy reason why strict adherence to *mens rea* requirements in this area of aiding and abetting is particularly important is that in many cases where a male parental-type figure is abusing a child, he may also be abusing the child's mother as well, and this may impact her actions in regards to her failure to protect. Advocacy groups have demonstrated the high rate and prevalence of domestic violence in American society. Shelters are proliferating across the country in an effort to provide safety to women and families fleeing domestic abusers. The

United States Civil Rights Commission Consultation on Battered Women conference held in 1978 gave rise to a national coalition to address domestic violence, and case law, too, has begun to recognize the impact that domestic violence may have on an abused woman's behavior. *See* The United States Commission on Civil Rights, Under the Rule of Thumb: Battered Women and the Administration of Justice (1982).

For example, in the case of *Ibn-Tamas v. United States*, 407 A.2d 626 (1979) the court considered whether it could hear evidence related to domestic violence in relation to self-defense on a homicide charge. Dr. Lenore Walker, author of *The Battered Woman* and expert psychologist, provided testimony for the purposes of showing that women who have experienced abuse may behave in counterintuitive ways. In Ibn-Tamas, Dr. Walker's testimony was offered to inform the jury about battered women, and to "explain why the mentality and behavior of such women are at variance with the ordinary lay perception of how someone would be likely to react to a spouse who is a batterer." In discussing the beliefs that battered women might hold, Dr. Walker testified that domestic violence can be used to make the abused person comply, and to punish, intimidate, and control. Although, as Dr. Walker explained, it is sometimes difficult for nonbattered people to understand, battered women "tend to believe their husbands are basically loving, caring men; the women assume that they, themselves, are somehow responsible for their husbands' violent behavior. They also believe, however, that their husbands are capable of killing them, and they feel there is no escape. Unless a shelter is available, these women stay with their husbands, not only because they typically lack a means of self-support but also because they fear that if they leave they will be found and hurt even more."

In these circumstances, battered women may exhibit "learned helplessness," where they realize that trying to leave or otherwise avoid the abuse will likely not be successful, and so they do not engage in efforts to do so. Compliance with the abuser's demands appears to be the only and the safest possible path. This may be true even when the abuser turns the violence towards the children; protesting or otherwise resisting this abuse may only lead to more detrimental effects. Thus, battered women may engage in *what looks like* passive acquiescence but is actually a means of harm avoidance.

If criminal liability for aiding and abetting were to rest only on a showing of presence, a duty to act and a failure to do so, many instances in which mothers were themselves in fear of abuse would likely lead to criminal conviction. This is so, despite the "reasonable" qualification to fulfilling the duty. As the judge stated in the jury charge, technically a "parent is not required to do the impossible or the unreasonable in caring for their children." In other words, a parent's duty to affirmatively aid does not require a parent to place themselves in danger of death or great bodily harm in coming to the aid of their children. But the duty is robust, in that parents do have the duty to take every step reasonably possible under the circumstances of a given situation to prevent harm to their children. In some cases, depending on the size difference, relative vitality, and history between the parties involved, it might be reasonable to expect a parent to physically intervene and restrain the persons attempting to injure the child. In others, it will be reasonable to for a parent to go for help or to merely verbally protest an attack upon the child. What is reasonable in any given case will be a question for the jury after proper instructions from the trial court.

Although the notion that a defendant need only make a "reasonable effort" to fulfill a duty to protect would seemingly provide a means to avoid conviction, the aforementioned tendency to blame mothers for the abuse their male partners inflict on their children, combined with a lack of understanding of some of the complexities and counterintuitive aspects of abuse highlights the dangers in relying on "reasonableness" to calibrate criminal liability appropriately. Dr. Walker's research shows that the actions of battered women are usually seen as "unreasonable," particularly when they do not leave the relationship immediately after they or their children are abused. Jurors will no doubt find it difficult to understand how someone could "allow" their child to be abused, and how failing to protest in the strongest possible terms or failing to fight tooth and nail to prevent the abuse from happening could possibly constitute reasonable efforts.[18]

The third reason suggesting that the scienter element in this context must be strictly adhered to concerns the troubling history surrounding race and allegations of child abuse or neglect. There is a history of white authorities using allegations of child abuse and neglect to justify intervening in minority families in ways that reflect discrimination. For example, the federal government recently passed the Indian Child Welfare Act, 25 U.S.C. § 1902 (Supp. II 1978), after it became apparent that a disproportionate number of children in those communities were being removed from their families, often on the premise of neglect or abuse. In fact, prior to this 1978 legislation, an estimated 30 percent of these children were removed and placed with white families on the grounds of alleged abuse or neglect. The defendant in this case is Black, and the court is aware that similar dynamics can impact Black families. Allegations of abuse and neglect and the interventions that

---

[18] The case record does not inquire into domestic violence of this nature in the instant case, but the record does hint at some troubling aspects of the relationship between Bishop Hoskins and Aleen Walden. At trial, the responding officer testified that Hoskins "claim[ed] to be a preacher" and that the officer was of the opinion that Hoskins had "a great deal of influence over [Walden]." The social worker Annette McCullers testified that Hoskins "purports to be a preacher" and that she "was aware of a following or two." The defendant's sister testified that the "Bishop" had "just two followers" – namely the defendant and the aforementioned Miss Devine. The defendant's sister also testified that "[the defendant's] relationship with Bishop Hoskins was she was so close to him none of us – she would not let us visit her, see her; wouldn't let us in [...] George Hoskins came on the scene and influenced her to come under him the way she has. It's not her. She is under some kind of influence." According to the defendant, the Bishop "was ordained by God," he was "a minister," and the defendant "believe[d] it's in God working through him."

flow from those have become increasingly criticized as imposing white "middle-class standards to poor and minority parents" and as being reflective of cultural bias. See Michael Wald, *State Intervention on Behalf of "Neglected" Children: A Search for Realistic Standards*, 27 Stan. L. Rev. 985, 998 (1975). If lower *mens rea* standards were applied to cases like this one, complicity doctrines could become a path to perpetuating the troubling tradition of separating Black families, which has persisted since the time of slavery.

Finally, the fourth policy reason to support the clear case law indicating that aiding and abetting requires the specific scienter of knowingly aiding, is that the aider and abettor is often punished as harshly, or sometimes even more harshly that the principal perpetrator of the crime. For example, in *State v. Smolin*, 557 P.2d 1241 (1976), a mother who was aware her child had been burned while in the care of her boyfriend, but nevertheless left the child in his care again, was found guilty of aiding and abetting (though she was not present at the time of the abuse) and sentenced to 3 to 20 years' imprisonment. The principal wrongdoer who inflicted the actual injuries, Robert Michael Berkowitz, on the other hand, successfully argued a double jeopardy issue when the initial statute he was convicted of was determined to be unconstitutionally vague, and in 1979 it was determined he could not be retried, and so he was not punished for this crime. Because aiding and abetting attracts such severe punishment, often resulting in practical terms in punishment that is greater for the aider and abettor than that imposed on the principal, it is important to uphold scienter requirements in this context.

Notably, many jurisdictions have enacted statutory provisions that operate in situations where a parent's actions or inactions are wrongful, but such scienter may not be present. In fact, as the defendant argued on appeal, North Carolina has such a statute. G.S.14-318.2 provides that "[a]ny parent of a child less than 16 years of age, or any other person providing care to or supervision of such child, who inflicts physical injury, or who allows physical injury to be inflicted, or who creates or allows to be created a substantial risk of physical injury, upon or to such child by other than accidental means" is guilty of the misdemeanor of child abuse. Section (b) states that this offense is "additional to other civil and criminal provisions and is not intended to repeal or preclude any other sanctions or remedies." As is clear from the language of the statute, this provision makes it a crime for any parent to permit the abuse of their child. The *mens rea* requirement here is less, and that is reflected in the lesser punishment attached to this misdemeanor crime. This statute demonstrates that the North Carolina legislature meant to distinguish between passive parental conduct which does not rise to the level of knowingly aiding and abetting, and to punish each proportionately.

These four policy reasons give even more heft to the already-clear case law on the elements of aiding and abetting. Silent presence with a duty to rescue may be evidence from which a jury can infer the defendant knowingly aided the crime but is not on its own equivalent to aiding and abetting. In this case, the weight of the evidence is such that a jury could infer that the defendant knowingly aided the crime, but because the jury was instructed they need not draw such an inference and could instead convict merely on a showing that the defendant was silently present while owing a duty to aid she did not fulfill, the verdict is set aside. The defendant is entitled to a new trial in which it is clear that aiding and abetting requires a *mens rea* of knowingly aiding.

We therefore order a new trial.

11

Commentary on *State v. Norman*

JOAN H. KRAUSE

In *State v. Norman*, the North Carolina Supreme Court upheld Judy Norman's voluntary manslaughter conviction for killing her abusive husband, reversing a Court of Appeals decision that had granted a new trial.[1] Focusing on the fact that J.T. Norman was asleep when he was shot, the Court found Judy failed to establish that she killed "due to a reasonable fear of imminent death or great bodily harm"[2] and was not entitled to a self-defense instruction. *Norman* is perhaps the most egregious example of a victim of domestic or intimate partner violence (IPV) who is unable to argue self-defense because she kills in "nonconfrontational" circumstances.

The doctrine of self-defense renders an otherwise criminal homicide permissible in certain circumstances. Although there are slight variations from jurisdiction to jurisdiction, a person generally may respond with deadly force if the person reasonably believes such force is *necessary* to defend against an *imminent* threat of death or serious bodily harm. That belief must be both *subjectively and objectively reasonable*; not only must the defendant believe the threat, but a *reasonable person* must similarly believe.[3] The defense was historically defined using male terms, including male pronouns in jury instructions.[4] Although feminists have questioned the assumption, the paradigmatic self-defense scenario involves a confrontation in which the actor, faced with an unanticipated and deadly threat, has no option but to respond in kind.[5] The further the facts diverge from the prototypical confrontation, the more difficult the defense. Victims of IPV (or "battered women," in the legal literature) face many barriers to these requirements. The act of killing in itself confounds expectations of how women are expected to behave. Without a typical confrontation, as when an abuser is asleep, it may be difficult to convince judges

---

[1] *State v. Norman*, 378 S.E.2d 8 (N.C. 1989) (*reversing State v. Norman*, 366 S.E.2d 586 (N.C. Ct. App. 1988)).
[2] 378 S.E.2d at 9.
[3] JOSHUA DRESSLER, UNDERSTANDING CRIMINAL LAW § 18.01 (8th ed. 2018).
[4] *See State v. Wanrow*, 559 P.2d 548 (Wash. 1977) (reversing because trial court framed instruction using male pronouns).
[5] *See, e.g.*, V. F. Nourse, *Self-Defense and Subjectivity*, 68 U. CHI. L. REV. 1235 (2001).

and juries that the defendant actually believed she faced an imminent threat, let alone that her belief was reasonable.

By the mid-1980s these cases had drawn public scrutiny, helped by dramatizations such as *The Burning Bed*, a book (and then TV-movie) describing how Francine Hughes set fire to her abusive husband's bed while he slept.[6] Advocates recognized that these issues were foreign to many jurors, and sought to introduce expert testimony to explain the relevance of abuse to self-defense: not only how the *defendant* could have perceived an imminent threat of deadly harm under these supposedly benign circumstances, but even more importantly, how that perception could be *reasonable*.

As Professor Mahoney has chronicled elsewhere, the psychological literature offered multiple competing analytical frameworks.[7] The framework that garnered the most support in court was the "battered woman syndrome" (BWS), developed by Dr. Lenore Walker in the 1970s to explain how women became trapped in abusive relationships. Walker adapted Martin Seligman's "learned helplessness" theory, which demonstrated that laboratory animals subjected to random electrical shocks continued to behave passively when given opportunities to avoid additional shocks; similar to the animals, Walker hypothesized that abused women "learn" they are helpless to control their fates.[8] Walker paired this with a three-stage "cycle of violence": a "tension-building" stage involving minor abuse, the "acute battering incident," and then a "calm, loving respite."[9] Together, Walker argued, these phenomena lead victims to believe they have no choice but to stay.

Perhaps because lawyers were attracted to "syndrome" evidence,[10] or perhaps because BWS did fit some defendants, BWS quickly became the dominant framework. Defense attorneys sought admission of expert testimony on BWS, jury instructions incorporating BWS, and even rulings that defendants should be compared to a "reasonable battered woman." In the years surrounding *Norman*, a number of states would admit BWS evidence by case law or statute, and some governors would use executive clemency to reconsider the convictions of women who had been precluded from offering such testimony at trial.[11]

From the outset, BWS was a problematic conceptual framework. "Learned helplessness" was an uneasy fit with the act of killing, an inconsistency highlighted by

---

[6] FAITH MCNULTY, THE BURNING BED (1980).

[7] *See* Martha R. Mahoney, *Misunderstanding Judy Norman: Theory as Cause and Consequence*, 51 CONN. L. REV. 671, 702–712 (describing different frameworks).

[8] Lenore E. Walker, *Battered Women and Learned Helplessness*, 2 VICTIMOLOGY 525 (1978).

[9] *Id.* at 531–532.

[10] Mahoney, *supra* note 7, at 704–705.

[11] *See* Joan H. Krause, *Of Merciful Justice and Justifiable Mercy: Commuting the Sentences of Battered Women Who Kill*, 46 FLA. L. REV. 699, 719–742 (describing ways in which different states addressed BWS evidence). Indeed, such clemency was later extended to Judy herself, although not more widely in North Carolina.

prosecutors. Women who successfully relied on BWS sometimes faced collateral custody consequences, with the evidence implying they were incapable of caring for their children.[12] Moreover, Walker's model came from interviews with a small, racially homogenous group of women, and was never designed to be a universal IPV model.[13] In its legal incarnation, BWS became an unrealistic, culturally limited construct that risked convicting women not because their actions failed to support self-defense, but because they did not fit the model of "good" battered women.

In the midst of this debate, Judy was tried for murder. Although Superior Court Judge John Gardner ultimately denied a jury instruction on self-defense, he appointed a forensic psychologist and admitted evidence that would have been relevant. The jury was instructed on first degree murder, second degree murder, and voluntary manslaughter (provocation), ultimately convicting Judy of voluntary manslaughter; she was sentenced to six years in prison, although the governor later commuted her sentence to time served.[14] A unanimous panel of the Court of Appeals reversed, finding the evidence sufficient to support a self-defense instruction.[15] As discussed below, a divided North Carolina Supreme Court disagreed and reversed.

THE NORTH CAROLINA SUPREME COURT'S DECISION IN *STATE V. NORMAN*

From the beginning of the North Carolina Supreme Court's decision, it is readily apparent how it will end. The opinion begins with a stark and unsympathetic description from Judy's statement to the Sheriff:

> She pointed the pistol at the back of her sleeping husband's head, but it jammed the first time she tried to shoot him. She fixed the gun and then shot her husband in the back of the head as he lay sleeping. After one shot, she felt her husband's chest and determined that he was still breathing and making sounds. She then shot him twice more in the back of the head.[16]

The Court summarized the "evidence tending to show a long history of physical and mental abuse by [defendant's] husband due to his alcoholism," including forced prostitution and a variety of physical abuse and "other indignities," but noted that no injuries required medical attention.[17] It described the escalating violence in the days before the killing, including Judy's suicide attempt and J.T.'s efforts to

---

[12] See Elizabeth M. Schneider, *Particularity and Generality: Challenges of Feminist Theory and Practice in Work on Woman-Abuse*, 67 N.Y.U. L. Rev. 520, 556–557 (1992).
[13] See, e.g., Linda L. Ammons, *Mules, Madonnas, Babies, Bath Water, Racial Imagery and Stereotypes: The African-American Woman and the Battered Woman Syndrome*, 1995 Wisc. L. Rev. 1003 (1995).
[14] Mahoney, *supra* note 7, at 676, 727 (describing trial and postconviction clemency requests).
[15] *State v. Norman*, 366 S.E.2d 586 (N.C. Ct. App. 1988).
[16] *Norman*, 378 S.E.2d at 9.
[17] Id. at 9–10.

thwart paramedics; J.T.'s interruption of her social services appointment; and multiple calls to the police. And the majority acknowledged that two experts testified Judy "fit the profile of battered wife syndrome" and that she felt she "had no choice" and it was "necessary" for her to kill.[18]

In North Carolina, "perfect" self-defense can be submitted to the jury when

> at the time of the killing it appeared to the defendant and she believed it to be necessary to kill the decedent to save herself from imminent death or great bodily harm.... That belief must be reasonable ... in that the circumstances as they appeared to the defendant would create such a belief in the mind of a person of ordinary firmness.[19]

North Carolina also recognizes "imperfect" self-defense, such as when the defendant is a nondeadly aggressor but the victim escalates the violence; while this does not justify the killing, it constitutes grounds for the lesser offense of voluntary manslaughter. Yet neither theory was available to Judy because both required evidence that she "reasonably believed" it was necessary to kill "to save herself from *imminent* death or great bodily harm."[20]

The majority focused on the fact that at the time of the killing, J.T. had been asleep for several hours; if anything, Judy initiated the final, fatal confrontation. Absent "an instantaneous choice between killing her husband or being killed or seriously injured," the majority concluded that "*all* of the evidence tended to show that the defendant had ample time and opportunity to resort to other means of preventing further abuse by her husband."[21] Rejecting both the expert testimony and Judy's own statements that she believed her husband would eventually kill her, the Justices stressed her "lack of any belief – reasonable or otherwise – that ... the drunk and sleeping victim" posed a threat.[22] They also expressed concern that relaxing the rigid imminence requirement might "legalize the opportune killing of abusive husbands by their wives solely on the basis of the wives' testimony concerning their subjective speculation as to the probability of future felonious assaults," and thus invite IPV victims to engage in "[h]omicidal self-help ...."[23]

In dissent, Justice Martin argued that the evidence satisfied the traditional requirements for self-defense. In addition to the statements of Judy and the expert witnesses, this included testimony from family members present in those fateful days, who "described circumstances that caused not only the defendant to believe escape was impossible, but that also convinced *them* of its impossibility."[24] Martin

---

[18] *Id.* at 11–12.
[19] *Id.* at 12.
[20] *Id.*
[21] *Id.* (emphasis in original).
[22] *Id.*
[23] *Id.*
[24] *Id.* at 18 (emphasis in original).

clarified that the question is not whether the threat is imminent *in fact*, but rather whether the defendant *reasonably believed* it to be so – a conclusion the jury could well have reached here. He drew from the expert testimony to explain the continuous nature of the altercation and stressed that as long as the evidence was enough to create reasonable doubt as to Judy's intention to kill, self-defense should have been submitted to the jury.

THE FEMINIST JUDGMENT

The *Norman* opinion has been widely criticized by feminists not only for its artificially narrow (mis)construction of self-defense, which rendered the expert evidence all but irrelevant, but also for its insistence on framing that evidence through BWS. The new dissent by Professor Martha Mahoney, writing as Justice Mahoney, adopts a feminist methodology that weaves together personal narrative, lived experience, and social science. Mahoney's dissent is rooted in a detailed reading of the trial record, which reveals that even the majority's horrifying summary of the abuse did not capture the full force of J.T.'s repeated threats, degradation, and ceaseless violence – all witnessed by the family members who testified on Judy's behalf. Mahoney also details the numerous times Judy had sought help, either to be stopped by J.T. (including at the food stamp office that very morning) or told incorrectly by law enforcement that there was nothing they could do.

Mahoney does a masterful job demonstrating how these facts support a claim of self-defense. Regarding the majority's dismissal of Judy's belief that J.T. would kill her as mere "speculation," she notes:

> The majority does not discuss her belief in his threats to kill in conjunction with the shared belief of her family members, his repeated threats to kill her that day, the speed and ease with which he could reach a knife, or the compressed time between when he fell asleep and she fired the gun. The legal question ... is what the history and her belief in the danger of death must mean in weighing the elements of self-defense.

Noting the troubling stereotypes invited by BWS, Mahoney clarifies that neither expert, in fact, "described separate standards for self-defense for battered women." In fact, Mahoney criticizes the Court of Appeals for its overreliance on BWS and learned helplessness, which arguably heightened the majority's fears of creating a new subjective defense.

Mahoney artfully debunks the majority's characterization of the expert testimony, pointing out that the court-appointed psychologist (Dr. Tyson) did not in fact testify about BWS, but rather the *coercive control* framework. Tyson emphasized "the importance of degradation and humiliation as strategies to break the spirit of a human being and make that person more vulnerable to abuse." Not only did Judy fear for herself, she also worried that J.T. would take his violence out on the children if she left. In one of her strongest points, Mahoney offers a quote from Tyson's testimony that was completely ignored by the majority: "Mrs. Norman didn't leave because she believed, fully believed that escape was totally impossible .... The law, she believed the law could not protect her; no one could protect her, and I must admit, looking over the records, *that there was nothing done that would contradict that belief.*" That evidence was relevant not only to Judy's own belief, but also to how a "person of ordinary firmness" would view the situation.

Mahoney argues that those beliefs were amply supported by the family members who "shared Judy's perception of deadly threat that day." Eyewitnesses feared for their own safety if they tried to intervene, and had seen that the police would not help. Indeed, the gun used to kill J.T. was taken from the purse of *Judy's mother*, who feared J.T.'s recent threats. That evidence ably refutes concerns that this is a purely subjective standard: as Mahoney notes, "Eyewitness perceptions are important to the core principle that gives the task of determining reasonableness to a jury of the defendant's peers. Shared terror is relevant to reasonable perception." Echoing feminist calls for engaging with lived experience,[25] Mahoney notes that imminence is "the product of circumstances ... [that] include the credibility of threats, the availability of weapons, and the availability of help or legal protection." She writes, "[f]rom prior experience and her experience that day, Judy Norman reached a *reasoned conclusion* that the law would not help her," and a person of ordinary firmness might well have agreed.

Finally, Mahoney reminds us of a core principle often overlooked: the "great bodily harm" encompassed by self-defense may well include *sexual violence.* J.T. regularly forced Judy into prostitution. Indeed, "[t]his daily sexual violence was so certain, so about-to-happen, that the majority treats it not as a threat but as a routine incident of abuse." Mahoney's dissent makes explicit the dangers of cloaking misogyny as jurisprudence, and warns of creating a defense that in reality helps only male defendants. Mahoney's cogent critique of BWS and coercive control could well have redefined the debate over IPV evidence, not only in academia but in case law. And her suggestion that sexual violence may support self-defense would have provided an opening for advocates to argue for changes in state law, years earlier than those efforts began in actuality.[26]

Mahoney makes clear how badly the legal system failed Judy Norman, both before and after the killing. When a victim of IPV believes she truly has no option other than to kill or be killed – and that belief is echoed by both eyewitnesses and experts – Mahoney implies that the entire *community* has failed. That societal responsibility echoes the core messages of feminist, vulnerability, and communitarian theorists,

---

[25] *See, e.g.,* SONIA KRUKS, *Women's "Lived Experience": Feminism and Phenomenology from Simone de Beauvoir to the Present* in THE SAGE HANDBOOK OF FEMINIST THEORY 75 (Mary Evans et al., eds., 2014) (discussing feminist critiques of concept of "lived experience").

[26] *See* Mahoney, *supra* note 7, at 75–80.

who argue that the fundamental role of government should be to provide support necessary for citizens to flourish and become functional members of society: "Respect for human dignity ... requires that the state actively support individuals in receiving the caretaking and conditions for human development necessary for them to become responsible, self-directing citizens."[27] The burden of Judy's lack of options should fall not on her, but on us all.

STATE V. NORMAN, 378 S.E.2D 8 (N.C. 1989)

JUSTICE MARTHA R. MAHONEY, DISSENTING

After enduring decades of abuse and thirty-six hours of rapidly escalating rage and lethal threats, Judy Norman shot her husband, John Thomas ("J.T.") Norman during his afternoon nap. That nap was a temporary pause of uncertain duration that let him rest from the exertion of beating, controlling, and transporting her all day, as he prepared to force her into prostitution that night. There is no dispute in the trial testimony about the facts of abuse or the timing of events. The questions on appeal are legal: the interpretation and application of those facts to the legal questions of whether the nap meant desistance from aggression or meant that the threats facing her could not be imminent, and the fundamental question of whether the jury should be allowed to consider self-defense. The Court of Appeals found error in the trial judge's failure to instruct on self-defense and ordered a new trial, finding no cessation in J.T.'s continuing threats and abuse, only a brief hiatus in his reign of terror. The majority here, finding no imminent threat and expressing fears of creating a new self-defense standard or potentially expanding self-defense law to rest solely on subjective perception, reverses the Court of Appeals and affirms her conviction.

I join Justice Martin's well-reasoned dissent but write separately to clarify the evidence, its relevance to self-defense, and the legal standard governing self-defense. The majority opinion states that Judy Norman had "ample time and opportunity to resort to other means of preventing further abuse by her husband." It concludes by warning that on these facts a jury instruction on self-defense would change the imminence requirement and undermine the requirement of reasonableness in self-defense. The factual analysis underlying those conclusions is mistaken in three crucial ways, all of which bear directly on the elements of self-defense: the timing that day, her options, and the harm she sought to avoid.

Time and opportunity go to the questions of imminence and necessity of using deadly force in self-defense. In ordering a new trial, the Court of Appeals relied on facts established at trial, on expert testimony, and on literature on "battered

---

[27] Maxine Eichner, The Supportive State: Families, Government, and America's Political Ideals 52 (2010).

spouse syndrome." The majority opinion, treating the appellate court's conclusion as based entirely on "battered wife syndrome," asserts that a self-defense instruction for Judy Norman would create a "battered woman defense" that could expand to any area and would rely entirely on the subjective perceptions of a defendant. Such an approach would, they fear, abandon our longstanding standard of reasonable perception by a person of ordinary firmness.

Supporting the denial of the self-defense instruction, the majority cites a law review article that says institutional change is preferable to relaxing the law of homicide. Marilyn Hall Mitchell, *Does Wife Abuse Justify Homicide?*, 24 Wayne L. Rev. 1705 (1978) (advocating institutional solutions to wife abuse; cautioning against self-help or creating a separate defense for battered women; and calling for reforms including shelters, improved warrantless arrests, and availability of protective orders). Institutional change is indisputably preferable to the death of any person. When the state charges someone with homicide, however, the facts and circumstances facing that defendant determine the issue of self-defense. The institutional changes North Carolina has made did not help Judy Norman in her circumstances.

Although the majority opinion recites some facts, the full factual record has significant bearing on the legal issues. Events developed in a compressed time period. Police did not help her, and she sought help from additional sources without success. She was not avoiding "further abuse" of the sort she had long experienced; rather, she was responding to a swift intensification of rage and danger, including repeated threats to use knives to maim and kill her.

Two grave threats of harm or death loomed as J.T. Norman slept. Violent forced sexual exploitation was so certain and so imminent that the majority treats it as a routine fact, not a threat of violence that would occur after he woke from a nap and be worse than ever given his state of escalated rage. J.T. had made repeated threats to kill Judy. His specific threat to kill immediately if she got legal help, and the failure of police to arrest him, foreclosed those possibilities for assistance. Testimony from her mother and daughter showed that they too believed his threats to kill her. The court-appointed expert found nothing in the records to contradict Judy's belief that the law would not protect her. Based on the testimony of the defendant, eyewitnesses, and experts, the jury should have been allowed to consider whether a person of ordinary firmness in her situation would have perceived apparent threat that made it necessary to kill to save herself from death or great bodily harm.

I.

Judy Ann Laws married John Thomas (J.T.) Norman when she was 15 years old and pregnant. Five years later, he began drinking and became abusive. After that, Judy could no longer hold a job. He said she did not make enough money as a waitress; he would come to her workplace and make her leave; he began forcing her into prostitution.

He hit her "most every day ... whenever he got drunk." She said that they "got along very well when he was sober" and that he was "a good guy" when he was not drunk. But his drinking and abuse continued. He beat her with his fists and with household items turned into weapons including bottles, glasses, an ashtray, a shoe, and a flyswatter. He had also beaten her with baseball bats, which have the capacity to be used as deadly weapons. *State v. Smith*, 121 S.E. 737 (N.C. 1924) (stating that "[a] pistol or a gun is a deadly weapon ... a baseball bat should be similarly denominated if viciously used").

During his attacks, she cried but never fought back. Beyond the physical violence and unpredictable terror, he called her degrading names including "bitch," "dog," and "whore." He forced her to sleep on the floor; sometimes he made her eat pet food from the cat or dog dish, act like an animal, or bark like a dog.

J.T.'s brutal control over his wife deprived her of all contact with one of her children for 12 years. Judy Norman gave birth to their fourth child prematurely after J.T. beat her and kicked her down a flight of stairs. The baby weighed only one and a half pounds at birth. J.T. forbade her to visit the hospital, and when the baby was released months later, J.T. gave the infant to his sister to raise. Judy did not see her son until he was 12 years old, when he found Judy and asked to live with her, and she agreed.

Judy's daughter Phyllis Norman and Phyllis's boyfriend Mark Navarra confirmed much of the evidence and testified to the violence with which J.T. forced Judy into prostitution. Phyllis stated that every day, Judy would beg him not to make her go out on the streets to sell her body; he would slap her and make her go. The Norman family had lived in Chicago for years. Navarra testified that during the period he lived with the Norman family there, J.T. "sent her out on the streets prostituting and if she didn't bring no money back, he'd send her right back out; cold, it was about two or three feet of snow on the ground.... [He] kicked her out of the house; ma[d]e her sleep in the car." When asked to describe Judy's clothing on those occasions, Navarra answered that she would have only a "[t]hin coat; maybe sometimes no coat, and sometimes no shoes, he used to take her shoes from her."

Judy tried to escape. She described having left her husband many times: "I've ... stayed all night in hotels to get away from him; he'd find me. I've walked to my son's house with no coat on ... in snow to get away from him." Whenever she left, "[h]e'd come and find me and he'd beat me up." She kept no money and had no way to get another place to live. She had nowhere to go. He threatened to kill her if she left.

They returned to North Carolina, living in a cluster of small buildings adjacent to or across from Judy's mother, Laverne Laws; Judy's sister; and Judy's grandmother. The household included three of their children (Phyllis, 17; John Wayne, 14; and Loretta, 6) as well as Phyllis's baby and Mark Navarra.

The presence of family did not provide protection. J.T. abused her physically and humiliated her in front of friends and family. Navarra said, "[H]e did it a lot when other people was around; he was showing off or something." When J.T. had friends over to drink, he forced six-year-old Loretta to say in explicit vulgar terms the sexual acts her mother performed for a living. Visitors laughed, and Judy hung her head in shame.

Every day, J.T. took Judy to the highway rest area or "truck stop" where he forced her to sell sex and beat her while she was there. He demanded that she bring back at least one hundred dollars. Sometimes Phyllis and Mark Navarra went with her to try to help her avoid J.T.'s violent attacks.

On the night of June 10 and morning of June 11, 1985, Phyllis and Mark took Judy to the truck stop; J.T. arrived later, already drunk. He beat her, saying that she did not have enough money; he punched her in the face and poured hot coffee on her. When she tried to escape, he slammed the car door against her. This was brutal coercion, but the family did not describe it as different from other days at the truck stop. On the way home in the early morning hours of June 11, the police arrested J.T. for drunk driving. Judy's mother Laverne bailed him out, and he was released in the morning.

J.T. reacted violently to the experience of arrest and jail, returning home in a state of rage. He began hitting Judy immediately and continued all day, slapping her and throwing things at her including glasses, ashtrays, and beer bottles. Laverne testified that by late afternoon, Judy was unusually nervous and frightened, acting "scared all the time."

The police received a call about a domestic quarrel, and an officer arrived after dark. Judy's face was bruised, and she was crying. She told the officer that J.T. had been beating her all day and that she "could not take it any longer." The officer advised her to go to the county jail to "take out a warrant on him." She told him that J.T. would kill her if she did that. At trial, she explained, "He always threatened me, 'Bitch, if you ever have me locked up, I'll kill you when I get out,' and I was scared, I was afraid he would." The officer told her he could not do anything for her until she got "a warrant in my hand where I could place him under arrest."

When the officer left, Judy took seventeen or eighteen "nerve pills." Phyllis realized what had happened and told her father that Judy had taken the pills. Judy's mother Laverne heard the threats that followed and testified that J.T. shouted that they should let her die. He threatened to cut Judy's heart out and cut off her breast. He cursed and said, "Call your brothers ... I'm not scared of your whole family ... I'll kill you, your mother and your grandmother."

Laverne called an ambulance, but J.T. fought the paramedics and refused to let them help Judy. Phyllis and Laverne managed to walk Judy past J.T. to the ambulance. The paramedics called for backup because of J.T.'s interference. The officer who talked with her earlier had not driven far when he got the backup call and returned to find a chaotic scene. J.T. was shouting that they should "[l]et the bitch die." When the ambulance left for the hospital, J.T. told Phyllis to take her "bastard" baby and get out. The Norman children fled and stayed at Judy's grandmother's house that night.

"Criminal sanctions for assault against an abusive spouse have not been traditionally pursued because of a reluctance by law enforcement officials to enter the domestic domain." Michael J. Duane, Comment, *North Carolina's Domestic Violence Act: Preventing Spouse Abuse?* 17 N.C. Central L. J. 82, 83 (1988). In 1979, North Carolina's Act to Provide Remedies for Domestic Violence, Session Laws-1979 S. B. 171, changed and clarified criteria for warrantless arrest for misdemeanors committed in and outside the presence of an officer.[28]

The officer's decisions are not before us for review, but the law gave him discretion to make an arrest for misdemeanors outside his presence when he had probable cause to believe the misdemeanor had happened and "physical injury may result" if no arrest is made. Arrest would have been required if a protective order had been in place, but there was none. Indeed, a protective order would have required Judy Norman to file a civil action in court, a more elaborate procedure than the warrant for which J.T. had promised certain death.

Instead, Judy had asked for the officer's help by providing information on J.T.'s assaults and on his threat to kill her if she tried to obtain a warrant. She made it clear that she believed his death threat. A little while later, when responding to the paramedics' call for backup and witnessing J.T.'s shouts that they should let her die, the officer threatened arrest unless J.T. went back into his house. The officer's decision not to arrest J.T that night became part of the circumstances that Judy Norman had to evaluate, reinforcing her belief that the law was not a source of help.

Judy Norman had learned the power of law as a defendant. In Chicago, she had been arrested for prostitution and more than once for shoplifting. She explained at trial that she had shoplifted food and sometimes clothing for her children. She received another message about the power of law and its absence after returning to North Carolina, when the officer decided not to arrest J.T. and told Judy she must get the warrant despite J.T.'s death threat.

Judy's mother Laverne Laws responded to J.T.'s lethal threats by arming herself. She testified that she thought J.T. "might have killed the whole family, and [I was] especially scared that he would kill [Judy]." Laverne's other daughter Janice carried a gun because of a violent attack some years earlier. After calling the paramedics, Laverne took the gun out of Janice's purse and took it away in her own purse.

---

[28] Chapter 561 Section 1 created §50A-1 on domestic violence and defined domestic violence to include "placing another person in fear of imminent serious bodily injury by the threat of force," Section 3 added §15A-401(b)), explicitly adding "assault, ... communicating a threat, or ... domestic criminal trespass, already committed or being committed by a person who is the spouse ... of the alleged victim ..." to misdemeanors for which warrantless arrests may be made of "any person who the officer has probable cause to believe has committed a criminal offense in the officer's presence," §15A-401(b) (1), or for misdemeanors *outside the presence of the officer* if there is probable cause to believe the misdemeanor occurred and physical injury may result if no arrest is made, §15A-401(b) (2). Section 4 created §15A-534.1, addressing pretrial release and detention, which applies the statute governing involuntary commitment to domestic violence arrests in which the defendant is an "inebriate" or mentally ill. *See* N.C. GEN. STAT. Chap. 15-A Article 20 §§ 15A-401(b) (2)-(3) and 15A-534.1(3) (1988).

The hospital emergency staff pumped Judy's stomach. Charlie Paige, a psychologist from the mental health center on call that night, had seen J.T. occasionally for mental health issues; he had seen severe bruising on Judy when she accompanied J.T. When Judy woke up, Paige found her groggy, anxious, and depressed. Paige encouraged her to get help and suggested prosecuting J.T. for abuse, Initially, she was very angry. She said she should kill J.T. for what he had done to her. Laverne had arrived at the hospital to help Judy. Eventually, Judy and Laverne agreed to go to the mental health center in the morning to explore bringing charges for abuse. Paige urged Judy to enter the domestic violence shelter, but Judy would not go to the shelter because she was concerned about her children and wanted to stay with them.

Mark Navarra and Phyllis Norman testified that J.T. was angrier than he had ever been on June 12 – the day after his arrest for drunk driving, the officer's decision not to arrest him for domestic violence, Judy's suicide attempt, and his resistance to the paramedics. Navarra pointed to J.T.'s reaction to his arrest, and Phyllis emphasized J.T.'s reaction to Judy's suicide attempt.

As Judy had agreed with Charlie Paige, she went to the mental health center on the morning of June 12. The staff advised her to sign papers to have J.T. committed for alcoholism treatment. Judy went home and told him, "J.T., straighten up. Quit drinking. I'm going to have you committed to help you." He answered, "If you do … I'll see them coming and before they get here, I'll cut your throat."

The same day, Judy went with Laverne to an appointment at the food stamp office, but J.T. arrived and demanded that she leave with him. Mark Navarra had driven J.T. to the food stamp office. Judy was still groggy from the pills, but J.T. forced her to drive home even though Laverne testified that the car swerved. J.T. punched her in the car; Mark Navarra also described another occasion on which J.T. had beaten Judy while she struggled to control the car.

Later that day, J.T. and Judy picked up J.T.'s best friend Lemuel Splawn to give him a ride to Spartanburg, South Carolina to get his paycheck. Again, J.T. made Judy drive though she was still struggling from the drug overdose. While she drove, he slapped her, then feigned sleep before kicking her in the side of the head. Splawn testified that during this trip J.T. threatened to "cut her breast off and shove it up her rear end."

Judy had not eaten in three days. There was no food in the house on June 12. Laverne sent some groceries, but J.T. made Judy put the food back in the bag and said nobody could eat it. Phyllis brought her a doughnut from Laverne, but J.T. smashed it into Judy's face. He continued to tell her she did not deserve to live, to beat her, to make threats to cut her throat and additional threats to cut off her breast. During that afternoon, six-year-old Loretta went to her grandmother Laverne's house and told Laverne that J.T. was beating Judy again. Laverne called police asking for help, but they told her they could not help without a warrant.

After the doughnut incident, Phyllis and Mark watched without interfering while J.T. put out a cigarette on Judy's collarbone. Mark testified that "It hurt her ….

[S]he was scared." Phyllis testified that she had not tried to stop her father because, "I was scared to do *anything*. I begged him not to hit her." (emphasis added).

The Court of Appeals was correct in describing a "nap" during the "late afternoon." A review of events shows that police arrived after the shooting at 7:30 p.m. June 12 was close to the longest day of the year; sunset would have been more than an hour away at their home in Spindale. That day, Judy had gone to the social workers regarding possible prosecution and settled temporarily on the strategy of commitment for alcoholism (though she gave up that approach because of J.T.'s death threat); she also went to the food stamp office. Judy and J.T. went out briefly for beer, returned home, then drove Lemuel Splawn to Spartanburg and back to get his paycheck. After that, abusive events at the Norman home included the doughnut incident and the cigarette burn.

After the cigarette burn, events moved rapidly. For clarity, terms from trial testimony that describe timing are italicized here:

When asked, "[E]xactly what happened after he smashed the doughnut on you and stuck the cigarette in your neck, what happened *after that*?", Judy answered that he "*set for a while*" cursing at her and then said, "[l]et's go lay down." Judy started to lie on the smaller bed, but he said, "[n]o, bitch ... [d]ogs don't sleep on beds, they sleep [on] the floor." He made her lie on the floor between the beds. At trial, she described the events that followed:

> Q. So what happened *then*?
> A. Well, *it wasn't but a little bit* till my daughter came in there and she says, "Daddy," says, "Let momma watch the baby while I go to the store." And, he says, "All right." So I got the baby and I had him on the bed. I was sitting in the floor watching him so he wouldn't fall off and J.T. *just finally went to sleep*.
> Q. What happened *then*?
> A. *The baby started crying* and I snuck up and took him out there to my mother's. I said, "Momma, watch him. I'm scared he'll wake J.T. up, and he'll start fussing again." And, I give her the baby. I said, "Give me something for the headache; my head is busting." [Laverne] says, "I've got some pain pills in my purse." *So I went in there to get the pain pills and the gun was In there, and I don't know, I just seen the gun, and I took it out, and I went back out there and shot him.*

After the shots, Phyllis ran into the bedroom and saw her mother with a gun. She testified:

> I grabbed the gun, and I hollered, "No," and she turned it loose to me .... I looked at my dad's head. I seen the blood and I dropped the gun, and I ran out of the room and hollered that he killed her. I kept on hollering, "He killed her."

When asked why she said that her *father* had killed her *mother*, Phyllis answered, "Because I would always think that he would kill her." Her father "always said that he would kill her. He kept on telling her and everybody else he would kill her... [He said it] the day he got shot. He would say it every day. It was constantly ...."

At trial, Judy's lawyer asked her why she had killed J.T. She wept while she answered:

> Why? Because I was scared of him and I knowed when he woke up, it was going to be the same thing, and I was scared when he took me to the truck stop that night it was going to be worse than he had ever been. I just couldn't take it no more. There ain't no way ... even if it means going to prison. It's better than living in that. That's worse hell than anything ....

The witnesses' testimony that J.T. was angrier than he had ever been corroborated Judy's stated belief that the violent exploitation and forced prostitution that night would be worse than ever.

Judy's lawyer asked whether she believed J.T. that day when he threatened to kill her. She answered: "Yes. I believed him; he would, he would kill me if had a chance. If he thought he wouldn't a had to went to jail, he would a done it."

In Judy's statement about her fear, the majority opinion sees only speculation about future harm. The majority does not discuss her belief in his threats to kill in conjunction with the shared belief of her family members, his repeated threats to kill her that day, the speed and ease with which he could reach a knife, or the compressed time between when he fell asleep and when she fired the gun.

The legal question in this case is what the history and her belief in the danger of death must mean in weighing the elements of self-defense. To analyze that question, it is important to review the expert testimony and the extent to which lay eyewitnesses shared her belief in lethal danger.

II.

Two forensic experts, a psychologist and a psychiatrist, testified at trial. That testimony was important in different ways to the analysis of both the Court of Appeals and the majority here. In finding that the defendant was entitled to an instruction on self-defense, the Court of Appeals emphasized the objective conditions that made it impossible for Judy Norman to escape abuse. Their opinion relies in part on concepts of "battered woman syndrome" and "learned helplessness," but it states clearly that "battered woman syndrome" is not a separate defense but rather evidence to be considered with all other evidence presented at trial. The majority of this court finds in the analysis by the Court of Appeals a dangerous relaxation of standards for self-defense, mere speculation rather than imminent threat, and the potential for creating a separate "battered woman's defense" that could expand to other contexts and would be based entirely on subjective rather than reasonable perception.

Courts often interpret expert testimony on battering as describing "learned helplessness" and passivity in battered women. In doing so, they reflect stereotypes about women and about domestic violence, missing the "circumstances which might explain the homicide as a woman's necessary choice to save her own life." Elizabeth M. Schneider, *Describing and Changing: Women's Self-Defense Work and the Problem of Expert Testimony on Battering*, 9 Women's Rts. L Rep. 195, 198 (1986). Judges may hear testimony this way whether or not lawyers emphasize passivity, *id.*, and the term "syndrome" may create images of a separate psychological defense, *id.* at 199.

At Judy Norman's trial, neither doctor described separate standards for self-defense for battered women. Dr. Rollins, the psychiatrist who had evaluated her competency to stand trial, had administered psychiatric tests and found her rational and competent. His records described her as having "marital problems," with a comment adding "battered woman syndrome." He described "battered woman syndrome" as the product of protracted abuse in which one partner achieves control of the other through physical and psychological domination, creating the belief that the abused partner is worthless and cannot get away. He testified that Judy was convinced that she could not escape from her husband's abuse.

The trial judge appointed forensic psychologist Dr. William Tyson as an expert. As a court-appointed expert, he could be deposed by either party; either party or the court could call him to testify; and either party could cross-examine him including a party calling him as a witness. See N.C. Gen. Stat. § 8C-1, Rule 706(a)-(b) (1983). Dr. Tyson hired an investigator and made an independent investigation. He interviewed medical personnel, family members, and police officers; he obtained records and documents rather than relying on the memory or opinion of any person.

Dr. Tyson's testimony applied a coercive control framework. *See, e.g.*, Lewis Okun, Woman Abuse: Facts Replacing Myths 113 (1986) (providing a psychologist's definition of "coercive control" as involving "a controller who takes enormous power—usually through confinement or isolation—over a victim he seeks to control by demanding compliance and violently enforcing that demand"); *see also id.* at 113–139 (comparing battered women to prisoners of war and noting that in some abusive relationships husbands use coercive control to force wives into prostitution); Susan Schechter with Lisa T. Gary, A *Framework for Understanding and Empowering Battered Women*, *in* Abuse and Victimization Across the Life Span 240, 243 (Martha Straus ed. 1988) (discussing the pattern of coercive control in battering).

Dr. Tyson testified extensively about obstacles that Judy Norman faced to finding help or escaping from abuse, focusing on the history of her attempts to find help, the difficulties she encountered, and other objective factors. He emphasized the importance of degradation and humiliation as strategies to break the spirit of a human being and make that person more vulnerable to abuse. Explaining coercion, Dr. Tyson linked the details of humiliation, such as forcing Judy to eat from pet dishes and bark like a dog, with the physical violence. He compared Judy's experience to the experience of prisoners of war and described the reasons for the combination of violence and degradation:

> It was part of the process that whenever you want to brainwash somebody, dehumanize them, degrade them, bring them completely under your power and remove whatever humanity they have; those are the kinds of things that you do. It's consistent with the kind of behavior that was observed in prisoner of war camps during the Second World War as practiced by the Nazis; it's consistent with the type of behavior, deprivation of information; deprivation of normal human functioning that was consistent in the brainwashing techniques of the Korean War. Anything that will reduce and degrade an individual's concept of themselves as human and make them totally dependent on the oppressor. It worked in Korea and it worked in J. T. Norman's home.

Dr. Tyson distinguished J.T.'s controlling violence from ordinary domestic abuse. Judy Norman's experience had progressed "far beyond what would be called '[w]ife battering or family violence,' and into a realm which could be only considered as torture, degradation and reduction to an animal level of existence, where all behavior was marked purely by survival ...." He distinguished J.T.'s violence from "disagreements or fighting between a husband and wife." He described "a *deliberate, studied, and effective* attempt to completely subordinate another human being[,] humiliating them and degrading them to the point where they became less than human." (emphasis added). Based on the difference between ordinary domestic violence and J.T.'s terrifying abuse and degradation, Dr. Tyson said Judy Norman fit and exceeded the profile of an abused spouse.

Dr. Tyson linked Judy's belief that her death was inevitable to the fear that, if she left the children behind, the violent abuse would transfer to them. When asked whether it reasonably appeared to the defendant that actual danger existed even while J.T. was asleep, Dr. Tyson addressed both Judy's actual belief and the rational factors supporting that belief:

> Yes ... [I]n examining the facts of this case and examining the psychological data ... Mrs. Norman believed herself to be doomed ... to a life of the worst kind of torture and abuse, degradation that she had experienced over the years in a progressive way; that it would only get worse, and that death was inevitable ... I believe she also came to the point of beginning to fear for family members and her children, that were she to commit suicide that the abuse and the treatment that was heaped on her would be transferred onto them. There is evidence that Mr. Norman had begun to make threats ...
>
> The answer very simply is, yes, I think Judy Norman felt that she had no choice, both in the protection of herself and her family, but to engage, exhibit deadly force against Mr. Norman, and that in so doing, she was sacrificing herself, both for herself and for her family.

His summary of the evidence explaining her belief that escape was impossible supported the reasonableness of her conclusion after her previous efforts:

Mrs. Norman didn't leave because she believed, fully believed that escape was totally impossible. There was no place to go ... [S]he had left before; he had come and gotten her ... She had gone to the Department of Social Services. He had come and gotten her. The law, she believed the law could not protect her; no one could protect her, *and I must admit, looking over the records, that there was nothing done that would contradict that belief.* She fully believed that he was invulnerable to the law and to all social agencies that were available; that nobody could withstand his power. As a result, there was no such thing as escape. (emphasis added).

When the experts said that Judy came to believe she could not get away and the law would not help her, they described her subjective assessment of the situation. Their description of her belief did not imply that Judy's subjective perceptions were not reasonable or predict whether a jury would assess her perceptions as reasonable. Dr. Tyson's statement that he saw nothing in the record to contradict her belief provided direct support for the reasonableness of her perception.

Obviously, recognizing actual belief does not preclude the reasonableness of that belief. Unfortunately, psychological testimony on battering sometimes confuses courts on the question of reasonableness. *See* Schneider, *supra*, at 199. When Dr. Tyson said, "It worked in Korea and it worked in J.T. Norman's house," his statement did not imply that either prisoners of war or Judy Norman had honest but not reasonable perceptions of threat. Put another way, the testimony of experts was relevant to her actual belief in apparent threat and whether it was necessary to kill and also, through analysis of this case and expert information on abuse and its patterns, relevant to whether a person of ordinary firmness would have had the same perception.

III.

Eyewitnesses are important because the credibility of J.T.'s death threats bears on the *reasonableness* of perceived apparent threat and the question of whether the jury should have received an instruction on self-defense. At least two eyewitnesses shared Judy's perception of J.T.'s deadly threat that day. The family's inability to help, to stop him, to provide food for her, or to save her from the deliberate cigarette burn demonstrates how terrified they were of J.T. The failure of law enforcement to protect her also left her family without support if they tried to protect her. Their paralysis supported Judy's perception of his dangerousness.

In the abstract, J.T.'s threats to kill might seem less credible because he repeated them so frequently. The response of the Norman family, however, showed that they took his threats seriously. Family members watched him torture Judy without trying to make him stop. Her mother tried to help with food, trips to see counselors and get food stamps, calling paramedics, and calling police – but she did not attempt to intervene physically.

Judy believed J.T.'s threats, and so did her family. When Judy attempted suicide, J.T. tried to block intervention and threatened the whole family, with specific threats to kill Judy, her mother, and her grandmother. Laverne found his threats so frightening that she armed herself. Phyllis showed her belief in the imminent deadly threat to her mother when she reacted to the sight of her dying father by shouting repeatedly that *he had killed her mother.*

Many domestic violence cases will not have so many witnesses, and witnesses must not be required. The wealth of evidence in this case was available because J.T. performed abuse in front of family and friends with no apparent fear of legal consequences.

The evidence showing that eyewitnesses found J.T.'s lethal threats credible and shared the defendant's fear speaks to the very essence of the reasonableness requirement in self-defense law – the question of whether others familiar with her circumstances would share her perception. When other witnesses with direct personal knowledge of the facts see no possibility of help or escape, the jury should be allowed to consider that testimony when weighing imminence and necessity *in the defendant's circumstances.*

The perceptions of witnesses were uncontradicted and expressed repeatedly. This evidence answers the majority's concern that expert testimony on the experience of battering would shift to a purely subjective standard of self-defense. The perceptions of other close eyewitnesses cannot be treated as relevant only to "subjective" belief. Eyewitness perceptions are important to the core principle that gives the task of determining reasonableness to a jury of the defendant's peers. Shared terror is relevant to reasonable perception.

To hold otherwise would create a new moral hazard in which the most lethal batterers could make more death threats and convince more people of lethal danger without adding to the evidence for *reasonable* self-defense. The perceptions of witnesses would not in themselves validate Judy's perception as reasonable, but their belief must be relevant to whether the jury should evaluate reasonableness. A juror could consider that evidence to determine whether Judy *and* the witnesses had evaluated the circumstances reasonably.

The expert opinion of Dr Tyson also supported Judy Norman's perception of threat. He described her many efforts to leave her husband and her conclusion from the fact that J.T. defeated those efforts. Her efforts to find help were also defeated. Dr. Tyson described Judy's experience seeking help at a hospital 13 years earlier in Chicago, an attempt that ended when J.T. arrived making threats. The doctor pointed to the same pattern when J.T. forced Judy to leave the food stamp office. When Dr. Tyson said that Judy believed the law would not help her, he also said that his review of the records found nothing to contradict her belief.

Dr. Tyson did not describe Judy as someone who failed to try find help; rather, he described how her every effort to get aid had been defeated before and during the time that J.T.'s threats to herself and her family escalated. Tyson used the word "studied" to describe the methods J.T. used to control Judy. J.T.'s violence and degradation of her were designed to and succeeded in persuading her that she could not escape. Inability to escape is relevant for evaluating the imminence of threat and whether it was necessary for her to kill to avoid death or great bodily harm. Dr. Tyson's explanation of J.T.'s deliberate abusive control would have helped the jury consider the reasonableness of Judy's perceptions.

IV.

Great bodily harm has been held to include sexual violence. Our courts have held the that deadly force can be used to defend against rape, forcible sodomy, and sexual assault by one man against another in prison. *State v. Hunter*, 286 S.E.2d 535, 540 (N.C. 1982) (summarizing authority on rape, holding forcible sodomy to be ground for deadly force in self-defense, and approving *State v. Molko*, 274 S.E.2d 271, 272 (N.C. Ct. App. 1981), which held that whether the defendant reasonably felt in imminent danger of a sexual assault by another man and whether he used more force than was reasonably necessary to repel the assault were questions for the jury).

When asked why she shot her husband, Judy Norman spoke first about the sexual violence she faced that night, saying that it would be worse than ever and beyond her capacity to bear. This was not a distant or uncertain threat. The violence would commence with transportation to the site at some point after he woke up; he took her there every night. She had never been able to resist the physical force with which he transported her and forced her into prostitution. This daily sexual violence was so certain, so about-to-happen, that the majority treats it not as a threat but as a routine incident of abuse. The majority says, "The law does not sanction the use of deadly force to repel simple assaults." But the looming threat of forced prostitution should not be characterized as a question of "simple assaults."

Our courts have not yet considered the application of *Hunter* and *Molko* to forced prostitution and violent sexual exploitation. The Model Penal Code allows deadly force in defense against sexual intercourse compelled by force or threat, § 3.04(2)(b), and defines sexual intercourse to include the form of sex that J.T. compelled Judy to sell, *see* § 213.0 (defining sexual offenses). Considering our prior holdings, the threat of what is now called "female sexual slavery," *see generally* Kathleen Barry, Female Sexual Slavery (1979), may justify deadly force in self-defense.

Imminent violent forced prostitution is one of the harms Judy Norman feared and needed to resist. But we do not need to decide here the application of *Hunter* and *Molko* to Judy Norman's circumstances. Although the defendant in *Hunter* described a threat that began with forcible sodomy, we decided that case on the issue of deadly force. *Hunter*, 286 S.E.2d at 541.

I agree with Justice Martin that Judy Norman does not seek to enlarge or change the law of self-defense; she relies on existing self-defense law in arguing that the evidence is sufficient to require a self-defense instruction. J.T.'s death threats – which

Judy and her family found credible – prevented her from getting a warrant for his arrest or signing commitment papers to treat his alcoholism. Combined with his violence, those threats established the danger and power with which he forced her into prostitution, persuaded her family of her mortal danger, and paralyzed them when he abused her in their sight. This case must be decided on the apparent threat of death or great bodily harm.

V.

The legal standard for self-defense is well-established:

(1) it appeared to defendant and he believed it to be necessary to kill the deceased in order to save himself from death or great bodily harm; and
(2) defendant's belief was reasonable in that the circumstances as they appeared to him at the time were sufficient to create such a belief in the mind of a person of ordinary firmness; and
(3) defendant was not the aggressor in bringing on the affray, i.e., he did not aggressively and willingly enter into the fight without legal excuse or provocation; and
(4) defendant did not use excessive force, i.e., did not use more force than was necessary or reasonably appeared to him to be necessary under the circumstances to protect himself from death or great bodily harm.

State v. Gappins, 357 S.E.2d 654, 659 (N.C. 1987).

The first element requires that it appeared to Judy Norman, and she actually believed, that it was necessary to kill her husband to save herself from death or great bodily harm. This element finds support in her testimony, her family's testimony, and the expert evidence at trial.

The threat must also appear to be imminent. *See State v. Mize*, 340 S.E.2d 439, 443 (N.C. 1986). But imminence cannot be defined solely by time – it is the product of circumstances. The context that determines imminence includes circumstances faced by the defendant and must include the credibility of threats, the availability of weapons, and the availability of help or legal protection.

The majority quotes Black's Law Dictionary to support its narrow discussion of imminence. But Black's definition for "imminence" places the need to act at that particular time in relation to whether help is possible: "immediate danger, such as must be instantly met, *such as cannot be guarded against by calling for the assistance of others or the protection of the law.*" Black's Law Dictionary 676 (5th ed. 1979) (emphasis added).

Judy Norman's inability to escape and failed efforts to get help were part of the context of imminence. She had left many times, but J.T. always caught her, forced her back, and beat her. She had followed advice and gone to the social workers to discuss prosecution or treatment for his alcoholism, only to be defeated by his threat that he would kill her before they could take him away. When she tried to get help, J.T. would intervene and prevent the help she sought.

The previous day, he had threatened to kill her, to cut her heart out, to cut her throat if she tried to have him committed, and to cut off her breast. That afternoon, before he fell asleep, J.T. had burned her with a cigarette in front of family members, denied her food for the third day, and threatened again to cut her throat and to maim her by cutting off her breast. His threats to kill or maim involved knives – and knives are ubiquitous. No significant time would have been required to lay hands on a knife in his home.

Her experience of the authority of law involved her own arrests for prostitution and shoplifting in Chicago – part of her struggle for survival – and the officer's statement in North Carolina, after she told him of the beatings and death threats, that she could not get help unless she went to the sheriff for a warrant. She told the officer that J.T. had threatened certain death if she obtained the warrant, but his position was that law required the warrant anyway.

J.T.'s violence and threats also kept her from going to the shelter. She was concerned for her children and wanted to stay with them. Dr. Tyson believed that after her failed suicide attempt she "came to the point of beginning to fear for family members and her children, that were she to commit suicide that the abuse and the treatment that was heaped on her would be transferred onto them."

The credible threat of death, combined with fear for the well-being of her children, cut off every avenue for help. The family did not believe she could get away; she did not believe she could get away or get help; and Dr. Tyson saw no options for help that she had overlooked. Put simply, in regard to the definition of imminence, Judy Norman had to meet threats that she could not guard against "by calling for the assistance of others or the protection of the law."

As to the second element – examining reasonableness for a person of ordinary firmness – I agree with Justice Martin's formulation: "Properly stated, the second prong of the question is not whether the threat was *in fact* imminent, but whether defendant's *belief in the impending nature of the threat, given the circumstances as she saw them, was reasonable* in the mind of a person of ordinary firmness." On the facts of this case, a juror could find that a person of ordinary firmness could reasonably perceive an apparent imminent threat of death or great bodily harm.

The majority, however, appears to modify our standard on imminence. In its concern that the Court of Appeals' reliance on "battered woman syndrome" might create a new defense, the majority cites cases on imminence and immediacy but then states without citing any authority, "The defendant was not faced with *an instantaneous choice* between killing her husband or being killed or seriously injured." But our cases have not required instantaneous or actual threat. In *State v. Spaulding*, 257 S.E.2d 391 (N.C. 1979), we granted a self-defense instruction to a prisoner armed with a knife who killed another prisoner who had threatened his life when that man approached – even though the apparent attacker showed no weapon and in fact was not armed.

There is no real danger here of doing away with the imminence requirement or creating a separate standard for self-defense. Unfortunately, "the term 'syndrome' and the psychological description of battered women that predominates in battered woman syndrome descriptions appears to conjure up images of a psychological defense – a separate defense and/or an impaired mental state defense" for the battered woman, Schneider, *supra*, at 199 – but that is not in fact the legal standard. If the jury had considered self-defense, the expert evidence would have aided the jury in evaluating the reasonableness of Judy Norman's perceptions as well as her actual beliefs.

From prior experience and her experience that day, Judy Norman reached a *reasoned conclusion* that the law would not help her and conclusions based on that unavailability of help. Threats that others also found credible had defeated her effort to have him institutionalized for help with alcoholism – the path advised by the social workers – and made it impossible to get the warrant the police officer demanded. A conclusion about unattainable options should not be categorized as merely "subjective" perception. The jury would consider whether a person of ordinary firmness would have reasonably perceived threat as Judy did. That inquiry does not substitute a subjective standard for the question of reasonableness.

There is a danger here for self-defense law, but it is not the separate standard the majority fears. The approach to imminence in this case may make it easier for male prisoners to get self-defense instructions when they kill other men than for Judy Norman to take that question to the jury – even though her beliefs were based on both lived experience and repeated threats and were supported by eyewitnesses and experts. Jurors could have concluded that her fears *and* her family's fears reflected the way a person of ordinary firmness would have perceived those circumstances. A reasonable juror might agree with the Norman family that threats of death are not discounted simply because they are repeated so often.

The third element in self-defense asks whether Judy Norman was the aggressor. J.T. had not retracted his threats to kill or his plans for forced prostitution. His threats to kill immediately if she invoked legal help had succeeded in stopping her from getting a warrant or signing commitment papers; Laverne Laws also testified to J.T.'s threats to kill Judy if she got a warrant.

J.T. had been attacking Judy for at least thirty-six hours with no cessation except when she was out of the home after her suicide attempt. His threats to the family were so violent that his children did not sleep there while their mother was at the hospital – his threat of violence did not diminish.

This case is very different from the *Mize* case invoked by the majority, in which we found the defendant to be an aggressor and affirmed the denial of a self-defense instruction. Mize killed a man who had never threatened him directly. Eight hours after hearing from others that the man wanted to get him, Mize took a shotgun to the man's trailer at about 3 a.m. and killed him. 340 S.E.2d at 442–443. J.T. Norman's direct threats and the common availability of knives to carry them out differentiate this case from *Mize*.

J.T.'s late afternoon nap was to be a prelude to his continuing forced prostitution of Judy and other acts of ongoing violence. Judy did not attack at another person's house, and she could not get away from her own. J.T. had not withdrawn from violence or ceased his threat, and the act of taking the baby to her mother's nearby house did not mean Judy could escape. She was not the aggressor.

The fourth element in self-defense asks for evidence that the force used was not excessive. Judy Norman had never before used force against her husband; nondeadly force had not been an option for her. She could not fight back or defend herself against forced prostitution, beatings, or other attacks. J.T.'s threats had been gruesome, and his abuse was designed to convince her of his dangerousness. His willingness to burn and starve her, threats to knife and kill her, and his attempt to deny her medical aid and let her die were all meant to convince her that he could hurt her unbearably and that her danger was mortal. As in his threats to kill if she got legal help, any attempt to resist with nondeadly force might have increased the risk of deadly and even fatal force being used against her.

The state has the burden of proving that the elements of self-defense were not present when Judy Norman killed her husband. Justice Martin is correct to remind us that in our jurisprudence the jury, not the judge, weighs the evidence. Judy Norman had the right to send the jury her claim of self-defense and to have jurors evaluate her actions and the evidence supporting her perceptions of threat.

12

Commentary on *Whitner v. State*

RUQAIIJAH YEARBY

During the 1980s and 1990s, the United States was experiencing the crack epidemic in many urban areas due to poverty, hopelessness, and lack of government support for safety net programs among other things.[1] Numerous women and men used crack during this time. However, the government and medical establishment focused primarily on the detrimental impact of the mother's use of crack on a child, particularly during pregnancy. Several medical studies were published regarding the connection between pregnant women's use of crack and poor outcomes for newborns.[2]

Many of these medical studies were poorly designed because they focused only on the impact of crack use on children without controlling for environmental impacts, such as lead and pollution exposure.[3] Furthermore, the use of crack and health outcomes was not compared to the use of other legal drugs such as cigarettes and alcohol to set a baseline for poor health outcomes that were only attributable to the use of crack.[4] These reports were then racialized, so that the problem was deemed a Black woman's problem, further supporting the welfare mother trope for Black women.[5] Most of these studies were discredited in the 2000s, and in fact, current research shows that the negative impact of alcohol on the unborn child is

---

[1] Michael Massing, *Crack's Destructive Sprint Across America*, N.Y. TIMES, Oct. 1, 1989, at 398.
[2] Jane E. Brody, *Widespread Abuse of Drugs by Pregnant Women Is Found*, N.Y. TIMES, Aug. 30, 1988, at A1; Susan Okie, *The Epidemic That Wasn't*, N.Y. TIMES, Jan. 26, 2009, www.nytimes.com/2009/01/27/health/27coca.html.
[3] Okie, *supra* note 2.
[4] *Id.*; Deborah A. Frank et al., *Growth, Development, and Behavior in Early Childhood Following Prenatal Cocaine Exposure: A Systemic Review*, 285 J. OF THE AM. MED. ASS'N 1613, 1613–1625 (2001). This study concludes that findings once thought to be specific effects of in utero cocaine exposure can be explained by other factors, including exposure to tobacco, marijuana, or alcohol, and the quality of the environment. This indicates that negative fetal health outcomes originally attributed to cocaine use during pregnancy are more likely due to exposure to tobacco, marijuana, alcohol, or a polluted environment during pregnancy.
[5] The Editorial Board, *Slandering the Unborn*, N.Y. TIMES, Dec. 28, 2018, www.nytimes.com/interactive/2018/12/28/opinion/crack-babies-racism.html.

greater than crack.[6] For example, research shows that alcohol use during pregnancy reduces nutrient uptake which compromises healthy fetus development, whereas the association between cocaine use and fetal development retardation is not completely mediated by nutrient uptake.[7] While another study found a relatively low frequency of detrimental acute effects from cocaine use during pregnancy compared with previous reports.[8]

The original studies and the racialization of the problem were a continuation of sexism and racism, which author Dorothy Roberts highlights in her groundbreaking book, *Killing the Black Body*. As Professor Roberts notes, the prosecution of Black women for drug use during their pregnancy is a continuation of America's systemic abuse of Black women's bodies.[9] This abuse started during slavery and continued with the government forcing Black women to be sterilized.[10] Black feminist theorists have also noted that, "Black women confront ... the 'overarching' and 'interlocking' structure of domination in terms of race, class, and gender oppression."[11] That Black women are imprisoned for drug use, while white women are provided with counseling, is an illustration of this problem. Black women are prosecuted because they are minority, women, and often poor. South Carolina was one of the many states undertaking these prosecutions, with the help of hospitals and medical personnel. The *Whitner* case is just one example of this issue.

In December 1991, Cornelia Whitner pleaded guilty to child neglect of her second child, while pregnant with her third child.[12] She received probation and was prohibited from using drugs and alcohol. On February 2, 1992, Cornelia Whitner gave birth to her third child, a son, at Easley Baptist Medical Center, where testing showed the presence of crack cocaine in his urine. The test results were given to the police and as result, on February 5, 1992, Cornelia was arrested at the hospital for child neglect. On April 20, 1992, while she was already in counseling, drug free, and taking care of her healthy third child, Cornelia pleaded guilty to child neglect. She was hoping for continued treatment to help her stay drug free; however, the judge sentenced her to eight years in prison for child neglect because her third child was born with crack cocaine in his urine.

Whitner appealed her conviction in a Post-Conviction Relief filing arguing that the circuit court lacked subject matter jurisdiction to accept her plea since the child

---

[6] Okie, *supra* note 2; Giorgia Sebastiani et al., *The Effects of Alcohol and Drugs of Abuse on Maternal Nutritional Profile during Pregnancy*, 10 NUTRIENTS 1008, 1011–1012, 1014 (2018).

[7] Sebastiani et al., *supra* note 6.

[8] Charles R. Bauer et al., *The Maternal Lifestyle Study: Drug Exposure during Pregnancy and Shortterm Maternal Outcomes*, 186 AM. J. OF OBSTETRICS AND GYNECOLOGY 487, 493 (2002).

[9] DOROTHY ROBERTS, KILLING THE BLACK BODY 150–202 (1997).

[10] *Id.*

[11] Ula Taylor, *The Historical Evolution of Black Feminist Theory and Praxis*, 29 J. OF BLACK STUDIES 234, 235 (1998).

[12] Chanapa Tantibanchachai, *Whitner v. South Carolina (1997)*, EMBRYO PROJECT ENCYCLOPEDIA (Nov. 30, 2014), https://embryo.asu.edu/pages/whitner-v-south-carolina-1997.

neglect statute on its face did not apply to fetuses. She also argued she had ineffective counsel because her lawyer failed to advise her that the neglect statute might not apply to her case.[13] She won her appeal and the State appealed to the Supreme Court of South Carolina.[14] The Supreme Court case is the opinion discussed in this chapter.

THE ORIGINAL OPINION

In the original opinion, the majority granted the State's appeal and denied Whitner's petition for Post-Conviction Relief. Specifically, the Supreme Court ruled that the circuit court had subject matter jurisdiction, Whitner's counsel was effective, she had fair notice, and the State did not unconstitutionally burden Whitner's right to privacy.[15]

Prior to this opinion, the South Carolina Supreme Court had ruled that the word "person" included a viable fetus in civil actions and for homicide.[16] Based on these precedents, the Court found the word "child" in the child neglect statute included a viable fetus, and thus, the Court had subject matter jurisdiction over the case. The child neglect statute, "forbids any person having legal custody of a child from refusing or neglecting to provide proper care and attention to the child so that the life, health, or comfort of the child is endangered or is likely to be endangered."[17]

The court did not discuss how the term "legal custody" modifies the meaning of child, nor did it discuss how this term would make defining child as a viable fetus different than other statutes. Significantly, their previous rulings that the word person included a "viable fetus" did not have this problem because they involved persons who were independent human beings. Yet, in the Whitner case, the court reasoned that a viable fetus is included in the term child because "the consequences of abuse or neglect which takes place after birth often pales in comparison to those resulting from abuse suffered by the viable fetus before birth."[18] However, this does not explain how a person would have legal custody over a fetus, which cannot survive separate from the mother's body. Furthermore, the court made this claim without any scientific or legal support. Moreover, the court said that there was no reason there should be a difference between prosecuting a third person versus the mother for harming a viable fetus, even if the "precise effects of maternal crack use during pregnancy are somewhat unclear." Since the court found that there was a crime, Whitner's counsel was not ineffective.[19]

---

[13] *Whitner v. S.C.*, 492 S.E.2d 777, 779 (S.C. 1997).
[14] *Id.*
[15] *Id.* at 779–786.
[16] *Id.* at 779–782.
[17] S.C. CODE ANN. § 20-7-50 (1993).
[18] Whitner, *supra* note 13, at 780.
[19] *Id.* at 782–784.

Furthermore, the court found that there were no due process issues because "it is common knowledge that crack use can harm a viable unborn child," so Whitner was on notice that this was a crime.[20] The court further noted that the right to carry her pregnancy to term without state interference did not apply here since the state's interest in the welfare of the fetus was significant.

THE FEMINIST JUDGMENT

In her feminist judgment, Professor Ahmed (writing as Judge Ahmed) denies the State's appeal and grants Whitner's petition for Post-Conviction Relief. Specifically, Judge Ahmed rules that the circuit court did not have subject matter jurisdiction because the word "child" in the statute does not include a fetus. Ahmed asserts that if it were otherwise, every action of a pregnant woman that endangered a fetus would constitute neglect, including smoking, drinking, eating shellfish, or even exercising improperly.[21] This would make the statute overly broad, be beyond what the legislature intended, and result in women being punished more harshly for child neglect than for drug possession.

Furthermore, Ahmed emphasizes the absence of reliable evidence that crack had negative short- or long-term health effects on a child. Thus, punishing Whitner under the child neglect statute was contrary to the medical evidence.[22] Ahmed also rules the law does not provide fair notice that her Whitner's actions were a crime, especially when the statute forbids "any person having legal custody of any child from refusing or neglecting to provide care and attention and endangers or is likely to endanger the child." If fetus is included in the definition of child, one has to ask what person has legal custody of a fetus? Thus, Ahmed holds, "given that the plain meaning of 'child' is that of a person who has been born, Whitner could not have known that using crack-cocaine during pregnancy could trigger criminal liability under the Children's Code for a fetus."

Finally, Judge Ahmed notes that the case "represents a problematic shifting of responsibility from the state to the individual pregnant woman and her caretakers," because it makes physicians and nurses representatives of the police, rather than the medical care takers of pregnant women who face health issues.

Ahmed's opinion in *Whitner* expressly relies on feminist legal theory by acknowledging the disproportionate burden on poor women, and in particular poor women of color. Ahmed notes that criminalizing drug use during pregnancy has not been

---

[20] *Id.* at 785–786.
[21] Kimberly M. Mutcherson, Feminist Judgements: Reproductive Justice Rewritten 152 (2020); Alma Tolliver, *Child Abuse Statute Expanded to Protect the Viable Fetus: The Abusive Effects of South Carolina's Interpretation of the Word "Child"*, 24 S. Ill. U. L. J. 383, 403 (2000) (discussing the possibility of prosecuting women for less culpable actions that are likely to endanger the fetus, such as eating too little or engaging in certain recreational activities).
[22] Mutcherson, *supra* note 21, at 152.

effective in addressing the issue of substance use during pregnancy, especially when not all women using substance abuse are treated the same. In fact, the primary ones being prosecuted are women of color. Even beyond the points raised by the feminist opinion, if the original court wanted to hold Whitner responsible for drug use during her pregnancy it could have done it without expanding the definition of who was a child. Instead, it simply could have found that Whitner violated her probation. However, it did not. As a result, many women have been charged under this law.

After the *Whitner* decision, the South Carolina Attorney General developed a protocol mandating the testing and reporting of pregnant women who use illegal drugs.[23] This policy was adopted by the Medical University of South Carolina, which led to the Supreme Court case, *Ferguson v. City of Charleston*, where the Court found that testing women without their consent violated the Fourth Amendment.[24] In short, not only was the government involved in punishing women, but also the medical establishment abused its authority and the trust of pregnant women seeking care.[25] Yet, the Supreme Court's decision in *Ferguson* did not end the prosecution of women for child neglect; the state has a mandatory child abuse reporting law requiring health care workers and providers to report pregnant patients who use drugs or engage in any behavior that may endanger the fetus. Moreover, the prosecution of women has not been equal. Black women were, and likely remain, disproportionately prosecuted. According to the National Advocates for Pregnant Women "virtually every woman arrested so far has been [Black] despite the fact that the Southern Regional Project on Infant Mortality found that the 'typical' chemical dependent woman is ... most likely white."[26] Furthermore, women were often arrested for legal drug use. For instance, a pregnant woman was arrested because she used alcohol during her pregnancy, while two women who had stillborn babies were charged with child neglect and homicide. The *Whitner* decision was also used as authority to try to force a mother to get a cesarean section against her will. The woman gave birth naturally while the court was deciding the case.[27]

Unfortunately, the actual *Whitner* decision remains good law. How many women have been prosecuted for ingesting drugs while pregnant? Clearly too many. Ahmed's

---

[23] Lynn M. Paltrow, Punishment and Prejudice: Judging Drug-Using Pregnant Women, Nat'l Advoc. for Pregnant Women (Jan. 31, 1999), www.advocatesforpregnantwomen.org/issues/whitner.htm.

[24] *Ferguson v. City of Charleston*, 532 U.S. 67, 83–86 (2001) (court ruled that, without consent, drug testing of pregnant patients and reporting positive results to law enforcement constitutes an unreasonable search in violation of the Fourth Amendment).

[25] Dorothy E. Roberts, *Punishing Drug Addicts Who Have Babies: Women of Color, Equality, and the Right of Privacy*, 104 HARV. L. REV. 1419, 1433–1450 (1991).

[26] Paltrow, *supra* note 23.

[27] *In re Baby Boy Doe*, 632 N.E.2d 326, 327–330 (Ill. App. Ct. 1994) (doctors sought a court order forcing Doe to undergo an immediate cesarean section after she refused the cesarean section based on her religious beliefs).

rewritten opinion shows the path the South Carolina Supreme Court should have taken, and suggests the many lives, of both mothers and children, that would have been spared by a more feminist judgment.

WHITNER V. STATE, 328 S.C. 1 (S.C. 1996)

JUDGE AZIZA AHMED DELIVERED THE OPINION OF THE COURT

On April 20, 1992, Cornelia Whitner (Whitner) pled guilty to criminal child neglect, S.C. Code Ann. § 20-7-50 (1985), because her child had been born with cocaine metabolites in its system by reason of Whitner's ingestion of crack cocaine during the third trimester of her pregnancy.[28] The circuit court judge sentenced Whitner to eight years in prison. Whitner did not appeal her conviction. Thereafter, Whitner filed a petition for Post Conviction Relief (PCR), pleading the circuit court's lack of subject matter jurisdiction to accept her guilty plea as well as ineffective assistance of counsel. Her claim of ineffective assistance of counsel was based upon her lawyer's failure to advise her the statute under which she was being prosecuted might not apply to prenatal drug use. The petition was granted on both grounds. The State appeals. We deny the appeal.

I. LAW/ANALYSIS

A. *Subject Matter Jurisdiction*

The State first argues the PCR court erred in finding the sentencing circuit court lacked subject matter jurisdiction to accept Whitner's guilty plea. We disagree.

Under South Carolina law, a circuit court lacks subject matter jurisdiction to accept a guilty plea to a nonexistent offense. *See Williams v. State*, 306 S.C. 89, 410 S.E.2d 563 (1991). The sentencing circuit court lacked subject matter jurisdiction because there was no offense. For the sentencing court to have had subject matter jurisdiction to accept Whitner's plea, criminal child neglect under section 20-7-50 would have to include an expectant mother's use of crack cocaine after the fetus is viable. All other issues are ancillary to this jurisdictional issue.

S.C. Code Ann. § 20-7-50 (1985) provides:

> Any person having the legal custody of any child or helpless person, who shall, without lawful excuse, refuse or neglect to provide, as defined in § 20-7-490, the proper care and attention for such child or helpless person, so that the life, health or comfort of such child or helpless person is endangered or is likely to be endangered, shall be guilty of a misdemeanor and shall be punished within the discretion of the circuit court.

---

[28] This rewritten decision reproduces portions of the original judgment.

The State contends this section encompasses maternal acts endangering or likely to endanger the life, comfort, or health of a viable fetus. Under the Children's Code, "child" means a "person under the age of eighteen." S.C. Code Ann. § 20-7-30 (1) (1985). The question for this Court, therefore, is whether a viable fetus is a "child or helpless person" for purposes of the Children's Code.

In interpreting a statute, this Court's primary function is to ascertain the intent of the legislature. *See, e.g., State v. Ramsey*, 311 S.C. 555, 430 S.E.2d 511 (1993). Of course, where a statute is complete, plain, and unambiguous, legislative intent must be determined from the language of the statute itself. *See, e.g., State v. Blackmon*, 304 S.C. 270, 403 S.E.2d 660 (1991). We should consider, however, not merely the language of the particular clause being construed, but the word and its meaning in conjunction with the purpose of the whole statute and the policy of the law. *See, e.g., South Carolina Coastal Council v. South Carolina State Ethics Comm'n*, 306 S.C. 41, 410 S.E.2d 245 (1991). Finally, there is a basic presumption that the legislature has knowledge of previous legislation as well as of judicial decisions construing that legislation when later statutes are enacted concerning related subjects. *See Berkebile v. Outen*, 311 S.C. 50, 426 S.E.2d 760 (1993); 82 C.J.S. Statutes § 316, at 541–42 (1953).

Neither of the words "child" or "person" include a "fetus" in any common understandings of the terms. While South Carolina law has previously recognized that viable fetuses are persons holding certain legal rights and privileges, we do not extend this reasoning to the case today, nor do we think it should be extended in the future. The intent of the legislature was not to hold pregnant women accountable for actions taken during their pregnancy that may or may not harm a fetus or child. In prior cases, we held that a viable fetus could be understood as a person in order to hold third parties liable for harm inflicted on a pregnant woman. Today we reject the idea that in order to hold an individual criminally or civilly liable for a crime committed against a pregnant person it is necessary to define a fetus as a "person." As discussed below, the plain meaning of "child" or "person" does not include "fetus."[29]

In 1960, this Court decided Hall v. Murphy, 236 S.C. 257, 113 S.E.2d 790 (1960). That case concerned the application of South Carolina's wrongful death statute to an infant who died four hours after her birth as a result of injuries sustained prenatally during viability. The Appellants argued that a viable fetus was not a person within the purview of the wrongful death statute, because, inter alia, a fetus is thought to have no separate being apart from the mother. We held in that case that "We have no difficulty in concluding that a fetus having reached that period of prenatal maturity where it is capable of independent life apart from its mother is a person." *Id.* at 263, 113 S.E.2d at 793. Four years later in *Fowler v. Woodward*, 244 S.C.

---

[29] Janet Gallagher, *Prenatal Invasions & Interventions: What's Wrong with Fetal Rights*, 10 HARVARD WOMEN'S LAW JOURNAL 9–58 (1987).

608, 138 S.E.2d 42 (1964), we interpreted Hall as supporting a finding that a viable fetus injured while still in the womb need not be born alive for another to maintain an action for the wrongful death of the fetus. We have also held that a viable fetus can be a person in the context of third-party criminal liability. In *State v. Horne*, 282 S.C. 444, 319 S.E.2d 703 (1984), the defendant stabbed his pregnant wife in the neck, arms, and abdomen. Today, we alter this rule. An unviable or viable fetus is never a person. It is not necessary for the court to view a viable fetus as a "person" in order to hold an individual civilly or criminally responsible for the harm that they cause a person who is pregnant.

In the case before us, Whitner is the pregnant individual who, acting out of addiction, took drugs that may have harmed her fetus. Whitner correctly argues an interpretation of 20-7-50 that includes viable fetuses would lead to absurd results obviously not intended by the legislature. Specifically, she claims if we interpret "child" to include viable fetuses, every action by a pregnant woman that endangers or is likely to endanger a fetus, whether otherwise legal or illegal, would constitute unlawful neglect under the statute. For example, a woman might be prosecuted under section 20-7-50 for smoking or drinking during pregnancy, or indeed even living with a smoker and thus exposing her fetus to second-hand smoke. In fact, the State's interpretation would permit the prosecution of a husband for smoking around his pregnant wife. Whitner asserts such results could not have been intended by the legislature and, therefore, the statute should not be construed to include viable fetuses. We agree.

We must also consider the current evidence on crack-cocaine use during pregnancy. Although Whitner ingested crack cocaine during the third-trimester of her pregnancy, the statutory language says that the act must "endanger" or be "likely to endanger" a helpless child. Indeed, the State seems to take it is a given that this element was met, i.e., that Whitner's use of crack cocaine likely endangered her fetus. This assumes too much. The evidence which suggests that crack-cocaine has short or long term health effects on the fetus or child is under scrutiny and has been contested.[30] As such, we fail to see how the State could have proved this element beyond a reasonable doubt. This is an independent reason why Whitner's conviction cannot stand.

We also note that outside of this jurisdiction, numerous cases have found that maternal conduct before the birth of a child does not give rise to criminal prosecution under child endangerment statutes. While the facts vary, one theme remains clear: Pregnant women should not be held liable for their actions during pregnancy even when they can be construed to cause harm to the fetus. *See, e.g., Johnson v. State*, 602 So.2d 1288 (Fla. 1992); *Commonwealth v. Welch*, 864 S.W.2d 280

---

[30] Claire D. Coles, *Saying "Goodbye" to the "Crack Baby,"* 15 (5) NEUROTOXICOLOGY AND TERATOLOGY, 290–292 (1993); Daniel R. Neuspiel, *Cocaine and the Fetus: Mythology of Severe Risk*, 15 NEUROTOXICOLOGY AND TERATOLOGY, 305 (1993).

(Ky. 1993); *State v. Gray*, 62 Ohio St.3d 514, 584 N.E.2d 710 (1992); *Reyes v. Superior Court*, 75 Cal.App.3d 214, 141 Cal. Rptr. 912 (1977); *State v. Carter*, 602 So.2d 995 (Fla. Ct. App. 1992); *State v. Gethers*, 585 So.2d 1140 (Fla. Ct. App. 1991); *State v. Luster*, 204 Ga. App. 156, 419 S.E.2d 32 (1992), cert. denied (Ga. 1992); *Commonwealth v. Pellegrini*, No. 87970, slip op. (Mass. Super. Ct. Oct. 15, 1990); *People v. Hardy*, 188 Mich. App. 305, 469 N.W.2d 50 app. denied, 437 Mich. 1046, 471 N.W.2d 619 (1991); *Commonwealth v. Kemp*, 434 Pa. Super. 719, 643 A.2d 705 (1994).

B. *Constitutional Issues: Fair Notice/Vagueness*

Because this issue may come up in future cases, we also elect to address Whitner's argument that the language of the statute is void for vagueness and does not provide fair notice. Whitner argues that section 20-7-50 does not give her fair notice that her behavior is proscribed. We agree.

The statute forbids any person having the "legal custody of any child" to refuse or neglect to provide care and attention in such a way as to endanger or is likely to endanger a child. The word child does not and should not include a fetus, viable or not. A person of ordinary intelligence would not think that a fetus is included in the definition of a child.

This court understands the plain meaning of "child" to only include individuals already born. Whitner could not have known that exposing her fetus to crack-cocaine during pregnancy could trigger criminal liability under the Children's Code. Whitner could not have anticipated that she would be punished for child neglect of a fetus. In addition, it is not clear that cocaine use during pregnancy harms a potentially viable fetus or child after birth. Whitner, therefore, could not possibly have had fair notice that she could be liable for potentially endangering her fetus given that it may not be possible to harm a fetus with crack-cocaine. *Cf. State v. Ashley*, 701 So. 2d 338 (Fla. 1997) (expectant mother may not be criminally charged with the death of her child resulting from self-inflicted injuries during the third trimester of pregnancy); *Stallman v. Youngquist*, 125 Ill. 2d 267, 531 N.E.2d 355, 359 (1988) (refusing to recognize tort of maternal prenatal negligence).

C. *Policy Considerations*

This case represents a problematic shifting of responsibility from the state to the individual pregnant woman and her caretakers. The law deputizes physicians and nurses to act on behalf of the police arm of the state. It forces physicians and medical providers to violate basic principles of provider patient confidentiality.[31] Further, by criminalizing and punishing pregnant women who face a health issue, addiction,

---

[31] *Id.*

the state disincentivizes prenatal care and undermines the future health of the child, the very entity it claims to care about. The focus on *crack* cocaine over other drugs suggests that the women who will be prosecuted will be racial minorities, particularly Black women.

It is the state that should ensure that pregnant individuals have the resources they need to give birth safely and with adequate attention to their various needs including addiction. It should be the state's responsibility to ensure that a child can remain united with their parent through adequate social support services during pregnancy and after birth. Prosecuting pregnant women shifts these responsibilities from the state to the woman and her medical providers.

As legal scholars have noted, this will have a disproportionate burden on poor women and poor women of color.[32] Criminalizing drug use during pregnancy and prosecuting women for being addicted to drugs is not the way to address the issue of substance use during pregnancy.

II. CONCLUSION

For the reasons stated above, the State's appeal is denied.

---

[32] Dorothy Roberts, *Punishing Drug Addicts Who Have Babies: Women of Color, Equality, and the Right of Privacy*, 104 HARV. L. REV. 1419 (1991).

13

Commentary on *United States v. Nwoye*

SHERRI LEE KEENE

In *United States v. Nwoye*,[1] decided in June 2016, the US Court of Appeals for the District of Columbia Circuit held that defendant Queen Nwoye was prejudiced at trial on extortion charges when her legal counsel failed to introduce expert witness testimony on the "battered woman syndrome" to support her duress defense. Specifically, the expert testimony could have supported Nwoye's claim that she was coerced into participating in the extortion by her controlling and abusive boyfriend.

The term "battered woman syndrome" was first introduced by psychologist Lenore Walker in the late 1970s, but continues to evolve in its use in the law.[2] Dr. Walker theorized that women who experience cyclical domestic abuse develop psychological paralysis or "learned helplessness" that renders them incapable of escaping their harmful relationship even when it might appear to others that they could safely do so.[3] Typically, expert testimony regarding battered woman syndrome is offered to support traditional self-defense claims, but courts have allowed this testimony to support duress claims as well.[4] That said, the use of the battered woman syndrome is not without controversy.[5]

---

[1] *United States v. Nwoye*, 824 F.3d 1129 (D.C. Cir. 2016).
[2] LENORE E. WALKER, THE BATTERED WOMAN xv (1979); Lenore E. Walker, *Battered Women and Learned Helplessness*, 2 VICTIMOLOGY 525 (1977–1978).
[3] Kelly Grace Monacella, *Supporting a Defense of Duress: The Admissibility of the Battered Woman Syndrome*, 70 TEMPLE L. REV. 699, 702, 709–711 (1997) (citing WALKER, THE BATTERED WOMAN, *supra* note 2, at 43).
[4] *See* Susan D. Appel, *Beyond Self-Defense: The Use of Battered Woman Syndrome in Duress Defenses*, 1994 UNIV. OF ILL. L. REV., 865–870 (1994); *United States v. Nwoye*, 824 F.3d at 1136 (listing cases and stating that most courts have found expert testimony on battered woman syndrome to be relevant to a duress defense).
[5] Some critics view the use of battered woman syndrome in support of a defense as "special treatment" for victims of domestic violence. Kit Kinports, *The Myth of the Battered Woman Syndrome*, 24 TEMP. POL. & CIV. RIT. L. REV. 313, 313 (2015) (noting criticism). For their part, proponents assert that expert testimony on battered woman syndrome merely provides abused women the opportunity to convince a jury that their choices, actions, and beliefs are reasonable. *Id.* at 321. In their view, expert testimony merely helps women to cut against existing gender bias that is so entrenched in the law that it is often invisible. Kathleen E. Mahoney, *The Myth of Judicial Neutrality: The Role of Judicial*

In the duress context, expert testimony of battered woman syndrome has been offered to explain why an abused woman did not take advantage of a seemingly reasonable opportunity to avoid committing an alleged crime. In general, to prove duress, a defendant must show that they were coerced to engage in a crime by the use or threat of unlawful force that a person of reasonable firmness in the situation would have been unable to resist.[6] Expert testimony about battering relationships can highlight the realities of the particular circumstance the defendant faced, including the increased risk of retaliatory violence by an abuser upon separation, and why escape was not the readily available option it might seem.[7]

While the use of battered woman syndrome assists some women, it also contains its own biases insofar as it claims a "typical" experience that may in fact vary among individuals, particularly where they differ with respect to other identities such as race. At best, expert testimony on battered woman's syndrome addresses one blind spot for decision-makers. Other blind spots may exist when it comes to women who don't fit the "typical" mode, such as women of color. Indeed, a defendant like Nwoye, a Black woman who was a recent immigrant, may have experiences that are at the intersection of several marginalized identities that go unrecognized by courts, which are typically made up of individuals who do not share these identities or vulnerabilities.[8] While the courts have made some strides to address potential biases through measures such as allowing an expert to testify about battered women's syndrome to support self-defense and duress claims, such accommodations should be recognized as addressing merely the tip of the iceberg.

THE ORIGINAL OPINION

In *Nwoye*, the District of Columbia Circuit's majority decision, written by then Judge Kavanaugh, held that trial counsel erred in not presenting expert testimony on battered woman syndrome to support a duress claim, and that this error amounted to ineffective assistance of counsel.

The facts at trial were relatively straightforward. Testifying in her own defense, Nwoye admitted to participating in a scheme to extort a married doctor with whom she previously had an affair by threatening to expose their relationship, but testified

---

Education in the Fair Administration of Justice, 32 WILLAMETTE L. REV. 785, 795 (1996). Such bias can perpetuate harmful myths, such as the common belief that a woman in an abusive relationship can just leave their abusive situation. Monacella, *supra* note 3, at 705.

[6] MODEL PENAL CODE §2.09 (2020).

[7] Lenore E. Walker, *Battered Women Syndrome and Self-Defense*, 6 NOTRE DAME J. OF L., ETHICS & PUB. POL'Y 321, 333 (1992).

[8] *See, e.g.*, Donna Coker, *Shifting Power for Battered Women, Law, Material Resources, and Poor Women of Color*, 33 U.C. DAVIS L. REV. 1009, 1014–1032 (2000); Roberta K. Lee, Vetta L. Sanders Thompson, & Mindy Mechanic, *Intimate Partner Violence and Women of Color: A Call for Innovations*, 92 AM. J. PUB. H. 530, 530–34 (2002).

that her boyfriend had coerced her to do so through his physical abuse and controlling behavior. However, Nwoye's counsel never sought to introduce expert testimony on battered woman syndrome, and the district court denied Nwoye's request for a jury instruction on duress, ruling that Nwoye had not presented sufficient evidence that there was no reasonable alternative to her participation in the extortion scheme.[9]

On direct appeal, Nwoye challenged the district court's decision not to give the duress instruction at trial. In denying her appeal, the District of Columbia Circuit found Nwoye had reasonable alternatives to participating in the extortion, pointing out that Nwoye was not always under her boyfriend's direct physical control. The Circuit also noted Nwoye's counsel had not offered expert testimony on battered woman syndrome, which the court suggested may have tipped the scales to justify a duress instruction.[10]

After Nwoye completed her sentence and term of supervised release, Nwoye filed a motion to vacate her conviction, claiming ineffective assistance of counsel. After the district court denied her motion, Nwoye appealed that denial and her case came back before the D.C. Circuit, and it is that judicial opinion that makes frequent appearances in criminal law casebooks. In finding Nwoye was prejudiced by her trial counsel's failure to introduce expert testimony, the Circuit found that expert testimony would have been relevant to the duress defense: "The reason, put simply, is that the duress defense requires a defendant to have acted reasonably under the circumstances, and expert testimony can help a jury assess whether a battered woman's actions were reasonable."[11]

Further, the Court found expert testimony on battered woman syndrome would have entitled Nwoye to a jury instruction on duress as such testimony would have helped to explain the effects of Nwoye's abuse. Specifically, the Court found expert testimony on the likelihood of Nwoye facing retaliatory violence from her boyfriend could have provided a plausible explanation for why she failed to extricate herself from the extortion scheme. According to the Court, "The concept of battered woman syndrome fits this case to a T .... Some outsiders may question why she did not just leave her boyfriend. But the expert testimony would help explain why."[12] The Court found that Nwoye's testimony concerning her boyfriend's abuse, supplemented by

---

[9] See *United States v. Nwoye*, 824 F.3d at 1133 ("To be entitled to an instruction on duress, Nwoye had to present sufficient evidence" (1) "that she acted under an unlawful threat of imminent death or serious bodily injury," and (2) "there was no reasonable alternative to participating in the extortion scheme").

[10] Judge Tatel dissented, asserting there was sufficient evidence presented at trial to warrant the duress instruction.

[11] *United States v. Nwoye*, 824 F.3d at 1136.

[12] *Id.* at 1139–1140 (noting that expert testimony on battered woman syndrome could have helped "dispel the ordinary lay person's perception that a woman in a battering relationship is free to leave") (internal citation omitted).

expert testimony on battered woman syndrome, would have constituted sufficient evidence from which a reasonable jury could find for Nwoye on a theory of duress.[13]

THE FEMINIST JUDGMENT

In her feminist judgment, Professor Mary D. Fan, writing as Judge Fan, concurs with Judge Kavanaugh's decision to find in Nwoye's favor on appeal, but does not agree that the error in the case was solely Nwoye's attorney's failure to bring expert testimony of battered woman syndrome to support Nwoye's duress defense. Fan notes that the framing in terms of ineffective assistance was forced by the procedural posture of the case coming in a postconviction motion after direct appeal was exhausted and therefore the bases for overturning the prior decision were constricted. While appreciating Judge Kavanaugh's opinion for giving Nwoye another opportunity to present her defense, Fan argues framing the error in terms of battered woman syndrome is a constrained lens that overlooks the larger harm of how courts interpret the duress defense. Fan rewrites the decision to discuss the empathy and experience deficit in how duress is construed by judges who ignore how for some defendants turning to law enforcement for help may not be a realistic or reasonable option.

Fan's opinion takes a more holistic approach, finding error in the trial court's refusal to grant Nwoye a duress instruction based on Nwoye's testimony of her entire experience, including that her abuser purported to be a law enforcement agent, making her fearful to turn to police for help. To be entitled to a duress instruction, Nwoye had to present sufficient evidence that she "acted under an unlawful threat of imminent death or serious bodily injury" and there was "no reasonable alternative to participating in the extortion scheme."[14] While Nwoye testified regarding her abuse, the district court found Nwoye did not provide sufficient evidence demonstrating that she had no reasonable alternative to participating in the crime. In affirming this decision on direct appeal, the Circuit substituted its own judgment and speculated Nwoye had a number of reasonable alternatives to participating in extortion that included reporting her boyfriend to police or to friends and coworkers when Nwoye was away from him, while at school or work.

Most notable to Fan was the Circuit's assertion that Nwoye could have gone to law enforcement to resolve her problems. For reasons also expressed by Judge

---

[13] In a dissenting opinion, Judge Sentelle indicated that, like the district court, he found Nwoye was not prejudiced by her counsel's failure to put on expert testimony of battered woman syndrome. The dissent noted the court's prior observations regarding Nwoye not always being under her boyfriend's direct physical control and speculating as to opportunities Nwoye had to contact law enforcement. It further emphasized that more deference should have been given to the trial court's determination on the matter.

[14] Id. at 1133.

Kavanagh in the original majority opinion finding ineffective assistance of counsel, Fan points out that a battered woman reasonably may not feel law enforcement can offer adequate protection from an abuser. But Fan's opinion goes a step further by declaring one does not have to be a battered woman to lack faith in law enforcement and noting that other compounding factors like Nwoye's race and recent immigrant status also may have influenced her perspective. Looking more broadly at the issue, Fan's decision criticizes the courts' refusal to recognize jurors might find that seeking the help of law enforcement was not a reasonable option for someone in the defendant's situation. Fan's opinion points out the court did not consider the possibility that Nwoye might reasonably believe law enforcement would not adequately protect her. To illustrate her point, Fan walks the reader through several court decisions in a variety of contexts where other courts made the same assumption, that going to US government officials was a reasonable option for defendants.

Recent events support Fan's view that the judges' perspective may not reflect that of defendants, let alone potential jurors. Notably, at the time Nwoye's postconviction claim was decided in 2016, there were nationwide protests around the country following the highly publicized deaths of unarmed Black men and boys at the hands of police, including Eric Garner and Michael Brown.[15] According to statistics gathered by the *Washington Post*, Black males were 34 percent more likely to be killed by police that year than white males.[16] And the disparities are not limited to Black males. By 2015, Kimberlé Crenshaw had already launched the #SayHerName campaign, calling attention to the police victimization of Black women and girls, who are far more likely to experience police violence than their white counterparts.[17] The more recent deaths of women like Sandra Bland, Breonna Taylor, Ma'Khia Bryant, and Deborah Danner at the hands of police have highlighted the increased risk of police violence faced by Black women.[18] Unfortunately, such violence extends to Black women who call 911 seeking help.[19]

---

[15] Daniel Funke & Tina Susman, *From Ferguson to Baton Rouge: Deaths of Black Men and Women at the Hands of Police*, L.A. Times, July 12, 2019, www.latimes.com/nation/la-na-police-deaths-20160707-snap-htmlstory.html.

[16] Kimbriell Kelly, et al., *Fatal Shootings by Police Remain Relatively Unchanged After Two Years*, The Washington Post, Dec. 30, 2016, www.washingtonpost.com/investigations/fatal-shootings-by-police-remain-relatively-unchanged-after-two-years/2016/12/30/fc807596-c3ca-11e6-9578-0054287507db_story.html?utm_term=.afc7e06d02af.

[17] *See* Mary Louise Kelly & Heidi Glenn, *Say Her Name: How the Fight for Racial Justice Can Be More Inclusive of Women*, NPR (Heard on All Things Considered) (July 7, 2020), https://www.npr.org/sections/live-updates-protests-for-racial-justice/2020/07/07/888498009/say-her-name-how-the-fight-for-racial-justice-can-be-more-inclusive-of-black-wom.

[18] *See* Michelle S. Jacobs, *The Violent State: Black Women's Invisible Struggle Against Police Violence*, 24 Wm. & Mary J. Women & L. 39 (2017).

[19] *See* Homa Khaleeli, *#Say Her Name: Why Kimberlé Crenshaw Is Fighting for Forgotten Women*, The Guardian, May 30, 2016, www.theguardian.com/lifeandstyle/2016/may/30/sayhername-why-kimberle-crenshaw-is-fighting-for-forgotten-women.

All of this police violence and killing naturally generates distrust. A study of 2,000 Americans conducted by the CATO Institute at the time this case was decided showed that 68 percent of white respondents had a favorable impression of police, compared to only 40 percent of Black respondents and 59 percent of Hispanic respondents.[20] Attitudes toward police are highly correlated to valuations of police confidence.[21] While 60 percent of white respondents believed that police effectively protect people from crime, only 38 percent of Black and 49 percent of Hispanic respondents held this view.[22] A substantial number of respondents also believed the system does not treat all groups of people equally. According to the survey, a majority of Americans, 58 percent, believed the criminal justice system fails to treat everyone fairly, with 45 percent of Americans saying that preference is given to white people.[23] Black Americans were more inclined to perceive bias, with 72 percent expressing a belief that there was a preference for white Americans.[24] The earlier referenced numbers concerning race, gender, and police violence provide just one justification for these beliefs.

Fan's opinion points out the problem Nwoye faced before the trial court and on direct appeal, where judges evaluating her case reviewed her facts through a lens that reflected their own perspectives and experiences. While judges are the gatekeepers at trial, Fan's decision aptly points out that the job of weighing evidence should be left to an informed jury, not judges who are far removed from the defendant's experience. In taking a critical approach to this case, Fan lays bare the assumptions underlying the court's decision-making in Nwoye's case and the need for courts to find ways to address bias in legal decision-making at a more fundamental level.

There remains the question: What makes Fan's opinion a feminist one? To be sure, Fan believes that Nwoye should have been allowed to mount a duress defense and call an expert witness on battered woman syndrome, and that her trial attorney's failure to offer such an expert amounted to ineffective assistance. But the same is true of Judge Kavanaugh's original opinion.

---

[20] *See* Emily Ekins, *Policing in America: Understanding Public Attitudes Toward the Police. Results from a National Survey*, CATO Institute, www.cato.org/sites/cato.org/files/survey-reports/pdf/policing-in-america-august-1-2017.pdf; CATO Institute Policing in America Report, Survey Methodology, www.cato.org/sites/cato.org/files/survey-reports/methodology/policing-in-america-survey-methodology_0.pdf.

[21] *See* Ekins, *supra* note 20, at 28.

[22] *Id.* Americans who are older, white, high income, conservative, and live in the suburbs expressed more confidence in police officers' ability to do their jobs. For example, 78 percent of respondents who identify as "very conservative" expressed confidence in local police compared to 46 percent of those who identify as "very liberal." *Id.*

[23] *Id.* at 32.

[24] *Id.* at 32.

As Abbe Smith recently noted in her essay, "Can You Be a Feminist and a Criminal Defense Lawyer?," feminism is not one-dimensional.[25] To the contrary,

> It is a movement, an ideology, and a method. Its most basic aim is to achieve gender equality, but this is a simplistic rendering of feminism. Feminism includes a range of socio-political movements and ideologies that seek to define and achieve the political, economic, social, and personal equality of the sexes.[26]

The range of ideologies include third-wave feminism, which among other things rejected the crude feminist essentialism of first- and second-wave feminism, and brought an intersectional analysis to the issue of gender inequality.[27] Given Fan's focus on Nwoye's intersectional identities, it would be easy to classify Fan's reading as consistent with third-wave feminism.

But to my mind, Fan's feminism goes beyond an intersectional analysis. And it goes beyond the issue of gender equality. At bottom, Fan seems to be suggesting that where judges are blind to the diversity of perspectives and experiences of the people appearing before them, a real danger exists that everyone's circumstances will not be fully appreciated if their realities differ from that of members of the court. Fan's feminism is impactful and speaks to inequality broadly. It leaves us with much to consider with regard to making our system more just for women, and for all.

UNITED STATES V. NWOYE, 824 F.3D 1129 (D.C. CIR. 2016)

CIRCUIT JUDGE MARY D. FAN, CONCURRING

Duress is a longstanding defense that injects empathy and humanity into the criminal law for people in desperate situations. *See* Model Penal Code, Part I Commentaries, vol. 1, at 368 (explaining rationale). The right to present a duress defense should be equal for everyone but in practice there is a judicial blindness to the situation of vulnerable people and communities in the United States who fear turning to the state for help. The trial court's erroneous preclusion of Queen Nwoye's attempt to argue duress exemplifies the refusal to recognize that jurors properly instructed about duress may find that a vulnerable person reasonably feared to seek help from law enforcement. The error was compounded when the decision on direct appeal treated Nwoye's fear about going to police for help as an unreasonable failure that requires some sort of syndrome to explain. *See United States v. Nwoye*, 663 F.3d

---

[25] Abbe Smith, *Can You Be a Feminist and a Criminal Defense Lawyer?*, 57 AM. CRIM. L. REV. 1569, 1573 (2020).
[26] *Id.*
[27] *See, e.g.*, Angela P. Harris, *Race and Essentialism in Feminist Legal Theory*, 42 STAN. L. REV. 581 (1990); Kimberlé Williams Crenshaw, *Mapping the Margins: Intersectionality, Identity Politics, and Violence Against Women of Color*, 43 STAN. L. REV. 1241 (1991).

460, 465 (D.C. Cir. 2011) ("[A]lthough Nwoye described some threats and physical abuse, her theory is devoid of the other usual indicia supporting a BWS [battered women syndrome] defense – expert witnesses testifying to the effects of isolation, financial dependence, or estrangement from family members").

I concur with Judge Kavanaugh's efforts to reach the just outcome in light of the unfortunate decisions below and the posture of this case, on a postconviction motion to vacate. His decision in Nwoye's case will be justly lauded as one of his notable opinions. Unfortunately, because of the posture of this case before us, we must characterize the error as one of ineffective assistance of counsel for failure to retain a battered women syndrome expert. The real error is not with defense counsel, who often have to suffer the slings and arrows of ineffective assistance claims by clients seeking postconviction relief after losing on direct appeal. The error is the recurring refusal of courts to recognize that jurors may find that going to U.S. officials for help is not a reasonable option for a person in the defendant's position. I write separately to address this problem in hopes that in the future, people will not be deprived of the right to mount a defense, as Nwoye was in this case.

Nwoye, at least, gets a second chance at a fair trial thanks to Judge Kavanaugh's decision here. But others who are not battered, nor a woman, or otherwise do not fit into the exceedingly confining "battered woman syndrome" box, have received no relief despite deprivation of the right to present a defense. *See, e.g., United States v. Gaviria*, 116 F.3d 1498, 1531 (D.C. Cir. 1997) (affirming denial of a duress defense to an incarcerated man whose teenage daughter was held by a coconspirator with a history of abusing his daughter because he failed to seek help from prison officials or others); *United States v. Alicea*, 837 F.2d 103, 106 (2d Cir. 1988) (affirming preclusion of a duress defense for women raped in Ecuador and forced to become drug couriers on threat of harm to their family, reasoning they failed to alert immigration and customs officials they were carrying drugs on arriving in New York). The reality is that often the reason people do not seek help from law enforcement when threatened is not a battered woman syndrome. It is unequal access to protection and to the ability to trust the state. A person on trial with liberty and life at stake should have the right to present these realities far different from the experience of persons fortunate enough to become judges, who may have blind spots in empathy and legal interpretation.[28]

---

[28] Former Chief Judge Kozinski of the U.S. Court of Appeals for the Ninth Circuit powerfully summarized this disjuncture between the experiences and understandings of judges and the persons at the receiving end of criminal law and procedure:

> There's been much talk about diversity on the bench, but there's one kind of diversity that doesn't exist: No truly poor people are appointed as federal judges, or as state judges for that matter. Judges, regardless of race, ethnicity or sex, are selected from the class of people who don't live in trailers or urban ghettos. The everyday problems of people who live in poverty are not close to our hearts and minds because that's not how we and our friends live. *United States v. Pineda-Moreno*, 617 F.3d 1120, 1123 (9th Cir. 2010) (Kozinski, J., dissenting).

I.

A recent immigrant to the United States, Nwoye met an abusive man she thought *was* law enforcement. We take her testimony as true for purposes of evaluating the denial of a defense, *see United States v. Glover*, 153 F.3d 749, 752 (D.C. Cir. 1998). Indeed, even the prosecution's star witness in the case testified that Nwoye described her abusive boyfriend as an FBI and CIA agent. Beginning in 2005, the self-proclaimed federal agent, Adriane Osuagwu, took "total control" of Nwoye during their relationship. He regularly beat her, monitored her, used her credit and ATM cards, and even bought and sold a house in her name without her knowledge or consent. She believed she could not call the police because he worked with the FBI. As she put it in her testimony, she believed the police and the FBI worked together for the government.

Osuagwu frequently beat Nwoye on her face and body and slapped her face with his shoe for even petty annoyances, such as taking too long to answer the door. When they were apart, Osuagwu controlled Nwoye by phone, even forcing her to wear a Bluetooth headset during her classes in nursing school so that he could constantly monitor her and confirm her whereabouts. Nwoye and her children moved in with Osuagwu. Osuagwu was the only person who knew Nwoye and the children lived with him. He repeatedly threatened to kill Nwoye and bury her inside the house.

In 2006, when Osuagwu learned about Nwoye's previous affair with a married doctor, Ikemba Iweala ("Dr. Iweala"), he coerced Nwoye into a scheme to extort Iweala. At the time of Osuagwu's scheme, Nwoye had been in the United States only five years. Her affair with Dr. Iweala had lasted a couple of months beginning in 2002, after she came across his name on prescription bottles while working as a pharmacy technician. Newly arrived in the United States from Nigeria, she was excited to meet a fellow Nigerian and was looking for a doctor. Their affair commenced after she visited his office. After the sexual relationship, they parted amicably and remained friends. It was not until Osuagwu learned of the affair that an extortion scheme began to unfurl.

Nwoye initially refused to introduce Osuagwu to her old friend but he beat her until she acquiesced. Over the next two months, Osuagwu, introduced as Nwoye's "cousin," demanded money on threat of ruining Dr. Iweala's successful career and life by exposing the affair to people, including Dr. Iweala's wife, who was a prominent Nigerian official, and the medical board. Osuagwu reminded Dr. Iweala of a news story regarding a doctor prosecuted for having sex with patients. Iweala succumbed to the threats and gave Nwoye and Osuagwu $185,000 over the course of six payments.

When Nwoye tried to resist participating in the continued extortion demands, Osuagwu beat her until she was "helpless." He threatened to strangle her and bury her body in the house if his scheme unraveled. He hit her when he felt she was not performing her role in his extortion scheme to his satisfaction. He made her initiate sex with Dr. Iweala in Dr. Iweala's vehicle, so Osuagwu could take a compromising photograph to further the extortion. When Nwoye met with Dr. Iweala to collect the money, Osuagwu would either monitor her in person, or over the phone, as her phone records document.

Osuagwu's claim to be an FBI agent kept Nwoye in his thrall and fearful of going to U.S. law enforcement for help. She thought the police "all work together for the government." Reporting him would only bring on more violence rather than help. She explained, "This is an FBI guy. He would find out." When one's abuser is a law enforcement official, she said, "Who are you going to tell?" Nwoye testified, "I was so scared. I didn't know who to talk to."

Indeed when Nwoye finally did seek help by reporting Osuagwu, she turned to law enforcement officials in her native Nigeria, the Economic and Financial Crime Commission – not law enforcement officials in the United States. By that time, Dr. Iweala had reported the extortion to the FBI in the United States.

Charged with conspiracy to commit extortion, Nwoye sought to explain to the jury that she acted under duress because of Osuagwu's violence and threats. The government wisely opted not to object to her telling the jury about the violence she experienced, and the trial judge correctly allowed Nwoye to tell her story of violence and coercion. After Nwoye's testimony concluded, however, the trial judge denied Nwoye's request that the jury be instructed on the duress defense, effectively barring the jury from considering the defense.

The trial judge ruled that a duress defense requires that the defendant have no reasonable legal alternative to committing the crime and that the evidence was "completely devoid in that particular factor." Noting that sometimes Nwoye and Osuagwu were physically apart, the judge reasoned "this guy wasn't holding a gun to her head every day, every minute," and there was not a "scintilla" of evidence that Nwoye lacked a reasonable opportunity to escape. Because of the judge's predetermination of these factors, the jury never had the opportunity to decide if Nwoye had no reasonable alternatives as a recent immigrant duped into believing she was in the violent control of an FBI agent.

Without the opportunity to present a duress defense to a properly instructed jury, Nwoye was convicted of conspiracy to commit extortion. The district judge sentenced her to 20 months of imprisonment, a three-year term of supervised release, a $100 special assessment, and restitution in the amount of $178,809.00 – though it was Osuagwu who took the bulk of the money that he extorted from Dr. Iweala. Apparently at least sympathetic to Nwoye, the Government moved to reduce Nwoye's sentence to 15 months. The district judge granted the government's motion for reduction of sentence, with all other conditions to remain the same.

On direct appeal, a split panel of our Court affirmed Nwoye's conviction, rejecting her contention that she should have been allowed to argue the duress defense to a properly instructed jury. *United States v. Nwoye*, 663 F.3d 460, 465 (D.C. Cir. 2011). Observing that "[t]his Court has affirmed denials of the duress defense even in quite harrowing situations," the two-judge majority concluded "Nwoye's testimony falls far short of the duress claimed in, and ultimately denied by, our precedents." *Id.* at 463. The panel reasoned that Nwoye "had ample opportunities to notify law enforcement either directly or indirectly." *Id.*

Nwoye was apart from Osuagwu three days a week while attending nursing school classes or working a hospital, the panel observed. "While there, she could have contacted police herself or asked teachers or classmates to do so or to help her escape Osuagwu's control." *Id.* The panel also noted that for two weeks, Osuagwu was thousands of miles away in California, with control maintained by constant telephone contact. The panel reasoned that "she could have turned off the phone, talked to her husband, her friends, or the police, and fled to safety with her children before Osuagwu could even get through airport security." Further envisioning options for Nwoye, the panel advised, "even if Nwoye wanted to avoid an open breach of her arrangement with Osuagwu, she could have explained any gap in their cell phone contact as the result of spotty cell coverage, a trip on the Metro, or a dead battery." *Id.*

Judge Tatel dissented from the panel's decision affirming the denial of a duress decision. A crucial part of his critique is important enough to quote in full:

> To the American-born, highly educated, legally sophisticated judges of this court, Nwoye's fears are unreasonable. They fault her for "provid[ing] no evidence of corruption beyond her conclusory assertion that police and FBI 'all work together for the government' and that anything she told the authorities would find its way to Osuagwu." ... But to obtain a duress instruction, she needed no evidence that police were *actually* corrupt or that they *actually* worked together or that they would *actually* tell Osuagwu that she reported him. She needed only a reasonable belief that the police would refuse to protect her, and reasonableness is quintessentially a question for the jury... [A] jury of Nwoye's peers, reflecting "the commonsense judgment of a group of laymen," *Williams v. Florida*, 399 U.S. 78, 100, 90 S.Ct. 1893, 26 L.Ed.2d 446 (1970), might well view the record very differently than do the judges of this court. The jury, observing the testimony of an abused woman and recent immigrant subject to the brutal control of a man she believed was part of American law enforcement and forced by him to participate in an unlawful conspiracy, might well believe her and conclude that she actually thought—and given her situation, reasonably thought—that any attempt to call the authorities would end in her ruin.

United States v. Nwoye, 663 F.3d 460, 468–69 (D.C. Cir. 2011) (Tatel, J., dissenting).

The wheels of appellate justice grind with deliberate speed, and by the time of the decision on appeal, Nwoye had served her sentence and term of supervised release. Yet a felony conviction punishes long after the prison time is served in terms of collateral consequences, such as immigration and employment problems for Nwoye, formerly a nurse. On March 7, 2013, Nwoye filed a petition under 28 U.S.C. § 2255 to vacate her conviction. The district court denied that petition, resulting in this appeal now pending before the Court.

II.

The duress defense requires sufficient evidence that the person acted (1) "under an unlawful threat of imminent death or serious bodily injury," *United States v. Bailey*, 444 U.S. 394, 409 (1980), and (2) the threat was so grave and immediate that it precluded "any reasonable, legal alternative to committing the crime." *United States v. Jenrette*, 744 F.2d 817, 820 (D.C. Cir. 1984). While the imminence requirement for a duress defense is sometimes depicted as the culprit in preventing people in desperate straits from claiming the shelter of the defense, scholars are showing that "the preclusion is the result of unfair application of existing law and not of its structure or content." Holly Maguigan, *Battered Women and Self-Defense: Myths and Misconceptions in Current Reform Proposals*, 140 U. Pa. L. Rev. 379, 458 (1991). "The legal standard of imminence is less the problem ... than judicial interpretation of the law in ways that keep questions of imminence from reaching juries." Lisa R. Pruitt, *Toward A Feminist Theory of the Rural*, 2007 Utah L. Rev. 421, 448 (2007).

Courts are sometimes more understanding that people in other countries, such as Colombia, cannot go to their government officials for help when threatened, see *United States v. Contento–Pachon*, 723 F.2d 691, 694 (9th Cir. 1984) (reversing the district court's denial of a duress instruction because the defendant's testimony raised triable issues of fact about the lack of reasonable alternatives to becoming a drug courier via his testimony that some police in Bogotá Colombia were actually paid informants for drug trafficking organizations and corrupt); *United States v. Chi Tong Kuok*, 671 F.3d 931, 950 (9th Cir. 2012) (reversing the denial of a duress defense because the defendant's testimony raised triable issues of fact regarding the lack of reasonable alternatives to his offense of exporting military-grade items to China because he claimed his family in Macau was monitored and threatened by Chinese intelligence and going to Chinese law enforcement for help was no reasonable recourse).

But courts have refused to acknowledge the plight of people and communities in the United States who fear going to law enforcement when denying defendants the right to raise a duress defense for jury consideration. For example, courts have refused to allow immigrants to explain their fears about going to the police in light of their familial history of past abuse by law enforcement authorities in their country of origin. *United States v. Jankowski*, 194 F.3d 878, 881, 883 & n.3 (8th Cir. 1999) (affirming the district court's refusal to allow the defendant to even mention his Polish national origin and familial history in which his father was beaten and jailed for five years for participating in the Polish solidarity movement to explain why he feared to go to the police explaining that, a Colombian may have reasonably feared to go to the Bogotá police because of well-documented police corruption but not someone in America). Similarly, courts denying access to the duress defense have held that fear of immigration consequences ensuing from seeking help is not a cognizable basis for not going to authorities. *See United States v. Salgado-Ocampo*, 159 F.3d 322, 327 (7th Cir. 1998), *as amended* (Nov. 4, 1998).

Courts affirming the denial of duress defenses by incarcerated persons have just assumed that inmates could obviously have told a prison guard or official about violence and threats from prison inmates and solved the problem. *See, e.g., United States v. Gaviria*, 116 F.3d 1498, 1531 (D.C. Cir. 1997) ("Second, Naranjo could have told a prison guard or a more senior prison official of his dilemma. Naranjo claims that he could not have reported Sanders's threats to a prison guard because many of the guards were corrupt but he provides no concrete evidence [beyond his testimony] in support of this assertion."); *United States v. Tanner*, 941 F.2d 574, 588 (7th Cir. 1991) (affirming denial of a duress defense reasoning the defendant could have sought help and protective custody from prison officials to escape). *See also United States v. Horr*, 963 F.2d 1124, 1127 (8th Cir. 1992) (cursorily dismissed inmates' account of the risk of greater violence that people who seek help from prison authorities face).

The substitution of a judge's imagination about what he or she would do if faced with a similar threat not only wrongly usurps the jury's role as the fact-finder, it also wrongly distorts the analysis and presents an inaccurate picture of the actual recourse reasonably available. Because of the wide difference in the life experiences and resources of people pressed into situations of duress and the judges who run the courtroom, it is all the more vital that judges do not substitute their opinions about what they would do for what is reasonable. While federal judges enjoy the professionalism and protection of U.S. marshals and other protectors on call, most people do not have access to such resources. The deference of the federal marshals or other law enforcement, including prison officials, to a judge is much different than interactions with a prison inmate or immigrant.

Intersectional vulnerabilities render access to law enforcement protection even more fraught. *See, e.g.* Kimberlé W. Crenshaw, *From Private Violence to Mass Incarceration: Thinking Intersectionally About Women, Race, and Social Control*, 59 UCLA L. Rev. 1418, 1435–1444 (2012) (discussing the intersecting vulnerabilities of gender, race, and unequally applied systems of social control including incarceration); Jennifer M. Chacón, *Producing Liminal Legality*, 92 Denv. U. L. Rev. 709, 730–732 (2015) (examining how intersectional vulnerabilities, produce liminality in immigration communities). The gap in access to state protection is even wider between judges and immigrants or incarcerated persons from minority racial or ethnic backgrounds. These intersectional vulnerabilities often are overlooked and unaddressed in cursory preclusion of attempts to present a duress defense.

The grim reality is that even in the United States, the government has limited ability to protect people from violence, and this includes protecting abused persons. Battered persons who have their accounts disbelieved, dismissed or who see violent abusers quickly released as misdemeanants despite inflicting brutal injuries face this painful reality. *See, e.g.*, Reva B. Siegel, *"The Rule of Love": Wife Beating as Prerogative and Privacy*, 105 Yale L. J. 2117, 2135–2161 (1996) (discussing the history and evolution of failure to protect spousal battering). Beyond this, people who seek help may incur the risk of further violence and retaliation. Fear of being disbelieved or ignored by law enforcement, perhaps based on prior experiences with law enforcement, also may render people afraid to go to the police for help when threatened. *See, e.g., United States v. Gonzalez*, 407 F.3d 118, 122 (2d Cir. 2005) (noting the defendant explained "she did not seek police intervention because she believed the authorities 'would not listen to her'" about the threats she faced). There is also evidence that battered persons of color are more likely to be arrested themselves when police respond to domestic violence calls, especially in mandatory arrests jurisdictions. *See* Mary Haviland et al., Urb. Just. Ctr., The Family Protection and Domestic Violence Intervention Act of 1995; Examining the Effects of Mandatory Arrests in New York City, Family Violence Project 1, 7 (2001).

Victims of domestic violence are sometimes thought of as being prisoners in their own homes. As such, it should be noted that incarcerated persons also face the dilemma of risking further violent reprisals – as well as potentially more punitive conditions of incarceration – if they go to authorities for help. *See, e.g., United States v. Haney*, 287 F.3d 1266, 1275 (10th Cir. 2002), *opinion vacated on reh'g en banc on other grounds of waiver*, 318 F.3d 1161 (10th Cir. 2003) (recognizing that a juror could have found that going to prison authorities would have ignited further violence from inmates). *But see United States v. Haynes*, 143 F.3d 1089, 1091 (7th Cir. 1998) (holding that fear of reprisal from other prisoners and being placed in administrative segregation upon attempting to seek help from prison authorities could not excuse an inmate's failure to turn to prison guards for help).[29]

---

[29] In the state courts, there is a countertrend to allow juries a chance at understanding the plight of prisoners subjected to sexual violence and afraid to go to prison authorities. *E.g., People v. Lovercamp*, 43 Cal. App. 3d 823, 830–831 (Cal. Ct. App. 4th Dist. 1974). For example, in *People v. Harmon*, the Michigan Court of Appeal considered a prison escape where the defendant proffered evidence of duress based on rapes and beatings by other prisoners and the risk of more violence if he sought help from prison officials. 220 N.W.2d 212, 213 (Mich. Ct. App. 1974). The *Harmon* Court reversed the trial judge's preclusion of a duress, holding:

> The time has come when we can no longer close our eyes to the growing problem of institutional gang rapes in our prison system. Although a person sentenced to serve a period of time in prison for the commission of a crime gives up certain of his rights, 'it has never been held that upon entering a prison one is entirely bereft of all his civil rights and forfeits every protection of the law.' ... The persons in charge of our prisons and jails are obliged to take reasonable precautions in order to provide a place of confinement where a prisoner is safe from gang rapes and beatings by fellow inmates, safe from guard ignorance of pleas for help and safe from intentional placement into situations where an assault of one type of [sic] another is likely to result. If our prison system fails to live up to its responsibilities in this regard we should not, indirectly, countenance such a failure by precluding the presentation of a defense based on those facts. *Id.* at 213.

Immigrants who fear deportation if they call the police and the effective destruction of their family by other means also face a brutal reality far removed from the position and power that judges enjoy. *See United States v. Salgado-Ocampo*, 159 F.3d 322, 327 (7th Cir. 1998), *as amended* (Nov. 4, 1998) (describing an undocumented defendant's fear of immigration status being uncovered when seeking help from authorities). Studies have found that the collaboration of local law enforcement with federal immigration officials on deportation chills help-seeking in immigrant communities, in myriad ways ranging from seeking prenatal care to calling 911 for help. *See, e.g.*, Scott D. Rhodes, et al., *The Impact of Local Immigration Enforcement Policies on the Health of Immigrant Hispanics/Latinos in the United States*, 105 Am. J. Pub. Health 329 (Feb. 2015); Mai Thi Nguyen & Hannah Gill, *Interior Immigration Enforcement: The Impacts of Expanding Local Law Enforcement Authority*, 53 Urb. Stud. J. 302, 14 (2015); Orde F. Kittrie, *Federalism, Deportation, and Crime Victims Afraid to Call the Police*, 91 Iowa L. Rev. 1449, 1451 (2006).

III.

The U.S. Supreme Court has at times recognized the unequal reality when it comes to trust in the state to protect rather than harm. More than a half century ago, in *Terry v. Ohio*, the Supreme Court acknowledged, using the unfortunate terminology of the times, "[t]he wholesale harassment by certain elements of the police community, of which minority groups, particularly Negroes, frequently complain." *Terry v. Ohio*, 392 U.S. 1 (1968). More recently, writing for four members of the Supreme Court in *Illinois v. Wardlow*, Justice Stevens cited data regarding the belief, particularly widespread among minority communities, that "contact with the police can itself be dangerous." *Illinois v. Wardlow*, 528 U.S. 119, 132 (2000) (Stevens, J., dissenting).[30] Observing that "these concerns and fears are known to the police

---

[30] Among the studies Justice Stevens referenced was a National Institute of Justice survey finding that 43 percent of African-Americans consider "police brutality and harassment of African–Americans a serious problem." *Illinois v. Wardlow*, 528 U.S. 119, 133 n.7 (2000) (Stevens, J., dissenting) (citing JOHNSON, AMERICANS' VIEWS ON CRIME AND LAW ENFORCEMENT: SURVEY FINDINGS, NAT. INSTITUTE OF JUSTICE J. 13 (Sept.1997)). Justice Stevens observed:

> The Chief of the Washington, D.C., Metropolitan Police Department, for example, confirmed that "sizeable percentages of Americans today—especially Americans of color—still view policing in the United States to be discriminatory, if not by policy and definition, certainly in its day-to-day application." P. VERNIERO, ATTORNEY GENERAL OF NEW JERSEY, INTERIM REPORT OF THE STATE POLICE REVIEW TEAM REGARDING ALLEGATIONS OF RACIAL PROFILING 46 (Apr. 20, 1999) (hereinafter Interim Report). And a recent survey of 650 Los Angeles Police Department officers found that 25% felt that "racial bias (prejudice) on the part of officers toward minority citizens currently exists and contributes to a negative interaction between police and the community." REPORT OF THE INDEPENDENT COMM'N ON THE LOS ANGELES POLICE DEPARTMENT 69 (1991); see also 5 UNITED STATES COMM'N ON CIVIL RIGHTS, RACIAL AND ETHNIC TENSIONS IN AMERICAN COMMUNITIES: POVERTY, INEQUALITY AND DISCRIMINATION, THE LOS ANGELES REPORT 26 (June 1999).

officers themselves, and are validated by law enforcement investigations into their own practices," the justices concluded that "the evidence supporting the reasonableness of these beliefs is too pervasive to be dismissed as random or rare, and too persuasive to be disparaged as inconclusive or insufficient." *Id.* at 134–135.

The body of evidence regarding the unequal risk of adverse outcomes in police encounters has only expanded exponentially since *Terry* in 1968 and *Wardlow* in 2000. Minority community members are more likely to be stopped and searched by the police – even though stops and searches of minority members yield less contraband, likely because race and ethnicity are being used as inaccurate proxies for suspiciousness. Andrew Gelman, Jeffrey Fagan, Alex Kiss, *An Analysis of the New York City Police Department's "Stop and Frisk" Policy in the Context of Claims of Racial Bias*, 102 J. Am. Stat. Ass'n 813, 815–817, 820–821 (2007); Tyler, Tom R., Jeffrey Fagan, and Amanda Geller, *Street Stops and Police Legitimacy: Teachable Moments in Young Urban Men's Socialization*, 11(4) J. Empirical Legal Studies 751–785 (2014). In law enforcement encounters, minority community members face a heightened risk of injury and death. *See, e.g.,* Mary D. Fan, *Violence and Police Diversity*, 2015 B.Y.U. L. Rev. 897–890 (calculating and reporting racial disparity ratios for deaths in law enforcement encounters for Hispanics and African-Americans from Centers for Disease Control mortality data); Andrew M. Burch, *Bureau of Justice Statistics, Arrest-Related Deaths, 2003–209 Statistical Tables* 6 tbl. 6 (U.S. Dep't of Justice ed., 2011) (revealing that nearly a third of people who died due to arrest-related killings between 2003 and 2009 were Black).

Some studies further report that minority community members are more likely to suffer police use of force though the data is mixed, likely in part because of the challenges of getting comprehensive data on police use of force and the conduct of studies in different jurisdictions and with different datasets. *See, e.g.* Joel H. Garner, Christopher D. Maxwell, Cedric G. Heraux, *Characteristics Associated with the Prevalence and Severity of Force Used by the Police,* Justice Quarterly 19(4): 705–746 (2002) (finding racial disproportionality in police use of force). *But see, e.g.,* William Terrill, *Police Use of Force: A Transactional Approach,* Justice Quarterly 22(1): 107–138 (2005); Philip Mulvey & Michael D. White, *The Potential for Violence in Arrests of Persons with Mental Illness,* Policing: An International Journal of Police Strategies & Management 37(2): 404–419 (2014) (not finding a significant association between race/ethnicity and police use of force in a dataset focused on arrests of persons with mental illnesses). In immigrant communities, where minority race and ethnicity often intersect with immigration status, rates of stops and arrests are higher despite lower involvement of immigrants in crime. Jose Torres, *Race/Ethnicity in Stop and Frisk: Past, Present, Future,* 9(11) Sociology Compass 931–939 (2015).

As discussed, in the body of this concurrence, the evidence has only grown more substantial since Justice Stevens's *Wardlow* dissent.

Minority and immigrant women experience intersectional risks potential harms in disparate police encounters. *See, e.g.,* Sherri Sharma, *Beyond "Driving While Black" and "Flying While Brown": Using Intersectionality to Uncover the Gendered Aspects of Racial Profiling,* 12 Colum. J. Gender & L. 275 (2003).

Unsurprisingly, in light of these heightened risks of harm that minority community members face, there is a substantial racial gap in trust in the police and government generally. *See, e.g.,* Elaine B. Sharp & Paul E. Johnston, *Accounting for Variation in Distrust of Local Police,* 26(1) Justice Quarterly 157–182 (2009) (studying variables accounting for the "gaping chasm" in the "race gap" when it comes to trust in local police); Melissa Marschall & Paru R. Shah, *The Attitudinal Effects of Minority Incorporation Examining the Racial Dimensions of Trust in Urban America,* 42(5) Urban Aff. Rev. 629–658 (2007) (noting the persistent racial gap in trust in the government that has spanned 35 years since the Institute for Social Trust began measuring political trust). One of the most frequent explanations given by social scientists for the trust gap is the "political reality model" viewing mistrust as a rational response to lacking political power and unequal treatment. Paul R. Abramson, *Political Attitudes in America* San Francisco, CA: W. H. Freeman (1983). There is some evidence that publicized accounts of police violence deter minority community members from calling the police for help or reporting crime. Matthew Desmond, Andrew V. Papachristos, David S. Kirk, *Police Violence and Citizen Crime Reporting in the Black Community,* 81(5) Am. Sociological Rev. 857–876 (2016) (reporting findings regarding deterred minority citizen crime reporting in Milwaukee after a highly publicized controversy over police use of force).

Unfortunately, as Justice Stevens observed in his remarkably frank *Wardlow* dissent, courts sometimes engage in an "ivory-towered analysis of the real world" that "fails to account for the experiences of many citizens of this country, particularly those who are minorities." *Illinois v. Wardlow,* 528 U.S. 119, 129 n.3 (2000) (Stevens, J., dissenting). As Judge Tatel suggested occurred here in his dissent on direct appeal, "American-born, highly educated, legally sophisticated judges" substituted their views for the reality faced by someone with far less resources, power, access to protection, and knowledge about the American system of law enforcement. *United States v. Nwoye,* 663 F.3d 460, 468–469 (D.C. Cir. 2011) (Tatel, J., dissenting).

Allowing the mere chance to argue duress to a properly instructed jury is far from granting a duress defense. It is simply allowing the defendant the constitutional right to present a defense, which the jury is free to credit or discredit as fact-finders. Arrayed against the vital right to mount a defense and the venerable rule that juries, not judges, should serve as factfinders, is concern about "wasting valuable trial resources." *United States v. Bailey,* 444 U.S. 394, 417 (1980). The *Bailey* Court set a high bar for prison escape defendants, denying a necessity defense based on violent and dangerous prison conditions, including frequent fires and beatings by guards, out of a "pragmatic" preference that trials for prison escape be "simple affairs" to conserve resources. *Id.* at 389, 397. 417. The concern for wasting trial resources is frankly overblown in a reality where approximately 90–95 percent of all criminal cases end by plea bargain, never entailing a trial at all. Lindsey Devers, Bureau of Justice Statistics, *Plea and Charge Bargaining: Research Summary* (Bureau of Justice Assistance, U.S. Dep't of Justice 2011). Moreover, as occurred in this case, defendants may still be allowed to testify as to the difficult circumstances surrounding the offense – but the jury is simply denied an instruction as to the law of duress and the opportunity to carry out its role as fact-finder surrounding the crux of the defendant's case.

Allowing a small subset of people facing the brutal realities of unequal access to state protection to exercise their constitutional right to present a defense if they squeeze their realities into "battered spouse syndrome" and get an expert to attest to this syndrome is no cure for the larger problem. The "battered spouse syndrome" box is exceedingly cramped and does not capture the realities that many people who experience violence and severely constricted alternatives face. Experts have critiqued the unfortunate legal pressures to force-fit the complexities of a person's situation into the syndrome's prototype of "an utterly dysfunctional woman" who suffers from "learned helplessness," "very low self-esteem," financial dependence, isolation and inability to think beyond the next beating. Martha R. Mahoney, *Legal Images of Battered Women: Redefining the Issue of Separation*, 90 Mich. L. Rev. 1, 37–39 (1991). *See also, e.g.*, Elizabeth M. Schneider, *Describing and Changing: Women's Self-Defense Work and the Problem of Expert Testimony on Battering*, 9 Women's Rts. L. Rep'tr 195–222 (1986) (discussing the dilemma of perpetuating the stereotypes about female incapacity that the women's rights and feminist movements sought to overcome because of legal pressures to fit clients' stories into the battered spouse syndrome profile). Here, Nwoye was a battered, but not a spouse. She was a married woman who had an affair with a married man. She was a recent immigrant from Nigeria. She was a professional woman. She believed her abuser was an FBI agent. In sort, she was a three-dimensional person who may have not checked every box of the "ideal" battered spouse. But this should not preclude her from mounting a defense.

There is one more thing to say about duress. Some duress decisions portray survivors of violence as seeking a concession to their "subjective vulnerability" or "*special vulnerability to fear.*" *United States v. Johnson*, 956 F.2d 894, 898 (9th Cir.), *opinion supplemented on denial of reh'g sub nom. United States v. Emelio*, 969 F.2d 849 (9th Cir. 1992). The suggestion that people who have experienced violence and have limited access to law enforcement protection are seeking a relaxed standard for some personal weakness is incorrect. The reasonableness of alternatives to succumbing to threats and violence is evaluated based on the circumstances and realities facing the defendant in the case, not the vastly different situation of judges whose task is to interpret the law, not decide the facts, a role reserved for a jury of the defendant's peers. *See Williams v. Florida*, 399 U.S. 78, 100, 90 (1970).

The foundational principles of fundamental fairness underlying constitutional protections for a fair trial "require that criminal defendants be afforded a meaningful opportunity to present a complete defense." *California v. Trombetta*, 467 U.S. 479, 485 (1984). As Nwoye's case shows, duress is often the entire defense of a person coerced into an offense, not just one of a grab bag of defenses. Denial of the right for a properly instructed jury to apply the law of duress to the facts proffered by the defendant effectively deprives a defendant of fair consideration by a jury of peers whose life experiences are likely closer to the defendant's than the presiding judge.

The jury is free to credit or discredit the defendant's account of no reasonable alternative – and should be allowed to do its job in evaluating the facts. Our court today gives Nwoye a measure of relief – if she force-fits her situation as a recent immigrant duped by a man claiming to be an FBI agent into the confines of battered spouse syndrome. Fundamental fairness requires more: equal access of all people to the right to present a duress defense even if their realities are different from the judges serving as gatekeepers, and their experiences, identities and circumstances different from the confining box of the "battered woman syndrome."

14

Commentary on *Erotic Services Provider Legal Education and Research Project v. Gascon*

AYA GRUBER AND KATE MOGULESCU

In the three years since the US Court of Appeals for the Ninth Circuit decided *Erotic Services Provider Legal Education and Research Project v. Gascon*,[1] discourse on criminalizing commercial sex has shifted dramatically, and the decision reflects an older mindset from which powerful decision-makers have quickly evolved. The shift came as the political branches to which the Ninth Circuit punted responded to the movements against mass incarceration and abusive policing that were gaining momentum. For example, in her 2016 brief in *Gascon*, then California Attorney General Kamala Harris urged the Ninth Circuit to uphold the state prostitution law.[2] Not three years later, as part of her 2020 presidential campaign, Senator Harris became the first mainstream US presidential campaign to publicly support the decriminalization of prostitution.[3] The pivot has been swift.[4]

In *Gascon*, the amici, a veritable *who's who* of the sex work debate, invited the Ninth Circuit to lend its voice to a pressing contemporary issue. However, mired in an older way of thinking, the court was unwilling to enter the fray and refused to do the most basic analysis of California's claimed rationales for criminalizing

---

[1] *Erotic Service Provider Legal Education and Research Project v. Gascon*, 880 F.3d 450 (9th Cir. 2018).
[2] *See generally* Brief of Appellee Kamala D. Harris, Erotic Service Provider Legal, Education & Research Project, 880 F.3d 450 (9th Cir. Nov. 30, 2016) (No. 16–15927).
[3] Melissa Gira Grant, Opinion, *Kamala Harris Brought Sex Work into the 2020 Spotlight. Here's What She Should Do Next*, THE WASHINGTON POST, Mar. 2, 2019, www.washingtonpost.com/opinions/2019/03/02/kamala-harris-brought-sex-work-into-spotlight-heres-what-she-should-do-next/.
[4] *See, e.g.*, Bryce Covert, *New York Moves a Step Closer to Decriminalizing Sex Work*, THE APPEAL, Feb. 9, 2021, https://theappeal.org/new-york-moves-a-step-closer-to-decriminalizing-sex-work/; Oralander Brand-Williams, *Washtenaw County Prosecutor Will No Longer Prosecute "Consensual" Sex Work*, THE DETROIT NEWS, Jan. 14, 2021, www.detroitnews.com/story/news/local/michigan/2021/01/14/michigan-prosecutor-no-longer-prosecute-consensual-sex-work/4157744001/; Chelsea Cirruzzo, *The Case for Decriminalizing Sex Work*, U.S. NEWS & WORLD REPORT, Jan. 11, 2021, www.usnews.com/news/health-news/articles/2021-01-11/calls-mount-to-decriminalize-sex-work-in-the-interest-of-public-health; Lisa Rathke, *Bill in Vermont Would Decriminalize Prostitution*, ASSOCIATED PRESS, Feb. 6, 2020, https://apnews.com/article/2f92fad4f8154f934183eb84b8048d39; Stephanie Ebbert, *Three Ways to Rethink Prostitution*, BOSTON GLOBE, Dec. 16, 2019, www.bostonglobe.com/metro/2019/12/16/three-ways-rethink-prostitution/Jr972r7C1TyQyQVNUByoRJ/story.html.

prostitution.⁵ By simply crediting the state's faulty justifications at face value, the decision highlights courts' tendency to blindly accept states' weak legal and policy arguments when it comes to criminal prostitution statutes. Whether because of discomfort with sex, sex exceptionalism, or paternalistic and moralistic attitudes toward women, courts regard prostitution as untouchable.

Judge Thusi's rewritten decision commendably does the work the Ninth Circuit refused to do. It scrutinizes the government's offered rationales for criminalizing prostitution and corrects many of the suspect claims the Ninth Circuit let stand. Still, the decision is relatively cautious in its vision of what is possible for those engaged in commercial sex when compared to the rapid movement toward decriminalization in jurisdictions across the United States and the world.⁶ The swiftly growing contemporary decriminalization movement is grounded in racial, gender, and economic justice and prioritizes protection of workers, immigrants, and LGBTQ individuals. To be sure, Judge Thusi's excellent opinion is vastly superior to the Ninth Circuit's, but additional foci would make it even more of a "feminist" judgment.

PROSTITUTION LAWS & ENFORCEMENT:
A BRIEF (INTERSECTIONAL) HISTORY

American prostitution laws, such as California's 647(b), have always been about "morality," whether morality born of religion, racial hierarchy, social convention, or even a sense of gender justice. The prostitution criminalization program arose in the late 1800s and expanded as the United States entered an extended period of social preoccupation with disciplining sexuality. Antiprostitution laws were driven by a diverse array of forces, including the evangelical revival that swept the nation in the mid-1800s and grew in response to the perceived debauchery of Civil War soldiers, the widespread fear of newly emancipated Black men's sexual prowess, press coverage of the "white slavery" crisis of young white girls trapped in exotic "dens of iniquity," and the activism of early feminist reformers concerned about women's exploitation *and* morality.⁷ In the twentieth century, as prostitution prohibitions and other laws outlawing disfavored sexual activity proliferated, the need for enforcement led to the growth of local and state police departments and notably

---

⁵ See generally *Gascon*, 850 F.3d.
⁶ See *supra* notes 3–4.
⁷ See generally AYA GRUBER, THE FEMINIST WAR ON CRIME: THE UNEXPECTED ROLE OF WOMEN'S LIBERATION IN MASS INCARCERATION (2020); Helen Lefkowitz Horowitz, *Victoria Woodhull, Anthony Comstock, and Conflict over Sex in the United States in the 1870s*, 87 J. AM. HIST. 403, 403–434 (2000); JESSICA R. PLILEY, POLICING SEXUALITY; THE MANN ACT AND THE MAKING OF THE FBI (2014); Mae Quinn, *From Turkey Trot to Twitter: Policing Puberty, Purity, and Sex-Positivity*, 38 N.Y.U. REV. L. & SOC. CHANGE 51 (2014).

the rise of the FBI.[8] This sex-regulatory era saw reformatories fill with "unruly" girls, mass arrests of gay men, formal and informal criminalization of interracial relationships, widespread brutality against Black men, and the confinement of sex workers to dangerous and stigmatized red-light districts.[9]

The second half of the twentieth century brought the sexual revolution, with its increased acceptance of liberalized sex. The changing norms coincided with shift in the constitutional regime governing state regulation of "intimate" and sexual affairs. Between 1965 and 1973, the Supreme Court protected individuals' rights to take and distribute contraception[10] and to choose an abortion.[11] It also significantly limited states' ability to criminalize sexual communications and images under obscenity laws.[12] Although the Supreme Court upheld the criminalization of consensual adult sodomy in the 1986 case *Bowers v. Hardwick*, sodomy laws, when enforced at all, were often restricted to cases of sexual violence.[13]

The increase in the demand for and supply of commercial sexual services and products sparked a legal effort in the 1980s and 1990s that united family-values conservatives and leftist feminists in the pursuit of stronger restrictions against pornography and prostitution.[14] During the infamous "sex wars," radical antiprostitution feminists, who regarded commercial sex as abusive male sexual domination of women, squared off against liberal and sex-positive feminists, who argued that prostitution criminalization harmed marginalized women and tightened the state's grip on female sexuality.[15] In the 1990s, the antiprostitution agenda received a boost with "quality of life policing" initiatives in cities like New York. In the name of "cleaning-up" the streets, police aggressively enforced prostitution laws, placing sex workers in a revolving door of jail, collateral consequences, poverty, and violence.[16] The weight of this antiprostitution policing, in New York and elsewhere, fell on women of color, particularly Black women.[17]

---

[8] *See generally* PLILEY, *supra* note 7.
[9] *See* Pliley, *supra* note 7; Jamelia Morgan, *Rethinking Disorderly Conduct*, CALIF. L. REV. (forthcoming 2021), https://papers.ssrn.com/sol3/papers.cfm?abstract_id=3552620.
[10] *Griswold v. Connecticut*, 381 U.S. 479, 485 (1965); *Eisenstadt v. Baird*, 405 U.S. 438, 453 (1972).
[11] *Roe v. Wade*, 410 U.S. 113, 153 (1973).
[12] *Miller v. California*, 413 U.S. 15, 23–24 (1973).
[13] *See Lawrence v. Texas*, 539 U.S. 558, 559 (2003).
[14] *See generally* GRUBER *supra* note 7; Kathy Abrams, *Sex Wars Redux: Agency and Coercion in Feminist Legal Theory*, 95 COLUM. L. REV. 304, 308 (1995); *See generally* CAROL S. VANCE, PLEASURE AND DANGER: EXPLORING FEMALE SEXUALITY (1984).
[15] *See generally* Abrams, *supra* note 14.
[16] *See generally* Aya Gruber, Amy J. Cohen, & Kate Mogulescu, *Penal Welfare and the New Human Trafficking Intervention Courts*, 68 FLA. L. REV. 1333 (2016).
[17] *See, e.g.*, Meredith Dank, Jennifer Yahner, & Lilly Yu, *Consequences of Policing Prostitution: An Analysis of Individuals Arrested and Prosecuted for Commercial Sex in New York City*, URBAN INSTITUTE (Apr. 5, 2017), www.urban.org/research/publication/consequences-policing-prostitution; *see generally* Kate Mogulescu, *Your Cervix Is Showing: Loitering for Prostitution Policing as Gendered Stop & Frisk*, 74 U. MIAMI L. REV. CAVEAT 68 (2020).

The end of the millennium witnessed another cultural shift, as the public appetite for demonizing homosexuality waned. In 2003, the Supreme Court's landmark decision in *Lawrence v. Texas* struck down a Texas statute criminalizing same-sex sodomy.[18] Justice Anthony Kennedy, author of the majority opinion, declined the invitation offered by LGBT advocates to treat the case as one about equal protection for sexual minorities. Instead, *Lawrence* was about sex, and specifically everyone's due process right to engage in adult, consensual, private sexual activity free from government interference.[19] Critics accused Kennedy of ignoring the equal protection angle to avoid the looming gay marriage issue.[20] But he explained that the liberty right prevented the government from criminalizing sodomy, even if applied equally.[21] The court opined that a moral objection to sodomy, even if traditionally shared by "the governing majority in a State," was "not a sufficient reason for upholding a law prohibiting the practice."[22]

With *Lawrence's* newly minted sexual liberty right, sex worker rights organizations began a renewed effort to assert the right to engage in private, adult, consensual commercial sexual conduct. But these organizations found themselves fighting on the new – and perilous – cultural terrain of contemporary human trafficking discourse. In the 2000s, the issue of sexual slavery once again rose to the fore of public discussion in ways that mirrored the Progressive-era white-slavery moment. By the 2010s, the media regularly covered spectacular and horrifying, if rare, tales of young children and vulnerable women sold into the sex trade and kept in physical bondage.[23] The antitrafficking rhetoric of some mainstream, even liberal, commentators was barely removed from the QAnon conspiracy talk of today. The most vocal anti-trafficking activist groups, which included many of the same 1980s antiprostitution feminists, painted *all* prostitution as human trafficking and all sex workers as coerced. They alternatively argued that even if not all sex work is coerced, it is the demand for commercial sex that leads to trafficking.[24] This particular narrative proved a boon to conservative moralists, vice squads, and the businesses interested in cleaning up the streets. It provided a vocabulary to communicate prostitution's spectacular harms to a public that might otherwise have arrived at the determination that adult consensual commercial sex is no big deal.

It was in this milieu that the Ninth Circuit decided *Gascon*.

---

[18] *Lawrence v. Texas*, 539 U.S. 558, 578–579 (2003).
[19] *Id.* at 564.
[20] *See, e.g.*, Andrew J. Seligsohn, *Choosing Liberty over Equality and Sacrificing Both: Equal Protection and Due Process in Lawrence v. Texas*, 10 CARDOZO WOMEN'S L. J. 411, 422 (2004).
[21] *Lawrence*, 539 U.S. at 575.
[22] *Id.* at 577.
[23] *See generally* Gruber, Cohen, & Mogulescu, *supra* note 16.
[24] SUPREME COURT OF THE STATE OF NEW YORK, APPELLATE DIVISION, FIRST DEPARTMENT & NEW YORK STATE JUDICIAL COMMITTEE ON WOMEN IN THE COURTS, LAWYER'S MANUAL ON HUMAN TRAFFICKING: PURSUING JUSTICE FOR VICTIMS 291–298 (Jill Laurie Goodman & Dorchen A. Leidholdt, eds., 2013).

THE ORIGINAL OPINION

The lawsuit, brought by Erotic Services Provider Legal Education and Research Project ("ESP"), a sex worker rights organization, sought relief under 42 USC § 1983, which provides a federal cause of action for state violations of constitutional rights.[25] ESP argued that California's SB 647 was unconstitutional. That law made it a crime to "solicit[]" or "agree[] to engage[] in...any act of prostitution."[26] ESP claimed, among other things, that the law violated due process by infringing on the fundamental liberty interest in adult, consensual, private sexual activity.[27] In addressing these contentions, the Ninth Circuit produced a one-sided and superficially reasoned opinion that evidenced both a preexisting bias against the sex worker rights position and ignorance about commercial sex.

ESP claimed that *Lawrence*'s establishment of a fundamental sexual liberty interest required heightened judicial scrutiny of SB 647. ESP's argument was that, *similar to* the sex at issue in *Lawrence*, sex worker's private, consensual, adult sex fell within *Lawrence*'s protection of "the most private human conduct, sexual behavior," that is "within the liberty of persons to choose without being punished as criminals."[28] The Ninth Circuit dismissed that argument on the sole ground that "whatever the nature of the right protected in *Lawrence*, one thing *Lawrence* does make explicit is that the *Lawrence* case 'does not involve ... prostitution.'"[29] Notice the sleight of hand. *Lawrence* made clear that the *case* facts did not involve prostitution. But the Ninth Circuit characterized that as a *substantive* declaration the liberty-right established could not involve commercial sex.

The distinguishing language from *Lawrence* relied on so heavily by the Ninth Circuit states in full: "The present case does not involve minors. It does not involve persons who might be injured or coerced or who are situated in relationships where consent might not easily be refused. It does not involve public conduct or prostitution."[30] Even accepting the Ninth Circuit's assumption that *Lawrence*'s language meant to limit the future reach of the liberty right, the sentence indicates a limitation against potentially coerced and nonconsensual sex and *public* sex. The *Lawrence* court grouped "prostitution" with "public conduct," and made clear throughout that the liberty right regarded *private* sexual conduct.[31] Thus, if the sentence constituted a substantive limitation, which it is not clear that it did, there is a compelling

---

[25] *Erotic Service Provider Legal Education and Research Project v. Gascon*, 880 F.3d 450, 454 (9th Cir. 2018).
[26] Cal. Penal Code § 647(b) (West, 2021). The statute defines prostitution as "any lewd act between persons for money." Cal. Penal Code § 647(b) (4) (West, 2021).
[27] *Gascon*, 850 F.3d at 454.
[28] *Lawrence v. Texas*, 539 U.S. 558, 567 (2003).
[29] *Gascon*, 850 F.3d at 456 (citation omitted).
[30] *Lawrence*, 539 U.S. at 578.
[31] See generally *id*.

argument to be made that limitation was about *public* prostitution offenses and not the private commercial sexual activity at the center of ESP's claim.

Despite its insistence that *Lawrence* itself foreclosed ESP's claim, the Ninth Circuit devoted a few sentences to "[t]he nature of the right" in *Lawrence*.[32] Here, the court argued that "the bounds of *Lawrence's* holding are unclear."[33] The court's alternative interpretations of *Lawrence's* liberty right were (1) a "right to private sexual activity among consenting adults" or (2) "the right to achieve a personal bond that is more enduring."[34] The court went on to presume that if it were the second, commercial sex would obviously be excluded because it is unconnected to an "enduring bond." The court concluded that "absent clearer language from the Court regarding the nature of the right *Lawrence* actually does protect," it could not extend the liberty right to commercial sex.[35] Later in the opinion, the Ninth Circuit made its view of commercial sex relationships clear: "the duration of the relationship between a prostitute and a client does not suggest an intimate relationship."[36]

The Ninth Circuit's reading of *Lawrence* to confer only the right to sex that achieves an enduring bond is difficult to support in the text. *Lawrence* states, "[w]hen sexuality finds overt expression in intimate conduct with another person, the conduct can be but one element in a personal bond that is more enduring. The liberty protected by the Constitution allows homosexual persons the right to make this choice."[37] In this passage, the court simply recognized one particularly pernicious aspect of the Texas law – that it denied homosexuals *any* avenue to express their bond through sex. But, importantly, the court was adamant that the case was not just about LGBT individuals' right to have sexual relationships. The liberty right applied equally to heterosexual people for whom sodomy statutes were a matter not of *whether* they could express personal bonds through sex but *how* they could have sex.[38] Suffice it to say, *Lawrence* did not preserve states' ability to criminalize sodomy between people not in a bonded relationship. Nowhere did *Lawrence* require long-term bonding for private, adult, consensual sex to merit constitutional protection.

Having decided that *Lawrence's* liberty right did not extend to commercial sex, the Ninth Circuit applied to SB 647 the basic due process test, "rational relation," which requires legislation merely to bear a rational relationship to a legitimate state interest, an extremely low bar.[39] To meet the "legitimate state interest" prong, the

[32] *Gascon*, 850 F.3d at 456.
[33] *Id.* (citations omitted).
[34] *Id.*
[35] *Id.*
[36] *Gascon*, 850 F.3d at 459.
[37] *Lawrence v. Texas*, 539 U.S. 558, 567 (2003).
[38] *Id.* at 575.
[39] *Gascon*, 850 F.3d at 457.

state needed only to point to a "conceivable" interest furthered by the legislation.[40] California, rightly sensing that *Lawrence* cast doubt on the legitimacy of states' interest in morality, articulated a more modern – and ostensibly feminist – set of interests behind the law: "discouraging human trafficking and violence against women, discouraging illegal drug use, and preventing contagious and infectious diseases."[41] California did not argue that it had a legitimate interest in preventing the exchange of sex for money *in itself*. Thus, by the government's own justification, to meet the second prong of the test, SB 647 had to bear a rational relation not to prostitution but to reducing human trafficking/violence against women, drug use, or disease.

The Ninth Circuit emphasized that the state only needed to provide "rational speculation" about SB 647's beneficial effects.[42] In concluding that SB 647 was rationally related to those goals, the court relied on dated and partisan research regarding the ills associated with prostitution, without considering whether SB 647 itself caused or exacerbated them. The evidence of SB 647's rational relation to preventing sex trafficking was that "82% of suspected incidents of human trafficking were characterized as sex trafficking, and approximately 40% of suspected sex trafficking incidents involved sexual exploitation or prostitution of a child."[43] These statistics deserve critical examination. Not only were they stale at the time the Ninth Circuit relied on them, but even if credited, they reflect only what law enforcement prioritized and pursued through investigation and prosecution, not the actual prevalence of human trafficking, the majority of which involves exploitation in labor sectors other than commercial sex.[44]

More importantly, merely stating that sex trafficking exists does not constitute proof that SB 647 had any positive impact on it. The other evidence accepted by the court was that "prostitutes" are addicted, diseased, and frequent victims of violence.[45] Such evidence might establish a relationship between *being* a sex worker and an increased risk of suffering certain harms, although correlation is not causation and it might be that similarly situated nonsex workers are even worse off. In any case, such evidence does not speak to whether SB 647 reduced, or even had the potential to reduce, these harms. The various harms afflicting sex workers highlighted by the court occurred *while SB 647 and similar laws criminalizing prostitution were in effect*. Consequently, the court's proof of rational relation was the mere speculation that without SB 647, the trafficking, violence, drug, and disease

---

[40] *Id.*
[41] *Id.*
[42] *Id.* (citations omitted).
[43] *Id.*
[44] *See, e.g.*, NATIONAL INSTITUTE OF JUSTICE, THE PREVALENCE OF LABOR TRAFFICKING IN THE UNITED STATES (Feb. 26, 2013), https://nij.ojp.gov/topics/articles/prevalence-labor-trafficking-united-states; *See also* Leila Miller, *Why Labor Trafficking Is So Hard to Track*, FRONTLINE (Apr. 24, 2018), www.pbs.org/wgbh/frontline/article/why-labor-trafficking-is-so-hard-to-track/.
[45] *Gascon*, 850 F.3d at 458.

problem would have been worse. The court hinged this finding on the commercial nature of prostitution, without any evidence that paid sex yields higher rates of the identified harms than noncommercial sex.

The Ninth Circuit's opinion makes only one mention of the actual, not speculative, relationship between criminalization and California's proffered interests in reducing violence and disease: "ESP maintains that the criminalization of prostitution makes erotic service providers more vulnerable to crimes, and does not significantly deter the spread of diseases."[46] Although the court credited without scrutiny the government's evidence that illegal sex work is rife with harms, it did not see fit to explicate, much less engage with, ESP's evidence that it was actually SB 647's criminalization of sex work that largely created those harms. Instead, the Ninth Circuit relegated such analysis to legislative consideration. Later in the opinion, when addressing ESP's First Amendment challenge, the court dispensed altogether with the pretense of connecting SB 647 with loftier goals than just outlawing prostitution for its own sake. The court described California's interest as "preventing the commodification of sex" and called the interest not just legitimate, but "substantial."[47]

Accordingly, the Ninth Circuit did a fair amount of work to place itself squarely in the camp holding that *"prostitution is bad* so criminalization must be *good."* As such, reducing prostitution activity, and demand for commercial sex, through criminal law passes constitutional muster. The decision, although proclaiming agnosticism to the legislative wisdom of prostitution criminalization, with its harmful rhetoric (labeling those who engage in sex work as "prostitutes") and empirically deficient presumptions holds tight to the contestable notion that commercial sex is itself a social harm that the government must fight.

THE FEMINIST JUDGMENT

From the outset of Judge Thusi's opinion, it is clear that the court would give fair consideration to the substance of ESP's liberty claim, rather than using interpretive maneuvering to avoid analyzing criminalization's real impact on those in the commercial sex industry. Judge Thusi showed sensitivity to the power of legal narrative to stigmatize disfavored groups. The original Ninth Circuit opinion described ESP as no more than a collection of "prostitutes" who "wish to perform sex for hire."[48] On the other hand, the rewritten opinion describes ESP as a "sex workers advocacy organization" that "seeks to empower the erotic community and advance sexual privacy rights through legal advocacy, education, and research" and "provides public education about the harms of the continued criminalization of prostitution and manages a clearinghouse of research to support erotic service providers."

---

[46] *Id.*
[47] *Id.* at 461.
[48] *Id.* at 454.

Like the original opinion, the rewritten judgment begins with ESP's claim that *Lawrence's* fundamental liberty includes commercial sexual activity. Judge Thusi correctly frames the issue as "whether there is a constitutional right to be free from government interference when engaging in private sexual activity, even where there is an exchange of money involved in this private activity."[49] The rewritten opinion rightly emphasizes that *Lawrence* starkly departed from past precedents by holding that moral objection to a sexual practice is not alone ground to outlaw it. As to *Lawrence's* observation that the case did not "involve prostitution," Justice Thusi interpreted this sentence as simply saying that the holding did not "*automatically* extend to prostitution."[50] She explained that *Lawrence* left open the possibility that a court could extend its liberty right, "much like *Lawrence* was an extension of the right to enter into an interracial marriage, the right to use birth control, and the right to have an abortion."[51] She added that "[a]ll of these acts were previously considered morally repugnant by the majority of Americans at some point."[52]

Judge Thusi further underscores that *Lawrence* grouped prostitution with *public* disorder, supporting the inference that its substantive limitation, if any, regarded public commercial sex. To make this interpretive point, the rewritten judgment offers an abbreviated history of prostitution laws showing, among other things, that they were initially about public disorderly conduct and not private morality.[53] Only later, in the twentieth century, did moralistic law-makers become preoccupied with private consensual sex, including sodomy and "indoor" prostitution.[54] Thus, prostitution occupies two distinct legal spheres: a public sphere, where regulation could survive *Lawrence*, and a private sphere, where regulation on moral grounds implicates fundamental liberty.

Unlike the Ninth Circuit, Judge Thusi does not avoid legal analysis by claiming that *Lawrence's* arguable lack of clarity on the sexual liberty right is grounds to ignore the case's reach.[55] Instead, Judge Thusi interprets the liberty right as "a fundamental right to be free from government interference when engaging in private sexual activity," an interpretation that hewed to the text in *Lawrence* far more than the Ninth Circuit's strained determination limiting it to "the right to achieve [an enduring] personal bond."[56] Thus, the rewritten opinion focuses on the crux of the controversy: whether an added financial element to private, adult, consensual sex changes its status under the Constitution. It answers this question in the negative.

---

[49] *Id.* at 14.
[50] *Id.* at 11 (emphasis added).
[51] *Id.* at 12.
[52] *Id.*
[53] *Id.* at 9–11.
[54] *Id.* at 7.
[55] *Gascon*, 850 F.3d at 456.
[56] *Id.*

Judge Thusi notes that the Supreme Court has consistently found that "commodification alone is not a sufficient basis for denying the existence of a fundamental right to be free from government interference while engaging in private sexual conduct." Understandably, the opinion seeks accuracy in describing commercial sex as "more complex than the stereotypes we see from television and the news." It demonstrates that commercial sex is not necessarily limited to one single transaction and can be long term, emotional, or intimate. SB 647's blanket prohibition outlaws all private commercial sex similarly, even "relationships [that] carry the same depth of more serious non-transactional relationships." In fact, the husband–wife relationship, considered by many the very exemplar of an "enduring personal bond," was once a quintessential "private economical relationship[]" as Blackstone put it.[57]

Here, the amount of time the rewritten opinion dedicates to proving that commercial sex can be loving and long lasting raises concern. The rewritten judgment delves deeply into the types of *relationships* that can emerge from consensual commercial sex as a way to position prostitution as a fundamental right of sexual intimacy. First, this gives too much credence to the view that *Lawrence* may have protected only sex that achieves an enduring bond. Just as *Lawrence* forbids the criminalization of private adult noncommercial sex that is quick, casual, and anonymous, so too could it protect private adult commercial sex, enduring or not. Moreover, in going to great lengths to identify ways in which commercial sex can create an enduring bond, the rewritten opinion suggests a divide between palatable commercial sex that mirrors "normal" (traditional heteronormative) relationships and commercial sex that is more "deviant." Affording fundamental rights protection to those engaged in the former but not the latter would leave the majority of sex workers still at the mercy of the carceral state.

The rewritten opinion, having decided that private sex work can be a protected liberty interest, applies a stricter test and requires that the legislation must be necessary to significantly further an important governmental interest. Like the Ninth Circuit opinion, it concedes that preventing trafficking, violence, addiction, and disease are important interests. However, the rewritten judgment scrutinizes California's claim that SB 647 actually furthers those interests. Judge Thusi carefully considers the evidence about criminalization's effect on California's proffered interests. She observes that criminalization can thwart anti-trafficking efforts by making it "more difficult for sex workers to report suspected sex trafficking." The opinion further cites studies linking prostitution decriminalization to decreases in trafficking. Similarly, Judge Thusi examines the relationship between criminalization and disease, referring to studies that "have demonstrated that sex workers are less likely to seek medical assistance under full criminalization." One of the starkest examples of the conflict between criminalization and public health involves the use of condoms

---

[57] WILLIAM BLACKSTONE, BLACKSTONE'S COMMENTARIES, *325.

as evidence to arrest and prosecute people for prostitution (and police officers shaming suspected sex workers for having prophylactics, which they then seize).

Regarding violence against women, the rewritten judgment cites research that criminalization has failed to protect sex workers from private violence and reinforced the conditions that make them vulnerable to violence. Moreover, the court acknowledges that violence against women includes *state* violence. Vice officers are notoriously abusive and degrading to women they suspect of prostitution. And, as Judge Thusi correctly observes, criminalization lands those arrested for prostitution, disproportionately women, in prisons and jails rife with sexual and other violence. The opinion concludes, "[a]ll of this evidence and research, when interpreted in the light most favorable to ESP, indicate that not only is the State criminalization of prostitution not necessary, it is counterproductive and may lead to an increase in sex trafficking and venereal diseases."[58]

Indeed, the evidence cited in the rewritten judgment casts serious doubt on whether SB 647 passes even the rational relation test's low bar. Yet, the opinion does not go this far and thus forgoes an opportunity to tease out this possibility. Ultimately, the rewritten judgment is at its most feminist when it emphasizes how the criminalization of commercial sex harms women, not when it endeavors to argue that prostitution creates enduring intimate bonds.[59]

CONCLUSION: THE DECRIMINALIZATION MOMENT

In January 2021, the recently seated prosecuting attorney in Washtenaw County, Michigan announced a new policy directive "regarding sex work."[60] In a stark departure from the outdated logic animating the Ninth Circuit's decision in *Gascon*, the prosecutor announced that his office would no longer prosecute charges "based solely on the consensual exchange, between adults, of sex for money."[61] Prosecutors in several other large jurisdictions have also recently indicated they will no longer charge and prosecute prostitution offenses.[62] Although a 2016 effort in federal court

---

[58] *Id.* at 21.
[59] *See generally* Laura A. Rosenbury & Jennifer E. Rothman, *Sex In and Out of Intimacy*, 59 EMORY L. J. 809 (2010).
[60] Office of the Prosecuting Attorney, *Policy Directive 2021-08: Policy Regarding Sex Work*, WASHTENAW COUNTY (2021).
[61] *Id.*
[62] Rebecca Rosenberg, *Brooklyn DA Eric Gonzalez Dismisses 262 Prostitution-Related Warrants*, N.Y. POST, Jan. 29, 2021, https://nypost.com/2021/01/29/brooklyn-da-gonzalez-dismisses-prostitution-related-warrants/; David Ganezer, *Prostitution, Trespassing, Disturbing the Peace, Driving Without a License and Loitering Are Now Effectively Legal in LA County*, SANTA MONICA OBSERVER, Dec. 10, 2020, www.smobserved.com/story/2020/12/10/news/prostitution-trespassing-disturbing-the-peace-driving-without-a-license-and-loitering-are-now-effectively-legal-in-la-county/5115.html; James Walker, *San Francisco's New DA Will Not Prosecute Prostitution, Public Urination Cases*; "We Must Think Differently," NEWSWEEK, Nov. 13, 2019, www.newsweek.com/san-francisco-district-attorney-public-urination-prostitution-not-prosecute-1471475.

to challenge New York's loitering for prostitution law as unconstitutional on its face and as applied failed, in February 2021, the New York State legislature repealed the law, striking it from the books.[63]

In recent times, sex worker and civil rights groups' organizing efforts have produced robust prostitution decriminalization initiatives in New York, the District of Columbia, and elsewhere.[64] Reading the Washtenaw County directive[65] or the comprehensive decriminalization bill pending in the New York State legislature[66] gives a sense of just how outdated, one-sided, and short-sighted the Ninth Circuit's treatment of the prostitution issue was. Things have changed dramatically, via legislative and executive action, and for the better. In the end, the *Gascon* decision may have sowed the seeds of its own irrelevance, and it – along with all the other cases where courts were mired in the past and unwilling to meaningfully scrutinize the "untouchable" commercial sex issue – may soon be a relic.

By contrast, Judge Thusi's rewritten judgment avoids that sidestepping and faulty reasoning. It engages deeply and thoughtfully with the issue of commercial sex. Yet, even this opinion lags somewhat behind the current movement of decriminalization and decarceration organizing and policy-making. In the short time since the original opinion, widespread support of programs to decriminalize or refrain from enforcing prohibitions on the sale, although not necessarily purchase, of sex has developed. In fact, this is becoming a mainstream position that unites anti-prostitution feminists and sex-worker advocates, and it is not – nor should it be – based on an overly rosy picture of the bonds created by commercial sex.

Prostitution statutes' particular perniciousness in the United States, and elsewhere, lay in the harms they exact on sex workers and other marginalized people. Police enforce these laws in unabashedly racist, sexist, xenophobic, and transphobic ways. This is true whether the sex work that is policed is loving and long term or emotionless and transactional. The rewritten opinion arrives at the correct outcome, and in doing so clearly lays bare the problems in the Ninth Circuit's original decision. The rewritten opinion does not pave the way for advocates to challenge prostitution criminalization under the rational relation test. Judge Thusi perhaps determined that courts will remain ever too skittish to entertain such analysis. But our current political moment shows what is possible, and we may get there nonetheless.

---

[63] Jimmy Vielkind, *New York Repeal of Anti-Prostitution Loitering Statute Is Approved*, WALL ST. J., Feb. 2, 2021, www.wsj.com/articles/new-york-repeal-of-anti-prostitution-loitering-statute-passed-by-lawmakers-11612303523; *see generally* Mogulescu, *supra* note 17.

[64] *See supra* note 4; *see also* Ken Duffy, *Report Renews Calls for Decriminalizing Sex Work in DC*, WTOP NEWS, Dec. 17, 2020, https://wtop.com/dc/2020/12/report-renews-call-for-decriminalizing-sex-work-in-dc/; Jesse McKinley, *Bills to Decriminalize Prostitution Are Introduced. Is New York Ready?*, N.Y. TIMES, June 11, 2019, at A19.

[65] Office of the Prosecuting Attorney, *Policy Directive 2021-08: Policy Regarding Sex Work*, WASHTENAW COUNTY (2021).

[66] S. B. S3075, 2021–2022 Leg. Sess. (N.Y. 2021).

EROTIC SERVICES PROVIDER LEGAL EDUCATION AND RESEARCH PROJECT V. GASCON, 880 F.3D 450 (9TH CIR. 2018)

JUSTICE I. INDIA THUSI DELIVERED THE OPINION OF THE COURT

This case raises questions regarding the constitutionality of Section 647(b) of the California Penal Code, which criminalizes commercial exchange for sexual activity. Plaintiffs Erotic Service Provider Legal, Education & Research Project; K.L.E.S.; C.V.; J.B.; and John Doe (collectively, "ESP") allege that Section 647(b) violates the following constitutional provisions: (1) the substantive due process right to sexual privacy under the Fourteenth Amendment; (2) the right to freedom of association under the First Amendment and Fourteenth Amendment; (3) substantive due process rights to earn a living under the Fourteenth Amendment; and (4) the First Amendment and Fourteenth Amendment right to freedom of speech. The trial court granted the State's motion to dismiss ESP's complaint for failure to state a claim upon which relief may be granted. The issue before us is whether the trial court erred in dismissing these claims. We hold that the trial court did err.

Accordingly, we reverse the trial court's dismissal of the complaint and remand for further proceedings consistent with this decision.

I.

The Erotic Service Provider Legal, Education and Research Project ("ESPLERP") is a sex workers advocacy organization based in San Francisco, California. ESPLERP "seeks to empower the erotic community and advance sexual privacy rights through legal advocacy, education, and research." *Complaint* at 6. ESPLERP provides public education about the harms of the continued criminalization of prostitution and manages a clearinghouse of research to support erotic service providers. It aims to "alter the current cultural climate of perceived sexual repression into one of sexual acceptance and freedom." *Id.* It is a member-based organization formed primarily of current and former sex workers, including escorts, adult film performers, exotic dancers, phone sex operators, and web cam performers. Many of its members remain anonymous in light of the continued criminalization of prostitution in California. ESLERP aims to publicly represent its members' interests. Plaintiffs K.L.E.S., C.V., J.B., and John Doe are members of ESPLERP and residents of California whose ability to enter into sex work transactions has been affected by California's criminalization of it.

Section 647 provides the following:

[E]very person who commits any of the following acts is guilty of disorderly conduct, a misdemeanor: (b) Who solicits or who agrees to engage in or who engages in any act of prostitution. A person agrees to engage in an act of prostitution when, with specific intent to so engage, he or she manifests an acceptance of an offer or solicitation to so engage, regardless of whether the offer or solicitation was made by a person who also possessed the specific intent to engage in prostitution. No agreement to engage in an act of prostitution shall constitute a violation of this subdivision unless some act, in addition to the agreement, is done within this state in furtherance of the commission of an act of prostitution by the person agreeing to engage in that act. As used in this subdivision, "prostitution" includes any lewd act between persons for money or other consideration.

Cal. Penal Code § 647 (2015). ESP filed a complaint that challenges this statute on its face and as applied to the plaintiffs. The State promptly filed a motion to dismiss the complaint for failure to state a claim upon which relief can be granted. The district court granted ESP leave to amend their complaint, but ESP declined to file an amended complaint. The court entered a judgment granting the State's motion to dismiss with prejudice. ESP appealed the district court's judgment, and we now consider the case. We have jurisdiction pursuant to 28 U.S.C. § 1291.

We review *de novo* the district court's order granting a motion to dismiss pursuant to Rule 12(b) (6). *See Stearns v. Ticketmaster Corp.*, 655 F.3d 1013, 1018 (9th Cir. 2011); *Kahle v. Gonzales*, 487 F.3d 697, 699 (9th Cir. 2007); *Davis v. HSBC Bank Nev., N.A.*, 691 F.3d 1152, 1159 (9th Cir. 2012). The complaint must provide "enough facts to state a claim to relief that is plausible on its face" to survive the State's motion to dismiss. *Bell Atl. Corp. v. Twombly*, 550 U.S. 544, 570, (2007); *Williams v. Gerber Prods. Co.*, 552 F.3d 934, 938 (9th Cir. 2008) ("Factual allegations must be enough to raise a right to relief above the speculative level."). "A claim has facial plausibility, when the plaintiff pleads factual content that allows the court to draw the reasonable inference that the defendant is liable for the misconduct alleged. The plausibility standard is not akin to a 'probability requirement,' but it asks for more than a sheer possibility that a defendant has acted unlawfully." *Moss v. United States Secret Serv.*, 572 F.3d 962, 964 (2009). In reviewing the complaint, this court must accept "all factual allegations in the complaint as true and construe the pleadings in the light most favorable to the nonmoving party." *Rowe v. Educ. Credit Mgmt. Corp.*, 559 F.3d 1028, 1029–1030 (9th Cir. 2009). This court has recognized, "Rule 12(b) (6) dismissals are especially disfavored in cases where the complaint sets forth a novel legal theory that can best be assessed after factual development." *McGary v. City of Portland*, 386 F.3d 1259, 1270 (9th Cir. 2004) (internal citations omitted). Indeed, "the court should be especially reluctant to dismiss on the basis of the pleadings when the asserted theory of liability is novel or extreme, since it is important that new legal theories be explored and assayed in the light of actual facts rather than a pleader's suppositions." *McGary*, 386 F.3d at 1270 (citing *Elec. Constr. & Maint. Co., Inc. v. Maeda Pac. Corp.*, 764 F.2d 619, 623 (9th Cir. 1985)).

II.

Plaintiffs raise both as applied and facial challenges to Section 647(b). An "as applied" claim challenges the statute as it applies to the specific situation of the individual plaintiffs. By contrast, a facial challenge asserts that the statute is unconstitutional on its face. See *United States v. Salerno*, 481 U.S. 739, 746–752 (1987). The State argues that the plaintiffs do not bring as applied challenges because they do not face the imminent threat of prosecution. However, the Supreme Court has noted that when the "plaintiff has alleged an intention to engage in a course of conduct arguably affected with a constitutional interest, but proscribed by a statute, and there exists a credible threat of prosecution thereunder, he 'should not be required to await and undergo a criminal prosecution as the sole means of securing relief.'" *Babbitt v. United Farm Workers National Union*, 442 U.S. 289, 298 (1979), quoting *Doe v. Bolton*, 410 U.S. 179, 181 (1973); *Steffel v. Thompson*, 415 U.S. at 459–462. We review the complaint in the light most favorable to the plaintiff and treat the complaint as both an as applied challenge and a facial challenge to Section 647(b).

A. *Fundamental Right*

The first issue is whether Section 647(b) violates the Due Process Clause of the Fourteenth Amendment. The Due Process Clause of the Fourteenth Amendment provides that no state shall "deprive any person of life, liberty, or property, without due process of law." U.S. Const. amend. XIV, § 1. The Supreme Court has described the two-step process for identifying fundamental rights: "First, we have regularly observed that the Due Process Clause specially protects those fundamental rights and liberties which are, objectively, 'deeply rooted in this Nation's history and tradition,' and 'implicit in the concept of ordered liberty,' such that 'neither liberty nor justice would exist if they were sacrificed.' Second, we have required in substantive-due-process cases a 'careful description' of the asserted fundamental liberty interest." *Washington v. Glucksberg*, 521 U.S. 702, 720–721 (1997) (citations omitted). As this court has noted, "[t]he Supreme Court has a long history of recognizing unenumerated fundamental rights as protected by substantive due process, even before the term evolved into its modern usage." *Raich v. Gonzales*, 500 F.3d 850, 862–863 (9th Cir. 2007). The Supreme Court has recognized the right to privacy as it relates to sexual matters and sexual intimacy as a fundamental right entitled to protection under the Due Process Clause in a number of cases. See *Skinner v. Oklahoma*, 316 U.S. 535 (1942) (the right to have children); *Griswold v. Connecticut*, 381 U.S. 479 (1965) (right to use contraception); *Eisenstadt v. Baird*, 405 U.S. 438 (1972) (right to access contraception); *Carey v. Population Services Int'l*, 431 U.S. 678 (1971) (right to distribute of contraception); *Roe v. Wade*, 410 U.S. 113 (1973) (right to have an abortion); *Planned Parenthood of Se. Pa. v. Casey*, 505 U.S. 833 (1992) (right to an abortion). The question for this court is whether the right to engage in consensual, private sexual conduct extends to sexual conduct that involves economic exchange. Even where the state government has determined that conduct is immoral or undesirable, it may not impinge upon individuals' fundamental rights unless the regulation is necessary to support an important government interest.

In *Bowers v. Hardwick*, Hardwick was charged with violating a Georgia statute that criminalized sodomy for engaging in sodomy in his bedroom home. *See Bowers v. Hardwick*, 478 U.S. 186, 189 (1986). The prosecutor elected to dismiss the charges until additional evidence became available to prove Hardwick's illicit conduct. *Id.* Hardwick challenged the constitutionality of the Georgia statute and claimed that he was in imminent threat of arrest as a "practicing homosexual." *Id.* Hardwick claimed that there was a fundamental right to engage in homosexual activity in the privacy of his home, but a majority of the Supreme Court rejected this argument. *Id.* at 190–191. The Court noted that homosexual activity is dissimilar from the rights articulated in its prior substantive due process rights cases: "[W]e think it evident that none of the rights announced in those cases bears any resemblance to the claimed constitutional right of homosexuals to engage in acts of sodomy that is asserted in this case. No connection between family, marriage, or procreation on the one hand and homosexual activity on the other has been demonstrated, either by the Court of Appeals or by respondent." *Id.* at 191. The Court further acknowledged that policymakers could assess the dominant morality that they would like to support. *Id.* at 196. The Court stated, "The law, however, is constantly based on notions of morality, and if all laws representing essentially moral choices are to be invalidated under the Due Process Clause, the courts will be very busy indeed." *Id.* This case emphasized legislatures' ability to legislate morality and downplayed the liberty interests at stake. But as Justice Blackmun wrote in his dissenting opinion, which was joined by Justices Brennan, Marshall, and Stevens, "This case is no more about 'a fundamental right to engage in homosexual sodomy,' as the Court purports to declare, than *Stanley v. Georgia*, was about a fundamental right to watch obscene movies.... Rather, this case is about 'the most comprehensive of rights and the right most valued by civilized men,' namely, *'the right to be let alone.'" Id.* At 199 (Blackmun, J. dissenting) (emphasis added).

Eventually, the Supreme Court overruled the morality-based approach from *Bowers v. Hardwick* in *Lawrence v. Texas*. *See Lawrence v. Texas*, 539 U.S. 558 (2003). In *Lawrence v. Texas*, the Supreme Court examined the scope of the constitutional right to privacy as it relates to sexual intimacy and stated the following:

> Liberty protects the person from unwarranted government intrusions into a dwelling or other private places. In our tradition the State is not omnipresent in the home. And there are other spheres of our lives and existence, outside the home, where the State should not be a dominant presence. Freedom extends beyond spatial bounds. Liberty presumes an autonomy of self that includes freedom of thought, belief, expression, and certain intimate conduct.

539 U.S. 558, 562 (2003). This fundamental right recognizes that people should be able to engage in private, consensual sexual conduct. *See Latta v. Otter*, 771 F.3d 456 (9th Cir. 2014) (Berzon, J., concurring) ("More recently, Lawrence clarified that licit, consensual sexual behavior is no longer confined to marriage, but is protected when it occurs, in private, between two consenting adults....").

After responding to a domestic disturbance, police observed Tyrone Garner and John Lawrence engaging in sexual activity and charged them with engaging in sodomy in violation of Texas criminal law. *Id.* at 562–563. Justice Kennedy, writing for the majority of the Court wrote, "The issue is whether the majority [of Americans] may use the power of the State to enforce these views [about morality] on the whole society through operation of the criminal law. 'Our obligation is to define the liberty of all, not to mandate our own moral code.'" *Id.* at 571 (quoting *Planned Parenthood of Southeastern Pa. v. Casey*, 505 U.S. 833, 850 (1992)). The Court reversed its decision in *Bowers* and held that the Texas statute criminalizing sodomy violated the Due Process Clause. *Id.* at 578. The Court noted that statutes that criminalize sodomy touch upon the "most private human conduct, sexual behavior, and in the most private of places, the home." *Id.* at 567. But in so holding, the Court noted that the case "does not involve public conduct or prostitution." *Id.* at 560. By listing prostitution with "public conduct," the Court appears to be particularly noting prostitution as a form of conduct that typically involved public conduct as is generally the case for street-based forms of prostitution. *Id.* at 578. In his dissenting opinion, Justice Scalia opined, "State laws against bigamy, same-sex marriage, adult incest, *prostitution*, masturbation, adultery, fornication, bestiality, and obscenity *are likewise sustainable only in light of Bowers' validation of laws based on moral choices.*" *Id.* at 590. (emphasis added). Justice Scalia was correct in observing that the basis for regulating consensual sexual activity between adults was undermined following *Lawrence*.

The *Lawrence* decision illustrates the importance of the right to engage in sexual conduct within the privacy of one's home without government interference. *Id.* at 567. This conduct may include reviewing obscene, sexual materials that otherwise would be criminalized outside the confines of one's home as the Supreme Court held in *Stanley v. Georgia*. *See Stanley v. Georgia*, 394 U.S. 557, 559 (1969). In that case, a defendant was convicted under Georgia state law of possessing obscene materials in his home. *Id.* at 558. The Court held that the First and Fourteenth Amendments prohibit making the possession of obscene materials a crime because "the individual's right to read or observe what he pleases ... is so fundamental to our scheme of individual liberty." *Id.* at 568–569 (internal citation omitted).

1. The History of Regulating Prostitution in California

The history of the criminalization of prostitution in California is instructive in evaluating the propriety of criminalizing this conduct. The State suggests that the criminalization of prostitution is merely a natural feature of American law when in fact its criminalization is relatively modern. Unlike many of the new crimes that populate state and federal court dockets, commercialized sex is a form of conduct that existed before the founding of this nation. In this way, it differs from the many computer, narcotics, and antitrust criminal laws that responded to new social and technological conditions. Prostitution has existed since Biblical times, yet *it was not criminalized* in the early years after the founding of this country. *See* Beverly Balos & Mary Louise Fellows, A *Matter of Prostitution: Becoming Respectable*, 74 N.Y.U. L. Rev. 1220, 1283 (1999); *Prostitution and Sex Work*, 14 Geo. J. Gender & L. 553, 554 (2013).

California criminalized aspects of prostitution in 1872, and only directly criminalized it in 1961. While prostitution itself was only directly criminalized in 1961, the public nuisance aspects of prostitution were regulated. Professor William Eskridge provides the background of California's regulation of prostitution:

> California's 1872 vagrancy law, as amended in 1891, made it a criminal offense to be an 'idle or dissolute person, or associate of known thieves, who wanders about the streets at late or unusual hours of the night,' or to be a 'lewd or dissolute person who lives in and about houses of ill-fame.' Both descriptions obviously referred to prostitutes but could be read more broadly. The vagrancy law was simplified and broadened in 1903 to make it a criminal offense to be either an 'idle, lewd, or dissolute person, or associate of known thieves' or to be a 'common prostitute.' As thus amended, the so-called 'lewd vagrancy' law became the most deployed criminal sanction against same sex intimacy in California. Unlike the state's sodomy law, it was broad enough to cover virtually any kind of erotic touching and, as a misdemeanor, carried no jury trial right. During the period 1880 to 1921, California jurisdictions vigorously enforced the state's vagrancy law.

William N. Eskridge, Jr., *Law and the Construction of the Closet: American Regulation of Same-Sex Intimacy, 1880–1946*, 82 Iowa L. Rev. 1007, 1036. In 1960, this statute was struck down as unconstitutional and revised in 1961. *See In re Newbern*, 350 P.2d 116 (1960) (holding that the statute was unconstitutionally vague). This revised vagrancy statute was frequently used to prosecute same-sex intimacy and other forms of erotic conduct that were deemed deviant, including sodomy. *Id.* This history is consistent with the approach of regulating prostitution as a public nuisance or vagrancy in other parts of the country.

In fact, the criminalization of prostitution in and of itself in the United States has its roots in the Progressive Era with the passage of the White-Traffic Slave Act ("Mann Act"), which purported to protect White women from the harms of forced sexual slavery. White-Slave Traffic (Mann) Act, ch. 395, 36 Stat. 825 (1910) (codified as amended at 18 U.S.C. §2421 (2000)). "In the early twentieth century, various anxieties about the loss of freedom and control seemed to converge in the phantasmic figure of the white slave. Most scholars agree that, global panic notwithstanding, there was no real 'traffic' in white women. The Mann Act was passed for the purported purpose of protecting white women from forced prostitution, but the broad wording of the law allowed police and prosecutors to selectively punish men involved in all manner of consensual behavior, especially Black and immigrant men who enjoyed premarital, extramarital, and cross-racial intimacy with white women." Sherally Munshi, *White Slavery and the Crisis of Will in the Age of Contract*, 30 Yale J. L. & Feminism 327, 342 (2018). Previously most states only regulated the public nuisance aspects of prostitution.

It is important to emphasize that in California, the statute that regulated conduct associated with prostitution also regulated sodomy – the same form of sexual intimacy that *Lawrence* held was protected from governmental interference. *Lawrence*, 539 U.S. at 567. Within this historical context, it is striking that the *Lawrence* majority opinion listed prostitution with public conduct, especially in light of the history of regulating the public nuisance aspects of prostitution. The question is whether it is still appropriate to criminalize all forms of prostitution in an era in which most prostitution transactions are facilitated through private communications on virtual platforms that eliminate the public nuisance aspects of it. *See* Br. of Plaintiff-Appellants at *10–11.

2. Regulating Intimacy

The State argues that prostitution does not involve the type of intimate relationships that the Court was discussing in *Lawrence*, alluding to Justice Kennedy's dicta in *Lawrence* that that case did not "involve public conduct or prostitution." *Lawrence*, 539 U.S. at 578. The government claims that it should be able to regulate commercialized forms of sex. ESP argues that they have a right to engage in sexual activity in their private spaces, and that the statute criminalizing commercialized sex infringes upon fundamental rights articulated in *Lawrence*. In *Lawrence*, the majority opinion clearly indicated that its decision did not automatically extend to prostitution. Given the dissenting opinion warnings that the case would be extended to prostitution and all forms of morality regulation, it is fair to presume that this sentence is a response to these warnings.

However, it would be misguided to assume anything further about the inclusion of this sentence. Some courts have interpreted it to mean that *Lawrence* decidedly prevents the recognition of the right to be free from interference when engaging prostitution transactions. *See U.S. v. Thompson*, 458 F. Supp. 2d 730, 731 (N.D. Ind., 2006); *State v. Romano*, 155 P.3d 1102, 1111 (Haw. 2007). This is a strained reading of the case. It is clear that the logic from the case can be extended and may very well lay the foundation for a finding that prostitution transactions should be free from government interference in the form of criminalization. Such a finding would be an extension of *Lawrence*, much like *Lawrence* was an extension of the right to use birth control and the right to have an abortion. *See Lawrence*, 539 U.S. at 567; *Griswold v. Connecticut*, 381 U.S. 479 (1965); *Roe v. Wade*, 410 U.S. 113 (1973). All of these acts were previously considered morally repugnant by the majority of Americans at some point. But the Supreme Court nevertheless held that the State may not interfere with individuals' right to engage in private activities, including the morally repugnant ones, where it would compromise their right to privacy. *Lawrence*, 539 U.S. at 567. The right is about being free from government intrusion into the most private aspects of one's life.

The question for this court to consider is whether the criminalization of prostitution interferes with a fundamental right to be free from government interference when engaging in private sexual activity. The State argues that prostitution transactions involve commercialized conduct, and the exchange of payment provides justification for State interference. However, the Supreme Court has held that the commodification of sex does not provide a basis for infringing upon the constitutional rights enshrined in the First Amendment in a number of cases. *Miller v. California*, 413 U.S. 15 (1973); *Carey v. Population Services Int'l*, 431 U.S. 678 (1977); *FCC v. Pacifica Foundation*, 438 U.S. 726, 745; *Sable Communications of Cal., Inc. v FCC*, 492 U.S. 115, 126 (1989); *Reno v. American Civil Liberties Union*, 521 U.S. 844 (1997); *Ashcroft v. Free Speech Coalition*, 535 U.S. 234, 243 (2002). Accordingly, commodification alone is not a sufficient basis for denying the existence of a fundamental right to be free from government interference while engaging in private sexual conduct.

Furthermore, the recent literature on prostitution suggests that the nature of the relationships that form the basis of these interactions are often more complex than the stereotypes we see from television and the news. For one, there is a growing trend for prostitution encounters that are described as "the boyfriend or girlfriend experience." *See* Adrienne D. Davis, *Regulating Sex Work: Erotic Assimilationism, Erotic Exceptionalism, and the Challenge of Intimate Labor*, 103 Cal. L. Rev. 1195, 1245–1246 (2015). These encounters involve sexual encounters that replicate the experience of being in serious relationship with the sex worker. *Id.* They may include exchange of intimate details about their personal lives, conversations about inner thoughts and worries, and regular dates, much like the conversations that a couple who are courting each other might engage in. *See* Elizabeth Bernstein, Temporarily Yours: Intimacy, Authenticity, and the Commerce of Sex 7 (2007). The purpose is to stimulate a deeper connection between the sex worker and the sex work client. Many of the sex work clients are men. *Id.* at 111. Many are also women. *Id.* at 86. There is an exchange of money for the continuation of the relationship, but many of these relationships last for as long as nontransactional relationships, and some last for years. *Id.* at 7.

These examples illustrate that the nature of prostitution encounters is not as black and white as the State suggests. In determining whether there is a fundamental right to be free from state criminalization in this area, it is important to appreciate the diversity and complexity of the sexual intimacy that is currently prohibited by the California statute. The State proclaims that there is no constitutional right to engage in prostitution. But much like the majority in *Bowers*, the State gets the issue wrong.

Bowers, 478 U.S. at 190–191. The question is not whether there is a constitutional right to engage in prostitution. The question is whether there is a constitutional right to be free from government interference when engaging in private sexual activity, even where there is an exchange of money involved in this private activity. The animating feature of the fundamental right is the right to be free from government interference in one's private life, not the measurable value of the sexual activity at issue.

Lawrence indicates that the question for courts to examine is not whether the sexual conduct itself is "entitled to formal recognition in the law," but rather whether it is "within the liberty of persons to choose [to engage in it] without being punished as criminals." Lawrence, 539 U.S. at 558. This is a different question that focuses on the liberty interests in being free from criminal sanctions in order to engage in private conduct. Should someone be criminalized for electing to engage in personal relationships through boyfriend experience engagements? Should the State be able to dictate how people cure their loneliness?

The empirical research suggests that the nature of sex work is remarkably diverse. As Phillip Hubbard has described, there are diverse categories of sex work that include street-based sex workers, escorts and dates, and brothel-based sex workers. See Phillip Hubbard, *Cleansing the Metropolis: Sex Work and the Politics of Zero Tolerance*, 41 Urban Studies 1687 (2004). It is important to recognize and understand the diversity of sex work in evaluating the nature of the privacy interests at stake here.

> [Often, commentators] equate prostitution with street prostitution. In the United States, Britain, The Netherlands, and many other countries, however, only a minority of prostitutes work on the streets (10–30%). Yet they receive the lion's share of attention, and findings on street prostitution are often presented as a feature of sex work per se.

Ronald Weitzer, *New Directions in Research on Prostitution*, 43 Crime, L. & Soc. Change 211, 214 (2005). There is a growing common space for sex work on the internet that sex work organizations argue allows them to screen clients and maintain additional safety in the screening process. See Campbell, et. al, *Risking Safety and Rights: Online Sex Work, Crimes and 'Blended Safety Repertoires,'* 70 Br. J. Sociology (2018). The move to online mediums to screen and advertise services has created a new space for sex workers that eliminates some of its visibility in public spaces. Id. This shift is significant because the public nuisance aspects of prostitution, which the Lawrence court appears to be alluding to in naming it with "public conduct," are reduced in online spaces. Lawrence, 539 U.S. at 558.

The only people who would enter into sex work in online spaces would be people seeking those services because surfing the internet allows people to select which spaces they enter and navigate only to those spaces. So, there is a decreased risk of a viewer accidentally being exposed to sexual solicitation. As the Supreme Court has recognized, "Unlike communications received by radio or television, 'the receipt of information on the Internet requires a series of affirmative steps more deliberate and directed than merely turning a dial. A child requires some sophistication and some ability to read to retrieve material and thereby to use the Internet unattended.'" *Reno v. Am. Civil Liberties Union*, 521 U.S. 844, 854 (quoting Reno v. Am. Civil Liberties Union, 929 F. Supp. 824, 845 (ED Pa. 1996)).

There is also empirical research that indicates that regular prostitution transactions often involve contact between repeat sex work clients and sex workers. Some of these people describe the relationship as intimate and resulting in a close bond. *See* Ann M. Lucas, *The Work of Sex Work: Elite Prostitutes' Vocational Orientations and Experiences*, 26 Deviant Behav. 513, 531 (2005). The relationship is clearly transactional in nature but nevertheless intimate and may involve emotional connection. On the other hand, there are people in this world who marry for money. There are people who have sex with their intimate partners with the expectation that their partners will shower them with gifts. There are people who go on dating websites with the goal of having meaningless sex. These relationships are also transactional in nature. And to arbitrarily draw the line, although the transactional and commercialized nature of intimate relationships exist on a continuum, would require undue government interference into a private, sexual conduct that undermines the right recognized in *Lawrence*. Even if a relationship appears to be repulsive or unseemly to some, which has been the case for sodomy, interracial relationships, and prostitution in this country, the government cannot unduly interfere with private sexual activity between consenting adults.

The trial court granted the State's motion to dismiss and determined that "the intimate association between a prostitute and client, while it may be consensual and cordial, has not merited the protection of the Due Process Clause of the Fourteenth Amendment." However, viewing the facts in the light most favorable to the nonmoving party, the sex work relationship may in fact involve a close emotional connection and involve intimacy. At this stage, it is for the finder of fact to determine this issue as there are facts under which the relationships may carry the same depth of more serious nontransactional relationships.

It is also questionable to suggest that the commodification aspect of the transaction eviscerates any rights to engage in sexual activity because it has no similar effect in the case of pornography, which the Supreme Court has recognized as entitled to First Amendment protection when not obscene. *Miller v. California*, 413 U.S. 15 (1973); *Carey v. Population Services Int'l*, 431 U.S. 678 (1977); *FCC v. Pacifica Foundation*, 438 U.S. 726, 745; *Sable Communications of Cal., Inc. v FCC*, 492 U.S. 115, 126 (1989) ("Sexual expression which is indecent but not obscene is protected by the First Amendment"); *Reno v. American Civil Liberties Union*, 521 U.S. 844 (1997); *Ashcroft v. Free Speech Coalition*, 535 U.S. 234, 243 (2002). Accordingly, we find that the government has interfered with a fundamental right to engage in private sexual intimacy in its criminalization of prostitution.

B. *Government Interest*

Nevertheless, our inquiry does not end just because we have found there may be a fundamental right under the Due Process Clause to be free from government intrusion when engaging in commercialized sexual transactions in a private space. The next question is whether the government regulation was nevertheless narrowly tailored to address a substantial governmental interest. This court has noted, "*Lawrence* applied something more than traditional rational basis review." *Witt v. Dept. of Air Force*, 527 F.3d 806, 817 (9th Cir. 2008). When the State intrudes upon the fundamental rights recognized in *Lawrence*, the governmental action must meet the following criteria: (1) it must advance an important governmental interest; (2) the intrusion must significantly further that interest; and (3) the intrusion must be necessary to further that interest. *Id* at 819. "This approach is necessary to give meaning to the Supreme Court's conclusion that liberty gives substantial protection to adult persons in deciding how to conduct their private lives in matters pertaining to sex." *Id.*

The State claims that the criminalization of prostitution aims to prevent the spread of venereal diseases and reduce the occurrence of sex trafficking. These are important governmental interests, but the State may not interfere with fundamental rights unless its regulation unless the governmental intrusion is necessary to further State interests. We address each of these interests in turn.

The State argues that the criminalization of prostitution is necessary in order to prevent sex trafficking. It argues that criminalization allows it to target pimps and johns who are exploiting young women who are forced into prostitution. Br. of Appellee at *27–29. However, there are already many legal tools available in criminal law that are specific to sex trafficking. *See, e.g.,* Ca. Penal Code § 236.1; 22 U.S.C.A §7101–7114. Sex trafficking is criminalized under federal law through 22 U.S.C.A §7101–7114 explaining that "[t]he purposes of this chapter are to combat trafficking in persons, a contemporary manifestation of slavery ... to ensure just and effective punishment of traffickers, and to protect their victims." 22 U.S.C.A. §7101(a). This statute targets sex trafficking. *Id.* In addition, California criminalizes sex trafficking through Ca. Penal Code § 236.1, both protecting adults and children stating, "A person who deprives or violates or deprives the liberty of another with intent to obtain forced labor or services, is guilty of human trafficking ... [and a] person who causes, induces, or persuades, or attempts to cause, induce, or persuade ... a minor... to engage in a commercial sex act, with the intent to effect or maintain a violation... is guilty of human trafficking." Ca. Penal Code § 236.1. These laws provide ample basis for criminalizing the conduct that has been defined as sex trafficking.

The State does not provide an adequate explanation for why it requires the ability to criminalize conduct that is not sex trafficking in order to prevent sex trafficking. It is not clear why the criminalization of prostitution would assist in addressing sex trafficking. Scholars have already argued that even well-intentioned programs that divert sex workers into human trafficking intervention courts may be problematic.

See Aya Gruber et. al., *Penal Welfare and the New Human Trafficking Intervention Courts*, 68 Fla. L. Rev. 1333, 1356 (2016). So, it stands to reason that outright criminalization for the purpose of helping sex trafficking victims would be even more harmful. In fact, ESP argues that criminalization makes it more difficult for sex workers to report suspected sex trafficking, and at this stage, the facts should be constructed to favor the nonmoving parties.

The State also argues that prostitution should be criminalized to prevent the spread of venereal diseases. Several counties in Nevada have legalized prostitution and have adopted a model of regulating prostitution in licensed brothels. *See* James R. Stout & Thomas S. Tanana, *Could California Reduce AIDS By Modeling Nevada Prostitution Law?*, 2 San Diego Justice J. 491 (1994). Some researchers have demonstrated that sex workers are less likely to seek medical assistance under full criminalization. *See* Tracy M. Clements, *Prostitution and the American Health Care System: Denying Access to a Group of Women in Need*, 11 Berkeley Women L.J. 49, 87–89 (1996).

Moreover, ESP allege that "when prosecuting cases under Cal. Pen. Code § 647(b), the Appellees use the fact of condom possession as evidence of prostitution-related offenses. By doing so, the Appellees discourage condom use and thwart safer sex practices." Brief of Appellees at *14 (citing Human Rights Watch, *Sex Workers At Risk: Condoms As Evidence of Prostitution in Four US Cities*, 2012). Thus, the enforcement of prostitution statutes itself may be a danger to the public health in discouraging sex workers to refrain from carrying condoms. One study found, "Sex workers reported that not only were they stopped and searched by police officers, because of the low threshold necessary for initiating a stop and search, police officers frequently took their condoms and commented on the number of contraceptives they had on their person." Meghan Newcomer, *Can Condoms Be Compelling? Examining the State Interest in Confiscating Condoms from Suspected Sex Workers*, 82 Ford. L. Rev. 1053, 1064 (2013). By encouraging sex workers to forgo condoms, the State policy may in fact exacerbate the spread of venereal diseases.

By contrast, numerous studies demonstrate the ways that continued criminalization of prostitution contributes to dangerous conditions for sex workers. *See* Olivea Myers, *Sex for Sale: The Implications of Lawrence and Windsor on Prostitution in the United States*, 5 Tenn. J. Race Gender & Soc. Just. 93, 106 (2016). Sex workers are less likely to seek government assistance for healthcare needs and to seek protection from police when they encounter violence. *Id.* Sex work organizations have reported that sex workers would be better able assist in the enforcement of sex trafficking violations if they did not face the continued stigma that comes from criminalizing their conduct. *See* Chi Adanna Mgbako, Katherine Glenn Bass, Erin Bundra & Mehak Jamil, *The Case for Decriminalization of Sex Work in South Africa*, 44 Geo. J. Int'l L. 1423, 1438 (2013). And there is a growing body of research that has been documenting the harms from criminalizing prostitution. After extensive research and data collection on the criminalization of prostitution, Amnesty International and Human Rights Watch have both indicated that the human rights approach to prostitution requires that it been fully decriminalized in order to decrease sex trafficking. *See* Rachel Marshall, *Sex Workers and Human Rights: A Critical Analysis of Laws regarding Sex Work*, 23 Wm. & Mary J. Women & L. 47 71 (2016). They argue, contrary to the State, that the criminalization is harmful for sex workers and sex trafficking victims who have been forced into the sex trades. *Id.*

Criminalization brings grave risks with it and may make the conditions of sex work more dangerous. *See* Sienna Baskin, Aziza Ahmed & Anna Forbes, *Criminal Laws on Sex Work and HIV Transmission: Mapping the Laws, Considering the Consequences*, 93 Denv. L. Rev. 355, 360 (2016). "These consequences include limitations on employment options, discrimination by employers, loss of access to public benefits–including public housing–and loss of the right to sue the police if they are victims of police violence. In some states, sex workers who have prior convictions of prostitution and are arrested again are subject to felony charges and mandatory jail time." *Id.* There are also issues with discriminatory enforcement of the prostitution statute. All of this evidence and research, when interpreted in the light most favorable to ESP, indicate that not only is the State criminalization of prostitution not necessary, it is counterproductive and may lead to an increase in sex trafficking and venereal diseases. In order for the State to interfere with a fundamental right, there must be a substantial interest that is narrowly tailored. At this stage, the State intervention fails to meet the heightened standard required to regulate fundamental rights.

C. *Other Claims*

ESP also argues that their rights to free speech, earn a living, and of freedom of association have also been violated by the criminalization of prostitution under Section 647(b). Because we conclude ESP's claims survive the State's motion to dismiss, and the district court focused on the substantive due process claim; we need not reach these claims at this time. However, there are important issues raised in these claims, namely the free speech concerns that may be implicated by the continued criminalization of prostitution under Section 647(b). This presents concerns about the overbreadth of the statute under the First Amendment, which may be an additional ground for finding the statute unconstitutional, which the Court need not reach here.

III.

For the foregoing reasons, the district court's judgment dismissing ESP's lawsuit is reversed, and the case is remanded for further proceedings consistent with this decision.

Printed in the USA
CPSIA information can be obtained
at www.ICGtesting.com
CBHW071330070324
5056CB00016B/28